LENINGRAD

Borderland: A Journey Through the History of Ukraine
The Shaman's Coat: A Native History of Siberia

LENINGRAD

Tragedy of a City
Under Siege, 1941–44

ANNA REID

BLOOMSBURY

LONDON · BERLIN · NEW YORK · SYDNEY

First published in Great Britain 2011

Copyright © 2011 by Anna Reid
Maps by ML Design

Images reproduced in the plate section of this book (with the exceptions
of those of pp. 3 (bottom), 7 and 8–9) are courtesy of the Tsentralniy
Gosudarstvenniy Arkhiv Kinofotofonodokumentov Sankt-Peterburga

The text paper image on p. 387 is courtesy of the Gosudarstvenniy Muzei Istorii Sankt-Peterburga

Bloomsbury Publishing Plc
49–51 Bedford Square
London WC1B 3DP

www.bloomsbury.com

Bloomsbury Publishing, London, New York and Berlin

A CIP catalogue record for this book is available from the British Library

ISBN 978 0 7475 9952 4

10 9 8 7 6 5 4 3 2 1

MIX
Paper from
responsible sources
FSC
www.fsc.org   FSC® C018072

...ext UK Ltd, Edinburgh
...n by Clays Ltd, St Ives plc

For Edward and Bertie

Contents

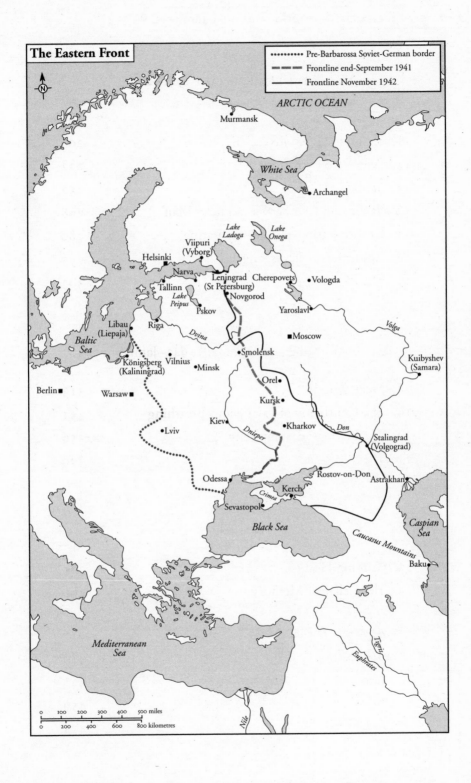

The Eastern Front

.... Pre-Barbarossa Soviet-German border
– – – Frontline end-September 1941
—— Frontline November 1942

ARCTIC OCEAN

Murmansk

White Sea

Archangel

Lake Ladoga
Lake Onega

Viipuri (Vyborg)
Helsinki
Narva
Leningrad (St Petersburg)
Cherepovets
Vologda
Tallinn
Novgorod
Lake Peipus
Pskov
Yaroslavl
Volga

Libau (Liepaja)
Riga
Dvina
Smolensk
Moscow
Kuibyshev (Samara)

Königsberg (Kaliningrad)
Vilnius
Minsk
Orel

Berlin
Warsaw
Kursk
Don

Lviv
Kiev
Dnieper
Kharkov
Stalingrad (Volgograd)

Odessa
Rostov-on-Don
Astrakhan

Kerch
Crimea
Caspian Sea

Sevastopol
Caucasus Mountains

Black Sea
Baku

Mediterranean Sea

Tigris
Euphrates

Nile

0   100   200   300   400   500 miles
0   200   400   600   800 kilometres

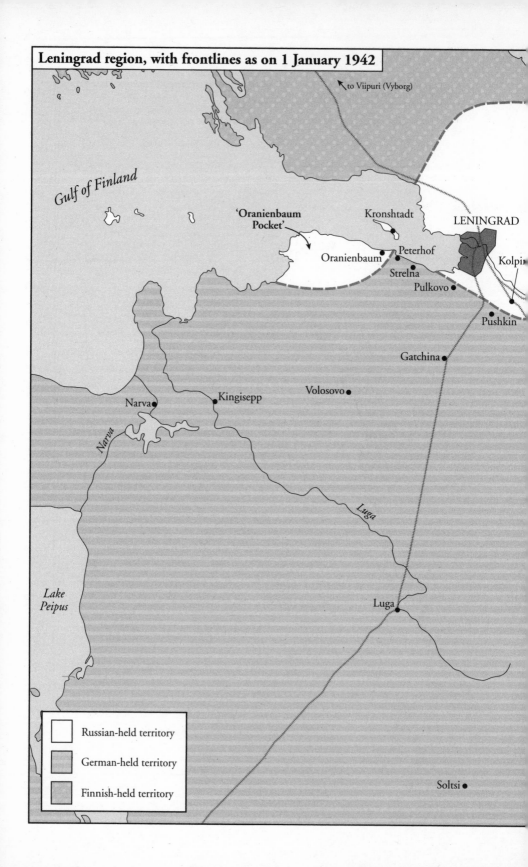

Leningrad region, with frontlines as on 1 January 1942

↖ to Viipuri (Vyborg)

Gulf of Finland

'Oranienbaum Pocket'

Kronshtadt

LENINGRAD

Oranienbaum
Peterhof
Strelna
Pulkovo
Kolpi

Pushkin

Gatchina

Volosovo

Narva
Kingisepp

Narva

Luga

Lake Peipus

Luga

Soltsi

Russian-held territory

German-held territory

Finnish-held territory

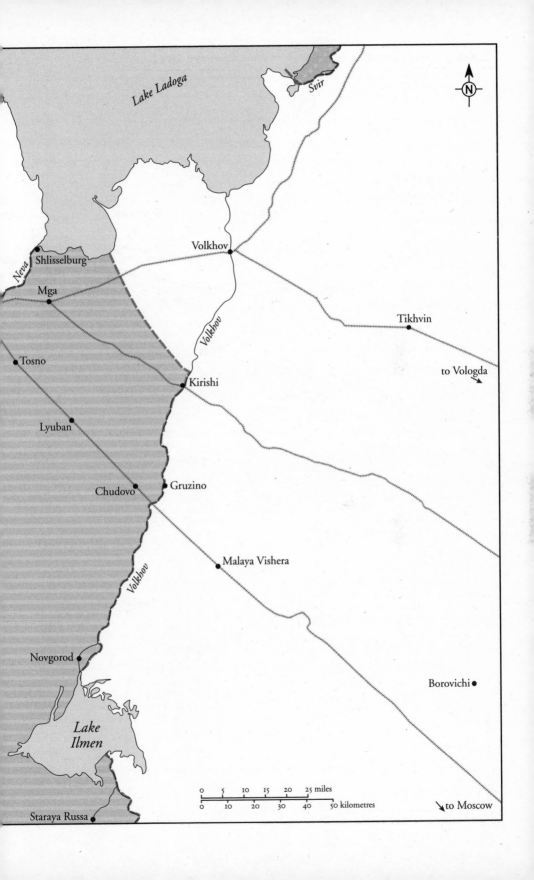

Lake Ladoga

Svir

Volkhov

Neva

Shlisselburg

Mga

Volkhov

Tikhvin

Tosno

to Vologda

Lyuban

Kirishi

Chudovo • Gruzino

Volkhov

Malaya Vishera

Novgorod

Borovichi •

Lake
Ilmen

| 0 | 5 | 10 | 15 | 20 | 25 miles |

| 0 | 10 | 20 | 30 | 40 | 50 kilometres |

to Moscow

Staraya Russa •

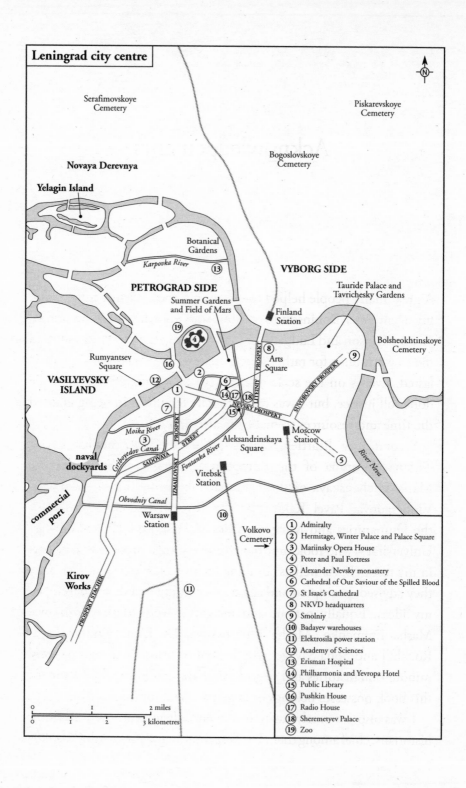

Leningrad city centre

Serafimovskoye Cemetery

Piskarevskoye Cemetery

Bogoslovskoye Cemetery

Novaya Derevnya

Yelagin Island

Botanical Gardens

Karpovka River

VYBORG SIDE

PETROGRAD SIDE

Tauride Palace and Tavrichesky Gardens

Summer Gardens and Field of Mars

Finland Station

Bolsheokhtinskoye Cemetery

Rumyantsev Square

Arts Square

VASILYEVSKY ISLAND

Moika River

Griboyedov Canal

Aleksandrinskaya Square

Moscow Station

naval dockyards

River Neva

SADOVAYA

Fontanka River

NEVSKY PROSPEKT

LITEINY PROSPEKT

SUVOROVSKY PROSPEKT

IZMAILOVSKY STREET

Vitebsk Station

commercial port

Obvodniy Canal

Warsaw Station

Volkovo Cemetery →

Kirov Works

PROSPEKT STACHEK

①	Admiralty
②	Hermitage, Winter Palace and Palace Square
③	Mariinsky Opera House
④	Peter and Paul Fortress
⑤	Alexander Nevsky monastery
⑥	Cathedral of Our Saviour of the Spilled Blood
⑦	St Isaac's Cathedral
⑧	NKVD headquarters
⑨	Smolniy
⑩	Badayev warehouses
⑪	Elektrosila power station
⑫	Academy of Sciences
⑬	Erisman Hospital
⑭	Philharmonia and Yevropa Hotel
⑮	Public Library
⑯	Pushkin House
⑰	Radio House
⑱	Sheremetyev Palace
⑲	Zoo

0 1 2 miles
0 1 2 3 kilometres

Acknowledgements

A great many people helped to create this book. First, I must thank my agent Peter Robinson for raising, and my editors Bill Swainson, George Gibson and Ludger Ikas for providing, the funds that allowed me to work on it for rather longer than the 872 days the siege itself lasted. Events on the scale of the siege of Leningrad can never be done full justice, but I was exceptionally fortunate in being granted the time and resources to make the attempt.

Second, my heartfelt thanks go to the five scholars – Dr Tatiana Voronina of the European University at St Petersburg, Maria Svichenskaya of the National Library of Russia, Dr Lyuba Vinogradova, Pavel Rakitin of the Russian State University for the Humanities and Michelle Miles of Freiburg's Albert-Ludwigs-Universität – who took time out from their own projects to take part in my research. As well as combing archives in Russia and Germany they advised, prompted and acted as sounding boards as I developed my ideas. Equally patient and insightful were Masha Bozunova, Masha Eremenko, Masha Kaminskaya, Dr Elena Khlinovskaya-Rockhill and Sofia Savage, who helped to translate dozens of voluminous oral histories and siege diaries. The credit for whatever merit this book possesses belongs in large part to all of them.

I was also extremely lucky in the encouragement given by fellow historians, chief among them Drs Sergei Yarov and Aleksandr Chistikov of the Petersburg branch of the Russian Academy of Sciences. Both were extraordinarily generous with their time and expertise, fielding rafts of questions and pointing me towards the latest debates and publications. In Freiburg Professor Ulrich Herbert and Dr Cornelia Brink fascinatingly explained German perspectives on the siege. In London Professors Orlando Figes and David Kirby, Simon Sebag Montefiore and in particular Antony Beevor – *velikiy vozhd* to all those of us posted to the Eastern Front – passed on wisdom and contacts and generally enlivened the long and solitary business of writing. So, too, did Judith Flanders, who found time between her own books expertly to pummel the final manuscript into shape. The last edits came under the eagle eyes of Richard Collins, Anna Simpson of Bloomsbury and Bernd Rullkotter, translator of the German edition.

Other busy people who gave interviews, made introductions or responded in detail to out-of-the-blue emails were Galina Afanasyeva of the St Petersburg zoo, Marion Beaton of Glasgow's Mitchell Library, Meriel Buxton, Felicity Cave, Dr Robert Dale of Newcastle University, Dr Alan Dangour, George Edgar, Olga Filochika of the Museum of the History of St Petersburg, Irina Flige of the St Petersburg branch of Memorial, Aleksandr Frenkel of the city's Jewish Community Centre, Deborah Hodgkinson, Virta Kaija of the *Helsingin Sanomat*, Olga Kalashnikova of Radio Baltika, Dr Nikita Lomagin and Dr Yekaterina Melnikova of the European University at St Petersburg, Dr Chiara Mayer-Rieckh, Giles Milton, Dr Yuri Nagovitsyn of the Pulkovo Observatory, Catriona Oliphant, Dr Vladimir Osinsky of the St Petersburg State University, Dr Siobhan Peeling of the University of Nottingham, Galina Retrovskaya of the St Petersburg Philharmonia, Nataliya Rogova of the National Library of Russia, Olga Smirnova and Renata Tairbekova of the BBC World Service, Dr Alexandra Smith of the University of Edinburgh, Tim Tzouliadis, Ludmilla Voronikhina of the Hermitage, Nicolas Werth of Paris's Institut d'Histoire du Temps Présent, Stephanie Williams, Dr Emma Wilson and Dmitri Zhuravlev of Petersburg's Military-Medical Museum.

Vladimir Nikitin of the State University's journalism faculty gave invaluable help in unearthing the photographs used to illustrate this book, many of which appeared for the first time in his ground-breaking collection *The Unknown Blockade*. Galina Stolyarova of the *St Petersburg Times* set me on my feet during my first few visits to her beautiful city, as well as supplying a stream of press tickets to the ravishing Mariinsky. Sergei Zagatsky showed me the original of his grandmother Klara Rakhman's siege diary, and transferred it to typescript. Sasha Orlov of the 'Poisk' organisation drove me round the battlefields of Myasnoi Bor, and Aleksandr Osipov gave me a tour of the Nevsky Pyatachok. (A commemorative museum, created entirely by himself, can be found above a shop in the village of Nevskaya Dubrovka.) At home, Commander Geoffrey Palmer hilariously recalled his years as a member of Britain's wartime Military Mission to Moscow; my thanks go to his widow Angelina Palmer. Lyubov Dvoretskaya brought my Russian up to scratch and Robert Chandler introduced me to the SEELANGS online forum, whose contributors came up with numerous useful leads and suggestions. Gisela Stuart MP responded to a plea on behalf of the historical and human rights society Memorial with a question to the prime minister in the House of Commons. The staffs of the London Library and of the School of Slavonic and East European Studies library were as helpful and efficient as ever, as was the unique John Sandoe's bookshop.

Most memorable of all were my interviews with siege survivors. Daniil Alshits, Irina Ivanova (née Bogdanova), Igor Kruglyakov, Anzhelina Kupaigorodskaya and Galina Semenova all consented to recall in detail a dreadful period of their lives, and have my most respectful gratitude and admiration. I am also indebted to the Bogdanov-Berezovsky, Hockenjos and Starodubtsev families for allowing quotation from unpublished family diaries. Last but not least come my husband, Charles Lucas, and our dear sons Edward and Bertie, to whom this book is dedicated. Without them I would have read more but understood less.

Introduction

This is the story of the siege of Leningrad, the deadliest blockade of a city in human history. Leningrad sits at the north-eastern corner of the Baltic, at the head of the long, shallow gulf that divides the southern shores of Finland from those of northern Russia. Before the Russian Revolution it was the capital of the Russian Empire, and called St Petersburg after its founder, the tsar Peter the Great. With the fall of Communism twenty years ago it regained its old name, but for its older inhabitants it is Leningrad still, not so much for Lenin as in honour of the approximately three-quarters of a million civilians who starved to death during the almost nine hundred days – from September 1941 to January 1944 – during which the city was besieged by Nazi Germany. Other modern sieges – those of Madrid and Sarajevo – lasted longer, but none killed even a tenth as many people. Around thirty-five times more civilians died in Leningrad than in London's Blitz; four times more than in the bombings of Nagasaki and Hiroshima put together.

On 22 June 1941, the midsummer morning on which Germany attacked the Soviet Union, Leningrad looked much the same as it had done before the Revolution. A seagull circling over the gilded needle of the Admiralty spire would have seen the same view as twenty-four years previously: below the choppy grey River Neva, lined by parks and palaces; to the west, where the Neva opens into the sea, the cranes of the naval dockyards; to the north, the zigzag bastions of the Peter and Paul Fortress and grid-like streets of Vasilyevsky Island; to the south, four concentric waterways – the pretty Moika, coolly classical Griboyedov, broad, grand Fontanka and workaday Obvodniy – and two great boulevards, the Izmailovsky and the Nevsky Prospekt, radiating in perfect symmetry past the Warsaw and Moscow railway stations to the factory chimneys of the industrial districts beyond.

Appearances, though, were deceptive. Outwardly, Leningrad was not much altered; inwardly, it was profoundly changed and traumatised. It is conventional to give the story of the blockade a filmic happy-sad-happy progression: the peace of a midsummer morning shattered by news of invasion, the call to arms, the enemy halted at the gates, descent into cold and starvation, springtime recovery, victory fireworks. In reality it was not like that. Any Leningrader aged thirty or over at the start of the siege had already lived through three wars (the First World War, the Civil War between Bolsheviks and Whites that followed it, and the Winter War with Finland of 1939–40), two famines (the first during the Civil War, the second the collectivisation famine of 1932–3, caused by Stalin's violent seizure of peasant farms) and two major waves of political terror. Hardly a household, particularly among the city's ethnic minorities and old middle classes, had not been touched by death, prison or exile as well as impoverishment. For someone like the poet Olga Berggolts, daughter of a Jewish doctor, it was not unduly melodramatic to state that 'we measured time by the intervals between one suicide and the next'.[1] The siege, though unique in the size of its death toll, was less a tragic interlude than one dark passage among many.

The tragedy arose from the combined hubris of Hitler and Stalin. In August 1939 they had astonished the world by putting ideology aside to form a non-aggression pact, under which they divided Poland between them. When Hitler turned on France the following spring Stalin stood aside, continuing to supply his ally with grain, metals, rubber and other vital commodities. Though it is clear from what we now know of Stalin's conversations with his Politburo that he expected to be forced into war with Germany sooner or later, the timing of the Nazi attack – code-named Barbarossa or 'Redbeard' after a crusading Holy Roman Emperor – came as a devastating shock. The new, poorly defended border through Poland was overrun almost immediately, and within weeks the panic-stricken Red Army found itself defending the major cities of Russia herself.

Chief victim of this unpreparedness was Leningrad. Immediately pre-war, the city had a population of just over three million. In the twelve weeks to mid-September 1941, when the German and Finnish armies cut it off from the rest of the Soviet Union, about half a million Leningraders were drafted or evacuated, leaving just over 2.5 million civilians, at least 400,000 of them children, trapped within the city. Hunger set in almost immediately, and in October police began to report the appearance of emaciated corpses on the streets. Deaths quadrupled in December, peaking in January and February at 100,000 per month. By the end of what was even by Russian standards a savage winter – on some days temperatures dropped to -30°C or below – cold and hunger had taken somewhere around half a million lives. It is on these months of mass death – what Russian historians call the 'heroic period' of the siege – that this book concentrates. The following two siege winters were less deadly, thanks to there being fewer mouths left to feed, and to food deliveries across Lake Ladoga, the inland sea to Leningrad's east whose south-eastern shores the Red Army continued to hold. In January 1943 fighting also cleared a fragile land corridor out of the city, through which the Soviets were able to build a railway line. Mortality nonetheless remained high, taking the total death toll to somewhere between 700,000 and 800,000 – one in every three or four of the immediate pre-siege population

– by January 1944, when the Wehrmacht finally began its long retreat to Berlin.

Remarkably, the siege of Leningrad has been paid rather little attention in the West. The best-known narrative history, written by Harrison Salisbury, a Moscow correspondent for the *New York Times*, was published in 1969. Military historians have concentrated on the battles for Stalingrad and Moscow, despite the fact that Leningrad was the first city in all Europe that Hitler failed to take, and that its fall would have given him the Soviet Union's biggest arms manufacturies, shipyards and steelworks, linked his armies with Finland's, and allowed him to cut the railway lines carrying Allied aid from the Arctic ports of Archangel and Murmansk. More generally, the siege remains lost in the gloomy vastness of the Eastern Front – an empty, snow-swept plain, in the public imagination, across which waves of Red Army conscripts stumble, greatcoats flapping, towards massed German machine guns. Worryingly often, during the writing of this book, friends turned out to think that Leningrad (on the Baltic, now called St Petersburg) and Stalingrad (a third of the size, near the present-day border with Kazakhstan, now called Volgograd) were actually the same place.

A slightly different form of vagueness afflicts Germans, for whom the Eastern Front was regarded until recently as a scene of military suffering rather than atrocity. Millions of Germans have to live with the fact that a parent or grandparent was a member of the Nazi Party; millions more have a father or grandfather who fought in Russia. It is easier to remember that they were frostbitten and frightened, or starved and put to forced labour in prisoner-of-war camps (almost four in ten of the 3.2 million Axis soldiers taken prisoner by the Soviets died in captivity[2]), than that they burned villages, stripped peasants of winter clothing and food, and helped round up and shoot Jews. More broadly, Leningrad cedes in the guilt stakes to the Holocaust: 'To be cynical', says one German historian, 'we have so many problematic aspects to our history that you have to choose.'[3] Strolling around the lovely medieval city of Freiburg, home to Germany's military archives, one comes across small brass plaques, engraved with names and dates, set into the pavement. They mark the houses from which local Jewish families were deported to the concentration camps. Leningrad's women and children, murdered by the same regime with equal deliberation, suffered out of sight and to this day largely out of mind.

The other reason the siege has been little written about, of course, is that the Soviets made it impossible to do so truthfully. During the war, censorship was all-pervading. Russians outside the siege ring, let alone Westerners, had only the vaguest idea of conditions inside the city. Soviet news broadcasts admitted 'hardship' and 'shortage' but never starvation, and Muscovites were amazed and horrified at the accounts privately given them by friends who made it out across Lake Ladoga. British and American media parroted the Soviet news bureaux. As the initial battles for Leningrad drew to stalemate the BBC's reports tailed off, and a year later London's *Times* reported the establishment of a land corridor out of the city with massive, unconscious understatement. Leningraders, readers were told, had suffered 'fearful privations' during the first siege winter, but with the coming of spring conditions had 'at once improved'.[4] Allied officialdom was equally in the dark. A member of Britain's wartime Military Mission to Moscow, a young naval lieutenant at the time, recounts how his only source of information was an actress friend, who got food to her besieged parents by begging a seat on a general's aeroplane.[5]

After the war, the Soviet government admitted mass starvation, citing a spuriously precise death toll of 632,253 at the Nuremberg war crime trials. Honest public description of its horrors, however, remained off-limits, as did all debate over why the German armies had been allowed to get so far, and why food supplies had not been laid in, nor more civilians evacuated, before the siege ring closed. The boundaries narrowed even further with the onset of the Cold War and with Stalin's launch, in 1949, of two new purges. The first, carried out in secret, swept up Leningrad's war leadership and Party organisation; the second, against 'cosmopolitanism' – codeword for Jewishness or any sort of perceived Western leaning – hundreds of its academics and professionals. The same year one of Stalin's cronies, Georgi Malenkov, visited the popular Museum of the Defence of Leningrad, which housed home-made lamps and a mock-up of a wartime ration station (complete with two thin slices of adulterated bread) as well as quantities of trophy ordnance. Striding furiously through the halls, he is said to have brandished a guidebook and shouted: 'This pretends that Leningrad suffered a special "block-ade" fate! It minimizes the role of the great Stalin!', before ordering the museum's closure. Its director was accused of 'amassing ammu-nition in preparation for terrorist acts' and sentenced to twenty-five years in the Gulag.[6]

With Stalin's death in 1953 and Nikita Khrushchev's rise to power, it finally became possible to focus on aspects of the war other than the Great Leader's military genius. As well as Khrushchev's 'Secret Speech' denouncing Stalin's Party purges, and the publica-tion of Solzhenitsyn's *One Day in the Life of Ivan Denisovich*, the 'Thaw' saw the opening, in 1960, of the first memorial complex to Leningrad's civilian war dead. The site chosen was the Piskarevskoye cemetery in the city's north-eastern suburbs, site of the largest wartime mass graves. Khrushchev's successor Leonid Brezhnev went further, making the siege one of the centrepieces of a new cult of the Great Patriotic War, designed to distract from lagging living stand-ards and political stagnation. Leningraders, in this version, turned from victims of wartime disaster to actors in a heroic national epic. They starved to death, true, but did so quietly and tidily, willing sacrifices in the defence of the cradle of the Revolution. Nobody grumbled, shirked work, fiddled the rationing system, took bribes or got dysentery. And certainly nobody, except for a few fascist spies, hoped the Germans might win.

Communism's collapse twenty years ago made it possible, in the words of one Russian historian, to start 'wiping off the syrup'. Government archives opened, giving access to internal Party memos, security service reports on crime, public opinion and the operations of various government agencies, the case files of political arrestees, political officers' despatches from the front, and transcripts of telephone calls between the Leningrad leadership and the Kremlin. Literary journals began publishing unexpurgated siege memoirs and diaries, and newspapers outspoken interviews with still-angry Red Army veterans and siege survivors. Not least, a great many photographs were published for the first time – not of smiling Komsomolkas with spades over their shoulders, but of stick-legged, pot-bellied children, or messy piles of half-naked corpses.

Though gaps remain – some material is still classified; some was destroyed during the post-war purges – the new material leaves Brezhnev's mawkish fairytale in tatters. Yes, Leningraders displayed extraordinary endurance, selflessness and courage. But they also stole, murdered, abandoned relatives and resorted to eating human meat – as do all societies when the food runs out. Yes, the regime successfully defended the city, devising ingenious food supplements and establishing supply and evacuation routes across Lake Ladoga. But it also delayed, bungled, squandered its soldiers' lives by sending them into battle untrained and unarmed, fed its own senior apparatchiks while all around starved, and made thousands of pointless executions and arrests. The camps of the Soviet Gulag, the historian Anne Applebaum remarks, were apart from, but also microcosms of, life in the wider Soviet Union. They shared 'the same slovenly working practices, the same criminally stupid bureaucracy, the same corruption, and the same sullen disregard for human life'.[7] The same applies to Leningrad during the siege: far from standing apart from the ordinary Soviet experience, it reproduced it in concentrated miniature. This book will not argue that mass starvation was as much the fault of Stalin as of Hitler. What it does, however, conclude is that under a different sort of government the siege's civilian (and military) death tolls might have been far lower.

For many Russians, this is hard to swallow. There is not much to celebrate in Russia's twentieth-century history, and the victory over Nazi Germany is a justified source of pride and patriotism. When Vladimir Putin, like Brezhnev before him, lays on lavish wartime anniversary celebrations, he finds a receptive audience. An element of tactful self-censorship also comes into play, because as well as flattering the regime the heroicised Brezhnevite version of the siege eased trauma for survivors.[8] It is hard – cruel even – to cast doubt on the doughty old woman kind enough to give an interview when she describes neighbours helping each other out, mothers sacrificing themselves for children, or good care in an evacuation hospital. She is not propagandising or myth-building, but has constructed a version of the past that is possible to live with. Paradoxically, public discussion of the blockade is likely to become franker once the last *blokadniki* have passed away.

The final point of retelling the story of the siege of Leningrad, though, is not to restore to view an overlooked atrocity, strip away Soviet propaganda or adjust the scorecards of the great dictators. It is, like all stories of humanity *in extremis*, to remind ourselves of what it is to be human, of the depths and heights of human behaviour. The siege's most eloquent victims – the diarists whose voices form the core of this book – are easy to relate to. They are not faceless poor-world peasants but educated city-dwelling Europeans – writers, artists, university lecturers, librarians, museum curators, factory managers, bookkeepers, pensioners, housewives, students and schoolchildren; owners of best coats, gramophones, favourite novels, pet dogs – people, in short, much like ourselves. Some did turn out to be heroes, others to be selfish and callous, most to be a mixture of both. As a memoirist puts it of the Party representatives in her wartime military hospital, 'There were good ones, bad ones, and the usual.' Their own words are their best memorial.

Brockagh

April 2010

Invasion: June–September 1944

PART I

Invasion: June–September 1941

'We will defend the city of Lenin' (Vladimir Serov, 1941)

One might say that Leningrad is particularly well suited to catastrophes . . . That cold river, those menacing sunsets, that operatic, terrifying moon

Anna Akhmatova

1

22 June 1941

Drive sixty kilometres south-west of what used to be Leningrad and you come to what Russians call dacha country: a green, untilled landscape of small lakes, soft dirt roads, tall, rusty-barked 'ship pines' and weathered wooden summer houses with sagging verandas and glassed-in porches. On the Sunday morning of 22 June 1941 Dmitri Likhachev, a thirty-five-year-old scholar of medieval Russian literature, was sunbathing with his wife and daughters on the sand martin-busy banks of the River Oredezh:

> The bank was steep, with a path leading along the top of it. One day, sitting on our beach, we overheard snatches of a terrifying conversation. Holidaymakers were walking along the path and talking about Kronshtadt being bombed, about some aeroplane or other. At first we thought they were reminiscing about the Finnish campaign of 1939, but their excited voices bothered us. When we returned to the dacha we were told that war had broken out.

At noon the Likhachevs gathered with other holidaymakers around an outdoor loudspeaker to listen to the formal announcement of war. The speaker was not Stalin, but the Commissar for Foreign Affairs, Vyacheslav Molotov. 'Men and women, citizens of the Soviet

Union', he began. 'At four o'clock this morning, without declaration of war, and without any claims being made on the Soviet Union, German troops attacked our country.' The text struck a note of baffled injury – 'This attack has been made despite the existence of a non-aggression pact between the Soviet Union and Germany, a pact the terms of which were scrupulously observed by the Soviet Union' – before ending with the more rousing 'Our cause is good. Our enemy will be smashed. Victory will be ours.' When the broadcast was over 'everyone was very gloomy and silent . . . After Hitler's *Blitzkrieg* in Europe, no one expected anything good.'[1]

All over Leningrad, quiet midsummer weekends were similarly violated. In her apartment in the city centre, near Potemkin's Tauride Palace, Yelena Skryabina had risen early so as to get some typing done in time for an outing to the countryside. The sunshine, the cool morning air coming in at the windows, the sound of her nanny shushing her five-year-old son Yura outside the door, all combined to give her 'a wonderful feeling of contentment and joy'. Her older son, fourteen-year-old Dima, had already left with a friend to see the fountains being switched on at the great baroque palace of Peterhof, out on the Finnish Gulf. At 9 a.m. her husband telephoned from his factory with a cryptic, agitated message to stay at home and turn on the radio. At noon, she and her mother listened to Molotov's broadcast: 'So this was it – war! Germany was already bombing Soviet cities. Molotov's speech was halting, as though he were out of breath. His rallying, spirited appeals seemed out of place. And I suddenly realised that something ominous and oppressive loomed over us.' When it was over she went outdoors, where she found crowds of people milling about the streets and elbowing their way into the shops, 'buying up everything they could lay hands on':

Many rushed to the banks to withdraw their savings. I was seized
by the same panic, and hurried to withdraw the roubles listed

in my bank book. But I was too late. The bank had run out of money. The payments had stopped. People clamoured, demanded. The June day blazed on unbearably. Someone fainted. Someone else swore vehemently. Not until evening did everything become somehow strangely still.[2]

At eleven o'clock on the same morning Yuri Ryabinkin, a skinny fifteen-year-old with a pudding-bowl fringe above big dark eyes, set off along Sadovaya Street for a children's chess competition in the gardens of the Pioneer (once the Anichkov) Palace next to the Anichkov Bridge. The policemen, he noticed, were carrying gasmasks and wearing red armbands – part, he assumed, of one of the usual civil defence exercises. He was setting out his chess pieces when he noticed a crowd gathering around a small boy standing nearby. 'I listened and froze in horror. "At four o'clock this morning", the boy was saying excitedly, "German bombers raided Kiev, Zhitomir, Sevastopol and somewhere else! Molotov spoke on the radio. Now we're at war with Germany!" . . . My head span. I couldn't think straight. But I played three games, and oddly enough, won all three. Then I drifted off home.' After supper he wandered about the tense, stuffy streets, queuing for two and a half hours for a newspaper – 'interesting talk' and 'sceptical remarks' ran through the line – until it was announced that there wouldn't be any papers, but 'some kind of official bulletin instead'. 'The clock', Ryabinkin wrote with adolescent portentousness in his diary later that evening, 'says half past eleven. A serious battle is beginning, a clash between two antagonistic forces – socialism and fascism! The well-being of mankind depends on the outcome of this historic struggle.'[3]

Leningraders should have been better prepared for the Second World War – the Great Patriotic War as they still call it – than other Soviet citizens, because they had had ringside seats at its prequel. Following the Nazi–Soviet pact of August 1939, the Soviet Union had occupied not only eastern Poland, but also, in June 1940, the Baltic states to Leningrad's west, and the lake-fretted southern marches of Finland, directly to its north.

The 'Winter War' with Finland in particular provided a foretaste of travails to come. The war was launched on 30 November 1939, three months after the invasion of Poland, and Russians expected it to be very short. '[We thought that] all we had to do was raise our voice a little bit', remembered Khrushchev, 'and the Finns would obey. If that didn't work we would fire one shot and they would put up their hands and surrender.'⁴ In fact the war proved a humiliation. Despite their tiny numbers – a population of 3.7 million compared to the Soviet Union's almost 200 million – the Finns put up a dogged defence, forcing the Russians to send in overwhelming numbers of troops. When the Soviet Union finally pushed Finland into surrender on 12 March 1941, annexing its second city of Viipuri (today Russia's Vyborg) and the whole of the isthmus between the Gulf of Finland and Lake Ladoga, it was at the cost of 127,000 Red Army fatalities. Via the rumours that leaked out of the military hospitals, Leningraders got their first intimation of the army's weaknesses in leadership, equipment and training. Soldiers lacked weapons, ammunition, winter clothing and camouflage ('We couldn't have been offered a better target', reminisced a Finnish fighter pilot of a column of troops crossing a frozen lake. 'The Russians weren't even wearing white parkas.') Most of all, they lacked good officers, thanks to Stalin's paranoid evisceration of the armed forces during the recent Terror. From 1937 to 1939 an extraordinary 40,000 officers had been arrested, and of those about 15,000 shot. Among them were three out of the five Marshals of the Soviet Union, fifteen out of sixteen army commanders, sixty out of sixty-seven corps commanders, 136 out of 169 divisional commanders, and fifteen out of twenty-five admirals. The survivors (44 per cent of whom had no secondary education) were mostly blinkered veterans of the

Civil War or overpromoted juniors too afraid of tribunal and execution squad to take the initiative or to adapt their orders to changing
circumstances.[5] The mistakes of the Winter War were repeated so
exactly during the first months of the German invasion that with
hindsight it resembles a warm-up for the main event. It certainly
seemed that way to Finns, who still call the Second World War –
during which they helped to besiege Leningrad but refused directly
to attack it – the 'Continuation War'.

In practice, though, for Leningraders as for most ordinary Russians,
the first twenty-two months of the Second World War had seemed
rather distant. 'Somewhere in Europe a war was on', one Leningrader
remembered, 'for a couple of years now – so what? . . . It wasn't
considered appropriate to worry about international events, to
exhibit, as they used to call it, "unhealthy moods".'[6] Though the
Finns had fought doggedly, the campaigns in Poland and the Baltics
had been quick and easy. Hitler's rampage across France and the Low
Countries in the spring of 1940 had moved Western-read intellectu-
als such as the poet Anna Akhmatova, who wrote unpublished verses
mourning the fall of Paris and London's Blitz. But most believed the
street-corner loudspeakers, the notice board 'wall newspapers' and
the agitators at the endless workplace meetings, who told them that
the capitalists were tearing each other apart, leaving the Soviet Union
ready to snap up the leftovers. Though the treaty with Hitler was
only temporary, any war with him would be fought on German soil
and be over almost before it had begun, brought to a halt by popular
revolution inside Germany itself. Hearing of the Nazi attack, workers at the Leningrad Metal Factory exclaimed, 'Our forces will thrash
them; it'll be over in a week. No, not in a week – we've got to get to
Berlin. That'll take three or four weeks.'[7] Even sophisticated observers, able correctly to interpret Hitler's April invasion of Yugoslavia (in
defiance of a Soviet–Yugoslav friendship pact) and Churchill's warning speeches, were shocked when what they had feared actually came

to pass. For Olga Fridenberg, a classicist and first cousin to Boris Pasternak, 'It wasn't the invasion that was incredible, for who had not expected it? . . . It was the upheaval in our lives, their sudden cleaving into past and present on this quiet summer Sunday with all the windows wide open.'[8]

Famously, the Soviet leadership was caught by surprise as well. 'Stalin and his people remain completely inactive', Goebbels confided to his diary a month before the invasion, 'like a rabbit confronted with a snake.'[9] Though historians still debate the rationale behind Stalin's pre-war foreign policy, it is clear that Stalin both expected war with Germany and convinced himself that with appeasement it could be delayed at least until the following year. Reports from the Soviet ambassador to Berlin were ignored, as was military intelligence of troop concentrations west of the new German–Soviet border. British warnings were dismissed as disinformation, designed to turn the Red Army into 'England's soldiers'. Notoriously, the trade commissariat continued to send grain, petroleum, rubber and copper to Germany right up to the very night of the invasion.

Stalin's plenipotentiary in Leningrad at the outbreak of war was Andrei Zhdanov, a plump, sallow-faced, chain-smoking son of a schoolteacher who had risen to be Party Secretary of Gorky (formerly and now again Nizhni Novgorod), thence to the Central Committee, and after the murder of Leningrad Party boss Sergei Kirov (probably at Stalin's hands) in 1934, to leadership of the Leningrad Party organisation and full membership of the Politburo. Devotedly loyal, and like Stalin a workaholic autodidact, he was one of the few people Stalin addressed with the familiar *ty* – equivalent to the French *tu* – rather than the formal *Vy*. Today he is best remembered for leading Leningrad's defence and for a tragic-comic post-war stint as cultural commissar, during which he denounced Akhmatova as 'half-nun, half-whore', and tinkled politically correct tunes to Shostakovich on the piano. In truth, he was a mass murderer: as well as overseeing the Leningrad purges of 1937–9, he had, like other Politburo members, toured them to the provinces – in his case, to the Urals and Middle Volga. His signature, together with Stalin's and Molotov's, is to be found at the bottom of dozens of death lists.

Like Stalin, Zhdanov was so confident that talk of an imminent German attack was premature that on 19 June he left Moscow for a six-week break at the Black Sea resort of Sochi. 'The Germans have already missed their best moment', Stalin reassured him. 'It looks as though they will attack in 1942. Go on holiday.' Through the afternoon of Saturday 21 June, as Zhdanov settled in at the seaside, the border guards' usual trickle of unsettling reports turned into a torrent: of yet more incursions into Soviet airspace, of covert movements of tanks and artillery, of pontoon bridges being built and barbed-wire entanglements cleared away. Shortly after nine in the evening, three deserters – a Lithuanian and two German Communists – crossed the River Bug to Soviet lines, and told interrogators of the orders that had just been read out to their units. The attack would begin at 0400, said the Lithuanian, and 'they plan to finish you off pretty quickly'.[10]

In the Kremlin, apprehension still vied with denial. The German Foreign Ministry, the Berlin embassy reported, was refusing to take its half-hourly calls. Sometime in the late evening the commissar for defence, General Semen Timoshenko, rang Stalin with the news from the German deserters, at which Stalin ordered him to assemble an emergency meeting of Politburo members and senior generals. On their arrival he paused in his pacing and asked, 'Well, what now?' Timoshenko and the chief of staff, General Georgi Zhukov, insisted that all frontier troops should be put on full battle alert. Stalin disagreed: 'It would be premature to issue that order now. It might still be possible to settle the situation by peaceful means . . . The border units must not allow themselves to be provoked into anything that might cause difficulties.' At half past midnight he finally allowed the order to go through – prefaced by a warning that the attacks might only be provocations, and calling for a 'disguised' response.

The meeting broke up at 3 a.m. An hour later Stalin had just gone to bed when he received a call from Zhukov. The major cities of the western Soviet Union – Kiev, Minsk, Vilnius, Sevastopol – were being bombed. 'Did you understand what I said, Comrade Stalin?' asked Zhukov. He had to repeat himself before he got a reply. War, even Stalin had to acknowledge, had begun.[11]

The first rule of foreign policy, the dinner-party truism has it, is never to invade Russia. Why did Hitler, very conscious of the disaster that befell Napoleon there, decide to attack the Soviet Union?

His aims, from the campaign's inception in 1940, were not those of conventional geopolitics. He did not want just to annexe useful territory and create a new balance of power, but to wipe out a culture and an ideology, if necessary a race. His vision for the newly conquered territories, as expounded over meals at his various wartime headquarters, was of a thousand-mile-wide Reich stretching from Berlin to Archangel on the White Sea and Astrakhan on the Caspian. 'The whole area', he harangued his architect Albert Speer,

> must cease to be Asiatic steppe, it must be Europeanized! The Reich peasants will live on handsome, spacious farms; the German authorities in marvellous buildings, the governors in palaces. Around each town there will be a belt of delightful villages, 30–40km deep, connected by the best roads. What exists beyond that will be another world, in which we mean to let the Russians live as they like.[12]

Existing cities were to be stripped of their valuables and destroyed (Moscow was to be replaced with an artificial lake), and the delightful new villages populated with Aryan settlers imported from Scandinavia and America. Within twenty years, Hitler dreamed, they would number twenty million. Russians – lowest of the Slavs – were to be deported to Siberia, reduced to serfdom, or simply exterminated, like the native tribes of America. Putting down any lingering Russian resistance would serve merely as sporting exercise. 'Every few years', Speer remembered, 'Hitler planned to lead a small campaign beyond the Urals, so as to demonstrate the authority of the Reich and keep the military preparedness of the German army at a high level.' As a later SS planning document put it, the Reich's ever-mobile eastern marches, like the British Raj's North-West Frontier, would 'keep Germany young'.

So surreal is this vision, so risible in its bar-room sweep and shallowness, that it is tempting not to take it seriously. What was the sense in occupying a country so as to destroy it? Where was the money for the new roads and cities to come from? The millions of willing settlers? The troops to hold half a continent in permanent slavery? For the Nazi leadership, though, it was no daydream. In July 1940, weeks after the fall of France, Hitler ordered the commander-in-chief of the army, Field Marshal Walther von Brauchitsch, and his military chief of staff, General Franz Halder, to start planning the conquest of the Soviet Union. Britain, Hitler argued, could not be invaded for the present, and the only way to persuade her to see reason and make peace was to eliminate the last continental power inherently hostile to the Reich. Brauchitsch and Halder were unconvinced (though less so than Halder claimed post-war), preferring to see Britain knocked out of the war first. ('Barbarossa', Halder wrote in his diary on 28 January 1941. 'Purpose not clear. We don't hit the British that way . . . Risk in the west must not be underestimated. It's possible that Italy collapses following the loss of her colonies, and we get a southern front in Spain, Italy and Greece. If we are then tied up in Russia, a bad situation will be made worse.'[13]) Equally doubtful was Foreign Minister Joachim von Ribbentrop, who regarded the pact with Molotov as his greatest achievement, and pointed out that the USSR was still punctiliously honouring its promises to supply grain and other commodities. Hermann Goering, head of economic planning and the second most powerful man in the Reich, worried about shortages of food and labour. But Hitler was at the height of his popularity and prestige, and used to browbeating subordinates: the waverers swallowed their doubts and accepted the inevitable. The only member of the leadership to take decisive action over the issue was the unstable Rudolf Hess, who made his bizarre flight to Scotland just six weeks before the invasion, apparently in hope of preventing a two-front war by negotiating peace with Britain.

The plan for Barbarossa was completed in December 1940, and a launch date set of 15 May 1941. Both date and design soon changed (Italy's calls for help in Greece and Libya forced a delay, and a two-pronged attack turned into a three-pronged one), but from its conception, the campaign was to be conducted with unprecedented harshness, a policy to which the army put up shamefully little objection. 'This war', wrote Halder after a two-and-a-half-hour address by the Führer to his assembled generals on 30 March, 'will be very different from the war in the west ... Commanders must make the sacrifice of overcoming their personal scruples.' In June High Command itself instigated the notorious 'Commissar Order', under which captured political officers were to be shot out of hand. Further orders authorised 'collective measures' against civilians 'who participate or want to participate in hostile acts', and removed military courts' right to try crimes – including rape and murder – committed by German soldiers against Soviet civilians. Individual officers were effectively freed to treat the Russians they came across as they saw fit. Also assumed from the outset was ruthless food requisitioning. The occupying troops were to live off what they could commandeer locally, even if it meant that civilians starved. 'The Russian has stood poverty for centuries!' joked Herbert Backe, state secretary in the Ministry for Food and Agriculture. 'His stomach is flexible, hence no false pity!' Goebbels quipped that the Russians would have to 'eat their Cossack saddles'; Goering predicted 'the biggest mass death in Europe since the Thirty Years War'.[14]

Most of all, the Bolsheviks were to be beaten quickly. This was to be a *Blitzkrieg*, or 'lightning war', of swift onward movement led by tanks and motorised infantry. The army should not wait to capture every centre of resistance on its race east, and above all it should not get bogged down in the sort of static, attritional fighting that had lost it the war of 1914–18. In all, the campaign was to take no more than three months; the first few weeks in major battles destroying the Red Army, the rest in mopping-up operations. Once conquered, the whole of European Russia would swiftly be transferred to civilian rule under four new Reichskommissariats, allowing most troops to come home.

Things didn't work out that way not only because Hitler was a fantasist, but because he radically misunderstood Soviet society. He vastly overestimated the power of Russian anti-Semitism, and underestimated patriotism and national feeling. He failed – in common with mainstream British and American opinion of the time – to see that most Russians, despite having been terrorised and impoverished over the preceding two decades by their own leadership, would tenaciously resist foreign invasion. 'Smash in the door!' he famously declared, 'and the whole rotten structure will come crashing down!' The crass slurs – 'the Slavs are a mass of born slaves'; 'their bottomless stupidity'; 'those stupid masses of the East' – endlessly repeated in his mealtime diatribes were a measure not only of his racism, but of intellectual laziness, of complacency in the face of a vast, fastchanging and secretive country of which he and his advisers knew very little. His misconceptions, ironically, mirrored Soviet ones about Germany: 'Too high hopes', one of Hitler's generals recalled later, 'were built on the belief that Stalin would be overthrown by his own people if he suffered political defeats. The belief was fostered by the Führer's political advisors, and we, as soldiers, didn't know enough about the political side to dispute it.'[15]

As the war progressed, rivalry increasingly broke out not only between the multiple, overlapping agencies responsible for the occupied Soviet Union, but between ideologues, intent on their Führer's grand vision of extermination, and pragmatists (many of them Baltic German by background), who advised something closer to the traditional colonial policy of co-opting ethnic minorities – in particular the Ukrainians – and reversing unpopular Communist measures, such as the closure of churches and collectivisation of land. But even if Hitler had understood the Soviet Union better, it is likely that he would have ignored the pragmatists' advice. The attack on the Soviet Union had rational justifications: it was to bring Germany agricultural land and oil wells, and eliminate an inimical regime. But it was also about race: a *Vernichtungskrieg*, a war of extermination. Bolsheviks, Jews, Slavs – they were vermin, brutes, cankers, poison; their very existence anathema to the National Socialist dream. Liquidating or enslaving them was not just a means to territorial domination, but part of its purpose.

2

Barbarossa

On the Sunday night of 22 June, as on every midsummer night, darkness did not fall on Leningrad. The sun slipped below the steel-blue waters of the Gulf of Finland to the west, but the sky above the rooftops remained a luminous pinkish violet, held in suspended animation until the small hours of the morning, when the sun rose again and bathed the city in full, disorienting daylight. At 2 a.m., Yelena Skryabina was woken by the deafening sound of anti-aircraft guns. Believing (wrongly – it was only a drill) that an air raid was in progress, she and her family joined their neighbours in the stairwell of their apartment building:

> Lyubov Nikolayevna Kurakina orated above the din. Her husband, a former Party member, has already served two years on a charge of counter-revolution. Her Communist sympathies were shaken by her husband's arrest, but last night, under the roar of the anti-aircraft guns, she forgot all her earlier resentment. With conviction she extolled the invincibility of Soviet Russia . . .
> Anastasiya Vladimirovna, our former landlady, sat on a large trunk, smiling sarcastically. She made no attempt to hide her hatred of the Soviet government and sees in this war and eventual German victory our only possible salvation. In

many respects I share her views, but that smile irritates me. Two sentiments entered the controversy: the wish to believe that Russia will not be destroyed, and the realization that only war offers any actual possibility that we will be freed from the terror of the regime.[1]

Skryabina was not the only Leningrader to have mixed feelings about the German attack. Everywhere, anger at Nazi aggression combined with anger at the government's evident unpreparedness for war, and among some, like Skryabina's reckless neighbour, with the feeling that German occupation might be a price worth paying for the end of Bolshevism.

When Likhachev returned to the city on Monday he found it sombre and quiet. In the university's Russian Literature department – housed in what had once been the customs house on the eastern point of Vasilyevsky Island, now called 'Pushkin House' – people were unusually talkative, though they 'looked around' as usual before speaking out: 'Everyone was surprised that literally days before a very great quantity of grain had been sent to Finland – it had been in the papers . . . A. I. Grushkin talked most, making fantastic suggestions, but all "patriotic".' At the Kirov Works informers recorded the reactions of ordinary workers. Speakers at a public meeting were predictably resolute: 'I cannot find words to describe the unthinkable treachery of the Fascist dogs', declaimed one. 'Our duty is to unite around the government and Comrade Stalin, to forget about ourselves and put all our strength into working for the front.' But in private, people were angry and frightened:

Comrade Martynov was overheard saying in private conversation: 'See, we feed Hitler our bread, and now he has turned against us!' E. P. Batmanova declared that she had heard that Hanko [a Soviet naval base west of Helsinki] has been taken by the Germans. Party members present rebuked her harshly, and explained to other comrades that such conversation is harmful and in the interest of enemy elements.

The following day 'canteen director Comrade Solovyov delayed lunch . . . because of problems with transport. Among those waiting the following conversation was overheard: "It's only the second day of the war, and already there's no bread. If the war goes on for a year we'll all die of starvation." '[2]

Overwhelmingly, though, the public mood in the first few days of the war was one of genuine patriotism. Even before orders for general mobilisation went out on 27 June, queues of would-be volunteers formed outside local Party offices, military recruitment centres and factory headquarters. Altogether, some 100,000 Leningraders volunteered in the first twenty-four hours of the war, well before officialdom had had a chance to call them up.[3] By Thursday 26th the Kirov Works was able to report that it had received over nine hundred applications for entry into the works militia and 110 new applications for Party membership. The district recruitment office had received over one thousand requests, from women as well as men, to be sent to the front.[4] On the day war was declared eight-year-old Igor Kruglyakov went with his father and uncles to the Karl Bulla photography studio on Nevsky Prospekt, to pose for a family portrait. The next day, he remembers, 'we went over to the Petrograd Side, to accompany my father to the military commission. I remember that *voyenkomat*, the courtyard was surrounded by buildings all the way round. There was a little checkpoint and he was quickly registered somehow or other. He went off that same evening.'[5]

Over the following few weeks, Party workers organised highly choreographed but nevertheless semi-voluntary drives to raise defence funds. At the Kirov Works, older 'veterans of labour' appealed to their colleagues to donate jewellery, money, bonds and other valuables, as well as one or more day's pay. So many items were donated that factory treasurers soon asked that they be delivered directly to the banks. Refusing, at a public meeting, to accept a Party official's invitation to forgo pay would have been hard. But as the historian Andrei Dzeniskevich – one of the first to mine Leningrad's wartime archives in the newly free early 1990s – points out, only genuine concern could have induced somebody to 'give up gold earrings or a single silver spoon, the existence of which nobody else knew about'.[6]

This wave of patriotic volunteerism also engulfed the city's intel-ligentsia, the social group, aside from army officers and senior Party officials, hardest hit by the repressions of the previous five years and thus with the most reason to hate the government. Despite the vast differences of context, the itch for action, among the young at least, was not dissimilar from that which propelled the jingo-fed schoolboys of Edwardian England into the trenches. 'Hello Irina!' an eighteen-year-old wrote to his girlfriend that June,

> I am going to witness something extraordinary and significant – I'm off to the front! Do you understand what that means? No you don't.
>
> It's a test of self – of one's opinions, taste, character. And that's not a paradox. Perhaps I'll be able to understand Beethoven's music better, and the genius of Lermontov and Pushkin, once I've been to war . . .
>
> Well, there's no time to write. Now I've got an advantage over you. I'm going to plunge into the vortex of life, while you're destined to keep on swotting away at your books. Am I overdoing it about the books? It's alright; maybe we'll see each other again one day. I hold your hands and squeeze them tight – Oleg.[7]

Older Russians, for whom the Soviet Union was a foreign and hostile country, felt a new identification with their homeland. 'In the dismay of the first few days', as the then thirty-nine-year-old literary critic Lidiya Ginzburg later put it, educated Leningraders wanted to be rid of loneliness, an egoism which intensified fear. It was an instinctive movement . . . the eternal dream of escape from self; of responsibility, of the supra-personal. It all found absurd expression in an odd feeling of coincidence. The intellectual now wanted for himself the thing that the community wanted from him.

Startlingly, people trained by necessity to disguise and hypocrisy, to never speaking their minds except to their oldest friends, suddenly found themselves sincerely in tune with the popular, state-approved mood. 'Those not liable for call-up', Ginzburg remembered, 'urgently wanted to do something – go to the hospital, offer their services as an interpreter, write an article for the paper, seemingly without wanting to be paid.' Officialdom did not always know what to do with them. They 'fell into a machine totally unadapted to such psychological material. With customary rudeness and mistrust . . . it threw people out of some sections and dragged them into others against their will.'[8]

One of the many who identified passionately with her country while loathing its government was Anna Akhmatova. Born in 1889 and brought up in Tsarskoye Selo, a palace town just south of Petersburg, she had won fame before the Revolution as a writer of lyrical, bittersweet love lyrics, travelled round Europe and been sketched – tall, lean and eagle-nosed – by Modigliani. The shadows began to lengthen in the late 1920s, when her ex-husband, the poet Nikolai Gumilev, was arrested and executed, one of the first prominent artists to fall victim to the Bolsheviks. Through the thirties, as all around friends disappeared into the camps, she turned to lecturing and translation, while continuing secretly to compose her own increasingly profound and wrenching poetry; each new work was committed to memory, then the manuscript burned. In 1938 her twenty-six-year-old son was arrested for the third time in five years and sent to the Gulag, where he remained at the outbreak of war. Despite all this, Akhmatova eagerly took up an invitation to make a patriotic broadcast to the 'women of Leningrad', and took her turn standing guard duty outside the Sheremetyev Palace on the Fontanka river, where she lived in a cramped and chaotic *ménage à trois* with her second ex-husband, the art historian Nikolai Punin, and his new wife and daughter.

Another writer who wrestled with the distinction between country and regime was the thirty-one-year-old poet Olga Berggolts. Out of fashion today, Berggolts became famous with *February Diary*, a cycle of vivid and by the standards of the time outspoken poems, written during the siege's first winter and broadcast early in 1942. At the war's start she was still unknown, a junior staff member at the city radio station. Fair and delicate, with a gentle, oval face and wide blue eyes, she knew and admired Akhmatova, but was a generation younger and had grown up a believing Communist, during the idealistic decade after the Revolution. Disillusion had not come until 1937, when her ex-husband was arrested (he was later secretly executed) and she was expelled from the Party and from the Writers' Union. Berggolts's own turn came eighteen months later, when she was taken to the prison behind the Ministry of Internal Affairs' headquarters on the Liteiniy, and kicked in the stomach until she suffered a miscarriage. Seven months later she was released – saved, ironically, by the Terror itself, which had just reached the upper levels of Leningrad's security services, purging her gaolers in the process.

By the time war broke out two years later, Berggolts had returned to the normal concerns of everyday life – a boozy flirtation with a colleague at the city radio station, hazy thoughts on a possible novel, arrangements for an illegal abortion for her sister. Her diary entry of 22 June reads simply 'WAR!', but on that day she also wrote a new, unpublishable poem, which tried to reconcile her fierce disillusionment with Communism as practised under Stalin with her love for her country:

On that day too I did not forget
The bitter years of persecution and sorrow.
But in a blinding flash I understood:
It didn't happen to me but to You;
It was You who found strength and waited.
No, I have forgotten nothing,
But even the dead and the victims
Will rise from the grave at your call;
We will all rise, and not I alone.
I love you with a new love
Bitter, all-forgiving, bright –
My Motherland with the wreath of thorns
And the bright rainbow over your head . . .
I love you – I can do no other –
And you and I are one again, as before.[9]

The men in charge of making sure that public anger at news
of the German invasion did not spill into disorder were Zhdanov
(who made it back to Leningrad on 26 or 27 June), Petr Popkov,
the hot-tempered chairman of the city soviet, and (with the declaration of martial law) Lieutenant General Popov, commander of the
Leningrad garrison. Actual fulfilment of the city leadership's orders
rested with the executive committees of the regional, city and fifteen
city district soviets. The entire structure took its cues from Moscow:
Popov's Order No. 1 of 27 June, for example, mandating longer
working hours, tighter travel restrictions and a curfew, was a verba-
tim copy of one issued by the Moscow garrison commander two
days earlier. 'It is difficult to avoid the impression', as one historian
puts it, 'that the Leningrad garrison commander actually copied his
order from *Pravda*.'[10]

This machinery, with its overlaps and overdependence on the
faraway Kremlin and on Zhdanov's office in the Smolniy, the gaunt
former girls' school that housed the Leningrad Party headquarters,

stayed in place almost until the city was surrounded. The creation on 24 August of a Military Council of the Leningrad Front, bringing together Zhdanov and army group commander Marshal Kliment Voroshilov, streamlined decision-making somewhat, but the problem of overcentralisation remained. Four days earlier Zhdanov had tried to offload some of his mountainous responsibilities by creating a second committee, not including himself, to have charge over the construction of fortifications, weapons production and civilian military training. Stalin immediately telephoned to complain that the new body had been formed without his permission, and insisted that Zhdanov and Voroshilov join it. Zhdanov was thus left with two almost identical committees, the second of which he wound up again ten days later. Fat, asthmatic, balding, his khaki tunic littered with dandruff and cigarette ash, he thereafter made no further attempts to delegate. The saying of the time – that not a volt of electricity was allocated without his consent – was almost literally true. Typical, among the mass of trivial documents in the archives bearing his signature, is an order that one factory deliver another nine tanks of oxygen.[11]

In a crisis, these men's first instinct was to make arrests. At one o'clock on the morning of the Friday following the invasion, Yelena Skryabina and her husband were woken by the doorbell: 'Anyone who lives in the Soviet Union knows what the purpose of such an especially long night-time ring is. It is the sound that means a search warrant or an order for arrest. But this time it turned out to be a summons from the draft board.' Four days later she heard that a colleague had been less lucky: 'They came at night, searched, found nothing, confiscated nothing, but took her away anyway. All I know is that the head of the institute where we both work is very hostile to her. It could be that the charge is "foreign ties".' Having spent longer than she meant to visiting the woman's family, Skryabina returned home to find her own family convinced that she had been arrested too.[12]

The most predictable victims of the new wave of terror that broke over Leningrad on the outbreak of war were the city's ethnic Germans. Descendants of German-speaking Balts, of the peasant settlers invited to plough the southern steppe by Catherine the Great, or of the numerous Germans who later came to make professional or service careers under the tsars, most had lived in Russia for generations and were indistinguishable from ordinary Russians save for their surnames. (Some tried to evade deportation by changing their names, others by pretending to be Jewish.[13]) In a procedure already well honed in the Baltics and eastern Poland, they were given twenty-four hours in which to prepare for departure, in overcrowded goods wagons, into what was euphemistically called 'compulsory evacuation' to the Arctic, Central Asia, Siberia and the Far East. About 23,000 ethnic Germans and Finns were thus deported in the summer of 1941, and another 35,162 in March 1942, across the ice of Lake Ladoga.[14] Among them were the Tribergs, who lived on the Nevsky above what had once been the family business, the well-known 'Aleksandr' shoe shop. 'They were just a family', a neighbour remembered sixty years later:

> They lived across the landing from us, on the same staircase of number 11 Nevsky Prospekt . . .
> There were three children, two boys and a three-year-old girl. The two older ones, twelve and sixteen years old, sometimes used to come round. I took German lessons from their mother and aunt, such beautiful, elegant, intelligent women. The boys' mother was especially kind, as well as highly intellectual. The elder son seemed to have inherited all his mother's talents, and those of his father too, an engineer who spoke several European languages. I can say with certainty that the country lost a future scholar when it lost this young man.
> More precisely, it lost them all. This is how it happened:
> In 1938 they arrested the father

In 1941 they likewise arrested the mother
In 1944 she was shot.

The sons were left orphans with nothing whatsoever: all their possessions were confiscated. As a consequence, the older son died from starvation, since they had nothing to trade for bread. The younger son remained with his aunt and her little daughter. They were living shadows: a woman dying from starvation and two dystrophic [emaciated] children. In this condition they were deported from Leningrad – over the ice of Lake Ladoga.

During the journey the aunt died and the two surviving children were separated, never to meet again. Thus perished a family, as the neighbour drily noted 'during the last war with the Germans, but not, strictly speaking, at the hands of the Germans'.[15]

Also deported or arrested in large numbers (71,112 up to October 1942, according to security service documents) were 'socially alien' and 'criminal-felonious' elements among the general population. In practice this meant the same sorts of people targeted during the 1936–8 purges: members of the old bourgeoisie ('de-classed elements'), peasants ('former kulaks'), ethnic minorities ('nationalists'), churchgoers ('sectarians'), the wives and children of earlier repression victims ('relatives of enemies of the people'), and anyone with foreign connections or knowledge of a foreign language ('spy-traitors'). As usual it could be fatal simply to air a grumble or state the obvious – the Soviet Union's first execution for 'spreading defeatist rumours' was recorded in Leningrad at the beginning of July. Hundreds of ordinary people were arrested for complaining about their working hours, predicting a bad harvest, or passing on news of the bombing of Kiev and Smolensk.[16]

One of the most notable Leningraders to vanish at this time was the absurdist writer Daniil Yuvachov, better known by his pen-name Daniil Kharms. A relic of the avant-garde 1920s, he cultivated a range of eccentricities, studying the occult, drinking nothing but milk and parading the neighbourhood around his Mayakovsky Street flat in a deerstalker, shooting jacket, plus-fours, saucer-sized pocket watch and checked socks. His scraps of prose and dialogue – unpublished until the late 1980s – capture the drabness and mad bureaucratic violence of his times with nightmare black humour. In one, a man dreams again and again of a policeman hiding in the bushes, and gets thinner and thinner until a sanitary inspector orders him to be folded up and thrown out with the rubbish. In another, inquisitive old women lean out of a window, tumbling one after another to the ground. In a third, friends quarrel over whether or not the number seven comes before the number eight, until distracted by a child who 'fortunately' falls off a park bench and breaks its jaw. Kharms was arrested in August and sent to the psychiatric wing of the Kresty prison, where he died, of unknown causes, two months later. Why was he picked out? 'Perhaps', as the siege historian Harrison Salisbury put it, just because he 'wore a funny hat.'

The volunteerism of the first few days of the war swiftly became mandatory. On Friday 27 June – before the rest of the Soviet Union[17] – the Leningrad city soviet issued an order mobilising all able-bodied men between the ages of sixteen and fifty, and all women, except for those caring for young children, aged between sixteen and forty-five, for civil defence work. Most were sent to the countryside to dig anti-tank ditches; the rest were put to work in the city digging air-raid shelters, camouflaging public buildings (the entire Smolniy was draped in netting, and amateur mountain climbers painted the Admiralty's gilded spire grey), and manning new fire-fighting, bomb-disposal and first-aid teams, as well as replacing factory workers drafted into the army. Much of the responsibility for making all this happen fell on the ubiquitous, disliked *upravdomy*, or apartment block managers, who were given the power to assign civil defence duties as well as to check residence permits and report on draft dodgers.[18]

For children, all this novel activity was rather fun. Yuri Ryabinkin helped build bomb shelters near the Kazan cathedral – 'now I have blisters and splinters on both hands', he wrote proudly – loaded sand – 'the boys modelled Hitler's ugly mug out of sand and started whacking it with spades' – played pool and more chess at the Pioneer Palace and read *David Copperfield*.[19] Little Igor Kruglyakov, finding himself left to his own devices, went out exploring – to the Tavrichesky Gardens, where silver barrage balloons swum like great whales above the gravel paths, and to the Suvorov Museum, whose janitor let him on to the roof to look at his racing pigeons. Blackouts – not very effective in the short, light summer nights – were introduced on 27 June, and phosphorescent badges, shaped like fireflies and roses, issued to children so as to prevent accidents. Attics were filled with sand and painted with flame-retardant limewash, and window glass pasted over with strips of paper or gauze, so as to reduce splintering. Applying the strips, wrote Lidiya Ginzburg, 'had a soothing effect, distracting people from the emptiness of merely waiting. But there was something poignant and strange about them too, reminiscent of a sparkling surgical ward, where there were as yet no wounded, but soon would be.' To others the strips looked light and decorative, like garden trellising or the carved window frames of prosperous peasant cabins. Some designs were imaginative – the inhabitants of a building on the Fontanka did theirs in the shape of palm trees, with monkeys sitting underneath – but the commonest pattern was two simple diagonals, and the resulting white St Andrew's Cross became a visual leitmotif of the siege.

Dmitri Likhachev, exempted from call-up for medical reasons, did military training alongside his colleagues from Pushkin House.

We 'white-ticketers' were enlisted into the Institute self-defence detachments, issued with double-barrelled shotguns and drilled in front of the History Faculty building. I remember B. P. Gorodetsky and V. V. Gippius among the marchers. The latter walked in comical fashion on his toes, leaning his whole body forward. Our instructor laughed silently along with everyone else . . .

Far-sightedly, Likhachev also stocked up on food, insisting that his family claim their whole, initially generous, bread ration, and dry slices on a sunny windowsill until they had enough to fill a pillowcase, which they hung on a wall out of reach of mice. He also insisted that they buy everything they could from the rapidly empty- ing shops, whose windows were now blocked with double screens of earth-filled planking. Later, he was to wish that they had bought more.

> In winter, lying in bed, I thought of one thing until my head hurt: there, on the shelves in the shops, there had been canned fish. Why hadn't I bought it? Why had I bought only eleven jars of cod-liver oil, and not gone to the chemist's a fifth time to get another three? Why hadn't I bought a few vitamin C and glucose tablets? These 'whys' were terribly tormenting. I thought of every uneaten bowl of soup, every crust of bread thrown away, every potato peeling, with as much remorse and despair as if I'd been the murderer of my own children. But all the same, we did as much as we could, and believed none of the reassuring announce- ments on the radio.[20]

Georgi Knyazev, director of the Academy of Sciences archive, was confined to a wheelchair by paralysis of the legs. Each day he pushed himself along the same 800-metre stretch of the Vasilyevsky Island embankment, from the bronze-plaqued 'Academicians' Building' where he lived, past a pair of sphinxes imported from Luxor by Nicholas I, the gabled Menshikov Palace and lime tree-filled Rumyantsev Square to the portico of the Academy. On the opposite bank spread the clas- sic Petersburg panorama: to the left, beyond Palace Bridge, the rococo hulks of the Hermitage and Winter Palace; just visible behind them, the Palace Square angel and topmost candy-swirl of the Cathedral of Our Saviour of the Spilled Blood; ahead, the Admiralty building with its needle spire; to the right, the egg-shaped dome of St Isaac's and Falconet's famous equestrian statue of Peter the Great – the 'Bronze Horseman' – rearing from its granite boulder. This stretch of pavement, this view, was what Knyazev called his 'small radius', the narrow aperture through which he was to observe the whole of the siege. Prosy and conventional (his diary is addressed, with unintentional irony, to 'you, my distant friend, member of the future Communist society, to whom all war will be as inherently loathsome as cannibalism is to us'[21]), he spent the first days of the war listening to the radio ('The peoples of Europe must surely rise in rebellion!') sorting out a first-aid kit ('for use in the event of burns or wounds'), and attempting to energise his staff, who showed a tendency to 'guard the sofa in the President's office' instead of the archive's depository. On 2 July he visited the archive administration headquarters, in the old Senate Building:

On the staircase which once heard the rap of Guards Officer Lermontov's sabre . . . there now hangs a length of rail on a thick cord, and next to it a metal rod – a beater. This is for use in the event of a gas alarm. On the upper landing it was dark, although blue lamps were burning. Walking along the corridor, which was in almost total darkness, I felt as though I were in a Meyerhold production.

The IRLI [Institute of Russian Literature] repository was a dreadful sight. I hardly recognised the workrooms. Everything was in chaos . . . Behind a statue of Aleksandr Vsevolovsky stood two large barrels of water, one of which was already leaking. There were boxes of sand and spades all over the place, and a fire hose stretched along the corridor. Outside the Pushkin room stood storage boxes, some empty, some full. I had to do them justice

– Pushkin's manuscripts were packed perfectly . . . But there was a lot of fuss and agitation. Right next to the boxes, a staff member was dictating an article on fascism to a typist. Someone else was writing out a list of what had to be packed . . . Everywhere, there were crowds of people carrying sandbags.

Yelena Skryabina decided to escape the war – and reduce her chances of arrest – by renting a dacha (their price had plummeted) near Pushkin, the town, formerly Tsarskoye Selo or 'Royal Village', that had grown up around the tsars' summer palaces. There she and her children spent their time wandering in the sunshine round the folly-dotted Catherine Palace park. 'Blue sky, blue lake, and the green frame of the shore. Peaceful. No voices audible. No one strolling the paths. Only somewhere, far away, the silvery walls of the palaces sparkling through the greenery.'[22] On weekly visits back to the city, though, it was impossible to shut out reality. She worried about gas attacks (unnecessarily as it turned out; gas masks were issued but never had to be used), and about famine, 'because all those news-paper reassurances about our massive food supplies are barefaced lies'. Her neighbour Kurakina whispered of the beatings her newly returned but now half-deaf and fearful husband had endured in camp; up in the cloudless sky high-flying planes left vapour trails, a sinister novelty to Leningraders, who thought them some sort of targeting device.

Not until 3 July, eleven days after the invasion, did Stalin make his first wartime broadcast. Unpolished but immediate – the rim of the glass clicking against his teeth as he took sips of water – it was, in the words of the BBC's Moscow correspondent Alexander Werth, 'a great pull-yourselves-together speech, a blood-sweat-and-tears speech, with Churchill's post-Dunkirk speech its only parallel'.[23] Opening with novel, almost beseeching informality – 'Comrades, citizens, brothers and sisters! I appeal to you, my friends!' – it called the nation to total war in the tradition of the struggle against Napoleon. Production was to go into overdrive, and 'whiners, cowards, deserters and panic-mongers' were to be put in front of military tribunals. Not a 'single railway truck, not a pound of bread nor pint of oil' was to be left in the path of the fascist enslavers' advance, and behind their lines partisans were to blow up roads, bridges and telephone wires and set fire to forests, stores and road convoys. 'Intolerable conditions' were to be created for 'the enemy and his accomplices', who were to be 'persecuted and destroyed at every step'. 'All the strength of the people', Stalin rounded off with sledgehammer emphasis, 'must be used to smash the enemy. Onward to Victory!'

The speech had a steadying effect, in Leningrad as elsewhere. In Moscow's cinemas, Werth remembered, audiences broke into frantic cheering whenever Stalin appeared on a newsreel, 'which, in the dark, people presumably wouldn't do unless they felt like it'.[24] Though in reality Stalin had grossly understated the success of Barbarossa, claiming heavy German losses, Russians now felt that they had heard the worst, and stood on firm ground. The seventy-year-old watercolourist Anna Ostroumova-Lebedeva (who had studied under Repin, Bakst and Whistler, and seen out three tsars) listened with her maid Nyusha in their flat near Finland Station on Leningrad's Vyborg Side. 'Today', she wrote in her diary, 'I listened, with heartfelt anxiety, to the wise words of Comrade Stalin. His words pour feelings of calm, hope and cheer into the soul.'[25]

She would have been less reassured if she had known how far the Germans had really got. For the Soviet Union, the first eleven days of the war were devastating. Arrayed against it was the largest invasion force the world had ever seen: four million German and Axis troops, 3,350 tanks, 7,000 field guns, over 2,000 aircraft and 600,000 horses. In the north in particular, the Red Army was heavily outnumbered, with 370,000 troops compared to the Wehrmacht's 655,000. (Numbers of guns, tanks and combat aircraft were roughly similar.[26]) The Germans were also better led and organised. Army Group North – one of three that attacked all along the Soviet–German border – was led by Field Marshal Wilhelm Ritter von Leeb, the sixty-five-year-old career soldier who had led the breaking of the Maginot Line. Under him, in command of the Sixteenth and Eighteenth Armies, came General Ernst Busch and General Georg von Küchler, fresh from victory in France. The Army Group's armoured spearhead was Panzer Group Four, commanded by General Erich Hoepner, with under him Colonel Generals Hans Reinhardt and Erich von Manstein, both among Hitler's most brilliant tank commanders. The Red Army's Northwestern Army Group, in contrast, had lost its leadership to Stalin's purges and was in the midst of traumatised reorganisation and redeployment. The bulk of its forces were understrength, and some had not even been issued with live ammunition. Its defences were also physically inadequate: by June 1941 the army had largely abandoned its bunkers along the old, pre-1939 frontier – the so-called 'Stalin Line' – but was still in the process of constructing fortifications further west.

Most of all, Germany had the advantage of surprise. When Soviet frontier guards woke to the sound of exploding shells in the early hours of 22 June, many had not yet even received Stalin's reluctant order of less than three hours earlier to go on to full alert. Flabbergasted and afraid to take the initiative, junior officers wired for orders: 'We are being fired upon!' ran a typical appeal, 'What shall we do?' The air force did not have time to mobilise either: Luftwaffe pilots were astonished to find Soviet aeroplanes lined up, uncamouflaged, on forward airfields, and even those that managed to take off proved easy targets. 'The Russian was well behind our lines', wrote a Finnish air ace of one, 'so I held my fire, though I am not at all sure that I could have brought myself to finish off such a lame duck . . . His inexperienced flying suggested that he could have hardly been more than a duckling.' In all 1,200 planes were destroyed at sixty-six bases in the first day of the war, three-quarters of them on the ground.[27] For the rest of the year the Germans had complete air superiority, and were able to strafe and dive-bomb as much as their resources – still depleted by the Battle of Britain – allowed. The fact that the air raids on Leningrad did not begin until early September was due to delay in repairing airfields that the Luftwaffe had itself earlier bombed, and the city would have been far more badly damaged had it not been for its hundreds of search-lights, anti-aircraft guns and 'listeners' – the acoustic devices, shaped like giant gramophone horns, that tracked the approach of what were often the same bomber crews who had blitzed London twelve months earlier.

With numbers, leadership, surprise and air superiority all on its side, Army Group North advanced at astonishing speed. Though Leningraders did not know it, three days into the war von Leeb's Panzer groups had already overrun most of Lithuania, and the follow-ing day they seized a bridgehead across Latvia's River Dvina, a line the tsarist armies had held for two years in 1915–17. 'It is unlikely I will ever again experience anything comparable to that impetuous dash', von Manstein wrote in his (notoriously selective) memoirs; 'It was the fulfilment of every tank commander's dream.' In Lithuania and Latvia, most of whose citizens rejoiced to see the Soviets pushed out, women handed the German cavalrymen bunches of flowers and nationalist militias joined in the fighting and the lynching of Jews.

As the German attack sped forward, the Red Army's commu-nications broke down. Shouted telephone calls were cut off mid-sentence; staff-cars dodged between smoking villages in search of command posts. Orders, when they arrived at all, bore no relation to reality, telling officers to deploy forces that no longer existed, or to defend points already far in the German rear. Typical was the experi-ence of the 5th Motorised Rifle Regiment. Like other border units, it was not part of the regular army but came within the sprawling security empire of the People's Commissariat for Internal Affairs, the NKVD. The outbreak of war seems to have taken the regiment completely by surprise. At ten o'clock on the morning of 22 June it was travelling along the road from Vilnius northwards to Riga when it was suddenly dive-bombed by German Stukas. 'The town of Siauliai burned', the regiment reported, and 'the German planes dealt brutally with the refugees and troops moving along the road. From this it became clear that war had begun.' The regiment took shelter in a wood, where a courier reached it with orders to proceed urgently to Riga, where 'disturbances' had broken out. On arrival, the regiment found the city in the grip of a rising by anti-Soviet Latvian partisans, who had set up machine-gun posts in church towers, attics and behind the top-floor windows of the city's Art Nouveau apart-ment buildings. Red Army and NKVD headquarters, the offices of the Latvian Communist Party and the railway station were all under attack. Rallying the local garrison, the regiment 'engaged the fifth columnists in hard fighting. Incoming fire from windows, towers or bell-towers was answered with fire from machine guns and tanks.' It shot 120 'scoundrels seized from amongst the fifth columnists' out of hand, and also took out reprisals against civilians: 'Before the corpses of our fallen comrades the personnel of the regiment swore an oath mercilessly to smash the fascist reptiles, and on the same day the bourgeoisie of Riga felt our revenge on its hide.'

It was not enough. Though demoralised and disorderly units of the retreating Eighth Army arrived in the city on 30 June, five days later the Soviets were forced to abandon Riga, retreating north into Estonia. The operation was a mess: Riga's railway bridge was blown up before all the Soviet troops had crossed; among those left behind was another border guard regiment, of which no further news was heard – as the 5th Motorised's report tersely puts it, 'since the officers and staff of the 12th Border Detachment did not emerge from the battle, no documentation survives'. On 10 July orders arrived from Zhdanov to stand fast at the River Navast, which the Germans had in fact already crossed. After a vicious two-hour battle, the Red Army withdrew in disorder to the town of Vykhma. 'In front of Vykhma there was literal butchery. As if drunk, the infuriated fascists strove to break out of Vykhma, but with fire and bayonets the fighters and commanders of the 320th Rifle Regiment and the 5th Motorised Rifle Regiment held down the enemy.' By this time not much of the 5th Motorised can have been left, because it was ordered to put itself under the command of another regiment in the same division, to retake its positions at Vykhma and to 'turn back, if necessary with fire, deserters'. It was an impossible demand: strafed 'incessantly' by German fighters, fleeing soldiers and civilians jammed the roads.[28]

While the Soviets bloodily exited Riga, to the east Reinhardt's panzers broke through the old 'Stalin Line' at Ostrov, on the pre-1940 Estonian–Soviet border. Here the Balts' whitewashed farmsteads and tidy fields gave way to Russia proper – an undrained, undyked landscape of alders, willows and reed beds, of scrubby birches and silver-weathered wooden cabins, their potato patches and haywire picket fences hidden behind stands of hogweed and rosebay willow-herb. On 8 July Reinhardt took the fortress and forty churches of the little medieval city of Pskov, a vital road and rail junction on the route east. Again, the Soviets blew up a vital bridge before all their retreating troops had crossed: 206 out of 215 machine guns were abandoned and stranded soldiers had to swim, clinging to floating logs. In seventeen days the Wehrmacht had advanced an extraordinary 450 kilometres, not only overrunning the whole of the recently acquired and dubiously loyal Baltics, but entering the Russian heartland and threatening Leningrad itself.[29]

In the city, few fully understood the approaching danger. It wasn't for want of trying. 'Waking up', wrote the young mother Yelena Kochina, 'we rush to our radios, and wash down the bitter pills of the news bulletins with cold leftover tea.' 'The thirst for information', Lidiya Ginzburg remembered, 'was fearful. Five times a day people would drop whatever they were doing and race to the loudspeaker. They would fall on anyone who had been a yard nearer the front line than they had, or to a government office, or any source of news.'[30]

The authorities did their best to keep the public in the dark. The Soviet Information Bureau, created three days into the war and known as Sovinform, was the only body authorised to issue communiqués. It kept its twice-daily reports deliberately vague, talking about fighting 'in the sector' of particular cities, and anonymous 'population points N' having been won or lost. (This convention dated back to the nineteenth-century novel. Gogol's *Dead Souls*, for example, opens with a carriage driving through the gates of an inn in 'the provincial town of N'.) Rather than admit defeats, it picked out barely credible incidences of individual heroism – what the war correspondent Vasili Grossman contemptuously called 'Ivan Pupkin killed five Germans with a spoon' stories. Major defeats were not reported until several days after the event. Fighting 'in the Pskov sector' was not reported until 12 July, four days after the city had fallen, and it was still being referred to as a 'battleground' twelve days later, after which it simply dropped out of the news.[31]

One of the practical results of this misinformation was that parents of children sent to stay in the countryside for their summer holidays often failed to fetch them home before they were engulfed by the German advance. Several of Yelena Skryabina's friends were thus almost caught out. On 8 July her neighbour Lyubov Kurakina, whose husband had just returned, broken, from the Gulag, succeeded in retrieving their children from Belorussia, by then already partially under occupation:

> She says she saw a German soldier just a few steps away from her. She said she wasn't afraid of him because they are people just like we are. What did worry her was that her Party membership card might be found hidden in her stocking . . . But everything turned out all right. She found her children. They rode part of the way home by train and part by truck, and some of the way they walked.

Another friend's husband was fortunate, as a 'dependable worker' – jargon for a favoured Party official – in having the use of a car to fetch their three-year-old daughter. 'This made it possible for him to circle through several villages and towns. Even so, he was lucky to find her. He brought her back dressed only in a little nightdress.'[32] The historian Anzhelina Kupaigorodskaya, aged eleven at the start of the war, remembers how the staff of her Pioneer camp simply abandoned their charges:

> We were supposed to be going on some sort of expedition, a hike. Then we were told it wasn't happening. Two or three hours went by and finally we were called into a line and told that Hitler had attacked us. Immediately everything changed. Before, the meals had been as good as in a sanatorium, but from then on all we got was *kasha* [boiled grains]. All the men disappeared, and the only adults left were the kitchen-ladies. Camp was supposed to have ended but nobody came to fetch us. We just wandered around. Nobody explained anything; there was some sort of rumour that we were going to be sent to Moscow, to live in the metro.

She got a message to her parents via another child, and they eventually came to collect her towards the end of July. 'I have no idea what happened to the rest of the children. Many still hadn't been picked up, and by then the Germans were already close.'[33]

Driven by fear of accusation of cowardice, even the army's internal communications were more rhetorical than factual. 'No sooner had the village of Polyana fallen under our fire' ran a report of 31 July, 'than the Germans jumped out of their cottages with their underwear down. Soldiers in the trenches also took to their heels . . . With cries of "Hurrah!" the battalion fell upon the fascists. Grenades, bayonets, rifle butts and flaming bottles came into play. The effect was stupendous.' On 2 July NKVD border troops holed up in a 'former kulak's house' outside Ostrov found themselves under attack from five enemy tanks: 'From the flaming premises junior *politruk* [political organiser] Broitman, already twice wounded in the chest, carried on firing at the enemy, not allowing him to open his tank hatches. Next to him the *starshina* [roughly, sergeant major] of the picket, Comrade Nagorsky, heroically struck at the enemy with a submachine gun. Bleeding profusely, they courageously covered the retreat of the picket to new lines. Both fell dead in courageous defence of their picket sector.'[34]

Closer to reality was a cynical joke of the time. A Red Army lieutenant is found sitting in an abandoned German lorry. He is told to move because otherwise he will get fired at. 'Who by?' he retorts. 'The Germans will think it's theirs, and our lot will run away.'[35] Throughout the war's first weeks, the Northwestern Army Group remained in near-total disarray. Internal reports repeatedly describe units as retreating 'as individuals and in small groups', a euphemism for complete disorder. Cut off by the German advance, large numbers of soldiers wandered the devastated countryside, trying either to return to Soviet lines or to surrender to the enemy. Leaflet drops told them to consider themselves partisans, and encouraged them with news of the new Soviet–British alliance.[36] So many were taken prisoner that the Germans simply herded them into the nearest available secure buildings, without any provision for food, sanitation or clean water. Men who did manage to rejoin their units were accused of cowardice, desertion or spying. Though the Red Army knew the terrain, its attempts at counter-attack were conducted, according to Halder, 'in a manner which plainly shows that their command is completely confused. Also, the tactics employed in these attacks is singularly poor. Riflemen on trucks drive abreast with tanks against our firing line, and the inevitable result is very heavy losses to the enemy.' By 3 July, Halder estimated, twelve to fifteen of the Northwestern Army Group's twenty-one infantry and armoured divisions had been wiped out.[37]

The confusion was intensified by a deadly round of scapegoating within the Soviet High Command. The most prominent victim was General Dmitri Pavlov, commander of the Western Army Group, who was arrested on 4 July and executed on the 22nd, together with three of his subordinates. General Kopets, head of Soviet bomber command, saved the NKVD the trouble by committing suicide on the second day of the war. Further down the line uncounted numbers of officers were shot on the spot by military tribunals, for 'cowardice' in making unauthorised retreats.[38]

From Moscow General Zhukov urged on the bloodletting. 'Commanders who retreat from defence lines without orders, treacherously squandering their positions', a telegram of 10 July thundered, 'have been going unpunished. Nor do your destruction battalions [of NKVD troops, responsible for rounding up deserters] yet seem to be operating; they have produced no visible results.' Representatives of the Military Council and military prosecutor were to 'quickly drive out to the forward units and deal with cowards and traitors on the spot'.[39] Hence the abject tone of many reports from the front, which typically insist that units have fought to their 'last round' before being forced to retreat.[40]

Significant for Leningrad was the fate of Kirill Meretskov, the burly, snub-nosed forty-four-year-old general who had commanded the disastrous first stages of the war against Finland and briefly been promoted to chief of staff, before losing the post to Zhukov. He was arrested in the first days of the war, having been named by his friend Pavlov as a member of a fictitious anti-Soviet conspiracy. In prison he was beaten with rubber rods by one of NKVD chief Lavrenty Beria's senior deputies – another former friend – before being recalled to duty in September. Cleaned up and in full uniform, he was affably greeted by his torturer on his way to Stalin's office. Bravely, he refused to act the amnesiac: 'We used to meet informally', he told the man, 'but I'm afraid of you now.' Having enquired after his health and kindly allowed him to sit, Stalin told him that he had been appointed Stavka's (High Command's) representative to the

Northwestern Army Group. Understandably reluctant, following this experience, to take the initiative or question orders, Meretskov was one of the Army Group's two or three most senior commanders for the whole of the rest of the war.[41]

Along with the bloodletting came a reshuffle of senior military appointments. Leningrad was unlucky in being assigned to Marshal Kliment Voroshilov. Sixty years old, vain and dapper, with a pencil moustache and small, pale blue eyes, he is often portrayed as a gallant but bumbling old warhorse (not least by Harrison Salisbury, who repeats the story that he personally led a group of marines – 'their blond hair tousled in the wind, their faces fresh, their chins grim' – in a bayonet charge outside Krasnoye Selo in September. Perhaps he did.) He was in fact not only militarily incompetent – as defence commissar he had presided over the disastrous opening stages of the Winter War – but, like Zhdanov, a desk-bound mass murderer, organiser of the purges that had wiped out most of the senior Red Army officer corps only four years before. Dmitri Volkogonov, in charge of the Soviet army's political education section before he became the first important *glasnost*-era biographer of Stalin, is eloquent: 'Mediocre, faceless, intellectually dim', Voroshilov was 'nothing more than an executioner, a henchman of the Executioner-in-Chief.'[42] Voroshilov's second-in-command, Marshal Grigori Kulik, was no better. Another old Civil War cavalryman and a crony of the sadistic Beria, he was a bullying, ignorant drunkard, whose incompetent direction of the 54th Army to Leningrad's south was largely to blame for the city's encirclement. Soldiers nicknamed his leadership style 'Prison or a Medal' – if a subordinate pleased him he got an award, if not he was arrested.[43]

While Stalin wiped out yet more of his top brass, Hitler and his staff, now headquartered in the specially built 'Wolf's Lair' outside Rastenburg in East Prussia, exulted. Hitler's after-dinner musings reached new heights. 'The beauties of the Crimea', he opined between midnight and 2 a.m. on the night Army Group North captured Riga, 'will be made accessible by means of an autobahn. The peninsula will be our German Riviera. Croatia will be another tourism paradise for us.' Russia's twin capitals apparently failed to offer the same leisure potential: three days later, as Pskov was taken, Hitler called Halder to a meeting and told him that it was 'his firm decision to level Moscow and Leningrad, and make them uninhabitable, so as to relieve ourselves of the necessity of feeding their populations through the winter. The cities will be razed by the air force.' So confident was he that the whole of European Russia was about to fall into his hands that he instructed Halder to start planning operations against the industrial cities of the Urals. Even cautious Halder admitted to his diary that things were evolving 'gratifyingly according to plan'. Barbarossa's initial objective – to shatter the bulk of the Red Army west of the rivers Dvina and Dnieper – had, he thought, been more or less accomplished. Though much remained to be done it was 'probably no overstatement to say that the Russian campaign has been won in the space of two weeks'.[44]

3

'We're Winning, but the Germans are Advancing'

Sovinform's economy with the truth meant that Leningraders quickly learned not to trust official news sources. '*Nashi byut*', they whispered to each other, '*a nemtsy berut*' – 'We're winning, but the Germans are advancing'. They also learned to interpret vague Sovinform language. *Ozhestochenniy boi* ('bitter fighting'); *uporniy boi* ('determined fighting'); and *tyazheliy boi* ('heavy fighting') suggested increasing levels of seriousness. 'Complex' situations were grave ones, and the worst communiqué phrase of all – 'Heavy defensive battles against superior enemy forces' – meant full retreat. 'From the veiled communiqués of the Soviet Information Bureau', wrote one Leningrader, 'it is nevertheless absolutely clear that the Red Army is unable to stop the German offensive on any one of the defence lines.'[1]

More reliable, though partial, were the kitchen-table confidences or overheard remarks of men newly returned from the front. In mid-August passionately anti-Bolshevik Lidiya Osipova, a pensioner living in Pushkin, thus discovered to her joy that the Germans were only fifty kilometres away: 'Yesterday an airman, eating at the aerodrome cafeteria, said to the girl on the till, "Now we're going to bomb the enemy in Siverskaya." Hence we know that Siverskaya has been taken by the Germans. When are they going to get to us? And will they really come? The last hours before release from prison are the hardest.' The so-called 'reports' by Party activists at her women's organisation were useless, 'like extracts from an illiterate wall news-paper . . . No commentary or questions are allowed. What we could have read for ourselves in fifteen minutes takes up a whole hour. Lord, when is all this going to end?'[2]

Guessing, though, was not the same as knowing, and hearsay filled the vacuum. Leningrad had not been bombed, it was rumoured, because Hitler was saving it as a present for his (mythical) daugh-ter; alternatively, Vasilyevsky Island would be spared because Alfred Rosenberg (chief of Hitler's *Ostministerium*) had been born there. A Red Fleet ship had been scuttled in the middle of the channel out to the Baltic; the Wehrmacht had a circular tank that spat out shells like a Devil's Wheel; and a German paratrooper had landed in the Tavrichesky flowerbeds, where he was lucky not to have been killed by old ladies armed with gardening forks.[3]

The authorities tried to halt the rumour mill. The city soviet's executive committee forbade its employees from discussing the war on the telephone, on pain of prosecution for 'disclosing military secrets', and yet more 'defeatists' were arrested in accordance with a new law making those accused of spreading 'false rumours provok-ing unrest amongst the population' liable to trial by military tribu-nal.[4] At the same time, the leadership indulged in some rumour-mongering of its own, diverting attention from disasters at the front by whipping up fear of spies, saboteurs and *raketniki* – 'rocket-men' – who were supposed to be using flares to signal to enemy aviation. Guidebooks and maps had to be handed in to a special department, as did bicycles, cameras and wireless radios. Tram and trolley-car conductors stopped calling out stops, street signs were painted over, and name boards removed from outside prominent buildings. It became hazardous to ask for directions or to appear in public in foreign-looking clothing. Dmitri Likhachev found himself trailed by small boys by reason of his pale grey coat ('light-coloured clothes', he remembered, 'were not usual in the USSR') and Yelena

Skryabina, having left her tall, bespectacled son Dima outside a shop for a moment, returned to find him being questioned by a policeman. She was able to persuade him of Dima's identity only by producing her husband's military certificate, and by pointing out that since Dima was not yet sixteen he couldn't possibly have a passport.[5] Another diarist, Yelena Kochina, found that she herself was not immune from the spy mania, which spread like 'an infectious disease':

> Yesterday near the market a little old woman who looked like a flounder dressed in a mackintosh grabbed me:
>
> 'Did you see? A spy for sure!' she shouted, waving her short little arm after some man.
>
> 'What?'
>
> 'His trousers and jacket were different colours.'
>
> I couldn't help but laugh.
>
> 'And his moustache looked as though it was stuck on.' Her close-set angry eyes bored into me.
>
> 'Excuse me . . .' I tore myself away. Before pushing off, she trailed me for several steps along the pavement.
>
> But . . . even to me many people seem suspicious, types it would be worth keeping an eye on.[6]

Though the mania continued well into the autumn, and the stories of *raketniki* seem to have been believed even by shrewd observers – like, for example, the Anglo-Russian BBC correspondent Alexander Werth – there is not a single reliable instance of a genuine foreign spy (as opposed to local sympathiser) ever having been discovered in the city.

Four weeks into the invasion the mood in Leningrad was one of disoriented anticipation, of disconnect between near-normality on the streets and the stunning news on the radio. 'It's just impossible to believe there's a war on', wrote the crippled archivist Georgi Knyazev. 'Everything's so calm, if only outwardly.' The weather continued hot and still, the fluff-covered poplar seeds Russians call *pukh* drifted along the gutters, and after work office clerks gathered as usual in Rumyantsev Square to play dominoes. Sitting out an air-raid drill in front of the Academicians' Building one evening, Knyazev watched a team of teenage girls shovelling a pile of sand into a lorry, while small boys in swimming trunks dived into the river off the glossy stone backs of the Luxor sphinxes. An Academician's wife stood guard duty wearing gloves and a hat. Chatting to the building's care-taker, Knyazev tried to introduce a 'mood of cheerfulness and perse-verance', but the man didn't understand why the war wasn't work-ing out the way it had in the films. '"It's awful", he said, "that the fighting is happening on our territory. There's so much destruction. Why did we surrender the old border defences just like that?" There was nothing I could say in reply. We have very little information. I still don't know how near, or how far, the Germans are from us. Is Leningrad seriously under threat or not?' The air, he noticed, carried a faint smell of smoke, from peat bogs deliberately set on fire so as to confuse enemy aviation.[7]

Anna Ostroumova-Lebedeva, the elderly artist who had been so reassured by Stalin's broadcast, lived opposite a military hospital. During air-raid drills she watched the wounded being stretchered down into bunkers, and medical students popping through trap-doors up onto the hospital roof. 'Still not a single bomb has fallen on Leningrad', she wrote on 21 July,

> though the sirens go off often. Last night there were air-raid warn-ings at 12.30 and again at 5.30 a.m., I woke up and the anti-aircraft guns were firing so loudly that I couldn't go to sleep again. I got dressed, went out into the courtyard and sat on a bench . . . It was a cloudless morning and though the sun hadn't yet reached the buildings, it shone brightly on the barrage balloons scattered

across the sky. They swam in the gentle blue ether like silver ships. One couldn't see their cables; it looked as though they were floating free.[8]

Though most public parks were closed for the excavation of air-raid shelters, she had permission to enter the Botanical Gardens:

The gardens were still in order, but not as carefully tended as usual. I got a great deal of pleasure from the wonderful hydrangeas; they grew in big urns in bunches of white, pink and pale blue, great explosions of unbelievable loveliness. Not a soul was there. The sun shone on the grass, and through the leaves of the trees. The light played across the bench, our dresses, the pages of our books. A cool breeze blew from the river. I was living in moments of quiet calm, and for a split second forgot that we're at war, that people are dying and cities burning.

One of the reasons the city felt so oddly quiet was that more than fifty thousand Leningraders, mostly women and teenagers, had been sent 100 kilometres to the south-west to build new defences along the so-called 'Luga Line'. Though the first construction brigades had started work on 29 June, the line was not formally sketched out until 4 July, when Zhukov ordered the Northwestern Army Group to take defensive positions from Narva (on the Baltic coast 120 kilometres to Leningrad's west) through Luga and Staraya Russa to Borovichi, 250 kilometres to the city's south-east. The line's strongest sector, behind the Luga River, was to consist of a fifteen-kilometre-deep series of minefields and anti-tank guns and barriers, with a gap between Luga and Gatchina through which the Red Army could retreat.[9] Work was also ordered on two inner rings, one running from Peterhof on the Gulf, through Gatchina to Kolpino, and the second round the city itself, from the commercial port at the Neva's mouth to the upriver fishing village of Rybatskoye.[10]

One of the thousands of teenage girls conscripted to work on the Luga Line was Olga Grechina, a seventeen-year-old student at Leningrad University. 'At the Department of Philology', she sardonically records in her memoirs,

> our idol Professor Gukovsky rousingly addressed a rally, urging us to enlist in the students' voluntary battalion. Everyone expected Gukovsky himself to enlist too, especially since many of our teachers were applying to be either translators or political workers. Instead, Gukovsky started making his appearance wearing green house slippers and leaning on a cane. Some said he had acute rheumatism; others cautiously hinted that he found calling others to action much pleasanter than acting himself. I really don't know if he was ill or not, but it was good that he was able to write his Gogol book.[11]

Though, if anything, anti-Bolshevik (her doctor father had been exiled to a tiny village clinic by the Revolution, and an uncle sent to the Gulag), Grechina employed no such stratagem, and in the third week of July found herself one of a group of female students waiting, amidst crowds of evacuees, at Moscow Station for a train to the Luga Line:

> There were worrying reports of strafing and bombing coming from the trenches – and especially from around Luga. But we hadn't been told where we were headed, and when we set off that evening we were cheerful, singing songs so as to distract ourselves from the anxiety inside. When we got off the train at Gatchina it was already dark. We were sent to spend the night in a park next to the Pavlovsk Palace, but never slept since the Germans started bombing a nearby airfield, and around us everything droned and shook. We were made to get up, and told to hide anything white and not to smoke. We started walking fast along a road already full of our units. The soldiers marched quickly and quietly; if one

made a sound the others shushed him for being careless. None of us had any idea where we were going or why, which made it all the more frightening. We were all desperate for something to drink, so much so that when the road went through a wood we drank muddy water from the roadside ditches.

In the morning, having marched twenty kilometres, the students reached a village, where they were distributed among local residents, two or three to a house. That afternoon their task was explained to them:

> It was to dig anti-tank ditches (1.2m deep) and breastworks (supposedly 1m high). Though our only tools were shovels, axes and stretchers [to carry soil], we set to work enthusiastically. The days were sunny and hot. We worked from 5 a.m. to 8 or 9 p.m., with a two- or three-hour rest after lunch. We were well fed but there was no tea, except for what our landlady made us from lime flowers. Physically it was very tough, and after two weeks, trying to lift a stretcher, I suddenly found I couldn't straighten up again.[12]

Grechina was lucky only to hurt her back. Yelena Kochina was one of many ditch-diggers strafed by German Stukas:

> Our whole laboratory dug anti-tank trenches around Leningrad today. I dug the earth with pleasure (at least this was something practical!) . . . Almost all the people working in the trenches were women. Their coloured headscarves flashed brightly in the sun. It was as if a giant flowerbed girdled the city.
>
> Suddenly the gleaming wings of an aeroplane blotted out the sky. A machine gun started firing and bullets plunged into the grass not far from me, rustling like small metallic lizards. I stood transfixed, forgetting completely the air-raid drill that I had learned not long before.

'Run!' someone shouted, tugging at my sleeve. I looked back.
Everyone who had been working in the trenches had run somewhere. I ran too, though I didn't know where to go or what to
do . . . Suddenly I saw a small bridge. I ran towards it. Under it
was a deep puddle. For a whole hour we squatted in this puddle,
and didn't do any more work for the rest of the day.[13]

Yelena Skryabina, hearing of the strafings and worried that her son
Dima might be conscripted to dig, thought the effort 'senseless –
a good way to kill people . . . No one is excused – young girls in
sundresses and sandals, boys in shorts and sports shirts. They aren't
even allowed home to change their clothes. How much use can they
really be? City youths don't even know how to use a shovel, much
less the heavy crowbars that they will need to break up dry clay
soil.'[14]

She was not wrong to be sceptical. Girls dug in bathing suits, with
bits of paper stuck to their noses to prevent sunburn. They dropped
their heavy shovels during the night-time marches or had to be sent
home with hopelessly blistered hands and feet. The peasant women
who cooked them *kasha* and spread out straw for them to sleep on
tut-tutted over the 'little ladies' from the city; the men overseeing
them shouted: 'You think you're actresses, that you've come to a
resort? You've come to save the Motherland!' Their initial enthusi-
asm quickly wore off: 'What did he think we were doing – playing
croquet?' one burst out when her professor of Marxism-Leninism,
out for a visit, asked if they were tired.[15]

Thin, patchy and in places overrun before it had even been
manned, the Luga Line was nonetheless also where the Wehrmacht
met its first, albeit temporary hitch. From Moscow, Zhukov ordered
the Northwestern Army Group to occupy the Luga Line on 4 July,
and the first divisions took up their positions the same day. On the
10th, with deployments and digging work still under way, Zhukov
ordered Voroshilov to launch a counter-attack against Manstein's 8th

Panzer Division, which was in an exposed position having pushed on east after taking Soltsi, just to the west of Lake Ilmen.

By this time, the *Blitzkrieg* was already being slowed by terrain and climate. Dust ground out engines; bridges were not strong enough to bear the weight of tanks, and turning off the main roads, as one German officer put it, was 'like leaving the twentieth century for the Middle Ages'. Nor could the Wehrmacht rely on its maps: 'All supposed main roads were marked in red', a general remembered, 'and there seemed to be lots of them, but they proved to be nothing but sandy tracks. Our intelligence was fairly accurate about conditions in Russian-occupied Poland, but badly at fault about those beyond the original Russian frontier.' Summer thunderstorms turned the dust into mud, passable for tanks but not for the lorries that carried their fuel, supplies and auxiliary troops. 'An hour or two's rain reduced the panzer forces to stagnation. It was an extraordinary sight, with groups of tanks and transports strung out over a hundred mile stretch, all stuck – until the sun came out and the ground dried.'[16]

Launched in 30° heat on 13 July, the Soviet counter-stroke caught the 8th Panzer Division by surprise, separating it from a motorised infantry division to its left and forcing it into a fierce four-day battle out of encirclement, during which it had to be supplied by air. Though the crisis was over by the 18th, it cost the division 70 of its 150 tanks, and helped force a pause of a vital ten days along the Narva and Luga rivers, while von Leeb and his commanders regrouped and debated what to do next. It was far, however, from the decisive victory that Moscow had wanted. At this point the Leningrad leaders, as they no doubt realised, edged perilously near the fate of General Pavlov of the Western Army Group, who had been arrested in the first week of the war and now awaited execution, together with his subordinates. The Northwestern Army Group's sacrificial lamb was the head of the Luga Operational Group, General Konstantin Pyadyshev, a respected and experienced specialist on military fortifications and holder of two Orders of the Red Banner. At the time, he simply disappeared; we now know that he was arrested for dereliction of duty by his commanding officer, General Popov, on 23 July, and died in prison two years later. A week later Zhdanov and Voroshilov got away with a summons to Moscow and a carpeting from Stalin for 'lack of toughness'.[17]

In Leningrad, the mood was one of rising anxiety. Two questions were beginning to predominate: food – would there be another famine, like the one during the 1920–21 Civil War? – and whether or not to evacuate.

Evacuation of valuables and of defence plant from the city had begun directly on news of the invasion, in expectation not of siege but of air raids. One of the best-prepared institutions was the Hermitage, thanks to the shrewdness of its director, Iosif Orbeli, who had risked accusations of war-mongering by discreetly stockpiling packing materials (among them fifty tonnes of wood shavings, three tons of cotton wadding and sixteen kilometres of oilcloth) months before. He immediately ordered that the museum's forty most valuable paintings be moved into the steel-lined vaults housing its famous collection of Scythian gold, and the following morning staff and volunteers began the gigantic task of moving, dismantling, crating and cataloguing the whole of its vast and wonderful collection, from winged Babylonian bulls to Fabergé's snowdrops in jade and crystal. 'We work from morning to late evening', wrote an art student:

> Our legs are throbbing. We take the paintings off the walls . . . There isn't the usual feeling of awe for the masterpieces, though we deliberately wrap up [Titian's] *Danaë* slowly . . . Downstairs the sculptors are packing things into crates. Orbeli is everywhere in the halls . . . The empty Hermitage is like a house after a funeral.[18]

Wherever possible, paintings were packed flat, but those too large to fit into a railway carriage had to be rolled, including, after much anguished indecision, Rembrandt's fragile *Descent from the Cross*. Only one painting – Rembrandt's *The Return of the Prodigal Son* – got a crate to itself, and only another three – two Leonardo *Madonna*s and Raphael's exquisite little *Madonna Conestabile* – were left in their frames. The rest – Giorgiones, Tiepolos, Breughels, Van Dycks, Holbeins, Rubens, Gainsboroughs, Canalettos, Velázquezes, El Grecos – were removed from their stretchers and the empty frames hung back in their usual places on the gallery walls. Houdon's magnificent sculpture of Voltaire, all beaky nose and twisted smile, was lowered down the three flights of a ceremonial staircase with the help of naval ratings, using wooden runners and a system of blocks and pulleys. The Chertomlyk Vase, a fourth-century BC silver ewer magnificently decorated with doves and horses, had to be filled with tiny pieces of crumbled cork, which two women spent the night patiently feeding through a crack in its lip with teaspoons.

After six days and nights of frantic activity, a first trainload of treasures – about half a million items in more than one thousand crates – left the city on 1 July. Originally intended for the evacuation of machinery from the Kirov defence works, the train was made up of two engines, twenty-two freight wagons, an armoured car for the most valuable items and passenger carriages for guards and Hermitage staff, with flatbeds for anti-aircraft guns at either end. Its destination, known only to a few, was Sverdlovsk in the Urals (formerly Yekaterinburg, the town in which Nicholas II and his family had been assassinated). A second train, containing 700,000 items in 422 crates, left on 20 July. Orbeli's packing materials had now run out, and an Egyptologist, Militsa Matye, was given charge of finding more. 'For almost two years', she marvelled later, 'some long smooth poles had stood in the corner of my office. I would never have believed that the time would come when I would wrap them round with fabrics from Coptic Egypt and send them to the

Urals.'[19] Pleading with shops and warehouses for everything from sawdust to egg boxes, she gathered enough to pack another 351 crates, but by the time they were ready the siege ring had almost closed, and they spent the war stacked in a gallery on the Winter Palace's ground floor.

Included on the second Hermitage train was Lomonosov's mosaic of Peter the Great's victory over the Swedes at Poltava, which hung (and still hangs) at the top of the main staircase of the Academy of Sciences building on the Vasilyevsky embankment. Knyazev oversaw its departure:

> No words can describe what I felt when they took away the Peter the Great mosaic . . . The Hermitage workers carefully removed it from the wall and carried it out to the waiting lorry. I accompanied them in what was, to be honest, an agitated state . . . Initially we discussed secure storage in the city, but now, in view of developments at the front, our only concern is to get as much as possible evacuated. I feel that evacuation with the Hermitage will be safer . . . But my heart aches. I came home quite drained.

A week later it was the turn of the Academy's most precious manuscripts:

> Altogether we packed thirty boxes. We've taken every precaution against damp and dust (rubber sheeting, cellophane, oilcloth, folders and paper), and made an inventory of all the materials, with a separate list for each box. With us all working flat out, it took two weeks. The boxes were wired round and sealed. I followed the lorry as far as the embankment. It was like seeing off someone near and dear – a son, a daughter, a wife . . . I watched for a long time as the lorry slowly (I had asked the driver to go carefully), drove across the Palace Bridge . . . Orphaned, I returned to the Archives.[20]

Another 360,000 items – among them a Gutenberg Bible, Pushkin's letters, Mary Queen of Scots's prayer book and the world's second-oldest surviving Greek text of the New Testament – left the Public Library (affectionately known as the 'Publichka') on the Nevsky.

Yelena Skryabina and Yelena Kochina, both working mothers, were among the many torn between evacuating with their children and colleagues, and staying behind with their husbands and elderly parents. 'I am faced', wrote Skryabina on 28 June,

> with a serious problem. And that is, that although I could take Dima and Yura with me, I would have to leave my mother and our elderly nanny behind. When I returned home with this news my mother burst into tears . . . Nana is overcome and silent. I am caught between two fires. On the one hand, I understand perfectly well that the children must be saved, and on the other, I pity these helpless old women. How can I leave them at the mercy of fate?

Like many, she also half believed the soothing propaganda:

> I can't believe there'll be famine in Leningrad. We are constantly being told of plentiful food stocks, supposedly enough to last many years. As for the threat of bombing – we are also constantly assured of the capabilities of our high-powered anti-aircraft system . . . If this is even half true, then why try to leave?[21]

Similarly reassuring, paradoxically, was the introduction of rationing on 18 July. At 800 grams of bread a day for manual workers, 600 grams for white-collar workers and 400 grams for dependants, plus ample monthly allotments of meat, cereals, butter and sugar, ration levels were generous ('this is not so bad; one can live on this', wrote Skryabina[22]) and even represented an improvement in diet for the poor. On the same day seventy-one new 'commission shops' opened, selling off-ration food in unlimited quantity though at high prices.

Unaffordable for many, especially given new restrictions on the withdrawal of savings, their lavish window displays nevertheless helped to instil a false sense of security. 'When you see a shop window full of food', thought Skryabina, 'you tend to disbelieve talk about an imminent famine.' Kochina was less complacent, rushing to buy the four and a half pounds of millet that was all that was left in her local commission store ('I hate porridge made from millet'), and she would have left for Saratov with her chemistry institute had it not been for her husband's opposition and her baby daughter's illness: 'Lena has diarrhoea and a fever. We'll have to put the evacuation off for several days. And in general, how does one handle sterile baby bottles on the road?'[23] The first of August found Skryabina still out at Pushkin, doing her best to ignore the war and enjoy the deserted palace parks. A niece had come to visit from the city: 'From her I found out about the rapid German onslaught. They are advancing on Leningrad. We have decided to stay in the country until Luga is captured.'

The deluge began a week later. On 8 August, in driving rain, Reinhardt's panzers began an assault on the northern sector of the Luga Line, near Kingisepp. In three days of chaotic fighting they broke across the Luga River in three places, at the cost of 1,600 German casualties. Manstein's 8th Panzer Division, recovered from the Soltsi setback, cut the Kingisepp–Gatchina railway line on the 12th. A Soviet counter-offensive near Staraya Russa, launched piecemeal from 10 August, failed, with massive losses of men and equipment. 'We pushed on a little further', wrote Vasili Churkin, in charge of manoeuvring a gun-carriage and six horses through woods sixty kilometres to Leningrad's south-west:

and on reaching the high road saw a huge, panicking crowd, running in total disorder towards Volosovo. On a cart lay an injured soldier, moaning and begging for his wounds to be dressed. Nearby a girl with a medical bag was walking along, but she wouldn't stop and help him, she was afraid to slow down. Behind you could hear the sound of clanking metal – German tanks. Someone shouted at the girl to help the injured man, and we turned around and quickly made our way back to where we'd left our guns. But guns and men had gone. Coming out of the woods into a clearing we saw Battery no. 4 being dragged along, under fire from tanks . . . A shell exploded right under the legs of the horse pulling the baggage cart. The horse fell and though the cart was carrying all our things, including our coats, we couldn't get to it because the tanks were already too close, even ahead of us.[24]

To the south, Küchler's Eighteenth Army advanced on the historic city of Novgorod, capital of one of the ninth-century Rus prince-doms and gateway to Lake Ilmen. Its fall on 17 August went unmentioned by Sovinform, which waited until the 23rd to report fighting 'in the Novgorod area'. Altogether, from 10 to 28 August the opposing Soviet 34th Army lost half its personnel, seventy-four out of its eighty-three tanks, 628 of its 748 guns and mortars, 670 trucks and 14,912 horses. To escape the slaughter, large numbers of soldiers either fled or mutilated themselves in hope of being invalided to the rear. Between 16 and 22 August more than four thousand servicemen were seized as suspected deserters while trying to get to Leningrad from the front, and in some medical units, a worried political report noted, up to 50 per cent of the wounded were suspected of self-mutilation. At Evacuation Hospital no. 61, for example, out of a thousand wounded 460 had been shot in the left forearm or left hand.[25]

Stalin's response to the disasters was a furious telegraph to Zhdanov and Voroshilov. If the German armies won more victories around Novgorod, he thundered, they might be able to outflank Leningrad to the east, breaking communications with Moscow and meeting the Finns on the far shore of Lake Ladoga:

> It appears to us that the High Command of the Northwestern Army Group fails to see this mortal danger and therefore takes no special measures to liquidate it. German strength in the area is not great, so all we need to do is throw in three fresh divisions under skilful leadership. Stavka cannot be reconciled to this mood of fatalism, of the impossibility of taking decisive steps, and with arguments that everything's being done that can be done.[26]

Three days later Stalin's fears came to pass when Chudovo, a town on the main Moscow–Leningrad railway line, was taken. On 22 August Zhdanov begged Stalin for reinforcements. The twenty-two rifle divisions of the Northwestern Army Group, he pointed out, were now fighting along a 400-kilometre front, and seven of them had almost no heavy weapons or radios. Another five divisions he did not include in his calculations, since their 'remaining fighting capacity' was 'low' – in other words, they had been wiped out. He needed forty-five to fifty fresh battalions, and new weapons for five divisions.[27]

On the evening of 25 August Lyuban, thirty kilometres north of Chudovo on the Moscow–Leningrad line, fell too. The following day Stalin telephoned, asking for a report. Voroshilov's second-in-command, General Popov, took the call, admitting that Lyuban had been abandoned and again requesting more troops – 'since the ones sent to us don't cover even half of our losses'; semi-automatic weapons for the infantry – 'who only have rifles'; and that Leningrad be allowed to keep rather than send to other fronts its own armoured vehicle production. Unwillingly, Stalin agreed:

> We've already let you have three days' worth of production, you can have another three or four days ... We'll send you more

infantry battalions, but I can't say how many . . . In a couple of weeks, perhaps, we'll be able to scrape together two divisions for you. If your people knew how to work to a plan, and had asked us for two or three divisions a fortnight ago, they would be ready for you now. The whole trouble is that you people prefer to live and work like gypsies, from one day to the next, not looking ahead. I demand that you bring some order back to the 48th Army, especially to those divisions whose cowardly officers disappeared the devil knows where from Lyuban yesterday . . . I demand that you clear the Lyuban and Chudovo regions of the enemy at any price and by any means. I entrust you with this personally . . . Tell me briefly, is Klim [Voroshilov] helping, or hindering?

'He's helping. We're sincerely grateful,' Popov prudently replied.[28]

On 26 August, also, Stalin finally allowed a retreat by sea from Tallinn, two hundred miles due west of Leningrad and the capital of Estonia. This operation – a 'kind of Dunkirk, but without the air cover' as Werth put it – was one of the biggest (and is one of the least remembered) of the military disasters that befell the Soviet Union in the first few months of the war. The man in charge was Admiral Vladimir Tributs, commander-in-chief of the Red Banner Baltic Fleet. Realising early on that the newly established Soviet naval base of Libau (now Liepaja), on the Latvian coast, was vulnerable in case of German attack, he had (bravely) sought and won permission to transfer his largest ships east to Estonia shortly before the war began. It was a prescient move: Libau fell two days into the war, and five days after that his flagship, the 7,000-ton cruiser *Kirov*, was lucky to escape Riga for Tallinn. To defend Tallinn, Tributs had at his disposal 14,000 sailors, a thousand or so police and the battered remnants, about four thousand-strong, of the frontier troops who had fled there from Riga, among them the 5th Motorised Rifle Regiment, now down to '150 bayonets'. Though Tributs conscripted 25,000 Estonian civilians into trench digging, most, like the Latvians, did not want to be 'defended'. Bursts of gunfire sounded around the city at night, anonymous hands pasted up pro-German flyers and a Russian officer was murdered coming out of a restaurant. The NKVD responded with its usual round of arrests, firing squads and tribunals.

On 8 August – the same day von Leeb began his attack on the Luga Line – Tallinn was surrounded by land, as the Wehrmacht reached the coast to its east. Tributs suggested two equally unpalatable ways out of the trap. Either he could mass his forces for a breakout eastwards towards still-unoccupied Narva, on the Estonian–Russian border, or he could sail them across the Gulf to the Finnish shore and fight back through Finnish lines to Leningrad. Stalin rejected both proposals: Tallinn was to be held at all costs.

The Eighteenth Army launched its attack on the evening of 19 August. Shells crashed among the cobbled alleys and steep red-tiled roofs of the old city, and among the clapboard summer houses and canvas bathing machines of Pirita beach. The *Kirov*'s guns replied, flashing orange from her anchorage in the harbour. The city's civilians watched and waited behind shuttered shops and barricaded doors. A week into the bombardment Tributs's second-in-command, Admiral Yuri Panteleyev, described the situation in his journal:

> Beat off strong attack on city during the night. Enemy has changed tactics, infiltrating in small groups . . . All airfields captured by the enemy. Our planes flew off to the east. Fleet and city under bombing and shelling. Lovely Pirita burning . . . Other suburbs also burning. Big fires in the city. Barricades being built at the approaches to the harbour. Smoke everywhere . . . Fire of ships and shore batteries has not slackened. Our command post at Minna Harbour constantly under fire.[29]

Later that morning Stalin finally gave permission to evacuate the fleet to Kronshtadt, Russia's historic island naval base at the head of the Gulf of Finland. While the defenders fell slowly back towards the harbour, setting fire to a power station, grain elevators and warehouses on the way, embarkation began of the Fleet's civilian entourage – officers' wives, Party officials, a theatrical troupe and senior Estonian Communists, including the president of the puppet Estonian Republic. The flamboyant war correspondent Vsevelod Vishnevsky, grandstanding at the quayside, insisted that his driver not simply remove his car's carburettor, but blow up the vehicle with a hand grenade. Loading of troops began the following day, and by the small hours of 28 August nearly 23,000 people and 66,000 tons of munitions had gone aboard a motley collection of 228 vessels, which formed up into four convoys outside the harbour mouth.[30]

Through the morning of the 28th the ships lay in the roads, rolling at their anchors in a force seven gale. By noon the wind had eased, and the signal went out to get underway. Stretched out over fifteen miles of sea, the convoys had an unenviable task ahead. Their equivalents at Dunkirk fourteen months earlier had had to cover fifty miles, through waters controlled by the Royal Navy. Tributs's ships had to travel 220 miles, over the first 150 of which they would be subject to attack by shore batteries, submarines and Finnish torpedo boats. The route was also thick with enemy mines – 'like dumplings in borscht'. At least a hundred minesweepers, Red Fleet commander Admiral Kuznetsov later calculated, would have been needed to clear a safe path; Tributs had thirty-eight, mostly converted trawlers. Nor, despite a last-minute plea to Zhdanov for air cover, did the fleet have any protection from the Luftwaffe, Zhdanov's orders having been issued 'with great delay'.

Under attack from Junkers 88 dive-bombers from departure, the convoys hit their first major minefield at six o'clock in the evening, off Point Juminda, forty miles east of Tallinn. The first ship to go down, at 6.05 p.m., was *Ella*, an Estonian merchantman. While rescuing survivors, a tug from the fourth convoy also hit a mine, and sank fifteen minutes later. Ten minutes after that an ice-breaker, the *Kristjanis Voldemars*, was sunk by bombs. *Vironia*, carrying civilians, was damaged in the same air attack and taken in tow by the *Saturn*. Less orderly now, the convoys steamed on eastwards, zigzagging to avoid the Junkers and fire from batteries on the point. The warships were too preoccupied with dodging or disentangling themselves from mines to give much protection to the transports, most of which had no anti-aircraft guns. The minefield's next victims, as dusk began to fall, were the sweeper *Krab*, then a submarine, which disappeared beneath the waves in less than a minute, then the *Saturn*, still towing the *Vironia*. A gunboat went down at 8.30 p.m., as the sun was setting, and another submarine at 8.48 p.m. Two minutes later a destroyer, the *Yakov Sverdlov*, took a torpedo aimed at the *Kirov* and sank in six minutes. 'Darkness', as Admiral Kuznetsov describes it,

> set in quickly. The ships steaming in the tail were sharply silhouetted against the background of the fires raging in Tallinn. Erupting out of the sea, huge pillars of flame and black smoke signalled the loss of fighting ships and transport vessels. With nightfall, the hideous roar of Nazi bombers subsided. But this didn't mean that the crews could relax, because of the danger still threatening from the water. In the darkness it was difficult to see the moored mines, now floating amongst the debris of smashed lifeboats.

Between 9 and 11 p.m. another nine ships were lost, including the transport *Everita*, the *Luga*, carrying three hundred wounded, and four more of the flotilla's eight destroyers. The *Minsk*, with Admiral Panteleyev aboard, lay wallowing after a mine exploded in one of her paravanes. The mine layer *Skoriy* ('Rapid') took her in tow, only herself to hit a mine and sink half an hour later. The best remembered casualty was the *Vironia*, with her gaggle of glamorous civilians. Listing to starboard and pouring smoke, she was already under tow when she hit a mine at 9.45 p.m. Soviet accounts describe dark figures leaping from the burning quarterdeck, the sound of the 'Internationale' drifting across the water, and the crack of revolvers as her officers took their own lives in the moments before she slid beneath the waves.

Shortly before midnight, the surviving ships anchored in the midst of the mines and waited for better visibility. With daylight, they weighed anchor and the carnage resumed. By the end of the afternoon six more ships had been sunk by mines and eight by bombs, and two tugs had been captured by Finnish patrol boats. Among the casualties were the transport *Five Year Plan*, with three thousand troops aboard, and the patrol ship *Sneg* ('Snow'), which had picked up survivors from the *Vironia*. Four more damaged ships, three of them transports, managed to beach themselves on the island of Gogland (Hogland to Swedes, Suursaari to Finns), from which troops (among them the remnants of the 5th Motorised Rifle Regiment) were picked up in small boats and taken to Kronshtadt. The remainder of the flotilla limped into port over the next four days. The whole operation had cost sixty-five vessels and perhaps 14,000 lives.[31]

It was the worst disaster in Russian naval history, at least twice as costly as the defeat of the tsarist navy by the Japanese – the first time an Asian power defeated a European one at sea – at Tsu-Shima in 1905. Later, arguments abounded as to what went wrong. Kuznetsov and Panteleyev both supported the decision to defend Tallinn, but thought that civilians should have been evacuated far earlier, blaming Voroshilov for not ordering plans in good time. The convoys would have done better to take to deeper water, running the gauntlet of German submarines but avoiding the shore batteries and most of the minefields. Obviously, they should also have included more minesweepers ('But where could we have got them?' asked Kuznetsov). Today's military historians question the defence of Tallinn itself, which cost about 20,000 soldiers taken prisoner and pinned down only four German divisions, making little difference to the fighting further east.[32]

The underlying problem, though, was that of the whole Soviet command: senior officers' well-founded fear of advocating retreat until it became inevitable, and inevitably disastrous. Instructive is the story of Vyacheslav Kaliteyev, captain of the *Kazakhstan*, the largest troopship in the flotilla. Knocked unconscious by a bomb that hit the bridge soon after departure on the first morning of the evacuation, he fell into the sea and was lucky to be picked up by a submarine, which took him to Kronshtadt. Meanwhile the *Kazakhstan* limped on, aflame, under her seven surviving crew, depositing her passengers on a sandspit before arriving at Kronshtadt four days later – the only troopship to do so. Immediately an investigation was launched. Why had Kaliteyev abandoned his ship? Why had he returned ahead of her? Had he deliberately jumped overboard? The crewmen who nursed the *Kazakhstan* home were rewarded with Orders of the Red Banner in a special communiqué from Stavka. Kaliteyev was executed by firing squad, for 'cowardice' and 'desertion under fire'.[33]

4

The People's Levy

'And what makes you think that I want to talk about the war?' eighty-year-old Ilya Frenklakh, retired to sun and sectarianism in Israel, scolded his interviewer six decades after the war's end:

> So, you want to hear the truth, from a soldier, but who needs it now? . . . If you speak the whole truth about the war, with real honesty and candour, immediately dozens of 'hurrah-patriots' start bawling 'Slander! Libel! Blasphemy! Mockery! He's throwing mud!' . . . But political organiser talk – 'stoutly and heroically, with not much blood, with strong blows, under the leadership of wise and well-prepared officers . . .' – well, that sort of false, hypocritical language, the arrogant boasting of the semi-official press, always makes me sick.

An apprentice textile worker at the start of the war, Frenklakh learned to fight not with the Red Army, but with the Leningrad Army of the *narodnoye opolcheniye*, literally translated as 'People's Levy' but more usually given as the 'People's Militia' or 'People's Volunteers'. A product, initially, of the wave of popular patriotism that broke over the city on news of the German attack, it turned into the vehicle by which the Leningrad leadership, to very little military purpose, squandered perhaps 70,000 lives in July and August 1941.

The *opolcheniye* was no Soviet invention. Scratch levies had helped
to defeat the Poles in 1612 and the French in 1812. Nor were its
members, to start with at least, conscripts. 'Most of us', Frenklakh
remembered,

> passionately dashed off to war as fast as possible . . . When the
> Military Medical Academy came along and started choosing
> people for medical training, nobody wanted to join this super-
> elite institution for one reason only – it would mean missing the
> first skirmishes with the enemy . . . In my platoon there was a
> *komsorg* [a junior Komsomol functionary] from the Agricultural
> Institute. He had tuberculosis, he actually coughed blood. He was
> offered a job in the rear, but refused it, and fell in one of the first
> battles.[1]

Among the volunteers the Vasilyevsky Island district soviet turned
away, according to Party documents, were 'professors, judges, directors, and some plain invalids – Sergeyev, with half his stomach cut
away; Luzhik – on one leg, and so on'.[2]

The novelist Daniil Alshits, now in his nineties and a grand
old man of the Petersburg literary establishment, was one of 209
students at the Leningrad University history faculty who signed up.
An orphan of Stalinism – his father had been exiled in the 1930s –
he was nonetheless a believing Communist. 'Very few families', he
explains,

> had not suffered under Stalin. And we students never believed in
> those fabricated trials [the show trials of 1936–7]. But you have
> to understand that we felt no hostility to Soviet rule. We thought
> that it was just Stalin overdoing things in eliminating his oppo-
> nents, that all these reshuffles at the top would soon be over. And
> everyone understood that Stalin was one thing and the country
> another.

When his knowledge of German meant that he was split off from his friends to train as an interpreter he was furious. 'We all wanted to go to the front to fight! Nobody wanted to be left behind!' In the event, the delay saved his life, since by the time he reached the front in late September the People's Levy was being wound up and all but thirty of his fellow students were dead.[3]

What began as a spontaneous, genuinely popular movement rapidly became official and near-compulsory. A Party organiser at the Kirov Works later described the transition. The first people to come to him with a request to be sent to the front, straight after Molotov's announcement of the German invasion, were five Red Cross girls:

> They were the very beginning of the People's Levy. (Of those five, I know that three were killed near Voronino, and one drowned in the Oredezh.) After them, other applicants began arriving in large numbers. Through the Sunday and Monday there were hundreds every few hours. We were accepting the applications but not sending people anywhere. By the end of Monday everything had reached such dimensions that we finally had to come up with some sort of specific reaction. I went to a member of the city Party Committee, Comrade Verkhoglaz, and asked him 'What do I do with all these people?' Other enterprises were in the same situation. The Partkom didn't answer immediately; it just told me to keep on accepting applications. Some seven or eight days later we were told to form a division of the *narodnoye opolcheniye*.[4]

On 27 June Zhdanov had asked Moscow for permission to form an *opolcheniye*, envisaging that it would form part of the army reserve. The following day he received a reply from Zhukov, approving a plan for seven volunteer divisions to 'reinforce' the Northwestern Army Group, and the scheme was officially announced on the 30th. Moscow's regional government followed suit with its own copycat *opolcheniye* proposal on 4 July – a feather in Zhdanov's cap, especially since his arch-rival Beria had strongly opposed the plan, wanting to keep all civilian militias, like the police, under his own NKVD's control. In a typical bit of one-upmanship, Zhdanov swiftly declared that Leningrad would match the bigger city's numbers, setting a target (never met) of 270,000 men in fifteen divisions.[5]

The first three Leningrad *opolcheniye* divisions, totalling about 31,000 volunteers, were called up from 4 to 18 July. Each was based on a city district, which meant that men from the same factories (and often from the same families) were able to stick together in the same units. The First Division were nicknamed the *Kirovtsy*, after the Kirov defence works, whose 10,000 or so applicants filled two regiments and three battalions, and the second regiment of the Second Division the *Skorokhodovtsy* – literally 'go-quicklies' – after the Skorokhod footwear manufactury. The remainder of the Second came from the Elektrosila power plant. Altogether about 67,000 factory workers signed up, the majority of them skilled men who had been exempted from the ordinary draft.[6] As well as creaming off the best of Leningrad's industrial workforce, the divisions also contained a great many of its engineers, scientists, artists and students. The Railway Engineering Institute produced 900 men for the *opolcheniye*, the Mining Institute 960, the Shipbuilding Institute 450, the Electrotechnical Institute 1,200. Seven battalions' worth signed up from Leningrad University. Not surprisingly, a disproportionate number of the first wave of *opolchentsy* were also Communists. Of the 97,000 men enrolled up to 6 July, 20,000 belonged to the Party and another 18,000 to its youth wing, the Komsomol.[7]

As Zhdanov's inflated targets bit, recruitment became more systematic. District soviets were given quotas, based on numbers of eligible residents, which they in turn parcelled out among local factories. Factory managers, now working flat out to evacuate or to convert to defence production, tried hard to hold on to key personnel, in some cases sending women instead of men. 'Production', the

Party official in charge of recruitment at the Kirov Works remembered, 'was stripped bare.' Managers 'proposed to the director and
the Partkom [factory Party Committee] that there should be a mech-
anism for deciding who should be allowed to go and who shouldn't.
But of course, a lot of people who shouldn't have been allowed to go
went all the same.'[8] A. I. Verkhoglaz, chief of the *opolcheniye*'s political department and a member of the city Party Committee, scolded
his agitators into greater efforts: 'You can't wait for patriotism, it has
to be taught!' They were not to 'hang about in warm, sleepy rooms
in headquarters', but to 'go to the factories and face people squarely.
Tell them "Take up your weapons!"'[9]

Resisting such appeals was hard, especially after Stalin praised the
Moscow and Leningrad *opolcheniya* in his broadcast of 3 July. 'One
volunteer', reported the Vasilyevsky Island soviet, 'a former Party
member, applied for exemption, but reappeared an hour later with
a request to withdraw his application, because he was so ashamed.'[10]
Another, pleading illness, was told that his health was 'of no significance. What is important is the very fact of volunteering, and thereby
displaying one's political attitude.' Likhachev despised the hypocrisy
of his bosses at Pushkin House:

All the men were registered. They were called in turn into the director's office, where L. A. Plotkin held court with the secretary of the
Party organisation, A. I. Perepech. I remember Panchenko emerging pale and shaking: he'd refused. He said that he wouldn't go as
a volunteer, and that he would serve with the regular army . . . He
was branded a coward and treated with scorn, but a few weeks later
he was called up as he'd said. He fought as a partisan and was killed
in the forests somewhere near Kalinin. Plotkin, in contrast, having
registered everyone else, obtained exemption on medical grounds.
In the winter he escaped Leningrad by plane. A few hours before
departure he enrolled a 'good friend' of his, an English teacher, on
to the Institute staff, and got her on to the plane too.[11]

Many people, it is clear, did not realise what they were signing up for, assuming that they would be used for civil defence or specialist work, or as a home guard in case the Germans actually entered Leningrad. Extracting oneself from the *opolcheniye*, however, was even harder than avoiding recruitment into it. Fifty-two actors and musicians, the Party files note, tried to 'refuse arms' – presumably thinking that their job should be to entertain the troops – 'but steps were taken to halt this phenomenon'.[12] A Comrade Ninyukov of the Botanical Institute

> kept saying that his work was extremely important, and asking to be dismissed. The same happened with Nikulin and Denisov from the Geology Institute. They have been sent back to their workplaces, where measures will be taken. Party member Taitz declared 'If the regiment can't use me according to my profession of engineer-metallurgist I don't want to be in the regiment.' The liberals from headquarters, instead of giving him the necessary rebuff, let him go back to his factory. And not until 11 July did the *zamkom* [deputy commissar] of the regimental political department start taking necessary measures.[13]

Reports on would-be draft dodgers were an excuse for coarse anti-Semitism:

> Sverdlin, a volunteer in the 3rd Sapper Battalion of the 2nd Sapper Regiment, a Jew, previously worked in a food shop. He applied to become a volunteer, but suddenly realised that the division was a fighting division and about to be sent to the front. He became distressed, announcing that when he joined the *opolcheniye* his wife had tried to hang herself, and had only been saved at the last moment. He was dismissed . . . In the artillery Communist Brauman burst into tears because he was afraid to go to the front . . . Komsomol member Peterson wanted to leave the

opolcheniye, but things were made clear to him and he was sent to work in the kitchens.[14]

But such backsliding was rare. Most people either itched to fight, like (Jewish) Frenklakh and Alshits, or found it easier simply to go along with the crowd. 'It was an unequal choice', as Lidiya Ginzburg put it, 'between danger close at hand, certain and familiar (the management's displeasure), and the outcome of something as yet distant, unclear, and above all incomprehensible.'[15]

Having created their people's army, the authorities treated it with deep suspicion. Born of a genuine grass-roots movement rather than by Party diktat, its members showed an unwelcome tendency to organise themselves, and to offer suggestions and criticism. Particularly hard to marshal were the thousands of intelligentsia volunteers. Of the 2,600 men of the 3rd Rifle Regiment of the First Division (recruited from the institute-packed Dzerzhinsky district), about a thousand, the Political Department apprehensively noted, were 'highly cultured types – professors, scientific workers, writers, engineers' – who needed to be 'planted' with educated officers whom they could respect. Requests to be used according to a specialism – radio engineers asking to become signal officers, mining engineers asking to become sappers – were nonetheless to be treated as 'manifestations of cowardice', and the regiment was subsequently stripped of 'moaners' and 'unstable elements'. In both of the first two *opolcheniye* divisions, volunteers initially chose their company commanders and 'political leaders' – the battalion-level entertainments officers-cum-propagandists-cum-informers known as *politruki* – by informal ballot,[16] a perilously democratic practice that was swiftly stamped out on Stavka's orders. The Political Department's best efforts, though, could not persuade them to initiate 'socialist competitions' with other units, or to adopt military formalities. 'Here are two examples', lamented one *politruk*,

from the Zhdanovsky and Kirovsky regiments. He used to be
an ordinary worker and is now an officer. In his unit he has
two of his former foremen – and of course, it's difficult to drop
the [familiar] Sasha, Vanya, Petya. Or take the following incident. A commander gives an order and says 'Repeat it.' And
his subordinate replies 'Sasha, why do I have to repeat it, do
you think I'm stupid?' . . . We have to force our commanders
to be stricter.[17]

Volunteerism, the Party bosses worried, might also mask treachery. Thirteen ethnic German and Estonian 'foreigners' were discovered to have signed up, as had an ex-Trotskyite, a White Finn, and
several Spanish and Austrian Communists. All were dismissed from
the *opolcheniye*, and their details passed to the NKVD.[18]

More practically, what were by 7 July 110,000 volunteers[19] had
to be transferred to barracks, equipped and taught to fight. In
this the authorities failed miserably, as the *politruki*'s frank reports
attest. The First, or 'Kirov', Division's volunteers were called up
on 4 July, and sent to improvised barracks in schools, a hospital,
a factory hostel and a dormitory of the Conservatoire, where they
slept on the floor or on bunks with no mattresses. They arrived, the
Political Department complained, straight from work, drunk after
the traditional conscription send-off and without proper clothing.
They sat listening to political lectures with their shirts off, banged
their newly issued rifles on their bedsteads to detach the bayonets,
hid quarter-litre bottles of vodka in their gas masks and bought
Eskimo lollipops from ice-cream sellers who were allowed to come
and go unhindered and might be spies. Worst of all, they were
not being trained. Theoretically, volunteers were supposed to have
sixteen hours' training. In practice, they had even less than this,
since they had not enough weapons or ammunition to learn with,
and almost no instructors (one per 500–600 soldiers, according to
one report[20]).

In practice, no adequate training could possibly have taken place in the time available. On 7 July, after three days in barracks, the men of the Kirov Division marched through the streets, followed by crowds of wives and children, to the Vitebsky railway station, where they entrained for the front. It was a piece of theatre, for a few stops out the army command sent them back again, to pick up basic equipment. Altogether, a volunteer remembered,

> we set off for the front three times . . . The first time was on 7 July. The command sent us back because we didn't have any kit. On 8 July our weapons arrived and were distributed. We set off again, and our uniforms were handed out on the way. Again we were turned back. By the 9th we were finally properly dressed and equipped: everyone with his rifle, and the officers with carbines.

But though the First Division had artillery, machine guns and a few sub-machine guns, it had no anti-aircraft guns, its mortars lacked sights and some of the rifles that had been issued were forty years old. ('Mine was made in 1895', one *Kirovyets* remembered. 'It was the same age as me.'[21]) The division finally arrived at its destination – a railway town between Luga and Novgorod – on 11 July, in the middle of an air raid.

Later *opolcheniye* units were even worse off. The Second Division also had no anti-aircraft guns, no automatic weapons save one machine gun, and such inexperienced gun crews that they had to 'learn how to use their guns while in battle'. The Third Division, *opolcheniye* commander Major General Aleksei Subbotin complained to Zhdanov, had half its designated artillery, no armoured shells, no grenades or Molotov cocktails, 'not a single mortar', insufficient cable for field telephones, only a handful of cars and motorbikes, and no gun oil for rifles, which meant that they hadn't been cleaned since being handed out. The third was nonetheless sent to man fortifications near Leningrad on 15 July, the actual day of its call-up.[22]

The Party saw the volunteers, internal records make clear, as cannon fodder. Meeting with his colleagues in the Political Department, Verkhoglaz praised their diversity – 'In our units you can see a professor marching alongside a student, a metalworker and a blast-furnace operator, or an architect doing target-practice alongside a baker' – but admitted that 'Since we don't have much preparation time, they must train while fighting, and fight while training.' Volunteers were 'not to be used for manoeuvres, only for defence . . . which is why they need to know how to use grenades and other primitive means of fighting off enemy attacks'.[23] The first division to be thrown into battle was the Second, which on arrival at the front on 13 July was immediately ordered to turn back German tank units from a bridgehead across the Luga River south-east of Kingisepp. The First and Third Divisions followed suit a week later, as the Wehrmacht's motorised divisions spread south along the Luga Line.

The result was near-universal panic and confusion. Unarmed, untrained, exhausted by night-time marches and sleepless days hiding from air attack, volunteers fled or fell into captivity in vast numbers. So many abandoned their ancient rifles that a special campaign was launched with the slogans 'Losing your gun is a crime against the Motherland' and 'A soldier's power is his weapon'. Mass flight in the face of tanks was so common that it got its own pseudo-medical name – *tankovaya boyazn*, or 'tankophobia'. Verkhoglaz even hinted to his subordinates that they should spread the rumour that the Germans were using dummies:

> The other day exactly this sort of incident was uncovered; it was spotted through binoculars. A colossal column of tanks was seen approaching. The tanks stopped, an officer got out and leant against one with his elbow, and his elbow made a dent. Well, as you know, elbows don't make dents on real tanks. This slight detail revealed the truth – the tanks turned out to be fake.[24]

Whether this absurd attempt at persuading men to fight panzers virtually with their bare hands had any success we do not know; it seems highly unlikely.

Brought to battle, the volunteers' lives were thrown away in the most primitive fashion. 'Russian attack method', German chief of staff General Halder wrote in his diary: 'Three-minute artillery barrage, then pause, then infantry attacking as much as twelve ranks deep, without heavy weapons support. The men start hurrah-ing from far off. Incredibly high Russian losses.'[25] One of those infantrymen was Frenklakh. 'You're so terrified that your legs root themselves to the ground', he remembered. 'It's extraordinarily difficult to make yourself get up, pick up your rifle and run. Once you're up it's fine – you just run forwards. But it wasn't just fear of being shot in the back of the head if you didn't that made you do it – you were high on a sense of duty.'

Officers who emerged from battle alive were subjected to the usual suspicious bullying. Verkhoglaz interrogated a *politruk*, Mikhail Serogodsky, after a disastrous engagement near Kingisepp at the end of July:

> Serogodsky: 'Nine hundred of us arrived at the railway station, and six hundred came out of the fighting there.'
> Verkhoglaz: 'Were the rest killed, or did they make off?'
> Serogodsky: 'Some went off towards Gdov, some were killed.'
> Verkhoglaz: 'I know exactly why some of them ran away – it was because you lost your head. You didn't understand that you have to lead. Thanks to your failure of leadership they ran away in animal terror.'

The remainder of the unit, Serogodsky continued, were ordered to 'consider themselves partisans', broke up into groups and headed into the woods:

> Verkhoglaz: 'The reason for your return from the rear?'
> Serogodsky: 'We had difficulties with food. For the last three days

until we met up with our units again, we fed off wild plants.
We were walking through deep pine forest and living off wood
sorrel. Extreme hunger forced us to rejoin our lines.'

Verkhoglaz: 'And your losses are how big?'

Serogodsky: 'Hard to say. In our detachment there are sixty-five
men left. That wasn't just deaths; twice I sent men out on
reconnaissance and they didn't come back.'[26]

Anger and despair come through the battalion-level reports as
well, their language burned clean of the usual political jargon. A
Commissar Moseyenko of the First Division explained, on 21 July,
why his unit had been forced to retreat:

> The battalion was defending itself against mortar fire, and could
> not open fire in return because it had no mortars of its own. The
> battalion had no communications with the regiment, the artillery
> or its own companies, as a result of which our artillery was firing
> at our own soldiers in their own trenches. The 1st Company of
> the battalion subjected the 3rd Company of the same battalion
> to fire.[27]

Another officer of the First Division complained of the lack of medical services:

> It isn't just that the situation with drugs is bad; we have no surgi-
> cal equipment at all. If the wounded need surgery we can't help
> them. There are no surgeons, no instruments, no nurses. There are
> the Red Cross girls – they are heroines, true, but that isn't much
> help to them. We haven't got enough first aid kits. There are no
> back-up stocks, only what the soldiers already have in their bags,
> that's all. One small bottle of iodine per bag . . . What can I say
> about medical transport? We should have 380 trucks; we have
> 170. There are no qualified doctors . . .

It was small wonder, he hinted, that officers often found their position unbearable:

> There was one unpleasant incident. The commander of the 1st
> Kirovsky Regiment shot himself. The reason, apparently, was
> cowardice, fear that [the regiment] was not properly armed. They
> say that fifteen minutes earlier he had given an excellent speech
> [to the troops], then walked out and shot himself. His actions
> have not been explained to the soldiers; they have been told that
> he was killed by diversionists.[28]

A senior lieutenant questioned why he had ordered a retreat on his
own initiative, replied, 'I don't know how to be an officer and I didn't
want lots of people to be killed through my fault', before bursting into tears.[29] A machine-gunner left a brisk note: 'I've decided to
take my own life. It's too difficult in the company. Signed, company
sergeant major Smirnov.'

On 16 July the High Command ordered the creation of four more
opolcheniye divisions, eventually comprising another 41,446 volunteers. Recruitment criteria were loosened to include 'white-ticketers', spectacle-wearers and the sons of 'enemies of the people', and
age limits extended from eighteen down to seventeen, and from fifty
up to fifty-five. Their grand new title of 'Guards Divisions' failed
to disguise the fact that they were even worse equipped than their
predecessors. The 3rd Rifle Regiment of the First Guards Division,
for example, had 791 rifles, ten sniper's rifles and five revolvers for
2,667 men.[30] Training was again abysmal or non-existent ('We're
teaching them to fight with stones', lamented an instructor). Thanks
to the profligacy of the past three weeks, the new divisions were also
acutely short of experienced officers – of the First Guards Division's
781 officers only eighty-two were 'cadres' – roughly speaking, professionals. To officer the Second Guards Division, commissars had to

scout the unoccupied Soviet Union, bringing men from as far away as the Urals.[31]

The new divisions were thrown into the same bloodbath as their predecessors. On arrival at the front on 11 August, the First Guards Division's orders were changed three times, with the result that some regiments had to march seventy kilometres in twenty-four hours. They were then thrown straight into action, despite lacking cartridges, shells and grenades. More ammunition could not be brought up from the rear, a Political Department boss reported to Zhdanov after a tour of the front, because the division had no fuel tanker, and had had to leave behind 390 horses for lack of harnesses and carts. Nor could the wounded be evacuated from the battlefield, since the medical unit had only four trucks. The 'high-ups' who descended on divisional headquarters were more hindrance than help:

> Every one of them feels that it's his duty to give an order or advice. A characteristic example: the divisional commander only found out that the 2nd Rifle Regiment had been ordered to attack on the evening of 12 August, when the order had already been carried out, under the command of a major general from group headquarters. In conversation with me, Major General Shcherbakov and brigade commissar Kurochkin both declared 'Everybody gives orders but nobody actually helps.'

A long list of requested supplies included water carts, an ambulance and a mobile field hospital, as well as twenty more mid-ranking officers and *politruki* to round up and rally retreating volunteers.[32]

The Second Guards Division was sent into the lines at Gatchina on 12 August, and cut to pieces two weeks later. During the battle, regimental commissar Nabatov reported, it became apparent that

A. Some of the soldiers don't know how to handle rifles or grenades. This contributed to their dispersal during fighting.

B. A number of soldiers were badly camouflaged, having failed to carry out orders to dig themselves in. As a result we suffered large losses from artillery fire and mortars.

C. During counter-attacks soldiers tried to keep close to one another instead of spreading out in proper formation. This meant more losses.

D. Soldiers do not recognise their neighbours to the left and right. Mistaking their own men for the enemy, they think they have been encircled.

E. A number of unit commanders do not know their own soldiers by name.

F. Some soldiers do not know how to use their first aid kits. As a result some, having suffered relatively minor wounds, bleed to death before they can be delivered to a medical point.

In between the bouts of carnage, volunteers sat out summer thunderstorms in half-built trenches, wet and hungry ('We sploshed about', as Frenklakh put it, 'like hippos in the zoo'). Units pleaded for tarpaulins, tents, field kitchens, underwear, razors, mess tins, water bottles, shovels, entrenching tools, helmets, and most of all for vehicles, communications equipment, weapons (the Third Guards had only three rifles for every four volunteers) and men who knew how to use them. 'The majority of volunteers', reported a *politruk* of a battalion of the Fourth Guards Division, sent to join the eviscerated Second Division, are untrained, or insufficiently trained, to shoot, so that in some cases they are unable to load their own rifles and their officers have to do it for them . . . Out of 205 listed as machine-gunners only 100 turned out actually to be acquainted with machine guns, the rest were just riflemen. A list of 'sappers' included more riflemen and ordinary labourers, but not a single explosives expert . . . Nor do they have any tools for repairing weapons, so that simple breakage of a machine gun's firing pin puts the gun out of commission.[33]

The decision formally to wind up the remains of the *opolcheniye* was taken on 19 September, and by the end of the month its remnants had been absorbed into the Red Army. Some 135,400 people, including substantial numbers of female auxiliaries, had served in it altogether.[34] The nearest we have to an official casualty estimate is from Zhdanov's deputy, Aleksei Kuznetsov, who stated, in a speech in the Smolniy the following year, that no fewer than 43,000 Leningrad volunteers were killed, taken prisoner or went missing in the first three months of the war. This is almost certainly far too low. The proportion of casualties in the First and Second Divisions, and in the Second and Fourth Guards Divisions, all of which were virtually annihilated before being officially wound up, was much higher, and hints dropped to Western journalists at the end of the war suggest loss rates of up to 50 per cent.[35]

Was the sacrifice worth it? The traditional interpretation is that though undertrained and underequipped, the *opolcheniye* held the Luga Line for a vital few weeks, winning time for the strengthening of Leningrad's inner defences. 'They couldn't be considered fully-trained soldiers', the director of the Kirov Works told Werth in 1943, 'but their drive, their guts were tremendous . . . they managed to stop the Germans just in the nick of time . . . The fight put up by our Workers' Division and by the people of Leningrad was absolutely decisive.'[36]

Today's historians are much less sure, crediting the brief late-July pause in von Leeb's advance more to rain and the regular Red Army. Even if the volunteers – bewildered, unarmed, leaderless – did make a difference on the battlefield, their loss undoubtedly represented a prodigious waste of skilled and educated manpower, especially given the Red Army's desperate need for officers shortly afterwards. (By the end of September 1941 the Red Army as a whole had lost an extraordinary 142,000 out of its total 440,000 officers. 'Basically to blame', reported General Fedyuninsky of a failed operation outside Leningrad in October, 'is weak leadership on the part of platoon and company-level officers, in some cases amounting to simple cowardice.'[37]) The military historian Antony Beevor is damning: 'The waste of lives', he writes, 'was so terrible that it is hard to comprehend: a carnage whose futility was perhaps exceeded only by the Zulu king marching an *impi* of his warriors over a cliff to prove their discipline.' Even harsher is *opolcheniye* survivor Frenklakh:

> There are moments I am ashamed of to this day. We repeatedly took to our heels, abandoning our casualties. Everyone was terrified of being wounded during a retreat, because if you couldn't walk there was almost no hope of stretcher-bearers picking you up. Your only chance was if a friend helped you . . . After the war I thought for a long time about '41, analysing the situation as it was then. All those fairy tales about mass heroism – they lie on the consciences of the writers and the *politruki*. There were some heroes of course, but there were also crowds of people who just panicked and fled. It was mass, completely unjustified, senseless sacrifice, at the pleasure of our moronic command.[38]

The last word should go to Stalin. In April 1942, wishing to humiliate Voroshilov, who had turned down an offered command, he circulated a note to the Central Committee listing Comrade (pointedly, not Marshal) Voroshilov's failings. Among them was the fact that while in command of the Northwestern Army Group he had 'neglected Leningrad's artillery defences, distracted by the creation of workers' battalions, poorly armed with shotguns, pikes, daggers etc'.[39] Voroshilov was a bad man and a bad soldier, but the disaster of the People's Levy was not his fault alone. He had learned his trade in the Politburo, whose members' most important life skill was the ability correctly to anticipate the wishes of Stalin himself.

'Caught in a Mousetrap'

Vera Inber arrived in Leningrad by train on 24 August. Fifty-one years old, she was, remarkably, both Trotsky's first cousin and a prominent member of the literary establishment, producing short stories that managed to pass the censors without descending into outright socialist realism. Her husband had just been appointed director of Leningrad's Erisman teaching hospital, a leafy complex of red-brick nineteenth-century buildings opposite the Botanical Gardens on the Petrograd Side. Having seen her daughter and baby grandson off into evacuation from Moscow, Inber was coming to join him.

The journey, in peacetime an easy overnighter, took two and a half days. Fresh bomb craters lined the tracks, and long factory trains rattled by in the opposite direction, machinery bulky under protective canvas. One could tell how long each one had been on the road, Inber noticed, by the freshness of the birch branches tied on to the wagon roofs for camouflage. Her own train, drawing towards Leningrad through dilapidated villages with picturesque backwoods names, came to increasingly frequent halts. 'We stopped at dawn', she wrote in her diary

and we are still here ... The carriage is fairly empty, and no one talks much. In one compartment an endless card game is in progress; a general whistles as he declares his suit, an army engineer knocks out his pipe on the corner of the table, over and over again. The sound reminds me of a woodpecker tapping its tree. The pipe smoke drifts into the corridor, moves in layers, thins out and is suspended in the rays of the sun. Everything is so quiet, it's as thought the train were resting on moss.[1]

They started to move again, through a heavily bombed wood. Trees lay charred and split; roots pointing upwards, earth scorched ochre. Passing through a station, Inber noticed its name – Mga. Normally one never took this route: already, the direct line from Moscow had been broken by the Germans.

Inber disembarked into an atmosphere of tense expectancy. The first thing she saw on leaving the railway station was a poster bearing the text of an appeal, signed by Zhdanov, Voroshilov and city soviet chairman Popkov and dated three days earlier. It was the first official acknowledgement that the Germans were now at the gates of Leningrad:

Comrades! Leningraders! Dear friends! Over our beloved native city hangs the immediate threat of attack by German-Fascist troops. The enemy is trying to break through to Leningrad. He wants to destroy our homes, to seize our factories and plants, to drench our streets and squares with the blood of the innocent, to outrage our peaceful people, to enslave the free sons of our Motherland. But this shall not be. Leningrad – cradle of the proletarian Revolution – never has fallen and never shall fall into enemy hands . . .

Let us rise as one man in defence of our city, our homes, our families, our honour and freedom. Let us perform our sacred duty as Soviet patriots and be indomitable in the struggle with the fierce and hateful enemy, vigilant and merciless in the struggle against cowards, alarmists and deserters; let us establish the strictest revolutionary order in our city. Armed with iron discipline and

Bolshevik resolve we shall meet the enemy bravely and deal him a crushing blow! [2]

In the eight days since she had decided to leave Moscow, Inber reflected, Leningrad's situation had become dramatically worse. Still, joining her husband had been the right thing to do. 'He always said "If war breaks out we should be together." And here we are – together.'

Over the next few days she saw little of him. He was frantically busy at the hospital; she made a broadcast for the city radio station ('Moscow and Leningrad, brother and sister, stretch out their hands to one other') and idled, feeling oddly surplus to requirements, round their airy new flat. Through the high windows the sun sparkled on the Karpovka river and the palm-filled glasshouses of the Botanical Gardens opposite. Inside, the walls were hung with fine old porcelain plates, their roses as fresh as the day they had been painted in the reign of Empress Elizabeth. What on earth would she do with them, she wondered, when the air raids began? Though there were ten to fifteen alerts each day – more like one continual drill with short breaks – everything seemed to be happening 'far away, beyond the horizon':

During alerts I go out on the balcony. Pesochnaya Street, always quiet, empties completely. Only the air-raid wardens in their tin helmets stand looking up at the sky. Occasionally a factory-school boy runs by – they have a hostel in one of the buildings in the Botanical Gardens. The woman tram driver had this to say about them: 'They carry on as if they owned the tram; hang on to the step, push their way on to the platform. But I don't mind any more – after all, they'll soon be off to the front to dig trenches.'[3]

Across the Neva on Sadovaya Street, Yuri Ryabinkin spent the radiant late summer days playing chess, sketching out study plans with his friend Finkelstein in case their school closed, and doing more chores around the flat now that his mother had dismissed the maid. Nobody took much notice of his sixteenth birthday, but as a treat he bought himself a chess book and five roubles' worth of supper at his mother's office canteen. Poring over books of military strategy, he came up with a plan to save his city. The whole population would be 'sent out into the forest' and the Red Army would feint a retreat, luring the Germans into a trap:

> Immediately, like lightning (even more so than the Germans on 22 June), our tank units will go over to a general offensive and push the Germans into a knot. Then all the might of our artillery – which in the course of the retreat will have occupied the most advantageous positions – will be hurled at that knot. After half an hour of firing our guns will move off a few kilometres, and the places they shelled be occupied by our troops. All the aircraft massed above them will bomb the remnants of the enemy. And as soon as the enemy falters he will be pursued by land, air and sea . . .

Ryabinkin knew, though, that this was a wish-fulfilment fantasy. 'But all this is impossible', he confided to his diary,

> There is no one to undertake such an offensive. And we have too few tanks . . . Every editorial shouts 'We shall not surrender Leningrad!' . . . But for some reason our army is not victorious; probably it doesn't have enough weapons. The policemen on the streets, and even some of the *opolcheniye* volunteers and regular soldiers, are armed with Mausers of goodness knows what vintage. The Germans are lumbering forward with their tanks and we are taught to fight them not with tanks but with bundles of grenades or bottles of petrol. That's how it is!'[4]

The elderly artist Anna Ostroumova-Lebedeva walked the city centre, making a mental record (sketching was forbidden) of the boarding up of Leningrad's public monuments. On the Anichkov Bridge, Klodt's plunging horses had already been rolled away for burial in the gardens in front of the Aleksandrinka theatre. Opposite St Isaac's, the outline of the equestrian statue of Nicholas I was still visible under layers of sandbags, which seemed to pour endlessly downwards in a fat, globular flow. The Alexander Column in Palace Square was covered in wooden scaffolding, but the poles did not reach its triumphant angel, who continued to brandish his cross against the blue sky. There had been debate about how to protect Falconet's famous statue of Peter the Great, the 'Bronze Horseman'. Some had suggested sinking it in the Neva, but now it too was being boarded up. Watching volunteers unload sand from a barge moored nearby, Ostroumova-Lebedeva wished she could join in: 'It was hot, the sun was burning. I stood there and watched, and felt ashamed that I wasn't working myself.' Though her sister and nieces had left Leningrad, she had decided to stay, partly out of reluctance to abandon familiar surroundings, but mostly out of a sense of solidarity with her city and sheer curiosity as to what would happen next. 'Everyone's worrying about the same question', she wrote on 16 August. 'Should we leave, and if so where for, and how? What does the future hold? How does one start all over again somewhere strange, having abandoned the comforting refuge of one's flat? Poor Leningraders! I want to stay. I definitely want to stay and witness all the frightening events ahead.'[5]

Failing to empty Leningrad of its surplus population before the siege ring closed was one of the Soviet regime's worst blunders of the war, leading to more civilian deaths than any other save the failure to anticipate Barbarossa itself. By the time the last train left, on 29 August, 636,283 people, according to official sources, had been evacuated from Leningrad. (This compares with 660,000 civilians evacuated from London in only a few days on Britain's declaration of war two years earlier.) Excluding refugees from the Baltics and elsewhere who passed through the city, the number falls to 400,000 at best. Just over two and a half million civilians were left behind in the city, plus another 343,000 in the surrounding towns and villages within the siege ring. Over 400,000 of them were children, and over 700,000 other non-working dependants.[6]

Why did more people unnecessary to Leningrad's defence not get away in time? To blame was a mixture of deliberate government policy, muddle and Leningraders' own faulty decision-making, exacerbated by an all-pervading culture of fear. Policy, from the outset of the war, was to prioritise industrial and institutional evacuation over that of the non-working population. On 3 July Moscow's new five-man State Defence Committee (headed by Stalin, and the supreme decision-making body of the war) decided to move twenty-six defence plants east, from Leningrad, Moscow and Tula. Leningrad's programme was accelerated at the end of the month, when the Wehrmacht reached the Luga Line. By the end of August ninety-two Leningrad defence manufacturies had been moved, together with 164,320 of their workers. Most went to the industrial cities of the Urals, where they resumed production, in hastily improvised new premises, with remarkable speed. It was a great achievement, but not as completely successful as Soviet accounts make out. The railway network, not surprisingly, became chaotically overloaded. Identical raw materials were simultaneously shipped in and out of the city, and some factories were dismantled when it was already too late for them to leave. More than two thousand carloads of machinery still awaited removal when the last railway line out of the city was cut, and sat idle in the freight yards through the first winter of the siege and beyond.[7]

The other, disastrous, evacuation programme of the first weeks of the war was that of children. On 26 June the Leningrad soviet announced the evacuation of 392,000 children to rural districts in the Leningrad, Kalinin and Yaroslavl provinces, with their schools, nurseries or children's homes but without their mothers. It was extremely unpopular. 'My heart thumped and my thoughts became confused', wrote Yelena Skyrabina on hearing the news. 'I didn't know what to do. The idea of separating from [five-year-old] Yura is so horrible that I am ready to do anything to keep him. I have decided to defy the order. I won't give up my son for anything.'[8] Many parents successfully evaded the order, but others put their children on to trains for Luga, Gatchina, Staraya Russa and other traditional summer-camp destinations to Leningrad's south and west. The first 15,192 children left on ten trains on 29 June. Yelena Kochina watched them being taken to the railway stations:

> Like frightened animals they filled the streets, moving towards the railway station, the demarcation line of their childhood: on the other side life without parents would begin. The smallest children were transported in trucks, their little heads sticking out like layers of golden mushrooms. Crazed mothers ran after them.[9]

Three weeks later the Wehrmacht had reached the Luga Line, and parents realised that, far from sending their children to safety, the authorities had actually put them in the path of the German advance. 'When we arrived in the village they put us in a cottage', fifteen-year-old Klara Rakhman wrote from near Staraya Russa. 'Oh yes, I quite forgot, while we were in the truck a German plane flew right overhead. That's evacuation for you!'[10] Retrieving a child was not easy, not least because the imposition of martial law had made it an offence to take unauthorised leave from one's job. (The archivist Georgi Knyazev defied the ban, giving one of his typists permission to go to Borovichi to fetch her daughters, aged twelve and nine.[11]) Lidiya Okhapkina, hampered by a new baby, could not fetch her young son herself, but managed to persuade a chance bread-queue acquaintance, a 'bespectacled, intellectual-looking woman in her early sixties', to do it for her. 'She told me that [her grandson] had been evacuated with Nursery School no. 21 (I remember the exact number), which meant that he had gone precisely to the place where we had sent Tolya . . . She asked how old my little boy was. I said he'd soon be six. I was lying, but he was sturdy and could walk a long way if he had to.' Applying to the district soviet for the necessary papers the following day, Okhapkina found herself one of a crowd of angry mothers. 'They were all agitated, making a lot of noise. Some were even shouting "Bring back our children! Better to have them die here together with us than to have them killed God knows where!"' Having got the right paperwork and handed it over to her new friend, together with as much bread as she could buy, Okhapkina settled down to wait. After a fortnight with no news she suddenly saw the woman standing in the courtyard with two small boys. Hugging her Tolya, she heard that their train had been bombed and that they had had to walk a long way, getting only a few lifts on lorries and carts.[12]

Incredibly, the city authorities actually tried to prevent such rescue missions. District Party Committee secretaries were instructed to forbid enterprise directors from giving staff time off to go and fetch children home, to reassure parents that their children were safe, and to 'liquidate all provocative rumours' to the contrary.[13]

A second round of evacuations, of mothers and children under fourteen, was announced in early August. Unsurprisingly, families now often preferred to take their chances at home. 'This time', wrote Skryabina,

> they are letting mothers go with their children. However, people have been so frightened by these first disastrously unsuccessful attempts that they use illness as an excuse to get a postpone-ment . . . There is still another fear – epidemics of typhoid, chol-era and other stomach disorders are raging along the railways. That, plus the fact that evacuation trains are exposed to bombard-ment. The family of the director of the factory where my husband worked left, and soon after came the news that their fourteen-year-old son had died of typhoid fever.[14]

Okhapkina, by contrast, desperately wanted to leave, but was delayed when Tolya got lost during an air-raid warning. By the time she found him at a police station the following day they had missed their train. 'I couldn't start petitioning all over again for evacuation papers. That incident decided everything – I remained in Leningrad.'

She may have been lucky to miss her slot, because the evacuation trains, instead of going east to Vologda province, were still being sent south, directly into the path of Busch's Sixteenth Army. Bombers preceded the panzers, hitting roads, railways and telegraph lines. The worst of the resulting tragedies occurred at Lychkovo, a small town just south of Lake Ilmen. A convoy of nursery-age children was going through the welcoming ceremonies at a collective farm forty kilometres away when news arrived that German parachutists had landed nearby. 'We were just being offered tea', recounts a survivor, 'when the farm director rushed up. I still remember his words – "There are Nazi paratroopers ahead!"'[15] The children were put in lorries and driven back to Lychkovo railway station, where several thousand more evacuees were already boarding a train. As they waited their turn a Stuka appeared overhead. 'He was flying so low', remembered a teacher. 'He'd take a look, press a button, and – bang! Later they claimed they hadn't known. What rubbish! It was a fine day and the children were dressed in their best, most colourful clothes. He could see exactly what he was hitting.'[16] The plane flew the length of the platform, bombing with methodical precision. Then there was a huge explosion, and when the smoke cleared the train's carriages lay scattered 'as if by a giant hand'.

There are accounts (strenuously denied) of the adults in charge of children's evacuation groups fleeing amidst the chaos, or getting their own children back to Leningrad but abandoning the rest. 'The station was on fire. We couldn't find anybody, it was absolutely horrible!' remembered a mother of her passage through Mga. 'The man in charge of our train sat on a stump with his head in his hands. He had lost his own family, and had no idea who was where.' Wandering infants were unable to give their names, and thus lost their families for good.[17] Returning to Leningrad, evacuation trains were met by mobs of enraged parents who behaved so threateningly that district soviet representatives were warned not to get off.

Other evacuation groups were spared air attack, but endured epic, circuitous journeys punctuated by long, hungry halts. A train that left for the Siberian city of Omsk towards the end of August carried 2,700 children between the ages of seven and sixteen. In peacetime the journey would have taken three days; now it took seven weeks. Most of the children, a doctor accompanying them remembered, carried food for the trip, but after a few days it started to go bad and had to be thrown out. Evacuation bases along the way only supplied flour and water, which she took outside during halts and cooked up into a sort of bread. 'Sometimes they got a little milk, but not regularly. They often went hungry. Occasionally we could pick things out of a field – tomatoes or carrots – but we couldn't wash them properly.' Measles as well as lice spread in the overcrowded carriages, killing five children en route.[18]

The awful rumours about the children's evacuation were not the only reason surplus civilians chose not to leave Leningrad. Many were tied to the city by relatives, or feared that a son or husband missing in action might come home to an empty flat. The siege survivor Irina Bogdanova describes how her grandmother sabotaged her family's evacuation with the Geology Institute, where Irina's mother worked. Though Irina, her mother and grandmother had been given permission to leave, Irina's aunt Nina, a defence worker, had not. As they drove to the railway station in the Institute's truck, her grandmother suddenly recalled that she had forgotten a trunk, and insisted on returning home to collect it. She then also insisted that there was no longer enough room for her in the lorry, and that she and Irina would go to the station by tram. This resulted in the whole family missing their train. Back home, Irina recounts, 'we sat on the sofa;

Mama hugged me and said, "All right then, we'll all die together"'.
So it was. Grandmother, mother and aunt all died of starvation in
February and March 1942. Eight-year-old Irina survived alone with
two corpses for ten days, before being picked up by a civil defence
brigade, which transferred her to an orphanage. Interviewed seventy
years later, sitting dressed in her best at a table covered end to end
with beautifully presented snacks, Irina admits she has 'been living
with this feeling of blame towards my grandmother for my whole
life. I think that she wanted to stay with Nina, and forgot the trunk
and refused to sit in the back of the truck on purpose.'[19]

For the unemployed, individual evacuation was theoretically
possible, but the bureaucracy involved was daunting, and unless put
up by relatives in unoccupied territory, they had no guarantee of
finding housing. In practice, people without jobs often managed
to inscribe themselves on to the staff of evacuating institutions, but
this required contacts and pull. A friend of Skryabina's, the wife of
a factory director, offered her a post as 'governess' to the factory
kindergarten, which was leaving for the Moscow region. A day later
she telephoned again, and 'between sobs, informed me that all our
plans had fallen through. When the workers learned that the factory
planned to send its so to speak "intelligentsia" off with the kindergarten, they revolted and nearly tore the factory committee apart.'
Skryabina was actually relieved: 'My agonizing problem has been
resolved by circumstances. It no longer depends on me. I no longer
have to worry about abandoning Mama and Nana; there will be no
parting.'[20]

Valerian Bogdanov-Berezovsky, the now forgotten composer of
Pilots and *Ballad of the Men of the Baltic Fleet*, decided to stay because
he didn't want to leave his mother, but also because he had just been
appointed chairman of the Leningrad branch of the Composers'
Union, the previous incumbent having failed to return from his
summer holiday. Others privately doubted whether German occupation would really be as bad as the propaganda made out. 'Can it really

be', wondered Skryabina incredulously, 'that they kill people just for being Jews?' In mid-August she turned down a second chance to evacuate in expectation, subtly implied in her diary, that Leningrad was about to be given up. 'If the war really is progressing at such breakneck speed then probably it will end soon. Why leave somewhere we are settled? Perhaps it would be wiser to stay in the flat. What should I do?' She nonetheless suspected provocation when an old schoolfriend sat down beside her on a bench and 'without any introduction, began talking about how happy he is that the Germans are just outside the city; that they are immeasurably powerful, and that if the city doesn't surrender today, then it will tomorrow . . . "And this", he said, showing me a small revolver, "is in case my hopes deceive me."' At Pushkin House a Jewish colleague of Likhachev's – the same Professor Gukovsky who Olga Grechina criticised for hypocrisy – appeared in the canteen rakishly attired in 'a peaked cap (worn somewhat to one side), and a shirt belted in the Caucasian style. He greeted us with a salute. Confidentially he told us that when the Germans came, he would pass himself off as an Armenian.'[21]

The art historian Nikolai Punin succumbed to simple fatalism. In the blacked-out, post-curfew silence of the evening of 26 August, the same day that permission finally came through for the Baltic Fleet to leave Tallinn, he sat at his desk restarting his diary, after a gap of five years, by the light of a lamp whose shade was made of blue wallpaper. For people of his generation, he wrote, death had never seemed far away. 'In reality they've been inviting us to die quickly these past twenty-five years. Many have died, death draws near, as near as it can. Why should we think of it, since it thinks of us so earnestly?' The sense of impending doom reminded him of the 1937 Terror, when he and all his friends went to bed each evening expecting a small-hours knock on the door and waiting Black Maria. Visiting the Academy of Sciences ('confusion and chaos') earlier in the day, colleagues had tried to persuade him to leave with them for Samarkand:

But that would mean getting drawn into the war. No, I'm not going. It's better to tilt at windmills while one still can. The lamp burns, it is quiet. Lord, comfort the souls ascending to heaven.

Not long ago I said to someone 'Now, there are two frightening things: war and evacuation. But of the two, evacuation is worse.' This is just a quip, it's true. But why didn't they evacuate us during the Yezhovshchina [the Terror]? It was just as frightening then.[22]

The background noise to agonised personal decision-making was strong popular and semi-official disapproval of those who were quick to leave the city. Evacuees were dubbed 'rats', or *bezhentsy* – 'refugees', but literally translated as 'runners-away'. Olga Grechina had an awkward parting with a pair of brothers, fellow students at the university, whose mother had wangled them places on an archaeological dig in Central Asia. 'I couldn't understand how healthy young people could agree to be evacuated when everyone else was trying to get to the front . . . Conversation was difficult. I didn't blame them for leaving; I was just terribly surprised that they had agreed.'[23] As perniciously and less inevitably, some district soviets paraded their faith in the leadership by actually discouraging civilian evacuation in their areas. As Dmitri Pavlov, wartime head of the national food supply agency, puts it in the best Soviet account of the siege, they 'viewed citizens' refusal to evacuate as a patriotic act and were proud of it, thus involuntarily encouraging people to remain'. The number of Leningraders evacuated through July and August, he thought, could and should have been two or three times higher.[24] Refusal to evacuate could, ironically, also be regarded as suspicious. A diarist noted the following rumour:

It's said that P. Z. Andreyev and S. P. Preobrazhenskaya (of the Mariinsky Theatre) refused to leave. 'Why?' they were asked. 'We're sure that Leningrad won't be surrendered,' they replied. But the administration thought to themselves, 'We know you.

It's already certain that Leningrad will have to be abandoned, and you want to go over to the Fascists! We'd better interrogate you, so as to see just what kind of Soviet people you really are.'[25]

By 25 August Leningrad was three-quarters surrounded. The railway lines west to the Baltics had been cut, as had the direct routes to Moscow. The only unbroken line ran to the east, splitting in two at the junction town of Mga, now itself the scene of heavy fighting. To the west, the Red Army had lost the whole of the Baltic littoral except for a sixty-kilometre stretch of Gulf shoreline to the west of Peterhof. Supplied via Kronshtadt, this 'Oranienbaum pocket' – named for one of the tsars' summer palaces – held out all through the siege, though to little strategic advantage and at dreadful cost. To the north, the Finnish army under General Carl Mannerheim, having recovered its pre-Winter War borders, had crossed into Russian Karelia and was advancing along the north-eastern shore of Lake Ladoga, in accordance with a promise to Hitler to 'shake hands' with the Wehrmacht on the River Svir.

The threat to Leningrad now absorbed all the Kremlin's attention. There is a school of thought, dating from Khrushchev's 'Thaw'-heralding 'Secret Speech' of 1956, which maintains that Stalin deliberately allowed Leningrad to be surrounded, out of suspicion of its liberal bent and record as a breeding ground for charismatic politicians such as the Old Bolsheviks Kirov (mysteriously murdered in 1934) and Grigori Zinoviev (shot after a show trial in 1936). But reading Stalin's furious – sometimes fantastical – harangues of the late summer and autumn, the theory dissolves. Though he clearly contemplated abandoning the city so as to save its armies, he equally clearly viewed this as a desperate last resort.

Sometime between 21 and 27 August, as German armour rolled through the railway towns to Leningrad's south, a 'special commission' set out to Leningrad from the Kremlin. Its members included Molotov, the chiefs of the air force, navy and artillery, trade commissar Aleksei Kosygin, and, most significantly, Georgi Malenkov, the thirty-nine-year-old rising star recently appointed to the State Defence Committee – the five-man chamber, headed by Stalin, that acted as the USSR's supreme decision-making body throughout the war. Despised by Zhdanov, who gave him the servant-girlish nickname 'Malanya' for his pear shape, smooth chin and high-pitched voice, Malenkov was also a crony of Zhdanov's archenemy, NKVD chief Beria. The commission's mission, officially to 'evaluate the complicated situation', was probably in reality to decide whether Leningrad should be abandoned. The journey alone proved how near to disaster it had already come. Having flown to Cherepovets, a railway town 400 kilometres to Leningrad's east, the group boarded a train which took them as far as Mga, where it was halted by an air raid. With fires twisting in the night sky and anti-aircraft guns hammering, the Kremlin grandees got out and stumbled along the tracks until they met an ordinary town tram, which took them to a second train that finally carried them to the city.

The commission stayed for about a week, during which Stalin continued to bombard Zhdanov with orders, now completely divorced from fast-changing reality.[26] On 27 August he telephoned the Smolniy with a dream-like scheme to post tanks 'on average every two kilometres, in places every 500 metres, depending on the ground' along a new 120-kilometre defence line from Gatchina to the Volkhov River. 'The infantry divisions will stand directly behind the tanks, using them not only as a striking force, but as armoured defence. For this you need 100–120 KVs [a type of heavy tank]. I think you could produce this quantity of KVs in ten days . . . I await your swift reply.'[27] The following day Zhdanov came up with his usual slavish agreement. Stalin's plan for a defence line 'of a special type' was 'absolutely correct', and he asked permission to postpone the evacuation of workshops belonging to the Izhorsk and Kirov weapons factories, so that their tank production be used to fulfil the scheme.

On 29 August the Germans took Tosno, only forty kilometres

from Leningrad on the Moscow road. They also reached the south bank of the Neva, cutting the forces defending Leningrad to the south-east in two. Spitting fury and paranoia, Stalin telegraphed Molotov and Malenkov alone:

> I have only just been informed that Tosno has been taken by the enemy. If things go on like this I am afraid that Leningrad will be surrendered out of idiot stupidity, and all the Leningrad divisions fall into captivity. What are Popov and Voroshilov doing? They don't even tell me how they plan to avert the danger. They're busy looking for new lines of retreat; that's how they see their duty. Where does this abyss of passivity of theirs come from, this peasant-like submission to fate? I just don't understand them. There are lots of KV tanks in Leningrad now, lots of planes . . . Why isn't all this equipment being used in the Lyuban–Tosno sector? What can some infantry regiment do against German tanks, without any equipment? . . . Doesn't it seem to you that someone is deliberately opening the road to the Germans? What kind of man is Popov? How's Voroshilov spending his time, what's he doing to help Leningrad? I write this because the uselessness of the Leningrad command is so absolutely incomprehensible. I think you should leave for Moscow. Please don't delay.[28]

How close Popov and Voroshilov came to a bullet in the back of the neck we can't tell. Malenkov and Molotov certainly heaped on the criticism, taking care not to spare Zhdanov either. Replying to Stalin the same day, they boasted that they had sharply criticised Zhdanov and Voroshilov's mistakes, which included creating the Defence Council of Leningrad, allowing battalions to elect their officers, holding back civilian evacuation and failing properly to build new fortifications. Worse, Zhdanov and Voroshilov were guilty of 'not understanding their duty promptly to inform Stavka of the measures being taken to defend Leningrad, of constantly retreating before the enemy, and of failing to take the initiative and organise counter-attacks. The Leningraders admit their mistakes, but of course this is absolutely inadequate.'[29] Stalin's response was curt: 'Answer: First, who holds Mga right now? Second – find out from Kuznetsov what the plan is for the Baltic Fleet. Third – we want to send Khozin as Voroshilov's deputy. Any objections?' According to Beria's son, on the commission's return to Moscow Malenkov urged Stalin to arrest and court-martial Zhdanov, but Beria dissuaded him.[30] Instead, Stalin made Malenkov his point-man on Leningrad: Stalin's wishes were to be transmitted to Zhdanov through him, and vice versa. This extraordinary arrangement, whereby Zhdanov communicated with Stalin via a man who had tried (as Zhdanov must at least have suspected) to have him murdered, continued for the rest of the war.

Zhdanov was spared; ordinary Leningraders were less fortunate. As the fighting rolled to and fro outside the city, Molotov and Malenkov stepped up the pace of terror inside it. A table drawn up by the Leningrad NKVD on 25 August gives a target number of 2,248 arrests and deportations, divided into twenty-nine categories, from Trotskyites, Zinovievites, Mensheviks and Anarchists, through priests, Catholics, former officers in the tsarist army, 'former wealthy merchants', 'White bandits', 'kulaks' and people 'with connections abroad', down to the catch-all 'diversionists', 'saboteurs' and 'anti-social elements', and simple thieves and prostitutes.[31] Their zeal had its usual results. At one collection point, a disgusted observer noted,

about a hundred people waited to be exiled. They were mostly old women; old women in old-fashioned capes and worn-out velvet coats. These are the enemies our government is capable of fighting – and, it turns out, the only ones. The Germans are at the gates, the Germans are about to enter the city, and we are busy arresting and deporting old women – lonely, defenceless, harmless old people.[32]

Among the victims was Olga Berggolts's elderly father, a doctor at a defence factory. Summoned to police headquarters at midday on 2 September, he was ordered to depart by 6 p.m. the same evening. 'Papa is a military surgeon who has faithfully and honestly served the Soviet government for twenty-four years', Berggolts wrote incredulously in her diary. 'He was in the Red Army for the whole of the Civil War, saved thousands of people, is Russian to the marrow . . . It appears – no joke – that the NKVD simply don't like his surname.'[33] Thanks to the Germans' advance and Berggolts's frantic string-pulling, he managed to stay in Leningrad until the following spring, when he was deported, half-starved, to Krasnoyarsk in western Siberia. The reasons? His Jewishness, his refusal to inform on colleagues and probably his relationship to Berggolts herself, for whose good behaviour he acted as hostage once her war poetry had turned her into a popular public figure.

At the end of August the glorious run of late summer weather broke. Rainwater gurgled down Leningrad's fat galvanised drainpipes, fanned over paving stones, dulled the greens and yellows of the stucco façades. Outside the city, seesaw fighting continued in the mud and wet. On 31 August, having changed hands three times, Mga finally fell, cutting the last railway line out of the city. 'Stavka considers the Leningrad Front's tactics pernicious', menaced Stalin. '[It] appears to know only one thing – how to retreat and find new lines of retreat. Haven't we had enough of these heroic defeats?'[34]

Vera Inber got the news from her husband, who had heard that a military hospital, loaded and waiting to depart for a week, had been told to detrain and return to quarters. The train she had arrived on herself, she calculated, must have been one of the last to get through. Yelena Skryabina, who had just ducked an evacuation order with a chit from her doctor, felt a chill of presentiment: 'The last transport left during the night . . . Leningrad is surrounded, and we are caught in a mousetrap. What have I done with my indecision?'[35] Seated at

his desk at midnight, Georgi Knyazev listened to the distant thump
of guns:

> Once again I have lit the lamp with the green shade . . . But what
> will be happening in a few days' time is utterly beyond imagina-
> tion. Examples of the destruction, the razing to the ground of
> dozens, hundreds of towns leap out from the scrappy newspaper
> reports like nightmares. Surely the same can't happen to a colossus
> like Leningrad? . . . Surely I am not going to see its death?

He had taken down some eighteenth-century silhouettes – of
Academicians, wigged and breeched, debating under delicate oak
trees – from his wall, but worried that the sphinxes outside on the
embankment – impassive, millennial – had not yet been sandbagged.
'They have simply been forgotten . . . Too much to do to bother
about them! And they sit there all alone, outside events.'

Beyond the civilians' rings of lamplight the battle for Leningrad
raged on. From Mga, the Sixteenth Army's 20th Motorised Division
pushed slowly northwards, opposed by a rifle brigade and exhausted
NKVD border guards. On 7 September it was reinforced with tanks
from the 12th Panzer Division and split the Soviet defence, pushing the border guards westwards towards the Neva, and the rifle
brigade eastwards towards Lake Ladoga. In heavy fighting it took
the 'Sinyavino Heights', a wooded ridge above a convict-manned
peatworks which was to become the scene of repeated Soviet breakout attempts and one of the bloodiest battlefields of the whole
Eastern Front. Finally, on 8 September, the Germans took the
fortress town of Shlisselburg, wedged like a nut at the Neva's junction with Lake Ladoga and guardian of the river route to Moscow
since the fourteenth century. With it, Leningrad lost its last land
link to the unoccupied Soviet Union. For the next year and five
months, Leningraders would only be able to reach the 'mainland' via
Lake Ladoga or by air. 'A grey mist', wrote Knyazev from his foggy

embankment, 'conceals the outlines of St Isaac's, the Admiralty, the Winter Palace, the Senate and the horses above the archway of the General Staff Building. And somewhere, just a few dozen kilometres away, are the Germans . . . It's incredible, unreal, like a delirious dream. How could it have happened? The Germans are at the gates of Leningrad.'[36]

PART 2

The Siege Begins:
September–December 1941

Bread ration coupons, December 1941

In order that we should understand things fully, the winter of nineteen forty-one was given to us as a measure

Konstantin Simonov

6

'No Sentimentality'

This was the beginning of the blockade. The mistakes had been made, the tragedy would now play out, with what from today's perspective feels like sickening inevitability. At the time, though, events still seemed to hang in the balance. Few anticipated a siege: either the Germans would quickly be pushed back, it was assumed, or Leningrad would fall.

Across the Eastern Front, the Wehrmacht now seemed poised for victory. In the north, von Leeb's Army Group North had surrounded Leningrad. Army Group Centre had captured Smolensk eight weeks previously and was now only two hundred miles from Moscow. Outside Kiev, Army Group South was in the process of encircling four Soviet armies, and shortly to capture the city itself. To the outside world, the Soviet regime seemed about to be overthrown or forced into a humiliating peace. ('Everyone is remarking in anticipation', wrote George Orwell in London, 'what a bore the Free Russians will be . . . People have visions of Stalin in a little shop in Putney, selling samovars and doing Caucasian dances.'[1]) On 4 September Stalin had sent a half-desperate, half-threatening letter to Churchill via his ambassador Ivan Maisky. The Russian front, he admitted, had 'broken down', and it was imperative for Britain to open a second front in France or the Balkans by the end of the year, diverting thirty to forty German divisions. If Soviet Russia were defeated, the ambassador added in conversation, how could Britain win the war? 'We could not exclude the impression', Churchill wired Roosevelt after the meeting, 'that they might be thinking of separate terms.'[2]

Zhdanov and Voroshilov only dared tell Stalin that Shlisselburg had fallen on 9 September, a day late. His telegraph in response – jointly signed, ominously, with Malenkov, Molotov and Beria – bristled with contempt:

> We are disgusted by your conduct. All you do is report the surren-
> der of this or that place, without saying a word about how you
> plan to put a stop to all these losses of towns and railway stations.
> The manner in which you informed us of the loss of Shlisselburg
> was outrageous. Is this the end of your losses? Perhaps you have
> already decided to give up Leningrad? What have you done with
> your KV tanks? Where have you positioned them, and why isn't
> there any improvement on the front, when you've got so many of
> them? No other front has half the quota of KVs that you have.
> What's your aviation doing? Why isn't it supporting the troops on
> the battlefield? Kulik's division has come to your aid – how are
> you using it? Can we hope for some sort of improvement on the
> front, or is Kulik's help going to go for nothing, like the KVs? We
> demand that you update us on the situation two or three times a
> day.[3]

Even before hearing about Shlisselburg, Stalin had decided to bring in new leadership. The previous day he had summoned his head of staff, General Zhukov, to the Kremlin and ordered him to fly to Leningrad with a note for Voroshilov that read simply 'Hand over command of the Army Group to Zhukov and fly to Moscow immediately'.

Forty-three years old, with a bald, block-shaped head, ruthless will, brilliant tactical sense and the courage to stand up to Stalin on military matters, Zhukov was the outstanding Soviet commander of the Second World War. He had made his name (and evaded, he suspected, the clutches of the NKVD) two years earlier, with the successful repulse of a Japanese incursion into Soviet Mongolia. Later he was to mastermind the spectacular encirclements at Stalingrad, and lead the Red Army in triumph to Berlin. The three weeks in the autumn of 1941 during which he stopped the Germans in front of Leningrad were to become part of a legend.

As recounted in his memoirs, Zhukov took off from Moscow on the same day that he saw Stalin, in grey, rainy weather. He took with him two trusted lieutenants from Mongolian days, Generals Mikhail Khozin and Ivan Fedyuninsky.[4] Approaching Ladoga the cloud cleared, and their plane was spotted by a pair of Messerschmitts, which chased them low over the water until seen off by outlying anti-aircraft guns. Having landed safely at an army airfield, the generals took a car straight to the Smolniy, where they were stopped at the gate by guards. They 'asked us to present our passes, which, naturally enough, we did not have. I identified myself, but even that didn't help. Orders are orders after all. "You will have to stay here," the officer told us. We waited outside the gate for at least fifteen minutes before the Commandant of Headquarters gave permission for us to drive up to the door.'

Zhukov walked in, as he tells it, on a mood of drunken defeatism. A meeting of Leningrad's Military Council was in progress; being planned were the demolition of the city's utilities and principal factories, and the scuttling of the Baltic Fleet. His arrival turned the mood around: 'After a brief conference . . . we decided to adjourn the meeting and declare that for the time being no measures were to be taken. We would defend Leningrad to the last man.'[5] All that night he kept the Council up discussing how best to strengthen the city's defences, particularly around Pulkovo, a small range of hills (site of Russia's oldest astronomical observatory) twelve kilometres to Leningrad's south. His improvisations included the adaptation of

anti-aircraft guns for point-blank fire against tanks, the secondment
of sailors to the infantry, and the transfer of naval guns from the
Fleet's trapped ships to the weakest sectors of the front. Among the
guns sent to Pulkovo were those of the cruiser *Avrora*, a blank shot
from whose forecastle gun had signalled the start of the October
Revolution. He also transferred part of the 23rd Army – facing the
'docile' Finns on the Karelian Isthmus – south to fight the Germans,
and abandoned plans to scuttle the Fleet. 'If ships have to sink', he
declared, 'let it be in battle, with their guns firing.' Khozin took over
as the Northwestern Army Group's chief-of-staff, and Fedyuninsky
went to inspect the 42nd Army at Pulkovo. Morale, he reported, was
cracking. Headquarters had lost contact with front-line units, and
was itself transferring to the far rear, into the basement of a Kirov
Works factory. 'Take over the 42nd Army', Zhukov ordered him,
'and quickly.'[6]

On the ground Zhukov's arrival made no immediate difference;
conditions remained chaotic. Vasili Chekrizov was a thirty-nine-
year-old chief engineer at the Sudomekh shipyard. Long-faced, with
large, earnest eyes and a wispy moustache, he had been demoted
and temporarily deprived of his Party card during the Terror.
This experience had failed, however, to make him worldly-wise.
A natural whistle-blower, he was to come into increasing conflict
with his corrupt bosses as the siege progressed, and never ceased
to be baffled at the gap between Party rhetoric and reality. On 1
September he had been sent with a team to a village near Pushkin,
to build reinforced firing points, nicknamed 'Voroshilov hotels'.
The scene he encountered was one replicated all along the Eastern
Front that month: streams of peasants, driving overloaded carts or
trudging with bundles over their shoulders; a mounted messenger
shouting as he pushed through the crowd; unshaven officers in
rumpled greatcoats; soldiers brewing tea on a park bench; a boy
tugging a goat on a piece of string. Chekrizov's suggestion that the
pillboxes be built further back, he confided to his diary, was not

appreciated. When dusk fell, he could see the fires of three burning villages.

Over the next two days the area came under increasingly heavy shellfire, forcing Chekrizov and his team to work by night. Lacking cranes or tractors, they hauled water in buckets and concrete blocks by hand. They shared their quarters with a group of eighteen- and nineteen-year-old nurses, who slept, like them, in shifts on the floor or on tables. 'Between the eleven of them', Chekrizov exasperatedly noted, 'only one has a blanket. For us it's the same, though at least we have coats. It's only our fourth day, but they've been here for a month and a half ... Could headquarters really not put them up somewhere better?' On 11 September he experienced bombing for the first time, and was startled at the fear and bewilderment on people's faces – 'It was interesting, like looking into a mirror. Did mine really look the same?' Two of his team – boys in their late teens, who a few days earlier had been swigging cognac and bragging 'partisan-style' to the nurses – were seriously injured in the attack, and one died overnight. Chekrizov accompanied the body back to Leningrad:

> At the factory the news was met with indifference, brushed aside. They wouldn't even let us set up his coffin there, so we took it home to his family. Their room is very small; even without the coffin there wasn't space to turn around. They buried him today. I wanted to go to the burial, but I couldn't bear it – or more precisely, I couldn't face his mother again. She is completely grief-stricken. Better not to see tears.

Back at the front, the confusion was worse than ever. 'Communications with Pushkin have been lost', Chekrizov wrote on the 16th. 'We went to Shushary, which is where our mobile gun emplacements are supposed to be going, but we've got nothing to transport them with, and we don't know what to do with them. The situation is the same all the way up the line.' At headquarters, where he went to plead for vehicles, 'ten people seemed to be trying to solve every problem':

> My impression is that they're mostly just ordinary bureaucrats in military uniform. Yesterday I'd finally had enough. I told them they were a mess. I suspect that many of them secretly agreed with me . . . Here's an example, something that actually happened in Pavlovsk. The lorry drivers delivering parts to us have to fill out consignment forms, each with a number of sections, just like in the city. The transport manager warned me that it all had to be done correctly, and that one particular driver was inexperienced and needed help. Completing his form took thirty minutes, and this on the front! Oh how we worship paper! The Germans probably have a simpler process for all of this . . .
>
> The rear is full of staff officers of every rank. Everyone runs around looking anxious. I'm sure a good half of them do nothing. Yes, in terms of leadership our army turns out to be rather weak. There's plenty of disorganisation in the factories, but it's ten times worse here . . . Will they never sort themselves out?[7]

While Chekrizov struggled to construct his soon-to-be-overrun pillboxes, a few miles away twenty-eight-year-old Anna Zelenova, a serious young woman with round spectacles, a pugnacious snub nose and hair cut in an emancipated bob, was organising the final evacuation of Tsar Paul's domed and colonnaded Pavlovsk Palace. It was a time, she remembered, 'of incredible hurry. The windows of the palace had been boarded up. There was no electricity so we worked by candlelight, or burned ropes and twists of paper.' Having loaded what turned out to be her last lorry to Leningrad, she dashed inside for a final check of the library:

> I went downstairs and ran along the desks and the cabinets, opening all the doors. And in the last cupboard I saw some portfolios.

I opened one and went numb. Here were all [the architect] Rossi's original plans. Then I opened the biggest one and circles danced in front of my eyes. Here were all Cameron's drawings – and Gonzago's, Quarenghi's, Voronikhin's. My instructions hadn't been followed. These priceless documents were going to be left behind.

The folders wouldn't fit into a standard crate so we had to make a special one. Fortunately the carpenters were still there. I gave them the measurements but they said 'We've got no more wood.' So I told them to break up a chest in which cushions were kept. While the crate was being put together I made up my mind to perform an act of vandalism. I was tormented by the fact that the unique tapestry upholstery on Voronikhin's furniture from the Greek Hall was being abandoned. We couldn't save the chairs, but we could save the tapestries. Every piece was held in place with hundreds of tiny gilt nails. I still probably couldn't have brought myself to touch them if at that precise moment a gun hadn't started firing. As it was I grabbed a razor blade and started slicing into the upholstery, cutting as close to the nails as I could. We laid the portfolios in the new crate, with the tapestries between them.

Next to be dealt with were the palace's sculptures, now looking painfully fine in the bare galleries. Too bulky to evacuate, they were manoeuvred down into an inconspicuous corner of the palace cellars and bricked in. To make the new wall blend with the old it was smeared with mud and sand. The outdoor statues – Apollo, Mercury, Flora, Niobe with her weeping children – were buried where they stood, dotted about the park. On the white marble of Justice and Peace a workman wrote, 'We'll come back for you', before disguising the newly turned earth with fallen leaves.

All around, the Red Army was now in full retreat. Entering the palace on the morning of 19 September, Zelenova was angry to see dusty military motorbikes carelessly parked among the lilac bushes of Empress Maria Fedorovna's Dutch garden. In her office, she found a major cranking the handle of a telephone:

> I was struck by how tired he looked. Someone was grunting on the other end of the line, and he replied (obviously not for the first time) that he hadn't hung up, that the line was bad, and that he hadn't got any more men. The person at the other end carried on angrily grunting away. The major very slowly put down the receiver and I started my speech. 'Please immediately tell your soldiers to remove their motorcycles from the private gardens!' He asked, 'Whose private gardens?' And this poor exhausted major had to listen to a whole lecture on Cameron.

That evening Zelenova received a call from Leningrad's museums administration, telling her that she had been made Pavlovsk's director – an empty promotion since she was also put formally in charge of its 'rapid evacuation'. 'Then the call was cut off, so I couldn't explain anything . . . I knew we had to leave, but how could we abandon all the crates we had prepared, and all the things we hadn't packed yet? No, let's keep on working!' Realising that no more lorries would arrive from Leningrad, she commandeered horse-drawn carts:

> After we had seen off the last of the cart-drivers a green MK [car] appeared. A short lieutenant jumped out and demanded, in an unexpectedly loud, bossy, voice, 'Who are you and what are you doing here?' I explained that I was director of the Palace museum and park, and that these were my colleagues. The lieutenant exploded: 'But everyone in the town has been evacuated!'
> 'We are arranging evacuation ourselves, and waiting for transport.'
> 'There won't be any transport! You're lucky that I came round

to check that everyone from divisional headquarters had gone. Get in my car this minute!'

'I can't go anywhere, even if you tell me to, because I'm here on the orders of the High Command' – and I gave him the number of the order.

'You don't understand! Pavlovsk isn't on the front, it isn't even on the front line. It's in the German rear!'

A siren went off, and Zelenova ran down to the palace cellars, which were being used as air-raid shelters. Stepping over samovars and sewing machines, she announced to a crowd of women and children that Pavlovsk had been abandoned, and that those who wanted to leave for the city would have to walk. As she was speaking a forester dashed in: 'There are German motorcyclists in the park. I saw them myself. By the White Birches!' The women, Zelenova quickly realised, were not going to move, so she went upstairs, emptied her desk drawer into a briefcase, and set off on foot in the general direction of Leningrad.

It took her all night to get there, stumbling in heeled shoes through fields and allotments, and crouching in ditches at the thump of artillery fire. On the way she passed the palace town of Pushkin, where the same sort of last-minute rescue effort – dinner services packed in new-mown hay, silver wrapped in Tsar Nicholas's naval uniforms – had been taking place as at Pavlovsk. Crossing the Alexander Palace park she saw Rinaldi's Chinese Theatre collapse in flames; at Kolpino the burning Izhorsky plant lit the sky like a false dawn. Nearer Leningrad the roads were less cratered, and she got a lift in an army lorry full of wounded, which dropped her where she could catch a tram into the city. At 10 a.m. she finally reached St Isaac's Cathedral, in whose 'dim, grim, cold and damp' vastnesses she was to live, together with the staff and rescued contents of all the other abandoned summer palaces, for the whole of the siege.[8]

On the same day that the Germans entered Pavlovsk they

also took Pushkin. Again their approach was acknowledged too late for orderly evacuation: at one point townspeople who fled to Leningrad were actually sent home again, because they lacked Leningrad residency permits. Fiercely anti-Bolshevik Lidiya Osipova watched with cynical detachment as friends and acquaintances tried to decide what to do. A split, she wrote on 17 August, had arisen between 'patriots' and 'defeatists': '"Patriots" try to get themselves evacuated as fast as they can, and the latter, including us, try by every means possible to evade it.' Like many, she preferred to disbelieve reports of Nazi atrocities. 'Of course', she wrote in her diary, 'Hitler isn't the beast that our propaganda paints him . . . People who feel sorry for Jews in Germany, negroes in America and Indians in India manage to forget our own pillaged peasants, who were exterminated like cockroaches.' Even some Jewish friends agreed. 'From many Jews we've heard this kind of thing: "Why should we go anywhere? Well, maybe we'll have to sit in camps for a bit, but then we'll be let out. It can't be worse than now."'

As the fighting grew nearer anxiety mounted. Osipova's neighbour, a former Party member, spent the night of 2 September

running back and forth from her room to the rubbish dump in next-door's courtyard, carrying armfuls of red-bound volumes of Lenin. In between chucking out the great genius's works, she came up to us for chats and a smoke. She bemoaned her lot and Soviet rule. I can see now that Soviet power is not doing very well, because N.F. is not someone who is ruled by her emotions. She was brought up under the Soviets and has seen every rung of the Party ladder, from the highest to the lowest. All this has turned her into a cynic; she has completely lost her faith in all the Communist rubbish, the idealistic dream. It's amusing to watch her, but she should beware of the Germans, since she's been a wife to three Jews and her daughter is half-Jewish. And she's got Communist feathers on her muzzle herself.

In the crowded half-darkness of the air-raid shelters, conversation became unusually free. People talked, Osipova wrote, 'about things that before the war we wouldn't have discussed even in our sleep, or when very drunk, except in the company of people we knew intimately. I'm sitting here writing my diary quite openly and nobody pays any attention.' As shells began to fall in Pushkin itself, she and her neighbours moved permanently into their cellars. Privately, Osipova longed for what she regarded as liberation. 'We sit here all day', she wrote on the 15th. 'The impression is of complete confusion. We asked – Where are the Germans? At Kuzmino. That means they'll get to us in about two hours.' Two days later the streets were still empty:

> No Germans yet. We walked into the town. Overwhelming silence . . . No sign of the authorities at all. If they are here, they are hiding. Everyone's afraid that it might be our lot coming, and not the Germans . . . If it is the Germans – a few unimportant restrictions, and then FREEDOM. If it is the Reds – more of this hopeless vegetable existence, and most probably repression . . .

The next day she had her first uneasy intimation that the Nazis really were a different breed from the Heine and Schiller of her schoolroom, when she picked up an anti-Semitic leaflet dropped by a German plane. 'What mediocrity, stupidity, coarseness. "A muzzle that asks for a brick!"; "Fight the Yid-*politruk*!" And what vulgar, mutilated language . . . Is it possible that we are mistaken, that the Germans really are as bad as Soviet propaganda makes out?' On the 19th the waiting was finally over. 'It's happened', she wrote exultantly in her diary, 'THE GERMANS HAVE COME! At first it was hard to believe. We climbed out of the shelter and saw two real

German soldiers walking along. Everyone rushed up to them . . .
The old women quickly dived back into the shelter and brought out
sweets, pieces of sugar and white bread.' 'NO MORE REDS!' the
entry ends. 'FREEDOM!'⁹

She was horribly wrong – or wilfully blind – of course. One of the
refugees from Pushkin into Leningrad was the composer Bogdanov-
Berezovsky, who before being sent with other musicians to load
timber at the Leningrad docks had lived in a wing of the Catherine
Palace. Shortly after Pushkin's fall he bumped into a former neighbour, who had witnessed the town's takeover before escaping to the
city on foot:

> She told us of awful things . . . An ordinary German language
> teacher at the Pushkin middle school took a 'leading role', volun-
> teering as an interpreter and identifying various Communists,
> among them sweet Anechka Krasikova from the Palace admin-
> istration. Anechka often used to drop round – pretty, young,
> always cheerful. Her little face wasn't even spoiled by pince-nez,
> though they didn't really suit her at all. Her husband and five-
> year-old boy managed to get away in time. But she was put in
> charge of the palace's air-raid shelters, in which much of the
> town was hiding, and so missed getting out either by truck or on
> foot. The fascists shot her and various others on the lawn oppo-
> site the parade ground, next to the Monogram Gates, having
> first made them dig their own graves. An elderly Jewish couple
> – the Lichters from the right-hand wing – were hanged. (The
> old lady was so proud of her boy, the *tankist*!) So were three Jews
> from the left wing. Two of them were the boys with sticking-out
> ears, aged about seven or eight, who were always dashing about
> outside our windows.¹⁰

The Germans' initial searches for Pushkin's Jews and Communists
were followed by an order that all Jews appear for 'registration' at

the Kommandant's office – opposite the 'Avant-Garde' cinema on the corner of First of May Street – on 4 October. Several hundred, mostly women, children and old people, did so. From there they were marched to the Catherine Palace and imprisoned in its basement for several days without food or water, before being taken out in groups and shot, either at the aerodrome or in one of the palace parks. Their clothes were thrown to a waiting crowd from a second-floor window of the Lyceum, the court school where Pushkin had studied. The round-ups continued for several weeks. On 20 October another fifteen adults and twenty-three children were shot outside the Catherine Palace. Having been left lying in the open for twelve days, some of the corpses were thrown into a bomb crater in the palace courtyard, and the rest buried in the gardens. There are examples of Jews being sheltered by non-Jewish neighbours, but examples, too, of denunciation – often motivated, as during the Terror, by desire for the victims' living space. The Catherine Palace's book-keeper and her husband, for example, were denounced by one of its carpenters, who took over their apartment in the palace's right wing and subsequently worked as an informer for the SS. Though the Leningrad area's Jewish population was relatively small (it lay outside the tsarist Pale of Settlement), altogether the German authorities murdered about 3,600 Jews in the region, nearly all in the first few weeks of occupation.[11]

At the same time that it lost Pushkin and Pavlovsk the Red Army was also driven out of Alexandrovsk, a small suburban town at the end of Leningrad's south-western tramline, and Pulkovo, defended to the last by the *opolcheniye*'s Fifth Guards Division, whose bones still lie, amid rampant shrub roses and philadelphus, in a benignly neglected mass grave next to the rebuilt observatory. Along the Gulf, Reinhardt's motorised divisions took Strelna and Peterhof, confirming the Soviet Eighth Army's isolation in the 'Oranienbaum pocket'. His attempts at counter-offensive having failed, Zhukov ordered the establishment of a new defence line, running from Leningrad's south-western outer suburbs through Pulkovo round to the Neva where it jinks northwards halfway between Ladoga and the Gulf. This time, he stated in a characteristically brutal Combat Order of 17 September, there would be no retreat:

1. Considering the exceptional importance [of the Pulkovo–Kolpino line], the Military Council of the Leningrad Front announces to all commanders and political and line cadres defending the designated line that any commander, *politruk* or soldier who abandons the line without a written order from the Army Group or army military council will be shot immediately.

2. Announce the order to command and political cadres upon receipt. Disseminate widely among the rank and file.

Three days later Stalin chipped in with orders that the troops around Leningrad should not hesitate, on pain of execution, to fire on Russian civilians approaching them from the German lines:

To Zhukov, Zhdanov, Kuznetsov and Merkulov,

It is rumoured that the German scoundrels advancing on Leningrad have sent forward individuals – old men and women, mothers and children – from the occupied regions, with requests to our Bolshevik forces that they surrender Leningrad and restore peace.

It is also said that amongst Leningrad's Bolsheviks people can be found who do not consider it possible to use force against such individuals . . .

My answer is – No sentimentality. Instead smash the enemy and his accomplices, sick or healthy, in the teeth. War is inexorable, and those who show weakness and allow wavering are the first to suffer defeat. Whoever in our ranks permits wavering, will be responsible for the fall of Leningrad.

Beat the Germans and their creatures, whoever they are . . . It makes no difference whether they are willing or unwilling enemies. No mercy to the German scoundrels or their accomplices . . .

Request you inform commanders and division and regimental commissars, also the military council of the Baltic Fleet and the commanders and commissars of ships.

[Signed] I. Stalin[12]

Finally the line held. On 24 September, when his forward units were only fifteen kilometres from the Hermitage – as far as the London suburb of Richmond is from Piccadilly Circus, or the Jersey turnpike from the Empire State Building – von Leeb finally acknowledged that his now exhausted and overextended armies could advance no further, and requested permission to move on to the defensive. Fighting petered out as the two sides retired to count their staggering losses. Within Germany's Army Group North, 190,000 men had been killed or wounded since the start of the invasion, and 500 guns and 700 tanks lost.[13] Soviet casualties were even heavier. In the same period the Baltic Fleet and Northwestern Army Group had together lost 214,078 men killed, missing or taken prisoner (POWs probably comprising 70–80 per cent of the total), and another 130,848 wounded – two-thirds of their original troop numbers. They had also lost 4,000 tanks, about 5,400 guns, and 2,700 aircraft.[14]

In traditional siege histories, these days in mid- to late September, with their exhausting battles and ruthless displays of military will, were when the tide turned in the defence of Leningrad. But newer interpretations put the emphasis less on Zhukov's (still undoubted) tactical brilliance, more on an earlier change of strategy on the German side. In this version, the Red Army did not so much beat off the Germans, as the Germans decide to focus elsewhere.

Since Barbarossa's inception, Hitler and his generals had nursed a simmering disagreement over whether Moscow or Leningrad was the more important strategic objective. Hitler's original directive of December 1940, which laid out the broad scheme for Barbarossa, had been clear: only once the Baltics, Leningrad and Kronshtadt had been taken, knocking out the Baltic Red Fleet and securing Leningrad's arms manufacturers, was the advance to begin on Moscow. The service chiefs, led by Chief of General Staff Franz Halder, disagreed. Russia's capital and biggest city should come first, they argued, and Leningrad second.

Put aside with Barbarossa's launch, the disagreement broke into the open again in mid-July, as von Leeb asked for more troops and equipment for his Army Group North. A parallel argument over whether to bypass surrounded Russian towns or capture them before advancing further was resolved in the generals' favour, but on Leningrad Hitler held firm. 'My representations stressing the importance of Moscow', Halder grumbled to his diary on 26 July, 'are brushed aside with no valid counter-evidence.' Ten days later, as the Wehrmacht approached Novgorod, Halder tried again, this time via General Paulus: 'At my request the commander of Army Group South raised points of high strategy, emphasising the importance of Moscow. The Führer again showed himself absolutely deaf to these arguments. He still harps on his old themes: 1. Leningrad, with Hoth [commander of Army Group Centre's 3rd Panzer Group] brought into the picture. 2. Eastern Ukraine . . . 3. Moscow last.' The following day Halder tried to recruit Chief of Operations Staff General Alfred Jodl to the cause. 'I put it to him that Leningrad can be taken with the forces already at [von Leeb's] disposal. We need not and must not divert to the Leningrad front anything that we might need for Moscow. Von Leeb's flank is not threatened in any way . . . Von Bock must drive with all his forces on Moscow. (Ask the Führer: Can he afford not to reduce Moscow before winter sets in?)'[15]

Increasingly irritated by von Leeb's pleas for more resources –
'Wild requests by Army Group North for engineers, artillery, anti-
aircraft guns' – Halder was driven to consider resignation by a
Führer Directive of 21 August, which flatly contradicted Army High
Command. 'OKH's [High Command's] proposals', Hitler declared,
'do not conform with my intentions . . . The principal object still
to be achieved before the onset of winter is not the capture of
Moscow, but rather, in the South, the occupation of the Crimea
and the Donets coal basin . . . and in the North, the encirclement of
Leningrad and junction with the Finns.' Not until these objectives
were met would forces be freed up to advance on the capital.

Halder was furious. Hitler's interference was unendurable, and
the Führer had only himself to blame for 'the zigzag course caused by
his successive orders'. High Command, now in its fourth victorious
campaign, should not 'tarnish its reputation' with his latest demands,
and Brauchitsch, the commander-in-chief, was being treated 'absolutely outrageously'. He suggested to Brauchitsch that they both
tender their resignations, but Brauchitsch refused 'on the grounds
that the resignations would not be accepted, so nothing would
change'.[16] The row was patched up ('Bliss and harmony', Halder
noted sarcastically on 30 August, 'Everything just lovely again') but
not resolved until 5 September, when Hitler finally agreed that if
von Leeb had not captured Leningrad within ten days, Hoepner's
Panzer Group Four would be transferred south to join von Bock's
push for Moscow.[17] In the event, von Leeb's protests and promises of
imminent victory meant that the transfer started three days late, but
Halder's point was won. 'The ring around Leningrad', he wrote on
the day the panzers swung south, 'has not yet been drawn as closely
as might be desired, and further progress after the departure of the
1st Armoured and 36th Motorised Divisions is doubtful . . . The
situation will remain tight until such time as hunger takes effect as
our ally.'[18]

The redeployment did not seem overwhelmingly significant at the time. On the German side it was seen as a temporary compromise; on the Russian, the sense of looming catastrophe only intensified. In retrospect, however, it was the point at which Germany missed her best chance of taking Leningrad. Never again, despite more than two years of near-continuous fighting, did Army Group North amass the mobility and firepower for a full-scale frontal assault on the city. Instead, it became the Eastern Front's poor relation, starved of reinforcements and unable to move troops into reserve for fear that they would immediately be redeployed elsewhere. While in the south and centre armies swept back and forth across the map, round Leningrad the front congealed – exactly as Hitler had planned that Barbarossa should not – into the mud and blood of positional trench warfare, during which neither side, despite repeated offensives, ever mustered the strength decisively to beat the other.

The Wehrmacht's change of strategy – from ground assault to starvation and air raids – was made official in a memo circulated to Army Group North under Halder's name on 28 September:

According to the directive of the High Command it is ordered that:

1. The city of Leningrad is to be sealed off, the ring being drawn as tightly as possible so as to spare our forces unnecessary effort. Surrender terms will not be offered.

2. So as to eliminate the city as a last centre of Red resistance on the Ostsee [the Baltic] as quickly as possible, without major sacrifice of our own blood, it will not be subjected to infantry assault ... Destruction of waterworks, warehouses and power stations will strip it of its vital services and defence capability. All military objects and enemy defence forces are to be destroyed by fire-bombing and bombardment. Civilians are to be prevented from bypassing the besieging troops, if necessary by force of arms.[19]

The concern to spare the German infantry was real. Street-fighting in Smolensk had cost Army Group Centre dear, and newly captured Kiev had just been thrown into chaos by the NKVD's detonation, by remote control, of dozens of large bombs. (Laid in major buildings and hotels, they killed several senior German officers.) A note of frustration was also starting to creep into Hitler's mealtime 'table talk'. His usual fantasising – 'In the East, the Germans will all be required to travel first or second class, so as to distinguish themselves from the natives. First class will have three seats on each side, second class four'; man-of-the-world travelogues – 'The dome of the Invalides made a deep impression. The Pantheon I found a horrible disappoint-ment'; and ragbag opinion-mongering – on Roman versus Inca roads, the design and pricing of washbasins and typewriters, the health-giving properties of polenta – was now interspersed with complaints about the stubbornness of the Soviet defence. 'Every [Soviet] unit commander who fails to fulfil his orders', he grum-bled over lunch on 25 September, 'risks having his head chopped off. So they prefer to be wiped out by us . . . We have forgotten the bitter tenacity with which the Russians fought us during the First World War.'[20]

The decision not to storm Leningrad also reflected the Nazi leaders' broader uncertainty about what to do with the twin Russian capitals once they fell into their hands – an uncertainty subconsciously driven, perhaps, by the memory of Napoleon's debacle at Moscow.* The initial conception was simply to raze both cities to the ground, in accordance with Hitler's millennial vision of a shining, new-built Eastern Reich. 'It is the Führer's firm decision', Halder had noted after a meeting in early July,

* Interviewed after the war, General Blumentritt recalled that he and his colleagues were gripped by the French general Armand de Caulaincourt's account of 1812: 'I can still see von Kluge trudging through the mud from his sleeping-quarters to his office, and standing in front of the map with Caulaincourt's book in his hand.'

'to level Moscow and Leningrad, and make them uninhabitable.'
This would not only 'relieve us of the necessity of feeding their
populations through the winter' but also deal Russia a devastating psychological blow, 'depriving not only Bolshevism but
also Muscovite nationalism of their wellsprings'.[21] Now, as Army
Group North closed the ring around Leningrad, staffers at High
Command began to weigh up – with extraordinary sketchiness
as well as inhumanity – what in practice should be the fate of its
civilians. A planning session of 21 September ran through the
options:

1. Occupy the city; in other words proceed as we have done in
regards to other large Russian cities.
   Rejected, because it would make us responsible for food supply.

2. Seal off city tightly, if possible with an electrified fence guarded
by machine guns.
   Disadvantages: . . . The weak will starve within a foreseeable
time; the strong will secure all food supplies and survive. Danger
of epidemics spreading to our front. It's also questionable whether
our soldiers can be asked to fire on women and children trying to
break out.

3. Women, children and old people to be taken out through gaps
in the encirclement ring. The rest to be allowed to starve:
   a. Removal across the Volkhov behind the enemy front <u>theoret-
   ically</u> a good solution, but in practice hardly feasible. Who is
   to keep hundreds of thousands of people together and drive
   them on? Where is the Russian front?
   b. Instead of marching them to the rear of the Russian front,
   let them spread across the land [i.e. German-occupied
   territory].
In either case there remains the disadvantage that the remaining

starving population of Leningrad becomes a source of epidemics, and that the strongest hold out in the city for a long time.

4. After the Finnish advance and the complete sealing off of the city, we retreat behind the Neva and leave the area to the north of this sector to the Finns. The Finns have unofficially made it clear that they would like to have the Neva as their country's border, but that Leningrad has to go. Good as a political solution. The question of Leningrad's population, however, can't be solved by the Finns. We have to do it.

In conclusion, the meeting came up with a three-stage scenario. First, the German government would 'clearly establish before the world' that since Stalin was treating Leningrad as a military objective, Germany was forced to do the same. It would also announce that once Leningrad had surrendered it would 'allow the humanitarian Roosevelt, under the supervision of the Red Cross' to transport civilians 'to his own continent, under a guarantee of free shipping movement. (Such an offer cannot, self-evidently, be accepted – this is just for propaganda.)' Meanwhile the city would be weakened by bombardment, then gaps opened in the siege lines to let civilians out. The remaining Leningraders would be 'left to themselves over the winter. Early next year we enter the city (if the Finns do it first we do not object), lead those still alive into inner Russia or into captivity, wipe Leningrad from the face of the earth through demolitions, and hand the area north of the Neva to the Finns.' This was not, the planners admitted, very satisfactory, and Army Group North still needed orders that could 'actually be carried out when the time comes'.[22]

German naval chiefs had similar misgivings – again, on practical and propagandistic rather than humanitarian grounds. Writing to his admiral on 22 September, the day after High Command's broad-brush planning meeting, a liaison officer attached to Army

Group North said that he personally doubted that Leningrad could be destroyed without a single German soldier setting foot in it:

> Four or five million people [sic] don't let themselves get killed so easily. I saw this for myself in Kovno, where the Latvians shot 6,000 Jews, among them women and children. Even a people as brutal as the Latvians could no longer bear the sight of these murders by the end. The whole action then ran into the sand. How much harder this will be with a city of millions.
>
> Besides, this would in my opinion let loose a worldwide storm of indignation, which we can't afford politically.

Razing Leningrad, he also pointed out, meant denying the Kriegsmarine the use of its naval dockyards, which might come in useful given that the final fight with Britain and America was still to come. 'After all, Leningrad can disappear at a later stage, when we have won the war at sea.' Like the army planners, he came up with the surreal suggestion of inviting the Allies to take off civilians in ships. 'If England and the USA refuse, world opinion will blame them for these people's demise. If they accept, we're rid of the problem and it will cost them considerable freight capacity.'[23]

Hitler – 'the hardest man in Europe' as he liked to call himself – was only irritated by this 'sentimentality'. 'I suppose', he declared over supper on 25 September, 'that some people are clutching their heads trying to answer the question – How can the Führer destroy a city like St Petersburg? Plainly I belong by nature to quite another species!'[24] He reiterated his determination not to waver in a notorious directive to Army Group North four days later:

Subject: the future of the City of Petersburg

The Führer is determined to erase the city of Petersburg from the face of the earth. After the defeat of Soviet Russia there can be no interest in the continued existence of this large urban centre. Finland has likewise shown no interest in the maintenance of the city immediately on its new border.

It is intended to encircle the city and level it to the ground by means of artillery bombardment using every calibre of shell, and continual bombing from the air.

Following the city's encirclement, requests for surrender nego- tiations shall be denied, since the problem of relocating and feeding the population cannot and should not be solved by us. In this war for our very existence, we can have no interest in main- taining even a part of this very large urban population.[25]

The formal orders – no acceptance of surrender; the city to be worn down by bombing and artillery fire; civilians to be fired upon if they approached the German lines – were issued by Jodl on 7 October. They did not, however, quite close down the debate. 'Today', Army Group North commander von Leeb confided to his diary, 'OKW's [Armed Forces High Command's] decision on Leningrad arrived, according to which a capitulation may not be accepted. [We] sent a letter to OKH [Army High Command] asking whether in this case Russian troops can be taken into captivity. If not, the Russians will keep up a desperate fight, which will demand sacrifices on our side, probably heavy ones.'[26]

Officers also continued to worry about the practicability of asking their men to fire on fleeing civilians. Returning from a tour of the front line on 24 October, von Leeb's head of staff passed on a divisional commander's opinion that his men would carry out such an order once, but that in case of repeated breakouts 'he doubted whether they would hold their nerve so as to shoot again and again on women, children and defenceless old men'. Though it was 'fully understood that the millions of people encircled in Leningrad could not be fed by us without this having a negative impact on our own country', such orders might cause 'the German soldier to lose his inner balance, so that even after the war he will not be able to hold back from acts of violence'. The sight of thousands of refugees streaming south through Gatchina and Pleskau, he noted, had already demoralised German troops repairing roads in the area, since 'where they are going and how they feed themselves cannot be established. One has the impression that sooner or later they will die of hunger.' Commander-in-chief Brauchitsch's response was to suggest that soldiers be spared the psychological strain of killing women and children close to by doing so from further away, with minefields and long-distance artillery. Once the Red Army units around Leningrad had surrendered, German units could even temporarily be transferred to quarters. 'Even then a large part of the civilian population will perish, but at least not right in front of our eyes.'[27]

In the event, the problems remained hypothetical. Leningrad's leadership never tried to negotiate surrender, nor did ordinary Leningraders ever attempt mass breakout. Germany did not follow her own, muddled, policy either. No gaps were ever left open in the German lines so as to allow disease-bearing starvation survivors to flee into unoccupied Russia; on the contrary, barges and lorries carrying evacuees across Lake Ladoga were repeatedly attacked. For the next three winters, the Wehrmacht prosecuted a classical siege, preventing, so far as possible, all movement of people and goods in and out of the city, and using air and ground bombardment to destroy food stocks, utilities, factories, hospitals, schools and hous-ing. ('It is particularly important', a Führer Directive issued just before the first air raids explained, 'to destroy the water supply.'[28]) Mass starvation, it should be stressed, was not an unforeseen, or regrettable but necessary, by-product of this strategy, but its central plank, routinely referred to with approval in planning docu-ments, and followed, once it set in, with eager interest by military intelligence.

It was a crime, as Germans have only recently begun uncomfortably to acknowledge, not of the Nazis, but of the army. Goebbels and Himmler were enthusiastic cheerleaders for exterminating Slavs, but had no major input to the decisions on Leningrad, which were the work of Hitler, Halder, Brauchitsch, Jodl and von Leeb. Though members of High Command began sharply to disagree with Hitler within weeks of the invasion of the Soviet Union, they did so only on narrow grounds of military expediency. Ethical considerations do not seem to have prompted a single senior officer to question a policy that directly led, not only foreseeably but deliberately, to the slow and painful death by starvation of about three-quarters of a million non-combatants, a large proportion of them women and children.

Nor was the army made fully to atone after the war. Jodl, signatory of the formal order to besiege Leningrad, went before the international tribunal at Nuremberg, was convicted of war crimes and hanged. Von Leeb, in contrast, got off extraordinarily lightly. Having retired pleading illness in December 1941, he was sentenced to a mere three years' imprisonment at Nuremberg. His replacement as leader of Army Group North, Georg von Küchler, though sentenced to twenty years, was released on compassionate grounds after only eight. Oddest were the fates of Halder and Erich Hoepner, commander of Army Group North's Panzer Group Four. Hoepner, though a fanatical racist – praised by the SS for his 'particularly close and cordial' cooperation in the murder of tens of thousands of Baltic Jews[29] – was persuaded by the prospect of defeat to join the July Plot to assassinate Hitler. When it failed he was arrested and executed, alongside the brave and decent von Stauffenberg and von Trott. Halder, though not involved in the plot, was imprisoned by Hitler in its wake, then freed by the Americans and spared prosecution at Nuremberg in exchange for giving evidence against his former colleagues. He went on to spend fourteen comfortable and respected years as head of the German section of the US Army's historical research unit, in which role he helped to establish the Cold War myth of the 'clean Wehrmacht', ignorant of the Holocaust and bullied into war by a crazed dictator. In 1961, when the unit was wound up, President Kennedy awarded him the 'Meritorious Civilian Service' medal – the highest honour a non-American can earn in US government service. The editor's foreword to the standard American translation of Halder's diary, published in the late 1980s, concludes with the remarkable words 'He was a distinguished soldier'.[30]

7

'To Our Last Heartbeat'

At five minutes to seven on the evening of 8 September the optical engineer Dmitri Lazarev was walking along Sadovaya when the usual cacophony of sirens, factory hooters and ships' foghorns sounded an air-raid warning. Standing under an archway with other passers-by, he heard the drone of engines overhead. He was already used to the silver specks, high in the sky, of German reconnaissance aircraft, but these were different: snub-nosed grey bombers, twenty or more, swimming low over the rooftops in strict, purposeful formation. Somewhere nearby, an anti-aircraft gun started to bark. Suddenly the avenue of sky between the rooftops was full of sparkling tracer bullets, and quickly dissolving puffs of white smoke. When the alarm was over Lazarev continued on his way to a cousin's flat on the Fontanka. There he found his relatives gathered on the balcony, gazing to the south. Beyond the curve of the canal a vast, spherical cloud was rising, black in places and blindingly white in others. Gradually it expanded to fill the sky, itself turned bronze by the setting sun. 'It was so unlike smoke that for a long time I could not comprehend that it was a fire . . . It was an immense spectacle of stunning beauty.'[1]

Vera Inber and her husband had gone, despite the day's endless alerts, to the Musical Comedy Theatre on Arts Square, to see Strauss's *Die Fledermaus*. They had also invited her husband's deputy at the

Erisman – a shrewd, clever man, Inber thought, with an amusing rural accent. During the interval there was yet another alert. 'The manager came out to the foyer to say a few words, his manner as casual as if he were announcing a change in the cast. He requested that we stand as close to the walls as possible, since – here he pointed to the domed ceiling – there was little protection overhead.' After forty minutes the all-clear sounded, and the operetta continued, though at a faster pace and omitting the less important numbers. Leaving the theatre, Inber and her husband still did not realise that the alert had been anything more than the usual false alarm. To their surprise they were met by their driver, though they had not asked him to wait. 'The car rounded the square and suddenly we saw black, swirling mountains of smoke, illuminated from below by flames. All hell had been let loose in the sky. Kovrov turned and said quietly "The Germans dropped bombs and set the food stores on fire."' Burning were oil storage tanks, a creamery, and thirty-eight wooden warehouses – known as the 'Badayev warehouses' after a pre-revolutionary owner – next to the Warsaw railway station, in which was stored a substantial proportion of the city's food.[2]

This first major raid was of incendiaries – narrow, flanged cylinders which began to smoulder on impact unless doused with sand by the civil defence teams standing guard on the city's roofs.[3] A second raid, at 10.34 on the same evening, nobody could mistake for a drill: it was of forty-eight high-explosive bombs, ranging from 250 to 500 kilograms in weight, and killed twenty-four people, mostly around the Smolniy and Finland railway station. Also hit was the city zoo, next to the Peter and Paul Fortress. A staff member, a child and seventy animals were killed, including the zoo's famous elephant, Betty, who had come to Petersburg from Hamburg six years before the Revolution. The monkeys were so traumatised, a zoologist noted, that 'for a few days afterwards they sat silently, in a sort of stupor, not even reacting to the shells falling all around'.[4]

Olga Berggolts sat out the raid in the hallway of her flat. 'For two whole hours my legs shook and my heart thumped, though outwardly I remained calm. I wasn't consciously frightened, but how my legs trembled – ugh!' As soon as it was over she ran to the Radio House to meet her colleague and lover Yuri Makogonenko. She loved her invalid husband, she confided to her diary, and knew that her affair with Yuri was 'a whim', but wanted 'one more triumph . . . Let me see him thirsty, frenzied, happy . . . before the whistling death.' She also wanted, despite the endless tension between loving her country and hating its government, to keep on working: 'Tomorrow I have to write a good editorial. I have to write it from the heart, with what remains of my faith . . . Nowadays I find it hard to put pen to paper, yet my pen moves, though my thoughts knock about in my head.'[5]

The blitz on Leningrad lasted off and on for the whole of the siege. It was at its most severe in the siege's first weeks, then fell off first with the diversion of the Eighth Air Corps to Moscow, and again with the onset of deep, aircraft-grounding winter cold, before resuming in the spring of 1942. Altogether, according to Soviet sources, about 69,000 incendiary and 4,250 high-explosive bombs hit the city during the war. Though their total tonnage was not nearly as heavy as that which landed on London, Leningrad was geographically a much smaller city, and not only bombed but also increasingly heavily shelled, the pattern of bombing by night and gunfire by day taking a relentless toll on nerves, sleep and lives. In all 16,747 civilians were killed by enemy fire in Leningrad during the war, and more than 33,000 wounded.[6]

For the young, the raids were initially rather exciting. Igor Kruglyakov, the eight-year-old who had had his photograph taken with his father and uncles on the first day of the war, enjoyed watching incendiaries slide down the mansard roof of the Suvorov Museum, sneaked into the local cinema for free by mingling with the crowd after all-clears, competed with his friends to collect shell fragments (the rule was 'finders keepers', even if the fragment was too hot to pick up), and was delighted when his family moved to a safer ground-floor flat in another building, because it meant that he could pet the pigs and calves which peasant refugees had penned up in its courtyard. Teenagers, firewatching through the lovely, frightening nights, had adolescent love affairs. 'Once, during a game of *flirt* [a parlour game]', Klara Rakhman wrote after a shift standing guard at her school, 'Vova write me a note – "What if I told you that I loved you?" I thought it was nothing but he carried on writing to me. I do realise that at a time like this it's silly to start anything, but it was his initiative . . . This evening he walked me home. I asked him whether what he wrote to me was true. He said it was.'[7]

Professor Vladimir Garshin, chief pathologist at Inber's Erisman Hospital (and Anna Akhmatova's lover), had no such compensations. For him, the raids meant a new sort of cadaver:

Shapeless lumps of human flesh, mixed with bits of clothing and brick dust, all smeared with gut contents. Relatives flooded in, some with faces motionless as masks, others screaming and shouting. It was hard to calm them down and make them answer questions, but we had to because there were death certificates to be filled out, and instructions to be taken on how to bury the dead. Those hours and days in the mortuary after raids I can never forget. Not the corpses – I saw lots in my decades of work – but the relatives . . . To a certain extent I was accustomed to taking on part of the burden of grief and horror, but there it went beyond all limits. By evening your soul was paralysed; I would catch myself wearing the same sympathetic expression and using the same formulaic words. You were left feeling completely empty.[8]

Leningrad had no underground system, and the government never provided equivalents of the mass-produced, do-it-yourself Morrison and Anderson shelters with which Londoners reinforced their homes during the Blitz. Instead, Leningraders took to the boiler rooms and stairwells of their apartment buildings, or to trench-like shelters dug in public parks and squares. They became accustomed to endlessly interrupted nights and days, to leaving cups of tea half drunk, pulling on coats and galoshes, dozing on benches and mattresses in dark, crowded basements ('rats ran along the pipes like tightrope-walkers') and to climbing back upstairs to a cold stove. In the deeper basements, the aeroplanes and anti-aircraft guns were hardly audible (such was the case in the Hermitage, though there were doubts whether Rastrelli's arches would hold), but in most, Leningraders braced themselves to the rising whistle of each approaching bomb ('one wanted to squeeze oneself into the ground'), to the thud and thunderclap of impact and explosion, followed by the drawn-out roar of collapsing buildings, tinkling glass, brick dust, screams. 'Everyone thinks "This one's for me"', wrote Berggolts, 'and dies in advance. You die, and it passes, but a minute later it comes again, whistles again, and you die, are resurrected, sigh with relief, only to die again over and over. How long will this last? . . . Kill me all at once, not bit by bit, several times a day!'[9]

Morning journeys to work, for those who had not decamped permanently to their factories or offices, turned into tallies of familiar landmarks damaged or destroyed. Bomb-sliced apartment buildings resembled stage sets or doll's houses, their banal domestic innards – sofa, cornflower-patterned wallpaper, coat hanging on a peg – brutally exposed. 'The cross-sections', wrote ever-analytical Lidiya Ginzburg,

illustrated the storeys, the thin strata of floor and ceiling. With astonishment you begin to realise that as you sit at home in your room you are suspended in space, with other people similarly suspended over your head and beneath your feet. You know this of course – you have heard furniture being moved about upstairs, even wood being chopped. But that's all in the abstract . . . Now the truth is demonstrated in dizzying, graphic fashion. There are skeleton buildings which have kept their façades . . . the sky shows through the empty window-sockets of the upper storeys. And there are buildings, especially small ones, whose beams and floors have collapsed under their crumbling roofs. They hang at an angle and look as if they are still sliding downwards, perpetually descending, like a waterfall.[10]

Vera Inber and her husband moved into the Erisman, allotting themselves a small room with two iron bedsteads, a cylindrical stove, a desk, a bookcase and an engraving of Jenner giving the first inoculation for smallpox. The ancient poplars in front of the windows, they tried to persuade themselves, would help protect them from blasts. Previously somewhat detached from events in Leningrad – her thoughts more with friends and relatives left behind in Moscow – the move put Inber at the centre of the hospital's life, which she was faithfully to record throughout the siege.

On 19 September, the day of one of the worst daylight raids (280 planes dropped 528 high-explosive bombs and about 2,000 incendiaries) she went to visit an old friend from Odessa, who she found sweeping her floor of fallen plaster while dead and wounded were carried out from the building next door. It was a long way from their shared pre-revolutionary childhood. 'I remember her', Inber wrote the next day, 'in the autumn of 1913, in Paris. She was so young, so gay, so attractive. A whole crowd of us went off to some fair. We ate chestnuts, rode on a carousel, looking out at Paris through falling leaves.' That day bombs hit the Gostiniy Dvor (an eighteenth-century shopping arcade on the Nevsky) killing ninety-eight, as well as four hospitals and a market in Novaya Derevnya ('New Village'), an old-fashioned working-class district of timber yards and nursery gardens on the north bank of the Neva estuary. Inber saw fifty wounded brought in, 'one a child of about seven years old. She kept complaining that the rubber tourniquet on her leg hurt. People comforted her, telling her that the pain would soon ease. Then she was anaesthetised, and the leg amputated. She came round and said, "Wonderful. It doesn't hurt any more." She had no idea that she had lost her leg.'

Four days later, at half past ten on a golden autumn morning, a huge bomb landed, but mercifully failed to explode, in the grounds of the Erisman, burying itself next to the fountain in the hospital's central courtyard. 'The strange thing', wrote Inber, 'is that I hardly felt the impact. My first thought was that a heavy door had banged.' She spent the tense ten days it took sappers to defuse it reading to wounded soldiers:

I was sitting on a stool in the middle of the ward, reading aloud a story by Gorky. Suddenly the sirens began to wail; the sound of anti-aircraft fire seemed to fill the entire sky, a bomb crashed, the windows rattled.

I sat on my stool, unable to lean back, as there was nothing to lean back against . . . surrounded by windows, and by the wounded – helpless people, all looking at me, who alone was healthy and mobile. I summoned up all my will-power. I let the drone of the aeroplanes go past, and read on, anxious that my voice might shake with fear. When I got home I felt so weak that I had to go and lie down.[11]

Shelling, many felt, was actually worse than bombing, since bombardments were not preceded by an alarm. From 4 September to the end of the year the Wehrmacht's heavy artillery pounded Leningrad 272 times, for up to eighteen hours at a stretch, with a total of over 13,000 shells. Worst affected were the factories to the south of the city, including the massive Kirov defence works and Elektrosila power plant, both situated just behind the front at the end of tramline no. 9. To the end of November the Elektrosila's buildings were hit seventy-three times. Fifty-four thousand residents and the whole or part of twenty-eight factories were moved northwards out of immediate firing range, into buildings emptied by evacuation. The rumour that some shells were filled only with granulated sugar, or held supportive notes from sympathetic German workers, was a soothing invention.

The danger from overhead was not all that occupied Leningraders, of course, for mid-September was also when the city seemed likeliest to fall. Though people could now hear the thump of artillery fire for themselves, most still did not know exactly where the fighting was going on. Sovinform's reports were as vague as ever: more reliable, the joke went, were the news agencies OBS – '*Odna Baba Skazala*', or 'One Gossip Said', and OMS – 'One Major Said'. That the front was very close was obvious, both from the shells landing in the streets and from the hundreds of peasant families camping out, together with their livestock, around the railway stations. More would have reached the city centre had the railway administration not been ordered to prevent them from boarding suburban trains.

One source of news was the thousands of civilian volunteers still building defence works in the outskirts of the city, among them seventeen-year-old Olga Grechina. After an unhappy stint bookkeeping in a munitions factory, where she had been bullied for her gentility and innocence ('You're like something out of a museum', her boss told her), she went back to trench-digging, this time in the north-eastern suburbs, near the present-day Piskarevskoye siege memorial. Conditions were much harder than in July, and the mood more sombre:

It quickly began to get cold, and though it was only the beginning of September we woke up to frosts. The food was poor – one bucketful of soup, mostly lentils, to feed everyone . . . Our women got no letters from their children in evacuation, nor from their husbands at the front.

One evening we were sitting in our landlady's room, listening to her only record, 'Little Blue Scarf'. Everyone started weeping inconsolably. This banal song, popular before the war, brought back so many memories. For each of the women its subject – separation from loved ones – had suddenly become very real.

Twice we were allowed to go home to wash, since many of us were infested with lice from the dirt and cold. It was the first time this had happened to me and I was alarmed and disgusted. I borrowed half a litre of kerosene from a neighbour (it was already unobtainable in the shops), and rubbed it into my hair, then spent until almost 2 a.m. trying to wash it out again with barely warm water . . .

After visits home people returned to the trenches in a sullen mood. It was getting even colder and we were digging horribly heavy blue clay. Lifting just one shovelful was hard. And even when stupid Tanka started modelling penises from this clay, it wasn't funny any more, and people began to get annoyed with her.

Stupid Tanka, though, gave sheltered, slightly snobbish Grechina what was to be the first of many lessons on the virtues of the Socialist Republic's working class. On Tanka's initiative the two girls dodged guards to steal two sackfuls of potatoes from an abandoned field. Together they lugged their booty to the nearest tramstop and caught a ride into the city. Chatting to Tanka on the way, Grechina was amazed to discover that she supported a widowed mother and crippled sister. A burning factory brought the tram to a halt, and they had to get out and walk. 'I was exhausted', Grechina remembered, 'and about to drop my sack, but Tanka said, "Have you gone mad?" and hoisted it on to her back . . . And then I began to understand how crude my judgement of other people had been before.'

On 14 September the brigade was ordered to stop digging and return to Leningrad. Grechina visited the university's languages faculty, where she had been due to start a degree. But academia now felt self-indulgent and naive. 'How on earth can you discuss abstract concepts with fires and bombing all around? I felt like a working person who suddenly finds herself in the company of the leisured.' Slipping out of a lecture early, she went to the faculty canteen and swapped ration coupons for horsemeat and *kasha*.[12]

Even official news sources now acknowledged that the city was in peril. On 16 September, a day of horizontal rain and the day on which Pushkin was abandoned, *Leningradskaya Pravda* ran a near-hysterical editorial, written by Zhdanov himself, titled 'The Enemy is at the Gates! We Will Fight for Leningrad to Our Last Heartbeat!' 'Each must firmly look the danger in the eye', it urged, 'and declare that if today he does not fight bravely and selflessly in defence of the city then tomorrow he will lose his honour, freedom and his native home, and become a German slave!' Next day's lead carried the clunking headline 'Leningrad – To Be or Not to Be?'[13] Factory militias were being trained in suicidal street fighting. 'Destruction of a tank', a manual promised,

> is first and foremost achieved by presence of mind, bravery, and decisiveness. One must not procrastinate, but display swiftness and dash . . . The fighter, having taken suitable cover [lamp posts, bollards and advertising pillars were suggested] should let the tank approach within 10–15 metres (at this distance the fighter will be in dead space; the tank will not be able to fire at him), swiftly break cover, throw the bundle of grenades under its caterpillar tracks, and just as swiftly take cover again. Exactly the same technique is used with inflammable bottles, the only difference being that the bottle is thrown at the rear part of the tank.

In the absence of grenades or Molotov cocktails, the manual blithely continued, tanks were to be disabled 'by the decisive and dextrous use of bayonet, rifle butt, knife, crowbar or axe'.[14] More convincing were the barricades being built – using steel 'hedgehogs' and concrete 'dragon's teeth' as well as steel joists, cobblestones and tram cars filled with sand – across the principal thoroughfares, and the bricking up of windows so as to turn them into firing points. Georgi Knyazev's Academicians' Building was filled with hurrying sailors carrying sandbags. He and his wife moved into his office in the Academy of Sciences, where they slept on camp beds under a bust of Lenin.

What Knyazev also saw the sailors doing – as he hardly dared note in his diary – was laying demolition charges next to the Lieutenant Schmidt (formerly the Nicholas) Bridge, westernmost of the two that connect Vasilyevsky Island to the mainland. 'By the Academy of Arts I was astonished to see sailors digging holes a short distance apart, putting something in them, laying bricks on top and sprinkling them with sand. Right opposite the sphinxes. Could it mean? . . . My heart skipped a beat.'[15]

If the Germans did take Leningrad, the destruction of its infra-structure and manufacturing capability was to be total. A 'Plan D' listing everything to be demolished was not made public until 2005. We now know that it included all the city's important factories, as well as its power stations, waterworks, telephone and telegraph exchanges, bakeries, bridges, railway network, shipyards and port – some 380 installations in total. (Aleksei Kuznetsov, Zhdanov's deputy, is credited with forbidding the mining of the Peterhof Palace, as well as with ordering the removal of machine guns from the Hermitage's roof, placed there in case paratroops landed in Palace Square.) At each listed institution a 'troika' of director, Party secre-tary and NKVD representative was instructed to draw up plans for the order in which machinery and buildings were to be destroyed, and for the quantity of explosive – or, for less important objects, of axes and sledgehammers – needed. The order to proceed with these 'special measures' was to be given by Kuznetsov, and responsibil-ity for seeing it carried out to rest with the regional branches of the NKVD.[16] Though the planning went forward in great secrecy, rumours leaked out, appalling factory workers. 'And what are we supposed to do once the factories have been blown up?' one man asked a friend. 'We can't do without factories. Even if the Germans come we have to work in order to eat. We won't blow them up.'[17]

Not a few factory bosses deserted their posts, as witnessed by a stream of reprimands and dismissals for 'showing cowardice', 'giving way to panic', misappropriation of funds and going absent without leave. In a memorandum to industrial managers of 5 September, Zhdanov complained of a rise in theft and embezzlement, as well as of jobsworth demands for overtime pay. The most prominent delinquent was the director of the large 'Red Chemist' plant, who ordered his bookkeeper to withdraw fifty thousand roubles, requisitioned a car and would have made good his escape had the bookkeeper not alerted the authorities.[18] Others, like First Party Secretary Nikonorov of Lodeinoye Pole, a small town east of Ladoga, drowned fear in drink. Instead of mobilising civilian resistance at the Wehrmacht's approach, a purse-lipped investigator noted, he 'occupied himself with the organisation of mass drunkenness, involving leading workers . . . Amongst the district police, drinking and card games flourished, chief of police Martynov personally taking part.'[19] By the end of the year 1,540 city officials 'unworthy of the high title of Member of the Bolshevik Party' had been stripped of their Party cards.[20]

At the same time, general security measures were tightened even further, the one which affected ordinary people most being the disconnection of domestic telephones. 'It gave me a strange feeling', wrote Vera Inber,

> when the phone rang, and a fresh young voice said, 'The telephone is disconnected until the end of the war', I tried to raise a protest, but knew in my heart that it was useless. In a few minutes the phone clicked and went dead . . . until the end of the war. And immediately the flat felt dead, frozen, tense. We are cut off from everyone and everything in the city . . . Only very special offices, clinics and hospitals are excepted.[21]

Checkpoints multiplied, and the streets on to which Nazi propaganda leaflets fluttered down were quickly cordoned off. ('We come
not as your enemies, but as enemies of Bolshevism!' ran one. 'If
your factories and storehouses burn, you will die of hunger! If your
houses burn, you will die of cold!') There were also new round-ups
(3,566 detentions between 13 and 17 September) of Red Army and
opolcheniye deserters, who were numerous enough to be described
by diarists as 'flooding' the city.[22] In the Ukrainian city of Lviv, the
NKVD had shot all its prisoners as the Wehrmacht approached.
In Leningrad it merely evacuated them to labour camps within the
siege ring, though the end result was similar. A survivor of a shipment across Lake Ladoga on 9 October remembers his voyage:

> The guards stood in two rows on the deck, driving a stream of
> prisoners down the steps into the hold. In the dark void a small
> flame flickered: a lieutenant stood there, vomiting swear words
> right and left as he hit out with a croquet mallet, trying to pack
> everyone in as tightly as possible. People stood squashed together,
> clutching their belongings. A long line of prisoners came down
> after me.
>
> By evening the hold had been packed full. It consisted of three
> compartments: one for men, holding about 3,000 people, one for
> women, of whom there were about 800, and a small corner into
> which were squashed two hundred German prisoners of war . . .
> From time to time a gasping prisoner would try to climb a little
> way up the steps, so as to gulp some fresh air. Shots would swiftly
> follow, and the unfortunate, having swallowed lead along with air,
> would tumble back down again . . .
>
> A metal hundred-litre barrel was lowered on a rope down
> through the hatch. A mass of prisoners immediately rushed
> towards it. Most had nothing to scoop up the water with, so they
> used their hands.
>
> [As the night progressed] conditions got even worse. To start

with we had been pressed tight, but at least it had been possible to stand on the floor. Now there was more space, but the floor had disappeared beneath a layer of corpses, on which it was hard to avoid standing or sitting. It was also starting to smell . . . When I left the hold I looked around: the floor had completely disappeared under a thick layer of decomposing dead.[23]

The security crackdown did not quite suppress all dissent. Swastikas materialised overnight on courtyard walls, and leaflets denouncing Stalin and calling for Leningrad to be declared a Paris-style 'ville ouverte' – a euphemism for surrender – were stuffed into stairwell mailboxes and sent anonymously to Party leaders. Widespread expectation of defeat was reflected in a dramatic fall-off in applications for Party membership – there were fewer in September 1941 than during the following February, when thousands of Leningraders were dying of starvation each day. Together with the departure of Party members for the front, this halved the size of the Leningrad Party organisation, from 122,849 full members on declaration of war to 61,842 at the end of the year. Numbers of Party cards reported 'lost' also rose sharply, though few were as unsubtle as a worker at the Okhtensky chemical factory, who asked his local Party secretary not to add his name to the membership list 'because that will make it easy for them to find out that I am a Communist'.[24]

The fence-sitters had justification, for the archives make it plain that Stalin seriously considered abandoning Leningrad not only during the mid-September crisis, but on into the late autumn and early winter, when his overriding priority was the defence of Moscow.

Hitler's plan for Moscow, code-named Operation Typhoon, had been outlined in a Führer Directive of 6 September. Eight hundred thousand troops and three panzer armies, comprising over a thousand tanks, were to make two great pincer movements to the city's south and west, encircling the Soviet armies defending its approaches. Launched on the 30th, Typhoon met its first objectives extraordinarily quickly. The small city of Orel, about two-thirds of the way along the main road from Kiev, is said to have been abandoned so fast that the German tank crews found themselves overtaking peacefully trundling trams. ('Why didn't you file anything about the heroic defence of Orel?' Vasili Grossman's editor angrily asked him on his return from a foray to the front. 'Because there was no defence', Grossman replied.) Five days into the offensive a Soviet reconnaissance plane spotted a twelve-mile armoured column approaching the town of Yukhnov, 120 miles north of Orel and only 80 miles from the capital. The news was so incredible that the air officer who reported it was threatened with arrest for 'provocation', and only believed once two more planes had confirmed the sighting.

On 6 October Stalin summoned Zhukov from Leningrad and put him in charge of Moscow's defence. Again, Zhukov found the army in a state of collapse: communications had broken down and ad hoc units were being formed from stragglers who had managed to escape being 'caught in the sack' of small-scale German encirclements. Of the 800,000 troops that had held the Central Front six weeks earlier, only 90,000 still stood between the Wehrmacht and the capital. Four days later, while conscripts laboured to dig a new ring of trenches around the Moscow suburbs, Hitler's press chief invited Berlin's press corps to the Ministry of Propaganda to hear a statement from the Führer. The remnants of the Red Army, it declared, were now trapped. Victory in the East was assured. The next morning's newspapers carried the headlines 'The Great Hour Has Struck!' and 'Campaign in the East Decided!'

In Moscow, where the crump of artillery could now be heard even from Red Square, it was decided to evacuate the government. The Praesidium of the Supreme Soviet, the defence commissariat and the Allied embassies all left on special trains for Kuibyshev (now Samara, on the Volga) on the 15th.* The following day, the ashes of a million hastily burned files twirling above the pavements, the city descended into anarchy. Police vanished; bosses fled in commandeered lorries loaded with rubber-plants and gramophones; workers looted and lynched. The director of a dairy, spotted trying to leave, was dragged out of his car and thrown head-first into a vat of sour cream. Order was only restored five days later. The whole inglorious episode became known as the 'big *drap*', a sardonic play on *drap*'s double meaning of 'medal ribbon' or 'skedaddle'.[25]

With Moscow teetering on the brink, Leningrad's abandonment seemed likelier than ever. A measure of how poorly its chances were now rated was senior generals' reluctance to take charge of its defence. On Zhukov's departure the command initially went to his deputy, Ivan Fedyuninsky, but he immediately began lobbying for it to be passed to Mikhail Khozin, who, he pointed out, had seniority, and under whom he had served in the past.[26] Khozin demurred, arguing that he could not leave the 54th Army, which he had just taken over from the loathed and incompetent Kulik. Zhdanov then tried to recruit Marshal Nikolai Voronov, a respected artilleryman and a native Leningrader, but he too turned the post down, arguing that he already had his hands full as deputy Commissar for Defence. After a fortnight of pass-the-parcel, Moscow intervened, and on 26 October the command was finally forced on Khozin, Fedyuninsky taking over the 54th Army.

For the rest of the year, Leningrad's role was to produce as much weaponry as possible, while continuing to evacuate defence plant and workers by barge across Lake Ladoga. (The despatch of the six thousand staff of the Izhorsk Works tank shop, together with their

---

* The British mission took a week to get there, thanks to frequent stops to let pass troop trains going the other way. Having omitted to supply themselves with food, its members had to bargain at farmhouses for provisions, and on arrival were put up, 'most uncomfortably', in a school.

families, was ordered on 2 October, and that of the Kirov Works, with 11,614 workers, a fortnight later.[27]) The ubiquitous slogan of the time – 'Everything for the Front!' – should more correctly have been 'Everything for Moscow!', for the bulk of Leningrad's depleted production went not to its own beleaguered defenders, but out of the siege ring to the Central Front. Stocks of coal and peat, which could later have saved homes from freezing, were used to power production of shells and mines, and transport capacity that could have been used to import food was given over to powder and explosives, which went into munitions that were immediately re-exported to the capital.

At the same time Stalin ordered Zhdanov to try to lift the siege. 'You must quickly break through via Mga to the east', he telegraphed the Smolniy on 13 October. 'You know yourselves that there are no other routes. Soon your food supplies and other resources will run out. Hurry, or we are afraid that it will be too late.'[28] Two days later Voronov flew into Leningrad to oversee the offensive and to set new, impossibly high production targets. At their first meeting Zhdanov pleaded for more munitions. In response Voronov demanded that Leningrad increase its own production of shells to a fantastical million a month. 'A million a month – that's madness!' Zhdanov exploded. 'It's a bluff! It's ignorant! You simply don't understand how munitions production works!'[29] Three days later Stalin demanded to know if his new offensive had been launched yet:

We sent you a directive ordering an immediate advance, so as to unite the *Lenfront* and the 54th Army. We've had no reply. What's going on? Why don't you answer? Is the directive understood, and when do you think the advance will begin? We demand a quick answer in two words. 'Yes' will signify an affirmative, and rapid fulfilment of the directive; 'No', the negative.[30]

On 23 October, the planned attack having been pre-empted by a German one threatening Tikhvin, a vital railhead for evacuation across Lake Ladoga, Stalin tore into the Leningraders yet again, in a message read out on the telephone by Marshal Vasilyevsky, deputy chief of general staff. This time Stalin explicitly admitted that Leningrad might have to be surrendered, emphasising the importance of extracting the encircled armies and Moscow's inability to come to Leningrad's aid:

> Judging by your indolence one can only conclude that you still haven't realised the critical situation in which the *Lenfront* troops find themselves. If in the course of the next few days you don't break through the [German] front and reconnect yourselves with the rear by restoring solid contact with the 54th Army, all your troops will fall into captivity. Reconnection is necessary not only for supplying the *Lenfront* troops, but especially so as to create an exit for the *Lenfront* troops to the east, in case necessity compels the surrender of Leningrad. Bear in mind that Moscow finds herself in a critical situation, and that she is in no condition to help you with new forces . . . We demand quick, decisive action from you. Concentrate eight or ten divisions and break through to the east. It's necessary either way, whether Leningrad holds on or is given up. For us the army is more important.[31]

Vasilyevsky reinforced the message personally in a call to Fedyuninsky's 54th Army on the same day. Unarmed reinforcements were being sent from Vologda, but beyond that the army had to rely on itself: 'Please bear in mind that in the present situation discussion is not so much about saving Leningrad, as about rescuing the *Lenfront* army.'[32]

The prioritisation of Moscow continued into November, as Leningrad's own civilian population started to die on the streets. Typical is a letter from Zhukov to Zhdanov of the 2nd. It opens

confidingly – 'My thoughts often return to the difficult and interesting days and nights when we worked and fought together. I
greatly regret not having completed the business, I was convinced
that I would' – but carries a sting in its tail. The Central Front's
generals had 'squandered all their troops; nothing but the memory
is left of them. From Budenniy all I got was a headquarters and
ninety men; from Konev, a headquarters and two regiments.' Could
Zhdanov send forty 82mm and sixty 50mm mortars on the next
air convoy, since 'you have them in excess, while we have none at
all?'[33] Zhdanov's counter-requests for more transport planes and for
deliveries of concentrated foods were fulfilled late or not at all.[34]
'You assigned us twenty-four Douglases', Zhdanov replied to yet
another of Stalin's demands for immediate breakout, transmitted by
Malenkov. 'So where are they? Get them sent as soon as possible.'[35]

Altogether, between 1 October and their virtual shutdown in
December, Leningrad's factories sent the Central Army Group
452 76mm field guns with over 29,000 armoured shells and 1,854
mortars of different sizes. With hindsight, they could arguably have
been better put to use outside Leningrad itself, since they were not
numerous enough to tip the balance in Moscow, but might have
done so south of Ladoga, where the Germans' foothold on the lake
shore was only ten miles wide. Had the Red Army then established
a secure land route out of the city – a year before it actually did
so – not only would hundreds of thousands of civilians have been
saved from starvation, but the city's defence factories could have
resumed normal production, to the benefit of the Soviet war effort
as a whole. As it was, the autumn's massive production effort crippled Leningrad, draining it of the resources either to break the siege
or – save at the cost of mass civilian death – to survive it.

8

125 Grams

Marina Yerukhmanova, nineteen-year-old descendant of Peter the Great's favourite Alexander Menshikov, was, like Olga Grechina, a studious, sheltered girl to whom war was to give a harsh emotional and social education. Her first war work was in a 'concert brigade' seeing off soldiers on their way to the front. 'The station platforms were covered with soldiers, sitting or lying, some with sobbing relatives. And then we appeared – four little girls with music stands and sheet music – and played quartets.' Though she had been given the opportunity to evacuate to Tashkent with the Conservatoire, she had turned it down, preferring to remain with her family. When the air raids began they moved to an aunt's safer ground-floor apartment – four adults, four children, four dachshunds and a baby squashing into a single room. The household saw its first death in early October, when Marina's stepfather, a naval officer de-listed during the 1937 purges, suffered a heart attack two days before papers arrived reinstating him to the service. The family were able to give him a religious funeral at the Spaso-Preobrazhensky Cathedral, and marked his grave with a large wooden cross (later stolen for fuel).

The death freed Marina and her younger sister Varvara to take jobs. They signed up as *druzhinnitsy* – unpaid auxiliaries, mostly teenage girls, who took on a wide variety of often dangerous wartime tasks under the direction of the police – at their mother's workplace,

the Hôtel de l'Europe, now requisitioned for use as a military hospital. Standing halfway down Nevsky Prospekt, the hotel – affectionately known as the 'Yevropa', or 'Europe' – was Leningrad's oldest
and grandest, founded in the 1830s and rebuilt, complete with lifts,
air bells and central heating, in the 1870s. To the Yerukhmanov girls
it seemed an 'Elysium . . . Everything was expensive and of good
quality – furniture, carpets, curtains, crockery . . . The showers still
had hot water, and the laundry still functioned, where a languid,
superior sort of woman handed us out our tunics. Everywhere order
and cleanliness reigned.' To start with they worked downstairs in
the kitchens, under a giant, red-haired 'tsar' of a head chef, who
was ceremoniously robed in full whites each morning and whose
stomach wobbled as he walked. Upstairs, slender Tartar waiters with
pomaded hair and 'theatrical' manners served the lightly wounded
in the ground-floor 'Big Restaurant'. 'They taught us how to lay the
tables, greet our "guests" . . . God preserve you if you served food
on cold plates.' The head waiter gave the girls 'scoldings, which he
loved to pepper with the most shocking swear words. The first few
times we didn't know where to look. Mama said firmly, "Children,
pretend you haven't heard."' Though officially forbidden to sleep on
the premises they quietly moved in, camping on a balcony above the
riotously eclectic 'Eastern' dining room, with its barrel-vaulted ceiling, vaguely Egyptian plasterwork and great stained-glass window
showing Viking longboats sailing down a river under the walls of an
ancient Rus kremlin. Though she worked fifteen-hour days without
pay, Marina remembered the hotel with gratitude: 'Our Yevropa hid
us and protected us, gave us time to catch our breath.'[1]

Marina's mother's first reaction, on hearing Molotov's announcement of war, had been to send her daughters out to buy soap, and
to light the stove, so that she could start making *sukhari*, the dried
rusks that are a traditional Russian standby in times of food shortage. Others did the same: by the time the siege ring closed, Marina

remembered, the only goods available for purchase were dried fruits and blanched almonds at the market, prohibitively expensive caviar in the shops and useless toys and sports equipment in the Passazh department store.

In 1941 a fifty-year-old Russian had lived through three major famines – the first of 1891–2, when drought hit the Volga steppe; the second of 1921–2, caused by grain requisitioning and the post-revolutionary Civil War, and the third of 1932–3, when the Bolsheviks violently collectivised peasant farms, condemning to death perhaps seven million people. Though privileged in normal times, Leningrad was particularly vulnerable, having always been dependent on food imports from the more fertile south. The bog-bound village of Myasnoi Bor, or 'Meat Wood' (just north of Novgorod and the site of a disastrous wartime encirclement in the spring of 1942), was named for the quantities of cattle which foundered there on their trek north to market in the capital. Though the collectivisation famine largely passed the city by, during the Civil War grass grew in the streets, so many were the Leningraders who fled to the villages in search of something to eat.

Despite all this, the Leningrad authorities went into the siege woefully underprepared. When the last road out of the city was cut on 8 September an estimated 2.8 million civilians were caught within the siege ring, 2.46 million of them in the city, and another 343,000 in its surrounding towns and villages.[2] Troops and sailors within the ring numbered about another 500,000, making approximately 3.3 million mouths to feed in all. (The Germans seriously overestimated Leningrad's population at more than four million, probably because they mistook the movement of families out of the vulnerable southern suburbs for the arrival of new refugees. They thus also overestimated how soon the city would begin to starve.[3]) On the same day that the city was cut off a junior trade commissar, Dmitri Pavlov, flew in from Moscow and started to make a detailed inventory of all food stocks held in warehouses, factories, army depots and other public institutions. At current consumption levels, he discovered, they would last not much more than a month. On hand were thirty-five days' worth of grain and flour, thirty days' worth of buckwheat, rice, semolina and macaroni, thirty-three days' worth of meat and live cattle, forty-five days' worth of oil and fats, and sixty days' worth of sugar and confectionery.[4] Planes were not available for a large-scale airlift (none ever seems to have been considered), and though the Leningrad Party had already requested that five trainloads of food be delivered to Lake Ladoga for transfer to the city by barge, there were no port facilities to receive them on the lake's shallow, sandbank-riddled western shore. (The decision to start building docks and warehouses, at the dacha village of Osinovets, was not taken until 9 September.[5]) Unless the blockade was broken quickly, Leningrad would have to survive on its own resources.

Failure to lay in adequate stores of food and fuel before the siege ring closed was due to the same lethal mixture of denial, disorganisation and carelessness of human life as the failure to evacuate the surplus civilian population. The most efficient and concerned administration could not have prevented serious shortage – emergency stocks did not exist, the trains were overloaded, the country's most fertile regions in the process of being overrun – but error, muddle and above all the leadership's refusal to face reality made the situation even worse than it need have been. Telling is a story that Anastas Mikoyan, the State Defence Committee member in charge of trade and supply, recounts in his memoirs. In the early days of the war a convoy of military supply trains travelling westward in accordance with out-of-date mobilisation plans found themselves unable to reach their destination. Knowing that Leningrad was reliant on grain from the south, Mikoyan ordered that they be diverted to the city:

Assuming that the Leningraders would be only too happy with this decision, I did not consult them in advance. Even Stalin only learned of it when he got a telephone call from Zhdanov. [But] Zhdanov told him that the Leningrad warehouses were packed as full as they could hold, and insisted that no foodstuffs over and above those already designated be despatched to them ... At the time none of us envisaged that Leningrad would be besieged. Consequently, Stalin instructed me not to despatch provisions in excess of agreed quantities without the prior consent of the city authorities.[6]

Zhdanov had earned points for zeal and successfully asserted himself against a rival; the trains went elsewhere.

Confusion and complacency continued to reign even after the siege had begun. 'Jurisdiction over food supplies', Pavlov remembered,

resided with ten different economic agencies. In the absence of instructions from their central offices in Moscow, each continued to issue food according to the usual procedures ... In mid-September the central administration of the sugar industry, located in Moscow, wired its Leningrad office to despatch a number of freight-car loads of sugar from Leningrad to Vologda. Leningrad had been blockaded since the 8th. There were many similar cases.

Though by the time Pavlov arrived in Leningrad the expensive 'commission shops' – opened in July so as to provide the reassuring sight of full shelves – had already been closed, off-ration sales through canteens and restaurants continued, constituting a substantial 8 to 12 per cent of all outgoings of oils, butter, meat and sugar. Production of beer and ice cream carried on, as did off-ration sales of luxury goods such as caviar, champagne and coffee.[7]

Most visibly, the authorities failed to redistribute food stores so as to minimise the risk of loss in air raids. The result was the spectacular Badayev warehouse fire of 8 September, which Leningraders at the time believed to have destroyed almost the whole of the city's food stocks – the air is described as filled with the smell of burning ham and sugar – and still remember as the trigger for their accelerating slide into starvation. ('It was when life ended', as Marina Yerukhmanova put it, 'and existence began.') Pavlov hotly disputes, in what is otherwise a rather impersonal account, the fire's importance, claiming that the warehouses held boxes of old paperwork and spare parts, and that the only foods destroyed were 3,000 tonnes of flour and 2,500 tonnes of lump sugar, most of which was reprocessed into sweets. In terms of public morale, however, the Badayev fire was unquestionably a catastrophe. 'Soon after', Yerukhmanova remembered,

> we were handed out eight kilograms of lentils, some canned crabmeat and a few other things. Everyone was unhappy that these handouts hadn't been ordered in advance of the fire, rather than once it had already happened. To give such instructions in those days would probably have needed a lot of courage. But how was it that they didn't have more foresight?[8]

Among the more successful of the Leningrad leadership's initiatives in the autumn of 1941 were its efforts to gather food from inside the siege ring and to devise food substitutes. First came a drive, hampered by lack of transport, to bring in the harvest from the unoccupied countryside to the city's east and north. For collective farmworkers (who did not qualify for rations) this meant a squeeze almost as severe as that which had caused the collectivisation famine of a decade earlier. A norm of what fell by November to fifteen kilograms of potatoes per person per month could be retained by the peasants themselves; the remainder had to be surrendered to requisitioning parties put together by local soviet executive committees. Peasants who hid their potatoes were 'held responsible under wartime law' – in other words, subjected to unspecified criminal punishment.[9] Extra hands were also conscripted from the city

– and carried home as much produce as they could. 'On the main roads and on suburban trams', a memorandum of 16 September complained, 'hundreds of people can be observed with sacks and baskets . . . Failure to take urgent measures to stop this anarchy will mean that the whole harvest is squandered into private hands.'[10] The squeeze on the countryside continued, via a mixture of compulsory purchase, requisitioning and 'donations', throughout the first siege winter, producing a total 4,208 tonnes of potatoes and other vegetables, livestock representing 4,653 tonnes of meat, over 2,000 tonnes of hay, 547 tonnes of flour and grain and 179,000 eggs. Three-fifths of the flour and grain came from peasants' private stores, as did over a quarter of the livestock and over half the potatoes.[11]

Within the city, institutions involved in food processing and distribution were ordered to search their premises for forgotten or defective stocks that could substitute for conventional flours in the production of bread. At the mills, flour dust was scraped from walls and from under floorboards; breweries came up with 8,000 tons of malt, and the army with oats previously destined for its horses. (The horses were instead fed with birch twigs soaked in hot water and sprinkled with salt. Another feed, involving compressed peat shavings and bonemeal, they rejected.) Grain barges sunk by bombing off Osinovets were salvaged by naval divers, and the rescued grain, which had begun to sprout, dried and milled. (The resulting bread, Pavlov admitted, reeked of mould.) At the docks, large quantities of cotton-seed cake, usually burned in ships' furnaces, were discovered. Though poisonous in its raw state, its toxins were found to break down at high temperatures, and it too went into bread. Altogether these substitutions, together with successive ration reductions, reduced Leningrad's consumption of flour from over 2,000 tonnes a day at the beginning of September to 880 tonnes a day by 1 November.

As autumn turned to winter the substitutions became more exotic, and the resulting foodstuffs, distributed in place of the bread, meat, fats and sugar promised on the ration cards, less nutritious. Flax-seed cake found in the freight yards, ordinarily used as cattle food, was used to make grey 'macaroni'. Two thousand tonnes of sheep guts from the docks, together with calf skins from a tannery, were turned into 'meat jelly', its stink inadequately disguised by the addition of oil of cloves. From the end of November onwards bread contained, as well as 10 per cent cotton-seed cake, another 10 per cent hydrolised cellulose, extracted from pine shavings according to a process devised by chemists at the Forestry Academy. Containing no calories, its purpose was solely to increase weight and bulk, making it possible notionally to fulfil the bread ration with a smaller quantity of genuine flour. The resulting loaves, which had to be baked in tins so as not to fall apart, were heavy and damp, with a clayey texture and bitter, grassy taste. To save on the two tonnes of vegetable oil used each day to grease the tins, an emulsion of water, sunflower oil and 'soapstock' – a by-product of the refinement of edible oils into fuel – was devised. It gave the loaves, Pavlov conceded, an odd orange colour, 'but the qualitative flaws were quite bearable, and the oil saved went to the canteens'.[12] Another of the Forestry Academy's inventions was a 'yeast extract', made out of fermented birch sawdust, which was distributed to workplace kitchens in sheet form and served up, dissolved in hot water, as 'yeast soup'.

The key to each person's fate during the siege, the basic template against which every life unfolded, was the rationing system. Every combatant country had one, and everywhere they were undermined by corruption, black-marketeering and fraud. In blockaded Leningrad, though, these faults were magnified; not only by the extremity of wartime conditions, but also by the brutality and incompetence of the Soviet regime itself. The consequences were magnified, too. Elsewhere, bad planning and weak management meant nagging hunger; dull, too-small meals. In Leningrad, they meant uncountable extra deaths.

Food, in the Soviet Union, had always been a means of coercion and reward, and at the extremes, of eliminating the useless while preserving the useful. As Lenin declared in a speech to an All-Russian Food Conference in 1921, in the midst of the Civil War famine,

> It is not only a matter of distributing [food] fairly; distribution must be thought of as a method, an instrument, a means for increasing production. State support in the form of food must only be given to those workers who are really necessary for the utmost productivity of labour. And if food distribution is to be used as an instrument of policy, then use it to reduce the number of those who are not unconditionally necessary, and to encourage those who are.[13]

This philosophy, encapsulated in the slogan 'You eat as you work', was trialled in the Soviet Union's first labour camps, on the White Sea's Solovetsky Islands. Prisoners were divided into three groups: those fit for heavy work, those fit only for light work and invalids. The first group were allotted 800 grams of bread per day, the second, 500 grams and the third, 400 grams. As predicted, the strongest, relatively well-fed, kept their health, and the weakest, fed exactly half as much, weakened further and died. The system, designed (unsuccessfully) to make the camps self-supporting, was subsequently copied throughout the Gulag.[14]

At the other end of the scale, food served as a means of delineating the hierarchy of Party and establishment. 'Closed' shops and restaurants were open only to Party members or employees of particular institutions, and workplace dining facilities more finely graded than those of the most self-important Wall Street bank. The war correspondent Vasili Grossman, in his epic autobiographical novel *Life and Fate*, describes the six different menus on offer at the canteen of the Moscow Academy of Sciences's Institute of Physics:

One was for doctors of science, one for research directors, one for research assistants, one for senior laboratory assistants, one for technicians and one for administrative personnel. The fiercest passions were generated by the two highest-grade menus, which differed only in their desserts – stewed fruit, or jelly made from powder.[15]

Another journalist, a British Communist called John Gibbons, spent the war working for Moscow Radio. During the winter of 1941–2, when food shortages were acute throughout the Soviet Union, he resented the fact that his workplace lunches consisted of dry bread and tea without sugar, while his boss, sitting in the same office, had ham and eggs. Though he accepted this as part of the system and 'no doubt quite right', it was nonetheless 'bloody unpleasant to *smell* the ham and eggs. All the more so as my boss thought it was quite normal, and never offered me even a scrap of ham.'[16]

Leningrad's rationing system operated similarly to the Gulag's. Though articulated as giving to each according to his needs, in practice it tended to preserve (just) the lives of those vital to the city's defence – soldiers and industrial workers – and condemn office workers, old people, the unemployed and children to death. When rationing was introduced in mid-July, initial allocations were the same as those for Muscovites – a generous 800 grams of bread daily for manual workers, 600 grams for office workers and 400 grams for children and the unemployed, plus adequate amounts of meat, fats, cereals or macaroni, and sugar. Astonishingly, the city soviet did not reduce the ration until 2 September, almost a fortnight after the direct railway line to Moscow had been cut. At Pavlov's insistence, the first reduction was followed by another ten days later, to 500 grams of bread for manual workers, 300 for office workers, 250 for dependants and 300 for children. To make up for the drop, rations of fat and sugar were simultaneously increased, with hindsight a terrible mistake. 'Looking back', Pavlov admitted later, 'it may be said that the fats ration, most clearly, and the sugar ration, should not have been increased in September. The approximately 2,500 tonnes of sugar and 600 tonnes of fats expended in September and October . . . would have been extremely valuable in December.' At the time, he added, nobody imagined that the city would remain cut off for that long.[17]

At its lowest, after a final cut on 20 November, the ration fell to 250 grams of bread per day for the 34 per cent of the civilian population classed as manual workers, and 125 grams (three thin slices) for everybody else, plus derisory quantities of meats and fats. For the lower category cardholders, this was officially the equivalent of 460 calories per day – less than a quarter of the 2,000–2,500 per day the average adult requires to maintain weight. Even these 460 calories were only the official figure: in reality bread, as we have seen, was seriously adulterated with 'fillers', meat disappeared, and there were days on which no rations were distributed at all. Today's nutritionists, who use siege survivors to study the long-term effects of foetal and infant malnutrition, estimate that just taking account of 'fillers' the real number was closer to 300 calories per day.[18] Had the second ration cut of 12 September been made just six days earlier, Pavlov later admitted, nearly 4,000 tons of flour would have been saved, and the final ration cut avoided.[19]

The allotments were also deadly in their crudeness, particularly as regards older children and adolescents. Children under twelve all fell into the same category, meaning that an eleven-year-old received no more than a toddler. From twelve to fourteen they were classed as 'dependants', even if in practice working and despite their fast-developing bodies' more than adult needs. A child turning twelve between the two ration cuts of 12 September and 1 October thus found that his or her bread ration actually dropped, from 300 grams per day to 250. The classifications, Pavlov admitted, were 'unjustified', but 'the situation made it impossible to feed them better'.[20] Equally unfairly classed as 'dependants' were non-working mothers, upon whom fell the physical burdens of queuing at bread stores, bartering and hauling fuel and water. Tellingly, 'dependants' were also allotted fewer non-food necessities: they received one box of matches, for example, as compared to workers' two. The nickname for the dependant's card was the *smertnik*, from the word *smert*, or 'death'.[21]

Diversion of rations from the productive to the unproductive was prevented by rules forbidding workers from taking food home to their families. An army surgeon, who had been forced to move into the hospital where she worked and thus leave her elderly mother living alone, asked permission to take home some of her own relatively generous ration. The request was turned down, but she nonetheless managed to smuggle her mother food via an orderly. 'I was ordered to report to the commissar', she wrote later, 'and he attempted to persuade me that I had no right to undermine my health, to deprive myself of food. I agreed, didn't protest, but told him that I couldn't do otherwise, that my sacred responsibility was to save my mother.'[22] Though in many workplaces, as here, the rules were not strictly enforced, in others employees' bags were searched as they left the premises.

The authorities did make some exceptions to their ruthless utilitarianism. On hearing that many of the city's elderly scholars were dying, Zhdanov is said to have personally ordered that a list be drawn up of the most prominent and that they be sent extra food parcels by municipal trade organisations.[23] One beneficiary was the artist Anna Ostroumova-Lebedeva, who on 20 January 1942 was astonished to open her door to a woman in a white coat carrying a box filled with butter, meat, flour, sugar and dried peas. 'This is Comrade Zhdanov', she wrote in her diary, 'who has noticed my age and taken it upon himself to send me food. I calculate that it amounts to roughly what one would get in a month on a worker's card.'[24] The delivery fed her and her maid Nyusha for ten days, but did not soften her attitude to the system as a whole. The dependant's card, she thought, was a death sentence and a 'disgrace', designed to rid Leningrad of old people and housewives – all 'superfluous mouths'.[25]

The biggest, inevitable, weakness of the rationing system was its vulnerability to corruption. The most romanticised Soviet accounts do not admit this at all, picturing the entire city, save for a few weak souls and saboteurs, as selflessly devoted to resisting the enemy. Even the more realistic ones, such as Pavlov's (published during Khrushchev's short-lived 'Thaw'), greatly understate the level of breakdown, detailing the measures taken to prevent forgery and ration-card fiddles on the part of the general population, but glossing over theft and bribe-taking within the food distribution network itself. Though 'egotists' and 'locusts' attempted to undermine the system, Pavlov concludes,

> the measures taken by the city Party organisation made it possible to protect the population from speculators, swindlers and spongers. The inhabitants' confidence in the established system of food distribution was maintained. There was little food, but each individual knew that his ration would not be given to anyone else. He would receive whatever he was supposed to receive.[26]

This picture, as both private and official records make clear, is far too rosy. Leningraders did not receive what they were supposed to receive – on the contrary, they queued for hours in the dark and cold, often to get far short of the designated ration, or nothing at all. Nor did they believe that the system was fair: every diarist complains of corrupt bosses and rosy-cheeked canteen workers and shopgirls; every diarist describes wangling extra rations themselves when possible, and trading on the black market.

The Party files, too, are stuffed with corruption cases. The chairman and deputy chairman of the Petrograd district soviet, one note records, instead of 'maintaining iron order' arranged regular off-ration food distributions for themselves and colleagues. 'Comrade Ivanov, moreover, converted his office into a bedroom for himself and his colleague Comrade Volkova, thus laying himself open to accusations of having sexual relations with a subordinate.'[27] There were similar goings-on in the Primorsky district Party Committee, twelve of whose members, led by its First Secretary and the district soviet chair, took special deliveries direct from the local Canteen Trust. 'Before the 7 November [Revolution Day] festivities', an NKVD investigator reported,

> the Trust issued the district committee with ten kilos of chocolate and eight kilos of caviar and tinned goods. On the 6th the committee telephoned the Trust demanding more chocolate . . . Altogether, 4,000 roubles-worth of food were misappropriated in November . . . Canteen no. 13 had cigarettes for all the committee members – 1000 packs – but Secretary Kharytonov told the canteen not to hand them out, saying 'I will smoke them all myself'.

Nikita Lomagin, the historian who has worked most extensively in Petersburg's security service archive, concludes from the fact that the report was not made until the end of December that the police had previously been taking a cut themselves. None of the Party officials involved, he also points out, lost his job.[28]

Instead of punishing dishonest officials, the leadership concentrated on preventing the public from cheating the system. One of Pavlov's first moves was to clamp down on unauthorised and duplicate ration cards. Record-keeping, he discovered on arrival in the city in September, had failed to keep up with the enormous population movements of the past two months, allowing Leningraders to take out cards in the names of friends and relatives who had gone into evacuation or to the front. Stricter checks and penalties cut the number of cards issued for October to 2.42 million, down 97,000 from the previous month. It was not enough, and on 10 October the city soviet passed a resolution, proposed by Zhdanov, to re-register all cards. Between 12 and 18 October Leningraders had personally to present proofs of identity at building managers' offices or work-places, and would receive a 're-registered' stamp on their ration cards in exchange. Unstamped cards would thereafter be confiscated on presentation. The measure cut the number of bread cards in circulation by another 88,000, meat cards by 97,000 and cards for oil and butter by 92,000.

Applications for replacement cards immediately started to rise. All the applicants, Pavlov remembered, 'told more or less the same story – "I lost my cards while taking cover from bombing or artillery fire." . . . Or if their building had been destroyed – "The card was in my flat when the building was hit."'[29] In response, it was ordered that replacement cards should be issued only by the central ration card bureau, and then only in the best-attested cases. For petitioners, this turned the application process from a familiar dreary tussle with petty officialdom into a fight literally for life – a 'weird combination', as Lidiya Ginzburg put it, of 'old (bureaucratic) form and new content (people dying of hunger)':

First there is the malicious secretary, who speaks in a loud voice, in studied tones of rejection, gently restraining her administrative triumph. Then there is the languid secretary, with beautiful, heavily made-up eyes, not yet dressed siege-fashion . . . She regards you without malice – her only desire is to rid herself of bother – and rejects your request lazily, even a little plaintively . . . Finally there is the businesslike secretary, who . . . prizes the official process itself. She turns you down majestically, with sermonising and reasons. And although the secretary is only interested in what she herself is saying, the applicant, who will likely be dead in a few days without a ration card, is comforted for a moment by these reasons.[30]

In December also, cards were made exchangeable only at designated stores. Since some stores were markedly better than others, getting registered at the store of one's choice became another life and death fight with bureaucracy. (The diarist Ivan Zhilinsky, despairing of his local Shop no. 44 – dishonestly run and overrun with 'granny-hooligans' – managed to swap to a more orderly Gastronom by bribing the manager with his fur hat.[31])

It is unrealistic to be too critical. No rationing system could have saved the whole population of Leningrad: the mouths were simply too many, the food supply too small. Nor was the system a fiasco: food was collected, distributed and queued for, in circumstances which could reasonably have been expected to cause complete social breakdown. It did, however, unarguably have serious and avoidable defects, costing uncountable thousands of lives. As the siege progressed, one of the most widespread frauds became concealment of the death of a relative so as to be able to go on using his or her ration card until it expired at the end of the month. Husbands, as Zhilinsky recorded of his neighbours in a subdivided wooden house in Novaya Derevnya, thus posthumously supported their widows and children. '[The families] store them away in the cold', he wrote in January 1942, 'and carry on getting bread with their cards. That's what's happened to Serebryannikov and Usachov – they're being kept in the laundry room. So are Syropatov and Fedorov. This is going on all over the city – so many more are dead, but hidden.'[32]

Falling Down the Funnel

In September still, golden days had alternated with autumn gales. In October the last of the summer came to an end. The first snow fell, unusually early, on the 15th, and ice, grey-white under the granite embankments and darkly transparent at its outer perimeter, began to creep across the canals.[1] Georgi Knyazev, wheeling himself along the Vasilyevsky Island embankment each morning, saw the military bustle that had invaded his 'small radius' fade away. The files of marching sailors, helmets strapped to their knapsacks, disappeared; so did the speeding, mud-spattered army lorries and the soldiers camped out with their horses on the yellowing grass of Rumyantsev Square. Shelling had ravelled the overhead tram wires along the Nicholas Bridge, and a warship blocked his view of the Senate House, her three funnels painted winter-camouflage white. Next to the still unsandbagged Luxor sphinxes a truck stood on chocks, two of its wheels missing. The sphinxes themselves looked like 'a couple of miserable naked pups, thrown out into the bitter frost'.[2]

This period – from September to the end of December 1941 – was, as the historian Sergei Yarov puts it, when Leningraders 'fell down the funnel'. Over the course of three months, the city changed from something quite familiar – in outward appearance not unlike London during the Blitz – to a Goya-esque charnel house, with buildings burning unattended for days and emaciated corpses littering the streets. For individuals the accelerating downward spiral was from relatively 'normal' wartime life – disruption, shortages, air raids – to helpless witness of the death by starvation of husbands, wives, fathers, mothers and children – and for many, of course, to death itself.

So swift was the transition, so anomalous its backdrop, that grapevine news of hunger deaths was at first greeted with incredulity. Lidiya Ginzburg wrote her forensic memoir of the blockade in the guise of an anonymous, composite 'Siege Man'. For him famine belonged 'in the desert, complete with camels and mirages'. He 'didn't believe that the inhabitants of a large city could die of hunger . . . On hearing of the first cases of death amongst their acquaintances, people still thought: Is this the one I know? In broad daylight? In Leningrad? With a master's degree? From starvation?'[3]

Yelena Skryabina, whose first reaction to the announcement of war had been to rent a holiday cottage at a knockdown price, similarly found the idea of death by starvation 'demeaning and absurd'. Though responsible for four dependants – her mother, two sons and an elderly former nanny – she returned to the city only in mid-August and thus began stocking up with food very late. On 15 September she made a trip to the city outskirts, to barter with villagers: 'I had cigarettes, my husband's boots, and some women's shoes . . . Everywhere I had to beg, literally implore. The peasants are already overloaded with valuable things; they don't even want to talk.' A few days later she managed, at the cost of endless queuing, to buy vodka, which she traded for potatoes with a 'drunk old woman . . . Lucky for us that there are still such old women around.'[4] Another lucky contact was a Tartar pedlar, who sold her chocolate and horsemeat for cash ('completely unbelievable these days, since money's worth nothing any more') and a bottle of red wine. Not all the inhabitants of her communal apartment, she noted in early October, were as fortunate:

People turn into animals before our eyes. Who would have thought that Irina, always such a quiet, lovely woman, would be capable of beating her husband, who she has always adored? And for what? Because he wants to eat all the time and can never get enough. He just waits for her to bring something home, and then throws himself on the food . . .

The most grisly sight in our apartment is the Kurakin family. He, back from exile and emaciated by years in prison, is already beginning to bloat. It's simply horrible! Of his wife's former love, there is little left. She is constantly irritated and argumentative. Their children cry and beg for food. But all they get is beatings. However, the Kurakins are no exception. Hunger has changed almost everyone.

Two lifelines helped prevent Skryabina's family from going the same way. The first was a pass to her military engineer husband's mess, from which she was able to bring home small but regular amounts of soup and porridge. The second was a fictitious job, arranged by a friend, for her fifteen-year-old son Dima, which allowed him an adult worker's ration. But though her younger son, five-year-old Yura, continued happy and lively, 'helping' the yardman to chop firewood and sweep snow, for teenage Dima even this was not enough:

He has lost interest in everything. He won't read or talk . . . he's even indifferent to bombing. The only thing that rouses him is food. He's hungry all day long and rattles through the cupboards, looking for something to eat. When he can't find anything he chews on coffee grounds or those abominable oil cakes which used to be fed only to cattle . . . Even in September he used to walk around the city looking for things to buy, took an interest in the military communiqués, met friends. Now he's like an old man, constantly freezing. He spends whole days standing next to the stove in his winter jacket, pale, with deep blue circles under his eyes. If he goes on like this he will die.[5]

Another job, arranged by Skryabina's husband, did not help. Attached as a messenger boy to a hospital, Dima was sent to and fro across the city in what was by now biting cold, often only to be cheated of the agreed-upon evening meal in exchange. The hospital's kitchen manager, Skryabina raged, was a thief: 'Only when Dima shows up with the director's son does he get everything – even meat patties. No wonder *that* boy is so well-nourished and rosy-cheeked.' On 15 December, having collapsed in the street, Dima took permanently to his bed – or in siege shorthand, 'lay down'. 'He lies quietly and won't talk at all, burying his face in his pillow. He no longer gets up to search for food in the cupboards and the sideboard . . . He's so tall and thin, and unbelievably pitiful . . . I look at him in horror. I'm afraid he will die.'[6] In a little over four months, Skryabina had gone from playing with her boys in the Catherine Palace park, to watching the elder of them waste away from simple want of enough to eat.

Olga Grechina lived with her mother and younger brother Volodya (Vova for short) in a grey-painted, ponderously ornate mansion block halfway down Mayakovsky Street, one of the shabby-grand boulevards leading off the Nevsky. Her father, a doctor, had died a few years earlier, and her older brother Leonid had been called up into the army. In October, having been released from trench-digging, she was able to visit Leonid at the village near Shlisselburg where he was stationed with his mortar battery. There he introduced her to his new medical orderly fiancée – an unsuitable girl, Olga couldn't help thinking, who insisted that they be photographed 'heads together, smiling, in the best village tradition', and seemed able to talk about nothing but curtains. Leonid and his fellow soldiers were cheerful – happy to have got out of the Kingisepp encirclements alive. But they had no bread or sugar and their horses were emaciated, tearing at the wooden porch to which they were tethered with huge yellow teeth. Nor did the unit have enough ammunition: 'Each battery gets five shells. When you let them off the Germans retaliate, and keep going for twenty-four hours, but there's nothing for us to fire back with.'

Soon after Olga returned to Leningrad her mother was hit by a car during the blackout. Though only slightly injured, she rapidly weakened and had to be helped down to the basement during raids. She also insisted on sharing her ration with the family dog, a beloved 'ball of fluff' called Kashtanka, so that Olga was half relieved when the animal was stolen – if the rumours were right, for food. The informal system of mutual favours whereby Russians got round shortages and bureaucracy – *blat* in Soviet slang – was now, Olga discovered, beginning to break down. To get medicine for her mother, she appealed to a former colleague of her father's, a Dr Mikhailov. The favour he owed the Grechin family dated back to 1916, when he had been caught saving 'self-shooters' – soldiers who had shot themselves in the left hand so as to be invalided out of the army – from execution by sending them to the rear. Instead of denouncing him, Olga's father had restitched the soldiers' hands so as to disguise the bullet wounds, and transferred him to another hospital. Mikhailov now worked in a clinic round the corner from the Grechins on Pestelya, a gracious, Italianate street book-ended by two perfectly proportioned churches. Olga found him

> besieged by old women – or that's how they looked then. He seemed to have sunk into old age himself as well. I asked him to come and see Mama, but he refused, saying 'You know we only make house calls in exceptional circumstances now, and she's already had diagnosis and treatment.' I was indignant, I remember, and berated him – He, having been educated in the humanitarian tradition, having taken the Hippocratic oath, refused to visit a sick person. He sadly heard me out, then said, 'If I come to

you, I won't be able to get home. For me everything is measured out: once a day I can get from Tchaikovsky Street to Pestelya. I haven't got the strength to do more. And if I don't get to work, what will happen to all these people?' And he pointed to the door, behind which waited all his patients.

Another doctor, whom Olga paid in advance for a house call, first advised, cruelly, that her mother be fed chicken soup and milk, then left the bedroom to write out a prescription for sedatives. After he had gone, Olga noticed that some sweets that had been sitting in a tin on the kitchen table had disappeared.

In November Olga and Vova both found jobs, Vova as a boilerman, which meant chopping and loading wood but provided a meal and warmth, and Olga in a polygraph machine-turned-ammunition factory, checking half-made shell casings and carrying them from workbench to workbench. Though the casings were heavy and greasy, and covered with steel shavings which cut her hands, the work earned her 230 roubles a week and as much soup ('really only hot water') as she could drink, plus some to take home to her mother. At the end of the month the family received news of its first death – Leonid's, killed in fighting near where Olga had visited him a few weeks before.

In early December swollen legs and infected sores on her hands stopped Olga from working, and she began to hear of the deaths of neighbours in her apartment block. The first to go (as was typical throughout the city) were low-status ancillary workers: the building's porter – 'a very neat, respectable man' – and his wife, then the yardman, then a 'small, mustachioed and gloomy plumber, who lived on the first floor and spent his time chasing the boys for hooliganism'. Next came the turn of the building's ordinary residents, starting with the husband of a singer, who lived with their mentally handicapped son on the floor above:

One December night at about 11 p.m. someone knocked on the door. I opened up, and there was our neighbour N with a small glass in her hand. She said, 'My son is dying – I beg you, give me a spoonful of sunflower oil. If I pour it into his mouth I might be able to save him.'

'But I don't have any oil!'

'Yes you do, you must have! You have to save my son!'

No, I insisted – but in fact I did have a hundred grams of oil, which by chance I had managed to get on my card somewhere or other. But I couldn't spare any for N – I was feeding Mama with it. If I gave it to N's son – who I had always found deeply unpleasant – then what would I give her? I got angry with N – saying no to her was excruciatingly shameful – and she left. In the morning her boy died. I felt like a murderer.[7]

As Leningraders' bodies began to fail, so did the arteries of the city itself. In October the power stations began to run out of fuel, reducing the electricity supply to a trickle. The trolley buses had long since been commandeered for use as ambulances; now the trams ground to a halt at random points on their routes, and began to gather frost and icicles. Their failure, as Ginzburg put it, 'restored the reality of city distances', lengthening streets and especially the windswept, shelterless Neva bridges. Snow went uncleared, so that all but major thoroughfares became impassable save for trodden-down, single-file paths, which traced new short cuts through bomb sites and the remains of fuel-scavenged fences. The patchworks of newsprint, wrapping paper, planks and plywood covering apartment-building windows lost the odd gaiety they had had at the start of the war. Now the boards had a 'funeral symbolism', they marked 'people jammed together, perishing, buried alive'.[8]

From 27 November residential buildings were banned from using electricity between 10 a.m. and 5 p.m., by which time it was anyway supplied very erratically or not at all. For light and heat,

Leningraders turned instead to the technologies of the village. Various sorts of home-made lamp were devised – an improvised 'bat' or storm lantern and the *koptilka*, or 'smoker', which consisted of a wick suspended in a small bottle, tin cup or upturned kettle lid. Both types burned dirtily, covering faces, hands and walls in sticky black soot. When kerosene ran out – a final two and a half litres per person was distributed in September – camphor, stain-remover, machine oil, eau-de-cologne and insecticide were burned instead. All rapidly disappeared from the shops and fetched increasingly outlandish prices in the street markets. The second vital piece of siege equipment was a small, usually home-made metal stove, or *burzhuika*, its pipe leading outdoors via a boarded-up or cushion-stuffed casement window. Into it went wood scavenged from bomb sites, furniture (in the street markets, wardrobes fetched more chopped up than whole), graveyard crosses, books and parquet tiles. Georgi Knyazev was advised by the Tartar wife of the Academy boilerman to feed his with dried faeces, as practised on the steppe. The *burzhuika* nickname – from the Russian for 'bourgeois' – came from the stoves' tubby shape, or from their greediness for fuel, or from the fact that it was the old middle classes who had resorted to them during the Civil War. (Metalworking equipment used to make *burzhuiki*, a crime report of January 1942 noted, was being stolen from factories and sold on the black market.) Third – and today most powerfully symbolic of the blockade of all – came the *sanki*, or child's sled, vital for transporting firewood, water and, finally, corpses.

Leningraders also had to master village skills. They learned that birch wood burned well and aspen badly, that dried maple leaves could substitute for tobacco, and how to light the resulting cigarette, rolled in newspaper, by holding a lens up to the sunlight, or by striking metal against stone. Oddly, few tried to ice-fish, probably because they lacked the necessary lines and drills. One man, a theatre producer, likened it to being in a time machine. The blockade had hurled Leningrad back to the eighteenth century – but worse, because people no longer owned fur coats, there weren't wells at every corner any more, and water had to be carried home in kettles instead of with buckets and yokes.[9] In most apartment buildings the water supply failed by degrees, starting with the top floor. When the last tap dried residents resorted first to neighbouring buildings, then to broken pipes and ice holes, cut by the fire brigade, on the frozen canals and river. Over time, spillages turned into icy hillocks, up which one had to push oneself and one's receptacle on hands and knees. Dmitri Likhachev was able to collect water from a fire hydrant, dragging it home on a sled in a zinc baby's bath. Less sloshed out on the way, he discovered, if he floated a few sticks in it first. His elderly father ('the most inconsistent and short-tempered man I ever knew') turned out to be unexpectedly good at chopping wood, being a veteran, like the *burzhuiki*, of the Civil War. Zoologists, Likhachev remarks, survived the siege, because they knew how to catch rats and pigeons. Impractical mathematicians died.

As the official ration dwindled and private stocks ran out, Leningraders also sought out their own, increasingly desperate, substitute foods. The commonest of these were *zhmykh* and *duranda* – the husks of linseed, cotton, hemp or sunflower seeds, pressed into blocks and normally fed to cattle. Grated and fried in oil, they could be turned into 'pancakes', the elaborate preparation of which helped give the comforting impression of a real meal. Also near-universally eaten was joiner's glue, made from the bones and hooves of slaughtered animals. Likhachev found eight sheets of it at Pushkin House, which his wife soaked in several changes of water then boiled with bay leaves to make a foul-smelling jelly, which they forced down with the help of vinegar and mustard. They also cooked up the semolina used to clean their daughters' white sheepskin jackets: 'It was full of strands of wool and grey with dirt, but we were all glad of it.' An art teacher searched the flats of evacuated friends: 'I rummaged in all the cupboards and took rusks of any kind – green, mouldy, anything . . . Altogether I collected a small bagful. I was extremely pleased to have got quite a good amount. Later one of my students brought me oilcake – three blocks this size. That was something tremendous – three blocks of oilcake!'[10] He also ate linseed oil and fish glue, used for mixing paints and priming canvases.

Substitutes were often dangerous. Even if not poisonous in themselves, they could cause diarrhoea and vomiting, or damage thinned stomach linings. Anything, though, was better than nothing. Glycerine contained calories, Leningraders discovered, as did tooth powder, cough medicine and cold cream. Factory workers ate industrial casein (an ingredient in paint), dextrine (used to bind sand in foundry moulds), tank grease and machine oil. At the Physiological Institute Pavlov's slavering dogs were eaten; at another, scientists shared out their stocks of 'Liebig extract' – a dried meat broth made from the embryos of calves and used as a medium for growing bacteria. One father brought home the maggoty knee of a reindeer, an air-raid casualty at the zoo.[11]

Eaten also were the vast majority of household pets. 'All day long', a wife wrote to her husband at the front, 'we're busy trying to find something to eat. With Papa we've eaten two cats. They're so hard to find and catch that we're all looking out for a dog, but there are none to be seen.'[12] One family, to save themselves embarrassment in front of neighbours, referred to cat meat by the French *chat*. Others swapped pets so as not to have to eat their own animal, or bartered them for other necessities. A teacher brought a handwritten advertisement, which she had found pasted up in the street, into her staff room. Reading 'I will trade 4.5 metres of flannel and a primus for a cat', it sparked a 'long argument – Is it moral to eat cats or not?'[13] Such squeamishness soon faded. 'Not all parents', a siege survivor remembered of her astronomer father's colleagues at the Pulkovo observatory,

> love their children as much as Messer and his wife loved their big pointer Graalya. Tender tears used to well in Yelizaveta

Alekseyevna's eyes as she watched the dog frisking on the grass. During the hunting season, Messer would take his darling prize-winner out every Sunday, setting off proudly and ceremoniously, with proper Germanic formality.

In January 1942 they ate her. Messer cut her throat while Yelizaveta Alekseyevna held her down. The dog was strong; they couldn't manage it on their own, so asked Pimenova for help, promising a piece of meat in return. But at the end of the whole operation all they gave her was the intestines.[14]

This was the period, also, when private stocks of food or trade-ables started to mean the difference between life and death. One family unearthed a suitcase full of 'fossilised' rusks, laid in twenty years earlier during the Civil War. Another, a ten-year-old diarist recorded, came upon a box of candles, which they were able to sell for 625 roubles – they had cost only eight kopeks apiece when his father bought them back in 1923. The classicist Olga Fridenberg kept herself and her mother going on a package of tinned food that they had earlier prepared for her brother prior to his depar-ture for the Gulag. Another woman traded her dead husband's clothes, bought on a pre-war visit to America. The trip had cost him his life – he had been shot as a capitalist sympathiser during the Terror – but the good-quality suits and jackets helped to save his family.

When there was no food to be had, fantasies took its place. Igor Kruglyakov, eight years old at the time of the siege, remembers going through the family box of Christmas decorations with his sister, looking for walnuts: 'Their insides were dry and shrivelled, but we ate them, they felt like food. We picked all the crumbs out of the cracks in our big, dirty kitchen table – again, they seemed like food. I can't say that it cheered us up, it was just a way to pass the time.' At the end of November his grandfather died of 'hunger diarrhoea' – possibly, Kruglyakov's mother agonised, because she had in desperation given him diluted potassium permanganate – the bright purple, all-purpose disinfectant known as *margantsovka* – to drink. The children, who not long before had been running round the streets collecting shrapnel, now stayed huddled in bed, leafing through a nineteenth-century book of birds and Madame Molokhovyets's *Gift to Young Housewives*, with its recipes for aspics, mousses, Madeira cake and suckling pig. 'For the first time in my life I read the words "Rum Baba". It had pictures too – quite simple ones, but they gave us pleasure.'[15] One of the most devastating documents on display in Petersburg's Museum of the Defence of Leningrad is an imaginary menu penned by a hungry sixteen-year-old, Valya Chepko. 'Menu', he neatly writes, 'for after starvation, if I'm still alive. First course: soup – potato and mushroom, or pickled cabbage and meat. Second course: *kasha* – oatmeal with butter, millet, pearl barley, buckwheat, rice or semolina. Meat course: meatballs with mashed potatoes; sausages with mashed potatoes or *kasha*. But there's no point in dreaming about this, because we won't live to see it!' He didn't, dying in February.

Sadder, perhaps, even than physical breakdown, was the way in which hunger destroyed personalities and relationships. Increasingly preoccupied with food, individuals gradually lost interest in the world around them, and at the extremity, with anything except finding something to eat. 'Before the war', wrote Yelena Kochina as early as 3 October, 'people adorned themselves with bravery, fidelity to principles, honesty – whatever they liked. The hurricane of war has torn off those rags: now everyone has become what he was in fact, and not what he wanted to seem.'

Her diary – written in the margins of old newspapers, on scraps of wallpaper and on the backs of printed forms – charts, with searing honesty, the gradual breakdown of her marriage. Immediately pre-war her mood is joyous, delighting in her new baby and doting husband. 'Dima is on holiday', she writes on 16 June, while watching him change a nappy. 'All day he's busy with our daughter: bathing her, dressing her, feeding her. His well-kept, sensitive designer's hands manage all this with amazing skill. His hair blazes in the sun, lighting up his happy face.' Six days later the young family was hit, like millions of others, with the announcement of invasion: 'I carried Lena out into the garden with her coloured rattles. The sun already ruled the sky. A cry, the sound of broken dishes. The woman who owns our dacha ran past the house. "Yelena Iosifovna! War with the Germans! They just announced it on the radio!"' Two weeks into the war the couple had their first serious quarrel, over whether or not Yelena should leave for Saratov with her institute. Yelena decided not to evacuate, and the closure of the siege ring trapped the whole family in Leningrad. Through September, Dima had hardly any sleep, firewatching with the local civil defence team at night and digging potatoes in an abandoned vegetable patch after work. Every morning, Yelena walked along the Neva embankment to the paediatric hospital which distributed the infant ration of soya milk:

The maples burn a feverish red, like dying embers. The leaves fall slowly, dropping straight into my hands. I take them home and put them on the windowsill, new ones every morning. These may be the last leaves of my life. A downpour of artillery shells whips along the embankment, landing on the Academy of Arts and the University. Sometimes shells land quite close and we see people fall.

At the hospital, Lena immediately drinks up her milk. When it is finished she cries bitterly, stretching out her little hands towards the white baby bottles . . . But they don't give her any more: three and a half ounces is the ration.

Dima, having been transferred to a defence factory where he worked as a lathe operator, received the manual worker's ration. 'During the midday break,' wrote Yelena, he brings me his lunch: a small meat patty and two spoons of mashed potato. Despite my protests he forces me to eat it all – 'Eat, please, you have to feed Lena. Don't worry about me, I'm full.' But I can see that this isn't true; all he's eating is soup. He can't keep going like this for long, and anyway I have less milk every day.

In early October, though the couple had already broken into their emergency reserves of potatoes and *sukhari*, Yelena's milk dried up. 'At night I drink a whole pot of water but it doesn't help. Lena screams and tears at my breast like a small wild animal (poor thing!). Now we give her all the butter and sugar we get on our ration cards.' On the 10th Yelena first recorded her suspicion that Dima was secretly eating *sukhari* in her absence. The rusks ran out four weeks later, leaving only fourteen ounces of millet with which to feed the baby ('Now I curse myself for buying only four and a half pounds at the commercial store. What a fool I was!'). No longer trusting her husband, Yelena started hiding the millet every time she left the apartment – 'up the chimney, under the bed, under the mattress. But he finds it everywhere.' On 26 November, returning home unexpectedly, she caught him in the act:

'Don't you dare!' I yelled, losing control of myself.

'Shut up, I can't help myself.'

He looked at me despairingly. He didn't even avoid my eyes as he's been doing these last few days. I shut up and my anger passed . . . After all, by giving me his lunches, he started going hungry before I did.

The millet ran out on 2 December. Two days later, the kindness of a stranger allowed Yelena to exchange coupons for macaroni. Roaming the streets in search of food for sale, she had spotted a horse-drawn cart laden with boxes:

A crowd dragged along behind the cart as if following a coffin. I joined this peculiar 'funeral procession'. It turned out that there was macaroni in the boxes, but nobody knew where it was being delivered. The driver remained stubbornly silent. Catching sight of a shop ahead we raced one another there and formed a line, exchanging abuse. We could have been trained animals. But the horse, squinting in our direction with his kind eyes, pulled the cart on past. Breaking away from our places, we ran after it. This happened five times . . .

At last the cart stopped at a shop. There was a long queue outside, looping round the corner . . . Gatekeeper to paradise, the shop manager counted off the 'faithful souls', letting them in ten at a time. I stood and gazed mindlessly. I don't know what was written on my face, but suddenly an old woman waiting in line asked me softly, 'When is it your turn?' I answered that I wasn't queuing, and that to start now would be pointless since there wouldn't be enough macaroni for everyone anyway. And I added, unusually for me, that I had a small child at home and didn't know how I was going to feed her.

The woman said nothing, but next time the shop door opened she shoved Yelena forwards, staying outside herself. 'I was so stunned that even when I had the macaroni there in my hands, which were trembling with excitement, I couldn't believe that what had happened was real.'

The time bought by this act of charity was short. Though Dima managed, at the cost of enormous physical effort, to make a *burzhu-ika* out of corrugated iron scavenged from a bomb site, by mid-December he had sunk into apathy and paranoia. No longer going to work or helping with the baby, he got up only to go to the bread shop, eating the makeweight piece, the prized *dovesok*, on the way home. His movements, wrote Yelena, were now those of a 'broken robot', his expression 'fossilised' and 'savage', his eyes rimmed with soot and the skin of his face stretched by oedema to a lacquer shine. Her own face had swollen, too – she looked 'like the back end of a pig'. Neither could think of anything but food:

> I pour four ladles of 'soup' [made of joiner's glue and crumbled bread] for Dima and two for myself. For this I get the right to lick the pot, though the soup is so thin that there's not really anything to lick. Dima eats his with a teaspoon so as to make it last longer. But today he finished his portion faster than I did. I happened to get a particularly hard piece of crust, which I was pleasurably chewing. I could feel him staring with hatred at my steadily moving jaws.
>
> 'You're eating slowly on purpose!' he viciously burst out. 'You're trying to torment me!'
>
> 'What do you mean? Why would I do that?' I blurted, amazed.
>
> 'Don't try to deny it, please, I see everything.'
>
> He glared at me, his eyes pale with rage. I was terrified. Had he gone mad?[16]

Vera Inber saw a corpse being dragged on a sled for the first time on 1 December. 'There was no coffin. It was wrapped in a white shroud, and the knees were clearly discernible, the sheet being tightly bound. A biblical, ancient Egyptian burial. The shape of a human form was clear enough, but one couldn't tell if it was a man or a woman.' By the end of the month this was a common sight. In October, the NKVD reported to Zhdanov towards the end of December, 6,199 people had died 'in connection with food difficulties' in Leningrad, a nearly 80 per cent rise on the usual pre-war mortality rate of about 3,500 deaths per month. In November the number had risen to 9,183, and, in the first twenty-five days of December, to 39,073. Each of the past five days, between 113 and 147 corpses had been picked up on the streets. Mortality rates were particularly high among men (71 per cent of the total), over-sixties

(27 per cent of the total) and babies (14 per cent). Despite the arrest of 1,524 'speculators', the report also noted, barter prices for food in the officially illegal but in practice tolerated street markets had risen to extraordinary heights. A rabbit-fur coat was worth one pood (sixteen kilograms) of potatoes, a pocket watch one and a half kilos of bread, a pair of felt boots with galoshes four kilos of *duranda*. In the last six days of December another 13,808 people died, bringing the month's total toll to almost 53,000.[17]

Progress was also being monitored in Berlin. Army intelligence and the Sicherheitsdienst, the intelligence wing of the SS, both regularly reported on conditions inside the city, collating information from informers, deserters and POWs. 'Illness', the Sicherheitsdienst reported on 24 November, had 'started to spread':

Women in particular are predisposed to serious throat infections, by reason of the insufficiency or complete absence of heating in domestic apartments, and breakage of window glass. The mortality rate amongst children is quite high. There have been cases of abdominal and spotted typhus, although one cannot yet speak of an epidemic. Numerous cases of dysentery have also been noted.[18]

A fortnight later another intelligence report, from von Küchler's Eighteenth Army, boasted successful artillery hits on a hospital, a House of Culture, the Mariinsky Theatre, a food warehouse, tram sidings and the offices of *Leningradskaya Pravda*. Casualties, it noted, were no longer being picked up by buses, but by horse-drawn carts – themselves often out of commission thanks to a shortage of forage. What German intelligence devoted most space to, though, was the onset of famine. The civilian ration, it was correctly noted, had been cut five times since the beginning of September, and 'bad organisation of food distribution' meant that card holders often got less than their allotment or nothing at all. 'There have been cases of increasingly weak workers falling unconscious in the workplace. The first starvation deaths have also been recorded. It can be concluded that in the coming weeks we will see further significant deterioration in the food situation of the civilian population of Petersburg.'[19]

The art historian Nikolai Punin made his last siege-winter diary entry on 13 December, sitting in his dark room overlooking the Sheremetyev Palace. Earlier, he had written of his longing that the churches be opened and filled with prayers and tears and candles, making 'less palpable this cold iron matter in which we live'. Now, he likened Stalin to the jealous Old Testament God:

De profundis clamavi: Lord save us . . . We are perishing. But his Greatness is as implacable as Soviet power is unbending. It is not important to it, having 150 million [people], to lose three million of them. His Greatness, resting in the heavens, does not value earthly life as we do . . . We are living in the frozen and starving city, ourselves abandoned and starving. I can't remember the snow ever falling in such abundance. The city is covered in snowdrifts like a shroud. It is clean, because the factories aren't working, and it is rare that smoke rises from the chimneys over the apartment buildings. The days are clear, and travel might be easy, but the city is buried like the provinces, white and crackling . . .

And everything is simple; no one says anything in particular. They don't talk about anything except ration cards or evacuation. They simply suffer and probably think, like I do, that maybe it's not their turn yet.

I feel the loneliness most of all at night, and the senselessness of petitions and prayers, and sometimes I cry quietly . . . And there is no salvation. And one can't even be imagined, unless you give in to daydreams. 'We turned our backs on Him,' I think, 'and He on us.' *Miserere* I mumble, and add – there it is, *dies irae*. Lord, save us.[20]

PART 3

Mass Death: Winter 1941–2

Death certificate, December 1941. The cause of death is given as 'dystrophy', a euphemism for starvation.

I think that real life is hunger, and the rest a mirage. In the time of famine people revealed themselves, stripped themselves, freed themselves of all trumpery. Some turned out to be marvellous, incomparable heroes, others – scoundrels, villains, murderers, cannibals. There were no half-measures. Everything was real. The heavens were unfurled and in them God was seen . . .

Dmitri Likhachev

The Ice Road

Lieutenant Fritz Hockenjos was thirty-two years old and commander of a *Radfahrzug*, or bicycle reconnaissance unit, within the 215th Infantry Division of General Busch's Sixteenth Army.[1] A forestry manager in civilian life, he came, like most of his men, from Lahr, a picture-perfect medieval town set amid rolling vineyards between the Rhine valley and the western edge of the Black Forest. He had a wife, Elsa, and two young sons, and his hobbies were hunting, bird-watching, photography and singing in the local church choir.

He entered the Soviet Union on 24 November in a heavily laden troop train. His first view of it, from the flat-bed carrying the train's anti-aircraft guns, was of the wide arable fields of Lithuania. 'Here is a landscape after my own heart! No barbed-wire fences or telegraph poles – just freedom and space!' Stopping at a country station to feed and exercise their horses, the soldiers were quickly surrounded by a friendly crowd of gawky teenage boys and women in felt boots and coloured headscarves: 'They all spoke a little German, joked with us . . . A lively barter trade began, and when the band got out and struck up a waltz, it wouldn't have taken much for the soldiers to start dancing with the girls, who looked as if they wouldn't have minded.' The next day they stopped at Riga, where they saw their first Russians – prisoners of war working on the railway track under a Latvian auxiliary:

They wear rags and have starved, blank faces. They look so hungry you think they're going to collapse at any moment. They came up to the train and started begging – I shrink from the comparison but there is no other – like animals. Our soft-hearted boys handed them bread, but the Latvian drove the poor devils off with the butt of his rifle. As they trotted away between the tracks they picked up sausage skins, bits of bread and cigarette butts, frantically stuffing everything into their mouths. The Latvian explained that in his camp about fifty prisoners die every day from hunger or illness, or are shot while trying to escape. But he also told us that the Bolsheviks, as they retreated, took with them half of Riga's children and sixty percent of the people of Dünaburg [today's Daugavpils]. All this chilled us; here in the East there's a damned hard wind blowing.

On the night of the 26th they reached the barbed wire and wooden watchtowers of the pre-1939 border with Russia itself. 'I was sitting by the window and blew on the frost-covered glass so as to be able to see out . . . In the pale moonlight I could see heather, moorland, felled forests, untilled fields, undergrowth.' From now on, the train had to be blacked out at night, and its wheels defrosted with blowtorches after every halt. Outside, the landscape remained 'always the same, always comfortless':

A few stunted willows and birches; otherwise, white monotony. A herd of small dark huts huddle forlornly; dark forests circle the horizon; it snows a little. We were stuck on an open stretch for several hours. Thickly wrapped figures were working on the tracks – women and old men. They looked up as we passed, but it was as if they didn't see us. Only the children waved or begged for bread – 'Pan [Sir], gib Brot!' they shouted. These were the first words we heard from Russians, and we were to hear them again and again.

On 28 November Hockenjos and his men disembarked from the troop train and took to the roads, which was already seething with soldiers, horses and long columns of prisoners. Pushing their heavily laden bicycles into a freezing wind, they crossed the River Volkhov on a pontoon bridge, passed through the ruined town and castle of Gruzino, then on from village to overflowing village looking for regimental command, which they eventually found 'squeezed into one small, smelly hut – staff officers, clerk, cartographer, messenger, telephone operator and radio operator all in one room'. Their own billet for the night was a cottage with a peasant woman and her three children. The family were not, the mother made haste to explain, Russians, but Latvians, descendants of Baptists exiled by the tsars for refusing to serve in the army. 'In 1938', Hockenjos gathered, 'the Soviets had come and taken all the men, and sent them to a labour camp near Archangel. We promised that when we found her husband there we would send him home. Adolf Hitler – who she recognised on a stamp – would put everything right!'

After supper their hostess played chorales on a harmonium, in return for which the young Germans showed her their family photographs, and amused the children by demonstrating the workings of their ink pens, pocket alarm clocks and the dynamo lamps on their bicycles. 'I asked her about "Kolchos, Komsomol and Komissar"; no – in the town there were no Party members and no commissar, but there was a *kolkhoz* [collective farm]. "Oh, Kolchos kaput! Gutt, gutt! Bolschewik – nix gut!"'

The next day the bicycle unit moved on to the village of Rakhmysha, eight kilometres behind the front line and its final destination. 'We have been given', Hockenjos wrote that evening,

a typical Russian hut, so sour-smelling that we almost reeled straight back out again. The walls are papered with old newspapers – against cockroaches, as we soon discovered. A table, a bench, a bed behind the stove and two pictures of saints are the only furnishings. The only metal objects are the stovepipe and the samovar ... Fedor, our host, is the archetypal Russian *muzhik*. His wife is unbelievably dirty and seems to be the source of all the unpleasant smells in the place. It's difficult to tell the children's ages, so it's hard to say whether the blonde girl with red cheeks, who reminds me of a little piglet with her round body and dirty feet, is their daughter or grand-daughter. A small runny-nosed boy called Kolya completes the family . . .

We don't talk a lot. We sit at the table or lie on the floor, smoking and drinking tea. From time to time Fedor comes out from behind the stove and picks cigarette butts out of the herring tin that serves as an ashtray. If there's nothing in it he takes a piece of newspaper, comes to the table, clicks his heels together and smiles, holding out the empty paper. Willynilly I then have to reach into my tobacco and give him a few strands, whereupon he makes a deep bow and retires behind the stove again.

The poverty of these people surpasses all our previous conceptions of the peasants' and workers' paradise. Fedor hasn't seen tea or sugar for years, and tobacco and paraffin are luxuries. Sitting in the embers of the fire is a pot filled with potatoes and some sort of unidentifiable broth, on which the family live from day to day. They drink hot water out of the samovar in old tin cans. When I gave little Kolya a roll of boiled sweets the old woman grabbed it from him and put one in each can, adding hot water.

Life now began to be frightening as well as uncomfortable. On the very evening of his arrival in Rakhmysha, Hockenjos was sent to deal with the first of what was to be a long series of Soviet guerrilla attacks:

Darkness falls at four, and in the gloomy light of the paraffin lamp the hours are long. So we all go to bed at eight – the Russians

climb onto the stove, and we bed down on straw ... At ten
o'clock someone knocks on the door and shouts 'Alarm! A field-
ambulance is on fire on the road to Glad. Shots have been fired.
Bicycle unit, go and investigate immediately!'

Arriving at the scene, the unit found the ambulance burned out and
its driver badly injured. 'We can't find any tracks through the forest.
A long-distance patrol? Partisans? By two in the morning we are
back lying on our straw.' Over the next five days three more trucks
ran over mines.

When not picking up casualties, the *Radfahrzug's* job was to
patrol the gaps between German-held villages along the straggling
front line. On the evening of 7 December, Hockenjos and his
men were ordered to pick up reinforcements from a neighbouring battalion. In the pitch-black darkness and forty-one degrees
of frost at six o'clock the following morning, they discovered that
their lorry, despite having been kept running most of the night,
would not start. Instead they set off on foot, the frost scorching
lungs and icing up eyelashes and nostrils. At nine the sun rose out
of the woods in a red haze, lighting up tiny ice crystals that hung
suspended in the motionless air. At ten they reached a command
post, by which time two men had already been disabled by frostbite. 'In five hours', wrote Hockenjos,

it will be dark again. We creep out and dive once more into
no-man's-land – a long row of dark figures in a bright aspen wood,
clumsy in the knee-deep snow and a frighteningly good target
against the white. We have neither snow-capes nor snow-shoes.

For a good hour we stumble through the tall, silent, snow-filled
forest. Here and there shells have made little clearings amongst the
spruce and pines. A larger clearing opens up, with a half-ruined
cabin. We think we see movement so I set up a machine gun at
the edge of the trees and send a group over. They find two shaggy

horses, who have been feeding off the cabin's thatched roof. They
gallop away, manes and tails flying.

Further on the woods thinned out and the snow reached the men's
hips. They crossed the tracks of what they guessed were wolf and elk.
From the south came the sound of heavy fighting, and they pressed
themselves against the trees when Russian fighters flew overhead.
At seven in the evening, four hours after the sun had set, they came
to a road, a neat stack of corpses and a line of huts – the village
of Gorneshno. 'Schnapps, tea, and army bread . . . Twenty of my
men have frostbite, mostly of the worst degree. The feet of some
have turned black, and they crawl to their quarters on hands and
knees.' The next morning Hockenjos was told that during the night
a field kitchen had driven over a mine, leaving only one survivor.
'We wait for our truck but it doesn't come. Instead a patrol comes

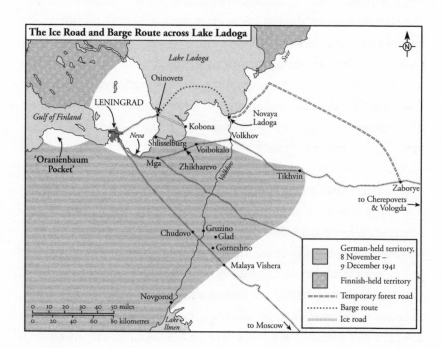

out of the forest with the bodies of the seven scouts we met yesterday. Their heads have been crushed and their noses and ears cut off.'
Hockenjos also heard the news, two days late, of Japan's attack on
the American fleet at Pearl Harbor. 'If that's not a world war', he
wrote with uncharacteristic acerbity in his diary, 'I don't know what
is. It seems that I might make captain after all.'

Hockenjos was in the rear of the second battle for Tikhvin, a town
175 kilometres to the south-east of Leningrad and the easternmost
point of the German salient over the River Volkhov. It was important because of its location, on the railway line along which supplies
were delivered for transport across Lake Ladoga to Leningrad. The
Wehrmacht's hold on Ladoga's southern shore, established when it
took Shlisselburg on 8 September, was tenacious but only thirty kilometres wide. Passing through Tikhvin, trains were able to unload at
Volkhov, twenty kilometres from the small port of Novaya Ladoga,
whence barges sailed, braving German air attack, to Osinovets, on
the lake's Soviet-held western shore. A small suburban railway line
covered the final forty-five kilometres into Leningrad. Twenty days'
worth of rations had thus run the blockade during the autumn.

On 8 November – at the height of the Battle of Moscow –
Tikhvin fell to the Germans, together with 20,000 troops, 96 tanks,
179 guns and an armoured train.[2] Its loss cut Leningrad's lifeline in
two. The closest supply trains could now get to Novaya Ladoga was
Zaborye, 170 kilometres to its east. Leningrad's Military Council
immediately ordered the construction, through almost virgin forest
and using conscripted peasant labour, of a new 200-kilometre road,
to be completed within a fortnight. The Council also ordered that
front-line troops' bread rations be cut for the first time, from 800
grams per day down to 600 grams. The allocation for rear units fell
from 600 to 400 grams. Another three ration cuts – one more for the
military, two for civilians – quickly followed. At the same time, ice
brought navigation across Ladoga to a close, the last barges reaching Osinovets on 15 November. Until the new road was completed

and the lake ice grew thick enough to carry trucks, no food could now reach Leningrad except by air. Though sixty-four planes, at Zhdanov's angry insistence, were eventually assigned to the route, only a third or fewer were operational at any one time, and they daily delivered only forty to fifty tonnes, mostly blocks of pressed and frozen meat.[3]

Watched with desperate attention by hydrologists, the ice thickened agonisingly slowly. (To estimate its likely rate of spread, one man consulted medieval records kept by the monks of Valaam, who each winter recorded the date on which pilgrims were first able to reach their island monastery on foot.) Ten centimetres of ice, it was calculated, was needed for a horse and rider, eighteen centimetres for a horse pulling a sled, twenty for a loaded two-ton truck. A road from Osinovets to the village of Kobona, on the nearest stretch of Soviet-held 'mainland' lake shore, would need a minimum of twenty centimetres of ice along the whole of its thirty-kilometre length.

On 17 November, when the ice was only ten centimetres thick, the first scouts ventured on to the lake, wearing life belts and carrying long poles. The following day the wind began to blow from the north, the temperature dropped and work began on clearing the route of snow, marking it and building bridges over crevasses. By the 20th the ice was eighteen centimetres thick, and the first transports – 300 horse-drawn sledges – set off, followed two days later by the first trucks, widely spaced. On the return journey, though carrying only a few sacks of grain each, several went through the ice. To spread weight, the next convoy towed sleds. To no avail: by 1 December only about 800 tons of flour – less than two days' requirements – had been delivered, and forty trucks had got stuck or broken down. The rough and narrow new overland road to Zaborye was even worse: the first convoy to set out along it, on 6 December, took fourteen days to make the round trip, and more than 350 trucks had to be towed or abandoned. Vasili Churkin, the artilleryman caught up in the chaotic flight from Volosovo back in August, was ordered to march across the ice on the windy, pitch-black night of 7 December. Slowed by frostbitten feet, he fell behind his unit and would have become completely lost if it had not been for red flashes from a lighthouse on the 'mainland' shore. He reached Kobona at 1 p.m. the next day, having passed ten flour-laden lorries with their back axles sunk through the ice, and a young soldier dying of exposure.[4]

No further convoys attempted this route. On 9 December, after a series of piecemeal attacks on the overextended German salient's southern flank, the Fourth Army, taken over by General Meretskov a month earlier, finally retook Tikhvin in heavy fighting, leaving up to nine thousand German dead.[5] Supply trains could now be unloaded at Tikhvin, and the truck route shortened to 160 kilometres – 130 kilometres overland by way of Novaya Ladoga and Kobona, and 30 over the lake. The liberation of two more railway towns, Voibokalo and Zhikharevo, allowed a further improvement: from 1 January supply trains were able to unload only thirteen kilometres from the lake shore, and the truck route was reduced to less than forty-five kilometres. Thereafter, deliveries over the Ice Road – in reality six different parallel routes – gradually improved. Though plagued by blizzards, bad management (the Road's first head, a Colonel Zhmakin, was sacked for incompetence), German bombing and bottlenecks along the small, underequipped Osinovets–Leningrad railway, a total 270,900 tonnes of food and 90,000 of fuel and other supplies were delivered by the time the ice melted again at the end of April.[6]

Less successful were November and December's attempts to lift the siege itself. On his departure for Moscow, Zhukov had bequeathed the Leningrad front a tiny, bloodily won bridgehead on the left bank of the Neva just to the south of Shlisselburg, the so-called 'Nevsky *pyatachok*', or 'Neva five-kopek piece'. Only two kilometres long and less than a kilometre deep, it looked significant on the maps but was in reality far too small and exposed (the Germans held a fortress-like

power station just along the river) to form the platform for a successful breakout. Successive attempts – on 2, 9, 11 and 13 November
– all failed, at enormous cost.

A parallel breakout attempt, over lake ice to Shlisselburg's north,
was a fiasco. On 13 November the 80th Rifle Division was flown
out of the 'Oranienbaum pocket' to Leningrad, force-marched to
Ladoga and then ordered to charge entrenched German positions.
A large number of men fell through the too-thin ice; others, emaciated and exhausted, dropped even before the attack began. Stalin
was furious at not being informed of the disaster: 'It's very odd that
Comrade Zhdanov seems to feel no need to come to the phone . . .
One supposes that in Comrade Zhdanov's head Leningrad isn't in
the USSR, but on some island in the Pacific Ocean.'[7] Zhdanov
scapegoated the hapless officers in charge, Colonel Ivan Frolov and
Commissar Konstantin Ivanov. Three hours before the attack began,
their sentencing document records, Frolov had 'declared to two Front
representatives that he did not believe in the successful outcome of
the operation' – words underlined in the copy sent to Zhdanov.
On 3 December both men were shot, for 'cowardice and defeatism'.[8] In total, of the roughly 300,000 Red Army troops employed
in the battle for Tikhvin and its associated offensives, 110,000 were
recorded as ill or wounded, and 80,000 as killed, captured or missing. On the German side, casualties were 45,000.

For the Eastern Front in general, the close of 1941 was nonetheless a genuine turning point. The Germans had encircled Leningrad
but failed to take it, and were also being brought to a halt outside
Moscow. In early November, slowed by slushy snow and Zhukov's
brilliantly organised resistance, Operation Typhoon had begun
to peter out. The psychological turning point was 7 November –
Revolution Day – on the eve of which Stalin gave a defiant speech in
the Mayakovsky metro station, followed by the magnificent gamble
of a full-scale military parade in Red Square. Faced with deepening
cold and mounting casualties, Hitler's generals asked permission to

dig in for the winter. 'The time for spectacular operational feats is past', Halder wrote in his diary on the 11th: 'Our troops can't be moved around any more.' Hitler disagreed, insisting that Moscow be taken by the end of the year. Reluctantly, his generals reanimated the offensive. 'Field Marshal Bock has himself taken charge of the Battle of Moscow, from an advanced command post', Halder noted on the 22nd. 'With enormous energy he drives forward everything that can be brought to bear.' Though the German divisions to the south were 'finished' – one regiment in his old 7th Division, Halder noted, was now commanded by a first lieutenant – in the north they still had a chance of success and were being 'driven relentlessly to achieve it. Von Bock compares the situation to the battle of the Marne, where the last battalion that could be thrown in tipped the balance.' A week later Bock telephoned Halder again. It was not the Marne that he compared the battle to now, but Verdun – 'a brutish chest-to-chest struggle of attrition . . . I emphasise that we too are concerned about the human sacrifice. But an effort must be made to bring the enemy to his knees by applying the last ounce of strength.'[9]

On 16 December – with his forward units tantalisingly within sight of the flash of Moscow's anti-aircraft guns – Hitler finally called a halt. Typhoon was over, but the eastern armies should hold their positions all along the line. More 'stormy discussions', 'mad outbursts' and 'dramatic scenes' followed, as his generals argued for withdrawal to firmer defence lines.[10] Three days later – twelve days after Pearl Harbor and eight after suicidally declaring war on the United States – Hitler sacked von Bock as head of Army Group Centre and Brauchitsch as commander-in-chief, and announced that he was taking over High Command himself. After another furious meeting at the 'Wolf's Lair' on 13 January, von Leeb asked to be relieved as well, and was replaced by the more pliable von Küchler. In the south, Runstedt was replaced by Reichenau, who promptly died of a heart attack. Altogether about forty senior officers resigned or were dismissed. From now on, Hitler's propensity to micromanage military operations would have full rein, with ultimately disastrous results.[11]

This was the point, most military historians agree, at which the whole war turned, not because it was when Germany started to retreat, but in the sense that from then on she stood no further chance of winning. With three great powers ranged against her, she had simply bitten off more than she could chew. In London, Churchill had no doubt. Nothing, he declared to his War Cabinet on 10 December, could compare to the US in warfare, and the Russian front would 'break Germany's heart'. From Leningrad to the Crimea, the Wehrmacht was in 'a frightful condition: mechanised units frozen, prisoners taken in rags, armies trying to stabilise . . . Russian air superiority.' On the state of the Wehrmacht he exaggerated, but his general point was sound: 'Germany is busted as far as knocking out Russia is concerned. The tide has turned and the phase which now begins will have gathering results . . . There should be no anxiety about the eventual outcome of the war. The finger of God is with us.'[12]

Tikhvin having been lost again, Fritz Hockenjos's *Radfahrzug* was ordered to retreat back behind the Volkhov. On 21 December they left their poverty-stricken billet in Rakhmysha, not before setting fire to barns and slaughtering sheep and chickens for the road. 'Women's wailing', Hockenjos wrote, 'followed us out of the village.' Again they pushed their bicycles along choked, snow-covered roads, past broken-down motorised columns and a stream of overladen peasant sleds, cows and goats in tow. The following afternoon they ran into fighting – shouts of 'oorah' up ahead, a burning lorry, injured horses standing in the middle of the road, heads drooping. When darkness fell they crept forwards in the shelter of roadside ditches: 'We came to lots of dead Russians, and then we were through, and ran as fast as we could. When we got to Glad we found the staff of the 2nd Battalion just sitting there, completely oblivious. I could have wept.'

At 3 a.m. they set off again, firing blindly into the woods either side
of the road in reply to shots from invisible Russians. With daylight
they came under heavy fire while passing a supply column:

> Bangs and whistles everywhere. The injured are brought in, coats
> and boots cut off. Open wounds leak dark blood. And next to
> all that people stand about, smoking and munching *Knäckebrot*.
> Only when there was lots of whizzing in the air did they take cover
> behind their vehicles or horses for a moment. I couldn't decide
> whether this was admirable equanimity or stupid indifference.

They were among the last troops back over the Volkhov at Gruzino,
crossing as darkness fell. Behind, the skyline glowed red where villages
burned. On Christmas Eve they reached Chudovo, a town on the
main Leningrad–Moscow railway line, and settled for the night in an
empty-windowed glassworks. 'We huddle with our cigarettes in front
of the great glass ovens', Hockenjos wrote. 'In one corner a Christmas
tree is being set up; in another some engineers are building tables
and benches. Someone is bashfully practising carols on a harmonica.
I have my notebook open on my knees and am writing a Christmas
letter to Els by the light of the flames. I have never felt further from
my love, nor closer to her, than this evening.' In the distance he
could hear the thump of shells, as the Russians 'threw suitcases' at
the railway station – it was amazing how fast they had brought up
their heavy artillery. When he and his men toasted Christ's birth at
midnight, it was with looted armagnac that they had brought with
them all the way from the Loire.

Sleds and Cocoons

At 60° north, Leningrad is on the same latitude as the Shetland Islands, and only a couple of degrees short of Anchorage. In midwinter, the sun rises at nine, hanging blindingly low in the sky until it sets again at three. Today, winter temperatures usually average around -10°C, but in January 1942 they dipped into the -30s. Head-high snow-drifts blocked the streets, metre-long glassy spears hung off the tram wires and the women turning rocket-casings at the Bolshevik plant were able to score a length of metal piping, tap it with a hammer, and break it clean through. During the short, bright days, for those with the energy to notice, the city looked extraordinarily beautiful – the air, free of the usual coal smoke, dazzlingly clear; the snow, unsullied by vehicles, a chemical blue-white. During the eighteen hours of silent, blacked-out darkness (the cold had grounded the German bombers), one felt one was living at the bottom of a well, or in the depths of the ocean.

Leningraders saw in the New Year as best they could. Vera Inber spent the first part of the evening at a poetry reading held in the red drawing room of the Writers' Union building on Shpalernaya, the long, rather dull boulevard, lined with government buildings, that runs from the centre of town to the Smolniy. A few small logs burned in the fireplace, and a single candle on the podium table. 'It was very cold. My turn came. I moved closer to the candle and started on the

first stanza of my new poem (I haven't decided on a title yet). It was
the first time I had read it in public. When I got to the part where
I curse Germany I could hardly breathe – I had to stop and start
again three times.' At midnight, back at the Erisman Hospital, she
and her husband went downstairs to the medical superintendent's
consulting room:

> We took with us our last bottle of Riesling. We poured the wine
> into glasses, but then the telephone rang. It was the doctor on duty
> in Casualty, reporting that he had forty dead bodies lying in the
> corridors and some even in the bathroom. He didn't know what
> to do. So the Medical Superintendent went down to Casualty, and
> we went back up to our room and bed.[1]

Vasili Chekrizov, returned from erecting pillboxes at the front,
spent New Year's Eve at the Sudomekh shipyard. For a month it had
had no electricity: 'We're doing damn all, and this hurts morale.
People should at least be allowed to go home, but the management keeps them here all day . . . I'm told that in Workshop no. 3
they're making eight to ten coffins daily – and that's just in our one
factory.' Leningraders no longer, he noted, took any notice of shelling: he had seen passers-by fight for bits of a broken wooden fence
in the midst of a bombardment; a colleague had seen a crowd tear
to pieces a newly killed horse. 'In an hour', he wrote as midnight
neared,

> 1942 will be with us. I'm sitting in our common room, lit only by
> the stove. In this respect at least, we're well off – we've got almost
> unlimited firewood. I'm sitting re-warming the coffee in my cup.
> Radio reception is good for once – New Year's Eve speeches . . .
> It's a hard way to meet the New Year – hunger and cold; people
> dying every day. But the speeches are full of optimism. The dark,
> difficult times are behind us. Though there's no improvement in

food supply you can almost smell the enemy's destruction and retreat.

Like thousands of others, he thought of his wife and son: 'How are Dina and Gelik? Did they get the money? If they did then they're all right. What luck that they aren't here. How could I have faced Gelik, seeing him hungry and not being able to do anything to help?'[2]

Yelena Kochina got up at four o'clock in the morning to queue for one of the bottles of wine distributed to mark the holiday:

> The hours ran silently after one another like grey rats, disappearing into the darkness. But I kept on standing and standing, repeating to myself the chant – 'Everything comes to an end, everything comes to an end . . .' The moon dimmed; the sky turned grey, then white, then blue . . . The night had passed. At three o'clock in the afternoon I got the bottle with its pretty little shiny cap.

She took the bottle straight to a street market, where she was lucky to trade it (with a sailor) for a large piece of bread. Back at home, she and her husband passed the evening together in grim, apathetic silence:

> Dima doesn't steal bread any more. For days at a time now he lies with his face to the wall . . . His face is covered with soot – even his fine pale eyelashes have become thick and black. I can't imagine him clean, smart and neat like he used to be. But of course I'm not much better. Lice torment us both. We sleep together – we've only got one bed – but even through padded coats it's unpleasant feeling the other's touch.[3]

Leningrad was now entering its period of mass death. In December, according to police records (certainly a substantial undercount), starvation and its related conditions – 'dystrophy' in a new coinage

– had killed 52,881 out of the city's civilian population of about two and a half million.[4] January's toll was 96,751 and February's 96,015.

The sight of death, already commonplace by the end of the year, now became universal. 'Early this morning', wrote a manager at the Lenenergo power station, '[the director] Chistyakov's father died. He's still lying on a daybed in Chistyakov's office. Next to him Chistyakov carries on working and eating, and takes rests on the same bed. Colleagues and visitors come and go – the dead man disturbs no-one.'[5] As if caught in Vesuvius's gas cloud, the corpses of the many who collapsed outside on the street also remained as they were, huddled in doorways or slumped against walls and fences. 'On the pavements', wrote Ostroumova-Lebedeva on 18 January,

> lots of wooden boxes have been erected, and filled with sand. There's no water, so these sandboxes are all we have to fight fires with. Today, walking along the street, I saw a very old woman sitting on one of these sandboxes. She was dead. A few buildings further on, on another box, a dead boy slouched. He had been walking along, became exhausted, sat down and died.

Vera Kostrovitskaya, a dance teacher at the Mariinsky ballet school and niece of the Franco-Polish poet Apollinaire, recorded the gradual stripping of a corpse that leant against a lamp-post opposite the Philharmonia:

> With his back to the post, a man sits in the snow, wrapped in rags, wearing a knapsack . . . Probably he was on his way to Finland Station, got tired and sat down to rest. For two weeks I passed him every day as I went back and forth to the hospital. He sat 1. Without his knapsack; 2. Without his rags; 3. In his underwear; 4. Naked; 5. A skeleton with ripped out entrails. They took him away in May.[6]

Shock and horror disguised themselves as gallows humour. The shrouded corpses pulled along the streets, sometimes two at a time, on sleds, prams, handcarts or sheets of plywood, were nicknamed 'mummies' or 'cocoons'. A 'strengthened supplementary food' ration – the *usilennoye dopolnitelnoye pitaniye* or UDP – sometimes issued to the dying became *umresh dnem pozzhe* or 'You'll die a day later'.[7] Saying goodbye, people told each other not to 'end up in the trenches' – referring not to the trench warfare of the front, but to the newly dug pits in the cemeteries. The soldiers who did the rounds of the streets picking up bodies dumped outside on the pavements called their job 'gathering flowers', because the heads of the dead were often wrapped in bright-coloured cloth, so as to make them easier to spot under the snow.[8] Bodies were also deposited in the open slit trenches in the parks, which formed impromptu mass graves when their props were looted for firewood, causing them gradually to collapse. The whole, as ever, was gloatingly recorded by German intelligence. On Prospekt Stachek (a long thoroughfare running through the south-western industrial suburbs), a report of 12 January noted, six people had collapsed and died, and their corpses been left lying. 'Such cases have become so common that nobody pays any attention to them, and general exhaustion is anyway such that only a few can give real help.'[9]

In part thanks to the design of the rationing system, mortality followed a clear demographic. In January 73 per cent of fatalities were male, and 74 per cent children under five or adults aged forty or over. By May the majority – 65 per cent – were female, and a slightly smaller majority – 59 per cent – children under five or adults aged forty or over. Children aged ten to nineteen made up only 3 per cent of the total in the first ten days of December, but 11 per cent in May.[10] Within a single family, therefore, the order in which its members typically died was grandfather and infants first, grandmother and father (if not at the front) second, mother and older children last.

The point at which an entire family was doomed was when its last mobile member became too weak to queue for rations. Heads of households – usually mothers – were thus faced with a heartbreaking dilemma: whether to eat more food themselves, so as to stay on their feet, or whether to give more to the family's sickest member – usually a grandparent or child – and risk the lives of all. That many or most prioritised their children is indicated by the large numbers of orphans they left behind. The lucky ones were put into children's homes; the unlucky had their cards stolen by neighbours, took to thieving on the streets or simply died alone.[11]

The physical symptoms of starvation, suffered in varying combinations by the large majority of Leningraders, were emaciation, dropsical swelling of the legs and face, skin discolouration ('hunger tan' in the slang of the time – faces are described as turning 'black', 'blue-black', 'yellow' or 'green'), ulcers, loosening or loss of teeth and weakening of the heart. Women stopped menstruating and sexual desire vanished. The optical engineer Dmitri Lazarev described how it felt in his diary:

For a long time I have wanted to write down what a person emaciated from starvation experiences. You sleep very little – six or seven hours. Throughout the night you continuously pull up your covers and tuck them in, for you are always cold. The cold pours along your spine and whole body. Your protruding bones ache, forcing you to keep changing position. All the time you are tortured by hunger; you can feel the emptiness of your stomach, and convulsively swallow your own saliva. It's difficult to perform any sort of physical movement, even the most insignificant. Before turning over in bed, you take a long time to gather your strength. You procrastinate, put it off. In your mind you repeat the necessary sequence of actions over and over again, before actually committing to them. The morning arrives and it's very hard to overcome your inertia, to get up and get dressed. During the day your movements are slow and careful. Despite wearing warm clothes you feel chilled, and are dogged by an unpleasant sensation of noise in your ears. Your own breathing and speech resonate as if in an empty vessel. Your feet swell, and deep cracks form in the skin of your fingers . . . You exist on the sidelines to everything going on around you. In the canteen, for example, you meet a friend, a colleague, and don't have the energy even to say hello. You look at him expressionlessly, and he returns the same look. Why waste strength on words?[12]

Lidiya Ginzburg describes starvation as a sort of premature ageing, combined with alienation from the body:

The mind hauled the body along . . . Let's say I move my right leg forward. The other one moves back, pivots on its toes and bends at the knee (how poorly it manages that!) then pulls itself off the ground and moves forward through the air . . . You have to watch the way it goes back, otherwise you might fall over. It was the most ghastly dancing lesson.

Even more insulting in its abruptness was losing one's balance. It wasn't weakness, nor staggering from exhaustion, but something else altogether. You want to put your foot on the edge of a chair to tie your shoelaces; but at that very moment your temples begin to thud and you are overcome with giddiness. The body has just slithered out of control and wants to fall like an empty sack into some incomprehensible abyss.

A whole series of foul processes went on inside the alienated body – degeneration, drying-out, swelling up, not like good old-fashioned illness. Some of these processes were imperceptible to the person stricken with them. 'He's already swelling up, isn't he?' they say . . . but he hasn't realised it yet . . . Then he suddenly becomes aware that his gums have swollen. He feels them with his tongue, terrified, then prods them with his finger. He can't leave

them alone, especially at night. He lies there with an intense feeling of something hardened and slippery, its numbness especially
frightening: a layer of dead tissue inside his mouth.[13]

In starvation's final stages, sufferers resembled barely animated
skeletons, with hollow stomachs, sunken cheeks, protruding jaws
and blank, frightening stares. 'His legs moved like artificial limbs',
Inber wrote of a man she saw being helped along the street. 'His
eyes stared madly, as if he were possessed. The skin on his face was
tightly stretched, the lips half open, revealing teeth which seemed
enlarged . . . His nose, sharpened as if it had melted, was covered
with small sores, and the tip had bent slightly sideways. Now I know
what is meant by 'gnawed by hunger'.[14]

Through January and February the city Party Committee issued a
stream of orders – on the manufacture of *burzhuiki*, chlorine tablets
and vaccines, on the 'holding to account' of pharmacy managers,
on the sorting of undelivered mail, on the provision of pillows and
linen to orphanages, the formation of teams of plumbers to repair
the sewage system, the delivery of 13,000 pairs of cotton socks to a
hospital. All fell into a void.

Among the many government agencies to cease functioning was
the fire service. Set alight by bombardment, home-made stoves or
by the twists of paper and splinters of wood used as torches once the
kerosene for 'bats' and 'smokers' ran out, buildings burned for days.
The health service was completely overwhelmed. 'In Hospital 25th
Anniversary of October', ran a report to Popkov, head of the city
soviet, of 12 February,

bedlinen has not been washed since 15 January . . . The wards
are completely unheated, so some patients have been moved into
the corridors, which have temporary stoves. Due to the very low
temperatures patients cover themselves not only with hospital

blankets but with dirty mattresses and their own coats . . . The
lavatories are not working and the floors are not being washed.

Of the hospital's 181 doctors only 27 were reporting for duty, of its
298 nurses only 163, and over a thousand corpses had piled up in its
mortuary and storage rooms. In the Raukhfus Children's Hospital,
which on some days had no heating at all, patients slept two or
three to a bed. They had not been washed or had their bedlinen
changed for six weeks, with the result that all had lice. Two hundred
and ninety-nine corpses awaited removal.[15] A pile of dead also grew
outside the Erisman's rear entrance on the Karpovka canal – overflow
from its mortuary plus neighbourhood fatalities deposited there by
relatives. 'Each day now', wrote Inber,

> eight to ten bodies are brought in on sleds. And they just lie there
> on the snow. Fewer and fewer coffins are available, so too the
> materials to make them. The bodies are wrapped in sheets, blan-
> kets, tablecloths – sometimes even in curtains. Once I saw a small
> bundle wrapped in paper and tied with string. It was very small
> – the body of a child.
>
> How macabre they look on the snow! Occasionally an arm or
> leg protrudes from the crude wrappings . . . It reminds me of a
> battlefield and of a doss-house, both at the same time.[16]

Dmitri Lazarev, who visited the Erisman to take leave of a friend,
described overflowing slop buckets – 'honey-buckets' – and the only
nursing as being done by visitors.[17] On 15 January its mortuary went
up in flames, the origin of the fire the still-smouldering quilted jackets, lined with raw cotton wadding, of workers killed in a factory
blaze. Overall, according to the city health department, 40 per cent
of those admitted to its seventy-three hospitals in the first quarter
of 1942 died in them. Wide discrepancies between different institutions – the Karl Marx Hospital reported 84 per cent mortality

among patients admitted in January, the October District Second
Children's Hospital only 12 per cent – suggest the figure may be less
than complete.[18]

Marina Yerukhmanova witnessed the rapid deterioration of conditions in the hotel-turned-hospital Yevropa. On 16 November a bomb
had landed just outside the main entrance, knocking out its electricity supply, and with it heating, lighting, stoves and lifts. Remaining
peacetime trappings – starched tablecloths, white-jacketed waiters
– quickly fell away, but the hospital managed to keep on operating
fairly normally until New Year, when its running water failed and
its lavatories froze. Thereafter it quickly descended into squalor and
disorder. Patients relieved themselves on the marble main staircase,
turning it into a 'yellow ice mountain'. They set up a black market
in the second-floor restaurant, and mugged the orderlies – many,
like Marina and her sister, gently reared 'Turgenev girls' – carrying
food along the dark corridors. *Shtrafniki* – dark-skinned, glittering-
eyed soldiers from the 16th Punishment Battalion, mostly former
convicts – took over the grandest bedrooms, pinning rugs over their
shoulders and twisting velvet curtains into turbans 'like the crew of
a pirate ship'. A grand piano was gradually stripped of its mahogany casing, which went into stoves for fuel, and the 'Eastern' dining
room with its stained-glass longboats was turned into a mortuary.

On 4 January, having been working fifteen-hour days carrying
buckets of hot water up four flights of ice-covered stairs, Marina
collapsed with stomach pains. A kind nurse put the girls and their
mother into what had been one of the hotel's cheaper bedrooms,
on the top floor. Its grey-painted walls were covered with fernlike
swirls of hoarfrost, the indoor temperature being eleven degrees
below freezing. What allowed them to make the room habitable was
Marina's mother's discovery of a half-litre bottle of alcohol in the
hotel's former pharmacy. With one half of it she bought *sukhari*,
and with the other paid a man to make a *burzhuika* out of a bucket.
Stoked with broken-up furniture and the hotel's old personnel files

– Marina and her sister leafed through application letters from long-gone wine waiters and pastry chefs before feeding them to the flames – the stove turned the room into the Yerukhmanovas' 'ark'. Two nurses moved in, one with her elderly mother; no gloomy talk was allowed and everyone got fully undressed daily, so that they could check each other's clothes for lice. The 'ark' could not, however, carry all. A first cousin, twelve-year-old Lesha, came to visit early in the New Year:

> The little boy had reached the last stage of starvation. He was all oedema – the liquid had swelled his body so much that it seemed as if his skin wouldn't hold . . . We somehow pulled him together, gave him something to eat. Like a stuck record, he kept repeating and repeating that he would die within a week, his mother maybe sooner, and so on and so on. And we sat and listened, but our feelings were so blunted . . . We lived only in order to live. Thought and emotion somehow came to a standstill.

All over the city, public institutions – schools, factories, banks, post offices, police stations, university departments – similarly ground to a halt, though employees with strength enough continued to turn up for warmth, companionship and the chance of obtaining a plate of watery soup in the canteen. 'In the mornings', Lazarev wrote of his Optical Institute, 'we sat round the stove in silence, heads bowed. We sat for hours, not moving, not talking. When there was no more firewood the stove went out. Though there was a big pile of wood in the courtyard nobody had the strength to chop it and carry it up the stairs. Instead, we sat out the wait until lunch in the cold. After lunch we went home.' The first to die (as in Georgi Knyazev's Academicians' Building and Olga Grechina's apartment block) were the Institute's ancillary staff. 'The old cleaning lady has just died of hunger', he wrote on 25 December. 'Only the day before yesterday she was dusting my desk. I'm told that she went home, lay down on her bed, stretched out her arms, sighed and died. Today, entering the lab, I saw the corpse of our recently deceased security guard in the next room.'

Unlike the cleaning lady, Lazarev had access to the Scholars' Building, a clubhouse for academics splendidly housed a few doors down from the Hermitage on the Neva. Through September *piro-zhki*, coffee and potatoes had been available there off-ration, though by New Year this had been cut to soup and sweet tea. 'In the freezing hall', wrote Lazarev

> a long queue winds up the marble staircase. People stand and wait in silence. Almost everyone carries a document case over their shoulder, with hidden inside it a container for carrying food back home to the family. The wait feels endless. It's especially cold standing next to the massive marble banisters – a perceptible wave of cold streams off them. At last our turn comes, and we enter the canteen. Frozen, in fur coats and hats, we sit down at the free tables. After some time a desultory conversation begins. A zoologist – tall and formerly overweight – complains that people of different sizes are all given the same food. 'Mark my words, bigger men . . .' But nobody listens to him, since Katyusha is approaching our table with her scissors and the matchbox for coupons. She is our favourite waitress – it seems to us that she serves up faster, and that her portions are a little bigger. People come to the canteen with their own plates and spoons. The respectable grey-haired professor licks his plate clean before hiding it in his gas-mask bag.[19]

Lazarev himself fell gravely ill in the spring, and was reprieved only by a providential secondment to a minelayer, which as well as providing him with proper meals allowed him to pass his ration cards to his wife and daughter.

The Leningrad Party Committee officially closed 270 factories over the winter, but most of the rest hardly functioned and even what remained of the defence plants managed only a little erratic repair work.[20] Olga Grechina, orphaned by her mother's death in January, stood guard duty at night in her semi-shut missile factory. Alone in the empty workshops she kept fear at bay by reading H. G. Wells's *The War of the Worlds* by the light of a 'bat' – the person on duty got the best book, as a distraction from the rats that scuttered 'loathsomely and incessantly' across the concrete floors. Off-duty she sat in the warmth of the janitor's room, stripping pine branches of their needles for processing into a vitamin C drink – another food supplement devised by the Forestry Academy. The job paid her a single meal at 2 a.m. each day, of soup and *kasha*.

Out of the 270 workers of Workshop 15 of Vasili Chekrizov's Sudomekh shipyard, 47 had died by the end of January. 'How many will die in February nobody knows. Only seventy appear for roll-call, or at the canteen. All the others are lying down . . . Skilled, qualified workmen, the backbone of the shop, have died . . . Only a few people are working on repairs, and you can't really call it work – in truth they're just marking time.'[21] The usual draconian punishments for absenteeism ceased to have any effect. At the Marti shipyard, a report to Zhdanov of early February complained,

> hundreds of people fail to appear for work, and nobody pays any attention. Every day the number absent without leave rises . . . After the district Party Committee told the management that their behaviour sheltered truants, in the course of two days they brought proceedings against seventy-two absentees. But this was not the end of [the management's] mistakes. Of the 72 cases half had to be sent back again, for lack of evidence.[22]

Academic life kept going for a remarkably long time. The Persianist Aleksandr Boldyrev was still taking tutorials in the Hermitage in late December (and scolding his students for turning in poor work). Nikolai Punin was doing the same until late November. At the Erisman Hospital the pathologist Vladimir Garshin lectured through the air raids, and held exams as usual at the end of the winter term, even as his students died in their hostels. (The single men, he noticed, collapsed first; girls and married couples lasted longer.) The only way to keep going, he thought, was to keep working:

> So we invent things for the laboratory assistants to do, just to keep them occupied. If you stop working, lie down, it's bad – there's no guarantee you'll get up again. One of the assistants died in the lab itself. She was found in the morning curled up in a ball underneath a warm shawl, wearing new brown felt boots. She hadn't gone home, it was too far. Another assistant's husband was killed in the street during an artillery barrage. She took two days' absence and then returned to work, her dropsy-swollen face even puffier from tears. She is silent. Does work go on? Yes it does, somehow. The important thing is not to give up. The examinations are happening, and I'm taking the orals – their presentations aren't bad! The lectures sank in after all! And the examiner, my assistant, grills them thoroughly but gently. Where do they get their strength from?[23]

Inber watched another Erisman doctor defend his thesis in the hospital's air-raid shelter; the toasts afterwards were drunk in diluted spirits.[24]

The higher-profile institutions especially persisted in a defiant, almost surreal facsimile of normal life right through the winter's worst days. On 9 February Inber attended a two-day Conference of Baltic Writers, organised by the Writers' Union. To prepare she darned extra gloves and stockings, swapped four canteen meals for two eggs and a small piece of dried-up cheese, and dipped into her private food stock for a bar of chocolate. The walk from the Erisman to the conference venue, in normal times a pleasant stroll from the

Petrograd Side to Vasilyevsky Island, took two hours, during which she passed snowed-in trams, a building that had been burning, unattended, all night, and a street flooded by a broken fire hydrant, the unexpected water giving off twists of vapour that caught the pink dawn light. At the end of a day of readings, reports and speeches she retired to a bunk set up behind a curtain in the tobacco-fugged conference hall. In the early hours she was woken by the sound of smashing wood. 'It was Z, who was using an axe to demolish the chair on which he had been sitting during the presentations. I watched him throw the pieces into the stove – helpless Leningrad chairs! I grew warm again and went back to sleep.'

At the Academy of Sciences Georgi Knyazev, confined more than ever to his 'small radius' because the cold had seized up his wheelchair, watched helplessly as his subordinates – to whom he had so recently given pep talks – died around him. 'Shakhmatova Kaplan and her sixteen-year-old son Alyosha', he wrote on 5 January, 'have died of dystrophy. The boy was extremely gifted and loved astronomy. He would undoubtedly have made a name for himself, perhaps even have become an Academician. The news greatly affected me and all our staff.' The following day a Commission on the History of the Academy of Sciences went ahead with a scheduled meeting, at which Knyazev presented a report ('perhaps my last') titled 'The History of the Heads of the Academy's Departments Throughout its Existence (1925–1941)'. As he read a 'poor wretch' lay outside in the courtyard, already stripped of his boots. Keeping up a confident façade, Knyazev admitted to his diary, was now almost impossible:

I try to smile when I'm with other people, to sound cheerful and optimistic, to raise their spirits . . . Only here, on these pages, do I permit myself to relax my self-restraint. Here I am as I really am. I saw Svikul, who has just lost her fifteen-year-old son Volodya, a modest youngster. Inconsolable grief, despair – these are pitiful words in comparison with what is expressed in her eyes, her sunken cheeks and quivering chin. I put my arms around her, hugged her, and that was all I could do.[25]

At the Hermitage, staff and their families – about two thousand people altogether – had moved permanently into twelve air-raid shelters in the palace vaults, where they slept on plank beds incongruously mixed with ancient Turkmen rugs and gilded palace furniture. Area-level windows having been bricked up, the rooms were almost pitch-black even in daytime. One, the office of museum director Iosif Orbeli, was supplied with electricity via a cable led in from Tsar Nicholas's old pleasure yacht the *Polar Star*, moored outside on the Neva. Otherwise, the only light came from icon lamps and 'bats' – fuelled, one memoir claims, with seal oil from the zoo. Several female members of staff, Boldyrev noted, bashfully produced long-hidden wedding candles – the tall, ribboned beeswax tapers held by bride and groom during the traditional Orthodox marriage service.

One of the most famous blockade-defying events of the winter was a symposium held by the Hermitage in mid-December, to celebrate the five hundredth anniversary of the birth of the Timurid poet Alisher Navai. A display was put together of porcelain decorated with scenes from Navai's verse (an artist from the old Imperial porcelain works, Mikhail Mokh, painted a small bowl in the style of a Mogul miniature); Boldyrev gave a paper and his fellow Persianist Nikolai Lebedev (so weak that he had to remain seated) read his own new Navai translation. The audience included Boldyrev's elderly mother, who insisted on contributing a small piece of bread with pork fat to the official lunch. It didn't matter, one attendee remembered, that there was not a single Uzbek amongst them – the event was 'a challenge to the enemy. Light was fighting darkness.'[26] Boldyrev, ever the realist, thought his old friend Lebedev's presentation 'bad and disorganised', but the translation itself 'wonderful – the bright clear language of Pushkin's fairy tales'. His own paper had been worth the effort too: 'In work lies the only happiness and satisfaction of our days. The worse the situation physically – up to a point – the brighter and fresher the workings of our minds.'[27]

Two months later Boldyrev heard of Lebedev's death, from starvation combined with dysentery. He had last seen him a fortnight earlier, in the Hermitage cellars:

> He and his wife were lying in cold and complete darkness, in the underground hell of the basement (shelter no. 3). He recognised me by my voice, and grabbed me like a drowning man clutching at a straw. They gave me 250 roubles, imploring me to buy bread and candles for them in the market . . . His last words to me were 'How I want to live, Sandrik, how I want to live!' He spoke with that amazing, melodious voice of his, with which he so inimitably read his marvellous, musical translations . . . At that point I was too squeezed myself to give real help, and couldn't buy him anything. Rather Galya, who did occasionally go to the market, didn't make it, not having the strength. And bread was hardly being sold for money anyway.[28]

Also celebrated as a manifestation of the defiant Leningrad spirit is the fact that some of its dozens of theatres and concert halls continued to function. The Musical Comedy Theatre – the *Muzkomediya* – stayed open almost throughout the winter, and concerts continued to be held under the crystal-less chandeliers of the Philharmonia into December. (Of the string players, an audience member noted, only the double bassists could wear sheepskin coats. The rest wore padded cotton jackets, which allowed freer movement of the arms.) It is claimed that altogether, Leningraders enjoyed over twenty-five thousand public performances of different kinds in the course of the blockade, and the image of artists flinging themselves into war work – Shostakovich on the roof of the Conservatoire, Akhmatova standing guard duty outside the Sheremetyev Palace, prima ballerinas sewing camouflage nets – is one of the key tropes of the siege.

At the time, however, many Leningraders were cynical. As one diarist noted of a concert given by the great violinist David Oistrakh (flown in from Moscow for the occasion), the audience were not the usual intelligentsia types, and appeared unusually healthy. He and his wife were by far the most 'dystrophic-looking' present.[29] Even a fervent Stalinist, watching crowds jostle for tickets to an operetta (*A Sailor's Love*) in March 1942, was reminded of bread and circuses.[30] One of the bitterest siege diary entries must be the following, written by Vera Kostrovitskaya, the dance teacher at the Mariinsky ballet school:

Since in April it became necessary to portray the rebirth of the city at the hands of the half-dead, L.S.T. [the school's director] got the vain idea that our school – or to be more accurate, what was left of it – would give the first [springtime] public performance at the Philharmonia.

Some of the girls had stayed relatively healthy, thanks to fortunate conditions at home, but they all had scurvy. The most talented of them, Lyusa Alekseyeva, couldn't dance the classics – her legs, covered with blue blotches, gave way and wouldn't obey.

I informed L.S.T. of the situation.

In reply there came a furious shout and threats to deny those who refused to dance their ration coupons for the next month . . .

The performance took place. We even had the 'dying swan' and other balletic nonsense. Petya, made up by me to look like a living person, 'danced' two numbers. To keep him going, the girls had brought him bread and *kasha*. I led him on stage and tried not to watch as he 'danced'. During the break he collapsed into my arms and vomited the *kasha* he had eaten.

There was no public audience at the concert, for there was none in the city. The first two rows were taken by arts administrators and representatives from the Smolniy and Party organisations. With her hair dyed red and dressed up like a model, L.S.T. shone during the *entr'acte*, accepting greetings and unnaturally loudly recounting her love for the children, whose lives she had been busy saving all through the winter.

Petya died soon afterwards, in an orphanage, and L.S.T. – one Lidiya Semenovna Tager – continued to flaunt a succession of new hats and fur coats, bought with food that she was able to obtain in her position as wife of the Leningrad Front's head of provisioning.[31]

Oddest, viewed from a utilitarian perspective, of the institutional stories is perhaps that of the Leningrad Zoo, a small and charming establishment, dating back to the 1860s, located behind the Peter and Paul Fortress on the Petrograd Side. The zoo had evacuated fifty-eight of its more valuable animals to Kazan before the siege ring closed, and others had been killed in the early air raids. The city soviet, instead of ordering the slaughter and consumption of the remainder, then allocated the zoo a special ration of hay and root vegetables, with which, by dint of extraordinary dedication and ingenuity, staff kept eighty-five animals alive through the winter. Foxes, ermines, raccoons and vultures, they discovered, could be persuaded to eat a 'vegetable mince' of bran, *duranda* and potatoes if it was first soaked in a little blood or bone broth, but for fussier tigers, owls and eagles it had to be sewn into the skins of rabbits or guinea pigs. When the zoo reopened the following summer the survivors – Verochka the black vulture, Sailor the Nilgai antelope and Grishka the bear – turned into celebrities. Undisputed star was the hippopotamus Krasavitsa, or 'Beauty'. The only hippo in the Soviet Union, she had been nursed through the winter by her devoted keeper Yevdokiya Dashina, who daily washed her with forty buckets of warm water hauled by hand from the Neva, and rubbed her baggy grey skin with camphor oil to stop it cracking.[32] A photograph from 1943 shows Krasavitsa and Dashina standing together in a muddy enclosure. Dashina holds out a piece of greenery; the hippo rests with her chin on the ground, squinting at the camera with a small, lashed eye. Behind the massive animal, on a railing, sit a row of large-kneed, shaven-headed children.

Achievements such as these, though, were specks of light in a vast darkness. More indicative of the state of the city as a whole were the activities of the Burial Trust, the agency in charge of morgues and cemeteries.[33] For the first few months of the war its 250-odd staff, twelve motor vehicles and thirty-four horses had coped with their increased workload fairly well. Some 3,688 burials – not much above the pre-war number – took place in July 1941, 5,090 in August, 7,820 in September, 9,355 in October and 11,401 in November. Though two out of eight designated new burial sites – pre-prepared in expectation of mass air-raid casualties – ended up on the wrong side of the front line, 80 to 85 per cent of bodies delivered to morgues were positively identified by family members and buried individually in the usual way. The rest were registered and photo-graphed by the police.

From December, however, procedures broke down completely, as 'mummy'-laden sleds began to fill the main streets leading to the big suburban cemeteries. Inside the cemetery gates, Trust staff (forty-six of whom died during the winter) were overwhelmed, leaving an opening for 'cemetery wolves' who brought their own crowbars and offered to dig individual graves in exchange for bread or money. Coffins could be had for temporary hire, as could actual graves, in which corpses were briefly deposited before being slung into trenches with the rest. One woman, depositing her dead father at the Serafimovskoye cemetery in March, could not afford an individ-ual burial, but agreed with workers that for twenty-five roubles they would place him on the edge rather than in the middle of a mass grave, having first removed him from his coffin. On her way out she noticed a grotesque piece of graveyard humour: a corpse propped vertically with a cigarette in its mouth, pointing trenchwards with an outstretched, frozen arm.[34]

Increasingly, relatives only made it as far as the new temporary morgues, opened in each of the fifteen city districts in part so as to shorten the funeral caravans on the streets, which as the Trust remarked made 'a bad impression on the population'. One such morgue is graphically described by the optical engineer Dmitri Lazarev, disposing of his dead father-in-law in late January:

The building manager wrote down the address on a scrap paper – Glukhaya Zelenina ['Lonely Green'] Street. He gave us a sled, and warned us that unless they are in coffins corpses can now only be transported through the streets after 8 p.m. Even for the time of year it was unusually cold – 35 degrees below zero. Nina, Nika and I tied Vladimir Aleksandrovich to a board with towels, and with great difficulty lowered him down the dark stairs. Nina stayed at home to put the children to bed; Nika and I dragged the sled to Glukhaya Zelenina . . . We pulled together at first, then took turns, so that the other person could turn his back to the wind and warm up his face and hands a little. The trip – in reality a fairly short distance – seemed never-ending. Finally we reached the gates of the morgue, previously a woodstore. The woman on the door, also half-dead from cold, was getting ready to go home, and in a martyred voice told us to hurry. We dragged the sled along a narrow cleared path through the yard to a big shed. Opening its door wide, in the moonlight we saw a mountain of corpses, half-dressed or sewn into sheets, and dumped in a heap like firewood. Impatiently, the woman indicated that the new delivery should be thrown on top of the mountain . . . There was nobody else there and she stood on the sidelines, clearly not intending to help. We untied the body from the boards and tried to lift it, but without success – our wasted muscles didn't have the strength. There was nothing for it except to try and drag it up the pile. The easiest way, it turned out, was to take it by the legs. Stumbling we began to climb, treading on slippery, frozen-solid stomachs, backs and heads. Despite the cold there was a suffocating stench. When, exhausted, we came to a halt, the head and shoulders of poor Vladimir Aleksandrovich still lay outside. The woman pushed at his head with the shed door, seeing if it would close. We needed to climb higher but couldn't. At last, in desperation, we gave a jerk and the body moved sideways, its head swinging to one side. At the same time the door closed, and something rattled. It was the woman fussing with the door latch, seeing if it would hold shut. For several minutes we stood in complete darkness, afraid to move . . . The door opened. Carefully, holding each other by the hand, we descended into the open, and all three of us sighed with relief. The woman (could she have been the morgue manager?) carelessly stuffed the paperwork into her pocket and the funeral was over.[35]

Sixteen more such morgues opened in April, several of them in disused churches, including the Trinity Cathedral and the chapel of the Alexander Nevsky monastery.

On 15 January the city soviet ordered the digging of more, bigger trenches at the Bolsheokhtinskoye cemetery (just across the river from the Smolniy), the Serafimovskoye cemetery in Novaya Derevnya, the old Lutheran cemetery on Decembrists' Island, and at the Piskarevskoye and Bogoslovskoye cemeteries in the far north-eastern suburbs. Though each of the fifteen district soviets was supposed to find four hundred workers to man new burial teams, only one actually did so, and the job was turned over to NKVD troops and civil defence units. The 'Komsomolets' excavators with which they started work proved unable to break the ground, which had frozen to a depth of one and a half metres, so instead explosives were used, together with heavier AK diggers.

A second order of 2 February instructed district soviets to come up with a daily total of sixty lorries with trailers, for the collection of corpses from morgues and hospitals. Five-tonne trucks were to transport one hundred corpses per trip, three-tonne trucks sixty corpses, and one and a half-tonne trucks forty. Drivers were incentivised with extra rations – 100 grams of bread and fifty of vodka for every second and subsequent delivery. As a result, the Burial Trust reported, for several days in February 'six to seven thousand bodies were delivered daily to the Piskarevskoye Cemetery alone . . . Five-tonne trucks piled high with corpses could be seen driving through town, their poorly covered loads reaching as high again as the sides of the vehicle, with five or six workers sitting on top.' Since the corpses were frozen stiff, to pack in the maximum number collection teams could use the same technique as for logs, some standing vertically so as to form a fence holding in the remainder.[36] At the cemeteries the excavators could not keep up with deliveries, creating enormous backlogs. The number of unburied corpses at the Piskarevskoye, the Trust estimated, reached 20,000–25,000 at its February worst, stacked in rows two hundred metres long and two metres high.

Though the conversion of brick kilns to crematoria in March, combined with decreasing mortality, gradually brought the situation under control, mass burial continued up to the end of May. At the Piskarevskoye (the largest of the sites) a total of 129 trenches were dug, filled and re-covered from 16 December to 1 May. The biggest six – four to five metres deep, six metres wide and up to 180 metres long – contained, the Trust estimated, about 20,000 bodies each. At the Bogoslovskoye a disused sandpit was filled with 60,000 corpses over five or six February days, an anti-tank ditch with 10,000, and bomb craters with another 1,000. Eighteen anti-tank ditches on the northern edge of the Serafimovskoye cemetery accommodated another 15,000. Altogether, the Trust reported, 662 mass graves were dug and filled in the city, not counting the use of pits, craters and trenches. How many dead they contained in total is still disputed, but the best estimate for the number of civilians who died during Leningrad's first siege winter is around half a million.[37]

12

'We Were Like Stones'

On 17 February 1942 Mariya Mashkova, head of acquisitions at the Public Library, a handsome, grey-blue, neo-classical building that curves round the corner of Aleksandrinskaya Square and the Nevsky, sat down to write:

> Day after day passes, and it already feels late to be starting a diary. Unrepeatable, terrifying things happen and are forgotten. The rest, the trivia, remain in the memory. A packet of letters arrived today and reminded me that away from Leningrad there's a different life going on, and people who can't imagine even a hundredth of what we're going through.
>
> Outside I can hear shelling. It didn't use to bother me, but now I think numbly, 'Somewhere a building is collapsing, people are being crushed.' But what's this compared to everything that's happened already? We are all ill. Olga Fedorovna [Mashkova's mother-in-law] is very bad – no surprise, since from room to room there are dead people, a corpse for every family. It has been almost a month since Anna Yakovlevna Zveinek died from starvation. She's still lying there in her freezing, dirty room – black, dried-up, teeth bared. Nobody is in any hurry to clean her up and bury her; everyone is too weak to care. Two rooms away lies another corpse – her daughter Asya Zveinek, who also died of

starvation, outliving her mother by twelve days. Asya died two steps from my bed, and Vsevolod [Mashkova's husband] and I dragged her away because it was too warm in our room for a dead body . . .

Almost in front of my eyes N. P. Nikolsky died, a friend of Vsevolod's and a [former] deputy to the Supreme Soviet. He was brought in on a sled, with the idea of placing him in a recuperation clinic so as to get him back on his feet . . . He fell into a coma and quickly died, in Vsevelod's office. He stayed there, on the sofa, for twelve days, since nobody could cope with burying him. Altogether, the Library has lost at least a hundred people . . .

People's attitude to death, and death itself and burial, have greatly simplified. At first it was very difficult. Make a coffin – it's hard to get one, 500–700 roubles – dig a grave, that has to be paid for in bread . . . Then rentable coffins appeared, and after that people were taken to the morgues on sleds, just wrapped in sheets and blankets. Thus I buried V. F. Karyakin, Zinaida Yepifanova's husband . . . and even my deadened nerves were barely able to handle everything I saw . . .

Asya moved in with us after her mother died . . . When she died, too, to my despair I couldn't use her ration cards, because a friend of hers had disappeared with them two days before. Card theft is frightening and commonplace . . . In shops and on the streets one often hears a piercing, tearing scream – and you know that someone's cards have been stolen, or that a piece of bread has been ripped from someone's hands. It is unbearably depressing, and what saves you is bestial indifference to human suffering.[1]

What was it like to live through this? Many diaries peter out in January or February, their authors either too weak to write or at a loss for words. Others condense into curt records of relatives' deaths and of food obtained and consumed. Yet others, like the poet Olga Berggolts's, become more prolix – long, repetitive outpourings of despair, disbelief, guilt, anger and terror. Ask one of the dwindling number of siege survivors today how they remember those months, and the reply will likely be the words '*kholod, golod, snaryady, pozhary*' – 'cold, hunger, shells, fires' – a set phrase whose long, rhyming syllables are both a shorthand and a litany.

Most obviously, the siege winter meant a narrowing of existence to the iron triangle of home, bread queue and water source – and to immediate family and neighbours. Sequestered in their dark and freezing flats, reliant on sleds, home-made lamps and scavenged fuel, Leningraders compared themselves to cavemen, to Robinson Crusoe and to polar explorers. Pre-war life, which at the time had felt so disorganised, now seemed to Lidiya Ginzburg's 'Siege Man' like 'a fairy tale':

> Water in the taps, light at the press of a switch, food in the shops . . . From that former time, an engraving hung above the bookshelf and a Crimean clay jug sat on the shelf – a gift. The woman who had given it was now in unoccupied Russia, and the memory of her had become a pale and unnecessary thing . . . In that winter's enveloping chaos it felt as though the jug and even the bookshelves were something in the nature of the Pogankiniy Chambers or the ruins of the Colosseum, in that they would never have any practical significance again.[2]

With narrowing of the physical world came narrowing of the emotions. Survivors describe themselves as having been 'like wolves' or even more commonly 'like stones' – automata drained of feeling or interest except that of prolonging their own survival. The sight of a stranger collapsing on the street, which in November and December had presented itself as a moral dilemma – should one stop and help, and risk failing to bring home food for one's own family, or pass on by? – in January and February hardly registered. On 13 January, setting out to the Scholars' Building for 'soy soup',

Aleksandr Boldyrev heard that a neighbour, 'grown completely old and dilapidated in the last couple of months', had collapsed outside on the pavement and been dragged indoors by passing soldiers. 'He's still there, in the stairwell, apparently dying. But I didn't go in, and went to get lunch. The journey there and back uses up all my strength, my little daily reserve. Golovan was also on his way to lunch, but his reserve was insufficient.'[3] Janitors, another diarist noted, asked people who sat down to rest on their buildings' doorsteps to move on, knowing that if they died there it would be their responsibility to drag the corpse to the morgue. If the person was well-dressed, however, the janitor would 'be more courteous, even offer a chair, because he knows that afterwards, he can take their clothes'.[4] The same shrivelling of the emotions occurred within families, the deaths of beloved husbands or parents provoking only relief at obtaining an extra ration card or anxiety about how to dispose of a corpse.

For almost everyone, it was impossible to think about anything except food. Obtaining it, preparing it, saving it, calculating how long it could be made to last – all became universal obsessions, as did memories of meals past. 'As he walked along the street', Ginzburg wrote of her 'Siege Man',

he would slowly go over everything he had eaten that morning or the day before; he would ponder what he was going to eat that day, or busy himself with calculations involving ration cards and coupons. He found in this an absorption and tension which he had previously known only when thinking through and writing about something very important . . . What was it so sickeningly like? Something from the previous life? Ah yes – being unhappily in love.[5]

Others became seized by 'bread mania', imagining themselves dipping slice after slice in sunflower oil, or nibbling an endless supply of

buttered rolls. (Varlam Shalamov, starving in the Kolyma goldmines
at the same time, wrote that 'we all had the same dreams of loaves
of ryebread, flying past like meteors or angels'.) New etiquettes grew
up around food. Some families ate everything they had obtained for
the day in one go; others spread it out into three 'meals'. Food could
be pooled and divided equally or according to need, or each family
member could eat 'according to his ration'. Food preparation was
spun out into elaborate rituals. The Zhilinskys, having reused their
tea leaves several times, mixed them with salt and ate them with a
spoon. Boldyrev's four-year-old daughter threw tantrums unless the
table was laid to an exact plan, and 'meals' accompanied with a set
form of words: 'The tea is so cold that flies and mosquitoes skate
and sled on it, and you can drink without a cup, without a spoon,
straight from the saucer.' ('This', wrote her father, 'is said about five
times with every cup, in a weird, almost sickly tongue-twister . . . A
childish reaction to the surrounding chaos.')[6] Traditions of hospi-
tality, inevitably, evaporated. 'I know she's hungry', wrote Klara
Rakhman of a schoolfriend's just widowed, lice-ridden mother who
came to beg for *duranda*: 'But she should understand that at such
times it's embarrassing to ask.' (Rakhman's own father, her 'darling
papochka', died in March.)[7]

At this period, too, Leningraders resorted to their most desperate food substitutes, scraping dried glue from the underside of
wallpaper and boiling up shoes and belts. (Tannery processes had
changed, they discovered, since the days of Amundsen and Nansen,
and the leather remained tough and inedible.) On sale in the street
markets was 'Badayev earth', dug from underneath the remains of
the burned Badayev warehouses and supposedly impregnated with
charred sugar. Together with another little boy, Igor Kruglyakov
slipped past guards to dig some up:

I found what I thought was a piece of sugar, and put it in my
mouth. I sucked it all the while we were walking home. It didn't

dissolve but it tasted sweet. When we got home I spat it out into my hand, and it was just an ordinary stone . . . Mama scolded us of course, but not wanting to hurt my feelings, pretended there was some sugar there. She mixed it with water and it was as though we drank sweet tea.[8]

Denying oneself food so as to give it to others – as hundreds of thousands of Leningraders managed to do – became an act of supreme self-control and shining charity.

In January Yelena Kochina and her husband moved in with friends. Revisiting her own flat on 1 February, Kochina found the door open and the furniture in pieces. '"Why are you chopping up our furniture?" I asked the woman next door. "We're cold," she answered laconically. What could I say to that? She has two children. They really are cold.' Returning four days later she found a corpse on her bed, 'so flat that the bedspread was slightly raised only by its head and feet. After chopping the leg off a chair I left, without inquiring whose body it was.' Two days later it had been joined by two more. 'Evidently the neighbours have set up a morgue in my room. Let them – dead bodies don't bother me.'[9]

The point at which Leningraders most often broke out of their 'caves' and realised the scale of the tragedy overwhelming their city was when they had to arrange the burial of a relative. When his crabby, wood-chopping father died in March, Dmitri Likhachev washed him with toilet water, covered his eyes with eighteenth-century rouble coins, sewed him into a sheet and tied him to a wide double sled, fashioned from two smaller ones joined by a piece of plywood. First he and his wife dragged the corpse to the Vladimir Cathedral, where a priest said the burial service and sprinkled it with earth, adding a second handful on behalf of a woman whose son had gone missing at the front. Next they took it to a newly opened 'mortuary' in the grounds of a concert hall, where thousands

of bodies lay piled in the open. When a lorry arrived to remove
bodies for burial, Likhachev tried to persuade the driver to include
his father in his first load. Otherwise, he feared, his shroud would be
torn open and his gold teeth pulled. The driver refused.[10]

Olga Grechina's mother died at home on 24 January. Determined
to give her the best possible funeral, Olga and her younger brother
Vovka bought a coffin, for bread and two hundred roubles, from
their building's yardman. Though it was slightly too short for lack
of wood, they did their best to make it presentable, lining it with a
sheet and edging it with lace unpicked from one of their mother's
shawls. Olga was even able to buy a bunch of decorative maidenhair
fern, from an otherwise empty florist on the Nevsky. 'The coffin
looked good', she remembered:

> I was pleased with my work, never thinking about what it was
> for . . . It was just very strange seeing this white figure under the
> sheet. Why, who is this? I took a look and it wasn't Mama, it was
> Death herself – a skull covered in skin, bones, hands that looked
> like chicken's claws. (I couldn't gut a chicken again for twenty-five
> years, I was so haunted by this memory.) Since it isn't her, I need
> to get rid of it as quickly as possible, then things will be all right
> again. With a sort of happy energy I began to organise. I arranged
> a grave, called our relatives . . .

The gathering was spoiled by her uncle Serezha, who arrived oddly
dressed and whined like a child, endlessly repeating that he wanted
soup (he died a few weeks later). With the help of the yardman's
son, they dragged the coffin on a sled from Mayakovsky Street to
Suvorovsky Prospekt, past the Smolniy and over the Bolsheokhtinsky
Bridge to the Bolsheokhtinskoye cemetery. As they approached
the cemetery gates, they more and more often passed 'mummies',
wrapped in bedlinen or old curtains, left at the side of the road.
One coffin had been improvised out of a sofa, and decorated with a

wreath made from curly ink-dyed woodshavings; a child lay in the case of an old-fashioned clock. Olga's mother got a 'real grave, dug to order but not very deep', and a cross made from planks, her name and dates inscribed in indelible crayon.[11]

Survivors of the siege have an irresistible urge to find a pattern to the deaths, a rationale behind who lived and who died. In one version the best – the 'noble, restrained, scrupulous' true Petersburgers – died first, elbowed aside in a Darwinian free-for-all. In the other (commoner) analysis restraint and scrupulosity were lifesavers: to survive it was vital to stay active, and to maintain certain stand-ards – to wash one's hair, shave, sweep the room, lay the table for 'meals', brush one's teeth with charcoal, not eat the cat, not lick one's plate and not let the slop bucket overflow or throw faeces out of the window. As one *blokadnik* puts it, 'When someone gave up washing his neck and ears, stopped going to work, ate his bread ration all in one go and then lay down and covered himself with a blanket, he wasn't long for this world.'[12]

These disciplines also applied to children. Yelena Kochina and her husband moved in with a colleague's extremely well-regulated family at the end of January, in (immediately disappointed) hope of a warmer room. His children, 'pale as potato shoots', spent the days sitting motionless side by side,

> as saturated with obedience as a sponge with water. N.A.'s wife Galya and her nanny work as if they were wind-up clocks. N.A. sets them going every morning, giving them their assignments for the day . . . He listens keenly to the work of his domestic machine, strengthening or weakening the load, increasing or decreasing the ration at just the right moment. He keeps the bread in his desk, weighing it out three times a day and handing to each their corre-sponding portion.[13]

Likhachev and his wife made their four-year-old daughters memorise poetry. They learned by heart excerpts from *Yevgeny Onegin* – the ball scene and Tatiana's dream – and Akhmatova's poem 'My Tartar Grandmother Gave Me', about a girl who pretends that she has lost a ring of black jet, which in fact she has given to a lover who sails away, never to return. The little girls behaved 'like heroes. We introduced a rule: no talking about food, and they obeyed! At table they never asked for food, were never naughty, but were terribly adult, slow-moving, serious. [All day] they sat close to the *burzhuika*, warming their hands.'[14] It was another household rule to wash daily, if only face and hands, and to excrete, once the lavatory had frozen, in the loft, to which, since they lived on the fifth floor, they had easy access. ('Fortunately', Likhachev notes, 'we had to go only once a week or even only once every ten days . . . When the weather grew warmer in the spring brown stains appeared on the ceiling in the corridor: we had been going in defined places.')

Crowded into a communal apartment on the Petrograd Side, Dmitri Lazarev's extended family was equally mutually supportive. Though two members of the household – a family friend and his father-in-law – died over the winter, the flat became (like Marina Yerukhmanova's room in the Yevropa) an 'ark'. He and his wife distracted the children – a six-year-old daughter and nine-year-old niece – by reading aloud pre-revolutionary detective stories and by playing charades. The one their daughter remembered was the word *blokada* – 'blockade'. For the syllable *blok* they acted out a scene from a poem by Aleksandr Blok; for *ad* – 'hell' in Russian – a devil sizzling a soul in a frying pan. For the whole word they pretended stumblingly to pull a sled across the room.[15]

But the diaries and memoirs, almost by definition, come from the families that managed to hold on, and hold together. Very many did not, and the descriptions of those who gave up the fight – the unanswered door; darkness, stink and cold; still figures under heaped blankets; muttered ravings – are numerous

The Neva embankment, summer 1941

Newsboard outside the offices of *Leningradskaya Pravda*, July 1941

Rally at the Kirov Works, June 1941

September 1941: bomb damage, and peasant refugees outside the Hermitage

October 1941: courtyard of the Young People's Theatre, after shelling

St Isaac's Cathedral and Falconet's statue of Peter the Great, boarded and covered with earth

Listening horns on the walls of the Peter and Paul fortress

Photographer: Boris Losin

Photographer: David Trakhtenberg

Washing clothes at a broken pipe, and scavenging meat from a horse killed by shelling

A 'well-fed type' and a 'dystrophic'; Ligovsky Prospekt, December 1941

The Nikitin family, January 1942. Nikolai Nikitin, a railway engineer, died of starvation-related illness in April 1942, as did his mother, seated left. His wife and children survived and were evacuated from the city the following December. The picture was taken by Nikolai's brother Aleksandr, who disappeared without trace during the winter of 1942–3.

February 1942, the peak of the mass death. In January, February and March 1942 at least 100,000 Leningraders died of starvation each month.

Evacuees on the Ice Road across Lake Ladoga, April 1942

Some of the thousands who died en route; Kobona, April 1942

Summer 1942: though outwardly the city returned to life, mortality remained high.

Victory salute; Troitsky Bridge, 27 January 1944

Reconstruction: Nevsky Prospekt, opposite the Beloselskikh-Belozerskihk Palace, 1944

Coming home: demobilised soldiers, July 1945

and near-identical. With a mixture of disgust and pity Mariya Mashkova recorded the disintegration of neighbouring families in number 18 Sadovaya Street – most, like her, employees of the Public Library. One neighbour, until recently head of a 'strong, alert, energetic' household, having seen her husband leave for the army, her parents fall to quarrelling and stealing as they died, and her daughter taken away to a children's home, ceased to care about anything except food: '[Her] overwhelming craving is to eat, to eat without end, savour and enjoy . . . Her husband's visits home frighten her – he might take her portion of bread. I recognise this state of mind – it's in me, in Olga, in everybody.'[16] Another turned on her ten-year-old son after he lost his ration card:

What never ceases to amaze me is the metamorphosis that has taken place in this loving mother, who we always used to tease for fussing so much about her Igoryok . . . Now she has turned into a wolf, stripped of humanity by hunger. Her only care is to snatch a piece of food from Igor, and her only fear that he will take a crumb of bread from her, or steal a spoonful of soup made from her grain. When I went to talk to her about getting help for Igor she didn't even listen to what I was saying. She was tormented by one fear – that he would get his hands on her card, or eat her bread. She categorically stated, 'I'm hungry, I want to live. I don't care about Igor and his hunger. He lost his card, let him deal with it himself.' She's not going to give him anything. She must survive and she's not interested in anything else. She hates and envies anybody who's still on their feet . . . Igor just stood there, not saying anything, and devouring a piece of bread which the neighbours had given him out of pity. She was shouting angrily, 'Don't believe his complaints! Look what a huge piece of bread he's stuffing down his throat, while I lie here hungry and weak!' Igor, despite the horror and tragedy of their situation, is calm and never complains. He may no longer be of sound mind.[17]

For those living in communal flats, whose kitchens, bathrooms and hallways were shared, neighbours' breakdowns could be very close indeed. Igor Kruglyakov, kept alive by the iron discipline of his mother and grandmother (no talk of death was allowed, and he and his sister were forced to stand outdoors in the snow for ten minutes each day to get light and air), heard the couple in the next-door room first quarrelling, then fighting, then thumps on the wall as the wife killed their baby.[18]

A consummate siege survivor was the Persianist Aleksandr Boldyrev. Good-looking, egotistical and possessed of a mordant wit, he had dodged the purges of 1936-7 by spending long spells in hospital with ulcers, or on research trips to remote parts of Central Asia. When war broke out he avoided the draft with the help of his lover, a colleague at the Hermitage, who interceded for him with the museum's director via her long-suffering husband. Though not a Party member, Boldyrev continued indefatigably to work his contacts through the siege, inscribing himself at the Scholars' Building and the Eastern Institute as well as at the Hermitage, and eating a daily 'lunch' at each. From the Hermitage he also managed to squeeze a manual worker's card and, remarkably, 1,417 roubles in compensation for his lost summer holiday. He also delivered historical lectures – on 'Peter's Fleet', 'The Literature of the Fraternal Peoples of Central Asia' and 'Today's Afghanistan' – to sailors on Leningrad's ice-bound ships. Sometimes these commissions meant a long walk across the city for no return, but usually they earned him a meal and a few Little Star cigarettes. His siege diary reads like an ever-changing to-do list of officials to be petitioned, debts to be called in and barter deals to be followed up – shifts he describes as like 'leaping from tussock to tussock through a bog'.[19] He managed, too, not to lose hope (the siege was always about to be lifted; England always about to open a second front) or his sense of humour. 'All the time', he wrote on 10 February, 'sitting, standing or lying, I am reminded of my extreme emaciation. Especially striking is the disappearance of my buttocks, the one really distinguished aspect of my person, of which I was very proud. Now I have no bottom at all; my pelvis and hip bones clink against the chair.'

Though his family was far from harmonious (his wife quarrelled relentlessly with his mother, and he with his wife), they continued to operate as a team, Boldyrev bringing home 'yeast soup' and 'jelly' from his various cafeterias, his wife donating blood (for which extra rations were given) and his mother queuing for bread. Most of all they were fortunate in having inherited valuables to trade. As well as the usual clothes and shoes, in the course of the winter they sold three watches – Boldyrev's own, his late father's and his wife's Longine – for ten kilos of flour and five of beef fat; an amber cigarette holder (for 200 grams of bread), two sets of silver dessert spoons (for two kilos of bread and 700 grams of meat), a silver cream jug and sugar bowl, porcelain teacups (sold to the old Fabergé shop on the Morskaya for 670 roubles, which bought a litre of sunflower oil) and his mother's wedding ring. This combination of perseverance, cooperation and luck just saved Boldyrev, his wife and daughter, but not his brother-in-law, uncle or mother, all of whom died of starvation between December and May.

At night, lying on a sofa next to a stove stoked with furniture and picture frames, Boldyrev read novels. On 19 December he finished *Great Expectations*: 'Indescribable delight – the only parts which grate are those repeated, oh-so-English edible passages.' The following day he started on Priestley's *The Good Companions* – 'Wonderful so far. Its main appeal is England, contemporary England' – which he finished 'with great regret – it was just the book I wanted'. Next came Kipling's heat- and light-drenched *Kim* ('heavenly pleasure') and Bulwer-Lytton's critique of the Regency criminal justice system, *Paul Clifford*. In March he read de Maupassant and Fenimore Cooper's *The Last of the Mohicans*, and in April Conrad's *Chance*, about a teenage girl shunned by society after her father's imprisonment.

That the blockaded Leningraders escaped confinement by reading is a siege cliché. ('I mostly read Balzac and Stendhal', a Kirov Works foreman is said to have told the Party hack Aleksandr Fadeyev, 'reporting' from the city in the spring.) It is, however, borne out by the memoirs and diaries. At the start of the war, according to Ginzburg, 'everyone' avidly read *War and Peace*, since 'Tolstoy had said the last word as regards courage, about people doing their bit in a people's war'.[20] Georgi Knyazev, on one of the days when his wife returned from the Academy's ration distribution point empty-handed, distracted himself with 'world history', the Hittites and (uncharacteristically) the French decadents.[21] On the pitch-black afternoon of 14 January, Vera Inber sat in coat and gloves reading *The Sun, Life and Chlorophyll* by the great nineteenth-century bota-nist Kliment Timiryazev, with its almost visionary description of plants transforming solar energy into life on earth. '"Unmeasurable surface of leaves"', she wrote in her diary. 'These words evoke in me a swaying ocean of green foliage and light particles flying towards us through the icy space of the universe.'[22] A Red Army lieuten-ant in charge of barrage balloons read Jules Verne's *The Mysterious Island*, from which he got (and successfully implemented) the idea of using the hydrogen inside the balloons themselves to fuel the engines which hauled them to the ground.[23] Mashkova scoured the second-hand bookshops for treasures from the hastily sold librar-ies of evacuees. For herself she bought Herzen, Dostoyevsky and *The Pickwick Papers* ('boring, pointless humour; I'm amazed it gets published, even for children'), and for her ten-year-old son Jules Verne, a life of Pissarro and Mayne Reid's adventures of the Wild West. Another siege survivor, aged ten at the time, recalls a similarly escapist reading list – Pushkin's fairy tales, Twain's *The Prince and the Pauper*, Darwin's *Voyage of the Beagle* and Ernest Seton Thompson's *Two Little Savages*, about a city boy who learns Indian woodcraft in the Ontario wilderness of the 1850s.

Leningraders also wrote – Knyazev his catalogues, Inber poetry,

Likhachev a history of medieval Novgorod, and Olga Fridenberg a paper on the origins of the Greek epics, until the contents of her inkwell congealed into a violet lump. Anna Ostroumova-Lebedeva, remarkably, never lost her appreciation of beauty, describing in detail the look of bare, frost-covered branches against the sky even in the depths of February. She tried to animate her increasingly lethargic teenage nephews, Petya and Boba – 'pale and thin as paper' – by setting up a still life for them to draw (Boba died, Petya survived). Mikhail Steblin-Kamensky, a folklorist and friend of Boldyrev's, studied Greek grammar and strove to convince himself that he had 'been presented with a singular opportunity to observe life at its most strange and remote'. He had often tried to imagine medieval Russia in time of plague or famine; now he could see it for himself. No wonder that the chroniclers had described a dragon swooping over the land, snatching children and breathing fire.[24] The archae-ologist Boris Piotrovsky, living in the Hermitage basement, wrote a history of Urartu, a lost seventh-century kingdom on the shores of Lake Van. 'Terribly cold', he scribbled in the margins, and 'Cold, it's hard to write'.[25] At the zoo, Nikolai Sokolov wrote up different species' reactions to artillery fire. Baboons and monkeys, he noted, became hysterical during shelling, but quickly became used to barrage balloons and showed only 'normal curiosity' towards search-lights and flares. Completely unruffled was the zoo's bear, which 'lay peacefully, sucking on its paw'. Similar sang-froid was displayed by a Siberian mountain goat: when a high-explosive shell landed in its enclosure it was found peering with calm interest into the resulting crater. The emu was 'completely unresponsive to anything' – thanks, Sokolov thought, to its 'limited intellect'.

As well as being read or written, books could, of course, be used as fuel. 'We warm ourselves', wrote Fridenberg, 'by burning memoirs and floorboards. Prose, it turns out, provides more heat than poetry. History boils the kettle to make our tea.'[26] Boldyrev sorted his books, like his furniture, into three categories – 'keep', 'sell' and 'burn'. One by one Likhachev dismembered and fed into his *burzhuika* the records of the proceedings of the pre-revolutionary Duma, saving only the volume covering its last session, a rarity. Olga Grechina burned her dead uncle's books of Roman law − nineteenth-century paper, she discovered, gave out more heat than the flimsy Soviet sort. Another family started with reference works and technical manuals, moved on to bound sets of journals, then to the German classics, then to Shakespeare, and finally to their blue and gold-bound editions of Pushkin and Tolstoy.[27]

Another siege cliché borne out by the diaries is the emotional sustenance Leningraders derived from the radio. Portable sets having been confiscated at the outbreak of war, they listened on fixed-wire loudspeakers, more than 400,000 of which had been installed in domestic apartments, as well as in outdoor public spaces, from the 1920s onwards.* Headquartered in the art deco 'Radio House' on the corner of Italyanskaya and Malaya Sadovaya streets, the city radio station continued to broadcast, despite power outages and shell damage to its transmission network, throughout the mass-death winter. Stories of its resuscitating power are legion: Olga Berggolts, collapsed in the street, picking herself up at the sound of her own voice reading her own poetry; a fighter pilot making it home 'on one wing' on hearing Klavdiya Shulzhenko − Russia's Vera Lynn − singing 'Little Blue Scarf'; the housewife, stumbling home to her family, 'handed' from loudspeaker to loudspeaker as if along a human chain. A (hammily Stalinist) programme for teenagers, titled 'Letter to my Friend in Leningrad' and broadcast on 7 December, delighted sixteen-year-old Klara Rakhman. 'What a wonderful letter!' she wrote in her diary: 'It very precisely expresses my thoughts. I'll put down everything I can remember of it.'[28] The writer Lev Uspensky, smoking a

---

* The system was admired by Hitler, who planned to install a loudspeaker in every Ukrainian village. They would not broadcast news, but 'cheerful music', giving Ukrainians 'plenty of opportunities to dance'.

late-night cigarette at a railway junction south of Ladoga, was startled to hear the words 'Leningrad speaking' echoing out of the fog
above his head. A time delay between loudspeakers attached to a
series of telegraph poles meant that the words overlapped, fading
into the distance. It sounded, he thought, as if a line of giants were
speaking, gently urging the German idiots to give it up, to go back
home before they got hurt.[29]

The most listened-to items were the Sovinform news bulletins,
broadcast at 11 a.m. and 11 p.m. daily. Having got hold of a radio
just in time for the Red Army's January offensives, Fridenberg and
her mother tearfully hung on the announcer's every word. They knew
the reports were untruthful, not to be relied upon – 'but all the same,
one listened and believed'.[30] Genuinely beloved were Berggolts's readings of her own verse, in particular her *February Diary*, a long poem
commissioned in February 1942 to mark Red Army Day. Though
censored, it managed to combine patriotism with an unusual degree
of realism and personal feeling, perfectly fitting the public mood.
The verses, a survivor remembers, were 'so simple that they just
stuck in your head. You'd walk along, muttering the lines . . . When
I had to climb up on to our library roof and stand there during the
shelling it was somehow a big help knowing them by heart.' Another
calls them 'splendid . . . they really shook us out of that animal
brooding about food'.[31] Other popular programmes were *Campfire*
– an imaginative magazine feature for children, which continued
long after the war – and, from the spring of 1942, *Letters to and from
the Front*, which enabled Leningraders to send each other (morale-
boosting) personal messages. The Radio House also broadcast to
Leningrad's besiegers. Headed by émigré Austrian Communists,
the brothers Ernst and Fritz Fuchs, its German-language section
featured defeatist interviews with German POWs and faked 'letters
from home', said to have been discovered in dead soldiers' pockets.
One described the bombing of Berlin; another, written by Berggolts,
waxed lyrical about Christmas in Bavaria – 'Do you remember the

smell of Christmas biscuits? Spices, raisins, vanilla? The warmth and crackle of Christmas candles?'[32]

In December and January programming shrank to a few hours per day. In the gaps, the radio broadcast the calm ticking (at fifty strikes per minute) of a metronome – the steady beating, for households whose sets still worked, of Leningrad's heart. What exactly the Radio House put out hardly mattered; the important thing was that the organism lived, that communication was maintained. Ivan Zhilinsky was one of the many diarists to record each day, even as his entries shrivelled to a bare record of food intake and deaths among neighbours, whether or not he had radio reception.

Much harder to gauge is how much solace Leningraders got from religious faith during the months of mass death.[33] By the late 1930s organised religion had been suborned or driven underground in the Soviet Union, following Stalin's closure or demolition of thousands of churches and monasteries, and execution, imprisonment or exile of their monks, nuns and priests. At the start of the war only twenty-one churches operated in the whole of the Leningrad diocese, the rest having been knocked down or turned into warehouses, garages, cinemas, planetaria or 'museums of religion'. The Cathedral of Our Saviour of the Spilled Blood – a multicoloured neo-Russian confection, filled with glowing mosaic, that is today one of Petersburg's chief tourist attractions – was only saved from demolition, ironically, by the outbreak of war.

With the German invasion, Stalin made a swift U-turn, allowing the Orthodox (but not the Catholic, Baptist or Lutheran) Church to play a tightly circumscribed role in public life in exchange for supporting the war effort. Some churches were reopened, the *Atheist* newspaper was renamed then closed, and Leningrad's Metropolitan Aleksei was allowed to make a patriotic appeal to the nation in which he invoked Russia's medieval warrior-saints Dmitri Donskoi and Alexander Nevsky but did not once mention Stalin. Priests were

allowed to take funeral services (as for Likhachev's father) and to
visit homes to administer the last rites. Crypts were used as bomb
shelters and as distribution points for kerosene, firewood, hot water
and clothing. (As a toddler, the poet Josef Brodsky sat out raids
underneath the martial white and gold of the Spaso-Preobrazhensky
Cathedral, round the corner from his family's flat on the Liteiniy.)
Leningrad churches also collected substantial defence funds – over
two million roubles by the end of 1941, which paid for a Dmitri
Donskoi tank column and an Alexander Nevsky air unit. So, too,
did the Choral Synagogue, the one remaining place of worship for
the city's 200,000-odd Jews.

Independent congregations, in contrast, were still ruthlessly persecuted. Typical was a small underground group discovered and liqui-
dated in the summer of 1942. It was led, the NKVD's case report
tells us, by a sixty-year-old known as Archimandrite Klavdi, who
had already served time in prison for 'counter-revolutionary activity'
and was now living in Leningrad illegally. His elderly, mostly unemployed followers included 'kulaks', former nuns, 'monastic elements'
and a nurse from the Lenin Hospital. Their crimes, according to
Klavdi's confession, included 'illegally trying to recruit believers',
'praising the pre-revolutionary order and living standards', and 'voicing disapproval of the methods of Soviet power'.[34] What became of
them we do not know, but it was probably similar to what happened
to Berggolts's doctor father, who in early 1942 was deported to
Siberia for refusing to inform on a Father Vyacheslav, an old friend
with whom he used to enjoy playing cards.[35]

How many Leningraders actually attended services during the
first siege winter is hard to say. Though one memoirist movingly
describes services at the St Vladimir Cathedral – choir wrapped
in shawls and felt boots, oil in the icon lamps frozen solid, the
sacraments taken with beetroot juice in place of wine – the diarists
of the time make no remark, even when recklessly frank on other
matters. Perhaps the packed Vladimirsky was a benevolent trick

of the memory; perhaps it only attracted crowds from the spring onwards, when surviving Leningraders had the strength to begin mourning their dead; or perhaps it was simply that it was the intelligentsia, on the whole, who kept diaries, and the working class who went to church. Educated Leningraders may have also found it harder to maintain what faith they had. Berggolts – Jewish by background and an idealistic Communist in youth – saw the siege as a collective punishment for having allowed the Revolution to be perverted, for the lies and moral cowardice of the purge years:

> What unhappy people we are! What did we wander into? What savage dead end and delirium? Oh what weakness and terror! I can do nothing, nothing. I should have ended my own life, that would have been the most honest thing. I have lied so much, made so many mistakes, that can't be redeemed or set right . . . We have to fight off the Germans, destroy fascism, end the war. And then we have to change everything about ourselves . . . (Just now Kolka [her husband] had [an epileptic] fit – I had to hold his mouth shut so he wouldn't frighten the children in the next door room. He fought terribly.) Why do we live? Oh God, why do we live? Have we really not suffered enough? Nothing better will ever come.

She had caught her mood from a friend, a traumatised survivor of the naval retreat from Tallinn, who had visited earlier in the day, incoherently mumbling 'For twenty years we have been in the wrong, and we're paying for it now.'[36]

Others found themselves returning to faith as their fear and suffering increased. Party members whispered prayers and crossed themselves in the air-raid shelters; Georgi Knyazev, self-styled humanist and worshipper of Turgenev, Tolstoy and Chekhov, by the depths of January mused through the eighteen-hour nights on the strength of the light fitting in his ceiling – he would hang himself, he had decided, if his wife died before him – and his 'favourite theme of Christ, that amazing teacher of love and mercy from faraway Galilee'.[37] A painter, dying alongside his wife, drew sketches of a fiery angel, of Christ – his skull-shaped head resembling those of the starving – and of the Virgin spreading her protective veil over the well-like courtyard of a blacked-out apartment block.[38] Old Believers and Seventh Day Adventists continued, as they had done since 1938, to hold services in secret, in their homes. The mother of one such family (whose husband, a priest, was already in prison) made her six children kneel for long hours on the floor, praying. When they became emaciated she let them kneel on pillows (two out of the six died).[39] Muslims and Buddhists also had to worship in secret, despite the fact that thousands were serving on the Leningrad front, and that the city possessed both a mosque and a magnificent Buddhist temple, built during the reign of Nicholas II and the tethering point of the barrage balloon that served as its wartime radio mast.

In sum, religious faith remained a private, risky source of consolation during the siege. Stalin's relaxation of the rules was opportunistic and temporary, and Leningraders knew it. A ten-year-old girl, taken into one of ninety-eight new orphanages that opened between January and March 1942, woke one night to see her class teacher kneeling, head bowed, at the dormitory window. The teacher whispered that she was praying for her son, who had gone missing at the front – and begged the girl not to tell anybody what she had seen.[40]

Svyazi

A not quite translatable word meant a great deal in the Soviet Union: *svyazi*, or 'connections' – the combination of string-pulling, exchange of favours and bribery by means of which citizens were able to work their way round the state's monopoly on goods and employment to get themselves everything from jobs, telephones and university places to a bucket of potatoes or a new pair of shoes. In peacetime, astute use of *svyazi* improved one's standard of living; during the siege it meant the difference between life and death.

If the typical Leningrader's first line of defence against starvation was immediate family, the second was his or her network of friends. Especially among the city's close-knit intelligentsia families, friend-ships – based on several generations of connection by marriage, education and profession, plus shared experience of fear and impov-erishment – could be both extensive and remarkably strong. Not unusual was the experience of widowed, childless Anna Ostroumova-Lebedeva, who was given small but heartening presents of food by old colleagues from her late husband's chemical research institute. 'My friend Petr Yevgenevich visited today', she wrote on New Year's Day 1942. 'He brought a handful of oatmeal for *kisel* [a thickened fruit drink], and Ivan Yemelyanovich brought three sprats.' The pair reappeared a few weeks later, this time with 200 grams of bread, dried onion, mustard powder, 'a tiny piece of meat, four dried white mushrooms, and four frozen potatoes (the first we've seen since the autumn). This is priceless treasure, and I was extremely grateful, especially since for the past week all we've had to eat is seaweed . . . A celebration!'[1] Similarly loyal were the retired railway clerk Ivan Zhilinsky and his wife Olga, who looked after an old friend whose family had departed into evacuation. They invited him to share wine and *duranda* at New Year – painstakingly cleaning their room and clothes beforehand, and giving him a wash and shave on arrival – took him in when his flat was made uninhabitable by shelling, and finally traded bread so as to give him a proper grave. If Olga had not also died of starvation, and Ivan been arrested by the NKVD, they would have adopted his children. Smaller acts of kindness could make all the difference, too: one siege survivor remembers the teenage girl next door bringing firewood filched from her job at a lumberyard – 'Not a lot of it, but for us it was everything.'[2] On a different level, Olga Grechina – aged nineteen and living completely alone – found human comfort in brief, heartfelt conversations with strangers on the street, who in January and February tended to walk together in pairs for fear of mugging:

It was interesting to observe people's contradictory impulses: on the one hand you fear that your most valuable possession, your ration card, might be stolen; on the other you want, even just for the short walk home, to be with someone who will listen. Never since have I experienced such an odd, uncontrollable desire to tell a complete stranger everything about myself . . .

Saying goodbye, each would thank the other for their company and wish that they might live to see victory. There was a new etiquette in this farewell, for the form of words was almost always exactly the same, whether spoken by a simple person or an educated one. The simple women, having heard my unhappy story, would commiserate with me and comfort me, saying that I was young and that everything would come again – home,

education, friends. In these naive but sincere good wishes I found
the vitamin I needed to live. And that was why I, like everyone
else, in reply to my companion's story would tell my own.[3]

Leningraders' second and most important ring of *svyazi* derived
from their workplaces. Having a job not only meant getting a
worker's ration card, but with luck, access to off-ration meals,
to firewood, to food parcels from affiliated organisations in the
unoccupied Soviet Union, and to a bed in one of the hundred-
odd recuperation clinics, or *statsionary*, opened from December
onwards on the orders of the city soviet. (Though many *statsionary*
were little better than dumping grounds for the dying, others saved
lives simply by providing patients with food without making them
queue.) Not all workplaces were equal. Among factories the best
supplied were the large, prestigious defence plants, though their
staff's chances of survival were pulled down to the civilian average
by the physical demands of their work, by targeted bombardment
and by the fact that even after call-up most defence workers were
quicker-to-starve men. At the Stalin Metal Works the fatality rate
was around 35 per cent, and in the Kirov Works, situated in the
vulnerable southern suburbs, somewhere between 25 and 34 per
cent.

During the production push of the autumn going absent without leave had meant criminal punishment and loss of the worker's
ration, but in the midst of mass death the rules ceased to be enforced.
Employees who failed to appear at work were automatically listed
as sick and kept their cards, so that in January 1942 837,000
Leningraders were still registered as workers despite the fact that 270
factories had been officially closed and most of the rest hardly functioned.[4] Among the many Leningraders with a purely notional job
was Yelena Skryabina. 'Friends', she wrote on 15 January 1942, 'have
found me a position in a sewing workshop. This puts me on first
category rations. The workshop does very little – there's no light or

fuel – but they hand out the ration just the same. Thus I get a little more bread, and at the moment every crumb is vital.'[5]

One of the most sought-after intelligentsia 'survival enclaves' – as one historian calls siege-winter workplaces – was the Radio House, whose director organised fair distribution of food that he regularly smuggled back to the office from the Smolniy's fabled Canteen no. 12. Though the amounts involved were small – a few lumps of sugar, a couple of meat patties, a bowl of *kasha* – the 'tremendous moral effect it had on us', as Olga Berggolts's lover Yuri Makogonenko recalled, 'is difficult even to describe'.[6] Radio House staff also received at least two special deliveries of food from Moscow, the first arranged by Berggolts's indomitable sister Mariya, who personally escorted a lorry-full of supplies over the Ladoga ice at the end of February. 'She took a roundabout route', Berggolts wrote admiringly, 'alone with the driver, in trousers and a short fur coat, armed with some sort of pistol . . . She slept in the lorry, chatted up the commandants, passed through villages just liberated from the Germans, collecting letters and packages for Leningraders along the way . . . I am proud of her, amazed by her – my wonderful quarrelsome Muska!'[7]

A second delivery was organised by Berggolts herself, who collected food and medicines for air transport to Leningrad while in Moscow giving readings of her *February Diary*. She would have been able to send more if it had not been for the Leningrad authorities, who mistrusted non-Party initiatives, did not want their own fail-ings shown up and possibly feared public anger if some institutions were noticeably better supplied than others. 'Zhdanov', Berggolts wrote furiously on 25 March, 'has just sent a telegram forbidding the despatch of individual packages to Leningrad organisations. This apparently has "bad political consequences". Thanks to this idiotic telegram we can hardly send anything to the Radio Committee.' Pleading was useless:

Today I had an appointment with Polikarpov, president of the
All-Union Radio Committee. It left a very unpleasant impression.
I addressed him badly, shyly – I would probably have done better
to be rude. I asked his permission to send the food package to our
Radio Committee, and in reply this smooth bureaucrat, obviously
uncomfortable in my presence, uttered stinking commonplaces:
'Leningraders themselves object to these packages'; 'The government knows who to help' and similar rubbish. 'Leningraders' –
this is Zhdanov!'[8]

Employment at the Radio House nonetheless enabled Berggolts,
though jaundiced and swollen with oedema, not only to survive
herself but to help friends. One beneficiary was the half-grateful,
half-resentful Mariya Mashkova, who more than once found herself
unable to tear herself away from the fried bread and coffee on offer
in Berggolts's warm, well-lit flat in order to return to crying children and dying mother-in-law in the darkness and cold of her own.
Berggolts gave her *sukhari*, oranges, biscuits, soup powder and
onions out of the first Radio House delivery from Moscow, and
bread, biscuits, soup powder, rice, buckwheat, sausages, chocolates,
vodka, tobacco and packets of vitamin C out of the second. 'I list all
this in such detail', Mashkova wrote in her diary after a celebratory
supper, 'because it's such a rarity – magical, unbelievable . . . To sit
with friends next to a cheerful samovar, to see bread lying sliced on
a plate in the normal way, to see the children eating as much as they
want . . . Not to worry about the diminishing loaf, to speak about
something other than food – is this not happiness?'[9]
    Another enviable enclave was the Writers' Union, run by the
novelist Vera Ketlinskaya. In January she applied to Zhdanov's
deputy Aleksei Kuznetsov for permission to send a fleet of lorries,
specially equipped with stoves and insulated with felt and plywood,
over the Ice Road to the 'mainland'. On the way out they were to
carry writers' families into evacuation, and on the way back, to buy

100,000 roubles' worth of food from collective farmworkers, who in return were to be entertained with 'modern literature' and 'literary evenings'. 'We are aware that all unscheduled trips are cancelled', she wheedled in a letter, 'but beg you to make an exception to this rule. Even in the most difficult times the Party and Soviet government have always taken particular care of literature. We remember Lenin's conversation with Gorky, about how our writers and scientists must be fed.'[10] Her lobbying worked and by early spring – well before other institutions returned to normal – the Union's canteen daily served barley soup, borscht, *kasha* and dessert.[11]

The Writers' Union also received special food deliveries from its Moscow headquarters; Vera Inber got a share of one in March: 'I was bewildered when I saw everything they had sent us. I grabbed a tin of condensed milk in each hand; I couldn't let them go.'[12] Lidiya Ginzburg cites these food parcels as an example of the Soviet hierarchy in action 'with unusual clarity and crudity'. Containing chocolate, butter, rusks and preserves, they were, she claims, divided according to work rate and seniority rather than need. Writers active in Union affairs got two kilos each, the less active a kilo and the inactive nothing at all.[13] One of several who loathed Ketlinskaya was Valerian Bogdanov-Berezovsky, head of the Leningrad branch of the Composers' Union, who fruitlessly begged her to admit his starving members since they had no clubhouse or canteen of their own.[14] Though wrung out by dysentery, which prevented him from making a meeting with city soviet chairman Popkov, he did manage to obtain eleven extra first-category ration cards, as well as three beds in a recuperation clinic set up in the Astoria hotel. He was then faced with the horrible task of allocating them:

I receive many acutely painful appeals. I was especially upset by a phone call from L. A. Portov, who several times, in a pleading voice, entreated me 'Do it. Do it now. If you wait a week, it will be too late. I won't survive.'

All the same I could only promise him a place on the waiting list, together with the much weakened Rubtsov and Peisin, since Rabinovich (long ill from tuberculosis), Deshevov (already hardly able to move) and Miklashevsky are all in an even worse state. When it comes to saving human life you can't make choices. The life of every Soviet person must be saved. But you do nonetheless have to choose, in the sense of deciding priorities. You mustn't be guided by judgements of each person's creative or practical 'worth' (these can only be subjective), but by objective indicators of how closely they are threatened by death.[15]

By the end of February, twenty-one out of the Union's eighty members had died of what Bogdanov-Berezovsky in his official report called 'exhaustion'.[16] So had his own mother, sister, brother-in-law, father-in-law and niece.

Workplace solidarity also often broke down. The acting direc-tor of Pushkin House, Dmitri Likhachev records, behaved cruelly, dismissing female staff – which amounted to a death sentence since it condemned them to dependants' rations – stealing the ration cards of the dying and finally throwing them out so as not to have to dispose of their corpses:

> I remember the death of Yasinsky. He had once been a tall, slim, very handsome old man, who reminded me of Don Quixote. During the winter he moved to the Pushkin House library, sleeping on a folding bed, behind the book stacks . . . His mouth wouldn't close and saliva trickled from it; his face was black, making an eerie contrast with his completely white, unkempt hair. His skin was taut over his bones . . . His lips became thinner and thinner and failed to cover his teeth, which protruded and made his head look like a tortoise's. Once he emerged from the stacks with a blanket over his shoulders and asked 'What's the time?' Then he asked if it was day or night (dystrophics' voices became slurred, as

the vocal chords atrophied). He couldn't tell because in the lobby all the windows were boarded up. A day or two later our deputy director, Kanailov, drove away everyone who had tried to settle down to die in Pushkin House, so as not to have to remove their bodies. Several of our ancillary staff – porters, caretakers, cleaning women – died like this. They had been drafted in, torn from their families, and then when they no longer had the strength to get home they were thrown out in thirty degrees of frost. Kanailov kept a close eye on all those who weakened, and not a single person died on the premises.[17]

In January 1942 Kanailov arranged his own evacuation across Lake Ladoga, offering friends places in his lorry if they carried his cases, which he stuffed with antique carpets and other valuables. The cases themselves – beautiful old ones in yellow leather – weren't his either, being part of a bequest from a book-loving illegitimate son of Alexander III. More Pushkin House valuables were stolen by sailors from a nearby submarine, who were allowed to move in – and appropriate Turgenev's sofa and Blok's bed – in exchange for supplying Kanailov's (slightly less corrupt) replacement with soup and electric light. 'In the spring', Likhachev remembered, 'when the Neva thawed, the sailors left the Institute one fine day without any warning, taking with them as much as they could carry. After they had gone I found on the floor a gilded plaque: Chaadayev's clock. The clock itself had disappeared. On what ocean floor does it rest now?'[18]

By far the best organisations to be connected to, to escape starvation, were the armed services, the food processing and distribution agencies, or Party headquarters at the Smolniy.

Front-line life, for soldiers in the trenches around Leningrad, was extraordinarily hard. They were brutally and capriciously disciplined, made to march long distances in filthy footcloths and ill-fitting boots, gouged ditches and dugouts out of the frozen ground with crowbars and pickaxes, slept outdoors on the snow wrapped in their greatcoats, waged a constant war against rats and lice, and during offensives went without hot food for days. Nonetheless their ration, even at its lowest, included a daily 500 grams of bread. Though in some units food was systematically stolen by the upper ranks, the full ration was possible to live on, and in general enough food circulated within the military so as to support not only servicemen and women but also their dependants.

Wives and girlfriends of officers stationed in the city itself were noticeably better off than the average, earning the resentful nickname 'defence ladies'. One such lived next door to Georgi Knyazev in the Academicians' Building. Wife of a military engineer, she traded small quantities of bread, sugar and rice for her neighbours' tablecloths, towels, carpets and lamps. Though the food was useful, it also proved, Knyazev wryly noted, that 'even in starving Leningrad, there are some well-fed types!'[19] In early February 1942 a smooth-faced, smartly uniformed officer appeared at Yelena Skryabina's door to serve her with evacuation papers. He seemed like a member of an alien species, 'literally a creature from another world who had accidentally landed on our planet . . . For the hundredth time you reflect on how differently situated those with power or advantage are, from ordinary people who have nothing but their ration cards.'[20] Servicemen also feature as the heroes of what siege historiographers call 'saviour stories' – the accounts, related by numerous survivors, of kind strangers turning up at the eleventh hour with life-saving gifts of food. Though part of siege mythology – one historian even likens them to the Great War's Angel of Mons[21] – many of these stories are undoubtedly true. Igor Kruglyakov remembers that 'just before or just after New Year we had a knock on the door from a young, rosy-cheeked pilot. He brought two boxes, from Father. One contained butter and flour, the second was full of *sukhari*. This saved us.' Skryabina's family was rescued by a completely unknown soldier who appeared one day on her doorstep with a pail of sauerkraut.[22]

Trips to the front itself were also highly prized, since they often involved being treated to what felt like lavish meals. An actress entertaining troops in mid-December wonderingly recorded the menu of a 'banquet' to celebrate the '140 Heroes of the Patriotic War' – 100 grams of alcohol per person, two glasses of beer, 300 grams of bread and one white roll, fifty grams of salted pork fat, two meat patties with buckwheat and gravy, a glass of cocoa with milk, sunflower seeds, a pack of Belomor cigarettes and a box of matches. She was also able to take 400 grams of boiled sweets back home.[23] Vera Inber joined a delegation that visited the Volkhov front in February 1942, bearing shaving kits, guitars and five automatic rifles inscribed with the words 'For the best exterminators of the German occupiers'. At breakfast she was thrilled to be served porridge, bread and a large chunk of butter. 'What a marvellous thing! Next time I shall without fail bring a spoon.' About a hundred workers' delegations made similar trips in November and December.[24] Other civilians managed to attach themselves to the warships moored around the city. Jobs aboard a submarine and a minelayer saved the engineers Chekrizov and Lazarev, and numerous writers and academics – like Boldyrev – earned themselves vital meals by giving readings or lectures to sailors. Visits home by front-line soldiers, in contrast, were forbidden, and doubly dangerous since a man walking alone through the streets in the small hours with a knapsack on his back made a tempting target for mugging or murder.

One of the surest survival techniques was to get employment in food processing or distribution. Leningraders with these sorts of jobs, unsurprisingly, seldom died of starvation. All 713 employees of the Krupskaya sweet factory survived; so did all those at the no. 4 bakery and at a margarine manufacturer. At the Baltika bakery, only twenty-seven out of what grew from 276 to 334 workers died, all the victims being men.[25] Canteen waitresses and bread-shop salesgirls were notoriously 'fat', as were orphanage staff – a friend

of Ostroumova-Lebedeva's, spotting 'Rubenesque' young women
in a newly reopened public bathhouse in the spring, automatically
assumed that they worked in bakeries, soup kitchens or children's
homes.[26] Menstruation having ceased for most during the winter,
women who gave birth in 1942 were also assumed to have worked
in a food plant or dining hall. (The only two pregnant women
Chekrizov saw during the whole of the siege were both waitresses in
his shipyard's cafeteria.)

A measure of such women's buying power was the fact that on
the black market the most saleable items were not those of practical
value, but fashionable women's clothes. Skryabina traded dress fabric
and a chiffon blouse for bread and rice with her former maid, now
the squirrel-jacketed mistress of a warehouse manager.[27] Boldyrev
bribed the 'tsaritsa of the kitchen' at the Scholars' Building with a
lace handkerchief and yellow silk pompoms. Likhachev's wife sold
two dresses at the Sitny market for a kilo of bread and 1,200 grams
of cattle cake.[28] Despite a crackdown in the summer of 1942, theft
and corruption continued to thrive within the food distribution
system throughout the siege. As one Leningrader complained in a
private letter (intercepted by the NKVD) in September of that year:
'There are people who don't know what hunger is, who've been positively spoiled. Look at the salesgirl in any shop, and you'll see a gold
watch on one wrist and a bracelet on the other.' This was only one,
the security men gloomily reported, of 10,820 similar complaints
picked up in just ten days.[29] Whistle-blowing was pointless: when
Lazarev's wife complained that the children in the paediatric hospital where she worked were getting less than half their allotted milk,
she found herself despatched out of town to spend twelve hours a
day digging the hospital's vegetable plot.[30]

Likeliest to survive – and most resented – of all were the apparatchiks at Party headquarters. 'I saw bread being delivered to the
Smolniy myself', an informer heard a woman hiss to her neighbour
in a queue in late January. 'They're not hungry there. If they had to

do without bread for a couple of days maybe they'd sit up and take notice, pay a bit more attention to us.' 'They're stuffing their faces', said another. 'We starve, and watch their fat mugs being driven about in automobiles. It's not fair.'[31]

Rank-and-file Party members – mostly ordinary workers – were not very much better off than ordinary citizens. Seventeen thousand Party members – 15 per cent of the total – are estimated to have starved to death in the first half of 1942. Though this was half or less of the overall civilian mortality rate of 30–40 per cent, the comparison is not direct, since the membership's demographic – mostly men, relatively few old people, no children – differed from that of the general population.[32] Food supply was unquestionably better, however, for the bureaucrats employed at Party headquarters. It is often said that Zhdanov ate ordinary workers' rations during the siege, but given the meals on offer in the Smolniy this seems highly improbable. Visitors came away with tantalising hints of abundant food – to Likhachev, attending a meeting about a book commission, it 'smelled like a dining room', and a Red Army supply officer remembered delivering smoked ham, sturgeon and caviar, left over from a shipment *out* of the city to officials' evacuated families.[33]

The best (and unique) first-person account of what Leningrad's elite actually ate comes from Nikolai Ribkovsky, an official in the Profsoyuz, the Party-sponsored trades union. Aged thirty-eight at the start of the war, Ribkovsky came from a peasant family, was a fervent Stalinist and a member of the generation of functionaries who did well out of the Terror, stepping swiftly into the shoes of their purged seniors. Prior to landing a job in the Smolniy in early December 1941, he lived like any Leningrader, worrying about his wife and son in evacuation ('I've saved a few bars of chocolate to send to Serezhenka'), queuing for the ordinary rations and becoming ordinarily emaciated: 'Is this my body or did it get swapped for somebody else's without me noticing? My legs and wrists are like a growing child's, my stomach has caved in, my ribs stick out from top to bottom.' His Smolniy post, as an instructor in the 'cadres department' of the city soviet, was a passport to a different world. 'For breakfast in the mornings', he wrote on his fourth day into the job,

> macaroni or spaghetti, or *kasha* with butter, and two glasses of sweet tea. Lunch – first course soup, second course meat. Yesterday for example, I had vegetable soup with sour cream, followed by a mince patty with vermicelli. Today for the first course, soup with vermicelli, for the second, pork with steamed cabbage. In the evening, for those still at work, free bread and butter with cheese, a bun, and a couple of glasses of sweet tea. Not bad. They only cut coupons for the bread and meat; everything else is off-ration. This means that with your spare coupons you can go to the shops and buy grain, butter and anything else available, and take a bit home.

Though many Smolniy staff were coming down with diarrhoea, the building was warm, clean and light, and its sewerage and running water worked normally. Other Leningraders, he noted, 'go to the bathroom right in their flats, and then empty it just anywhere, and don't wash their hands before eating . . . Meeting such people – and you meet them quite often – is unpleasant.'

In March 1942 Ribkovsky was sent to the city soviet's 'Rest House' – effectively a hotel – in a dacha village to the north of the city:

> The surroundings are lovely. Little two-storey dachas with covered porches, surrounded by soaring pines, reaching right up to the sky . . . After a walk in the cold, tired and a little hazy in the head from the forest smells, you come home to a warm, cosy room, sink into a soft armchair and gratefully stretch out your legs.
>
> The food here is like in a good peacetime Rest House: varied, delicious, high-quality. Every day there's meat – lamb, ham,

chicken, goose, turkey and sausage. For fish – bream, Baltic herring and smelt – fried, poached or in aspic. Caviar, smoked sturgeon, cheese, *pirozhki*, cocoa, coffee, tea, 300 grams of white bread and of black bread every day, thirty grams of butter and to top it all off, fifty grams of wine and good port with lunch and dinner . . . We eat, drink, spend time outdoors, sleep or just do nothing while listening to the Pathephone, swapping jokes and playing dominoes or cards . . . I am almost unaware of the war, which reminds us of its presence only by the distant bang of guns, though we are only a few dozen kilometres from the front.

The district soviets, he added defensively, were said to do themselves no less well, 'and several organisations have recuperation clinics with which ours pale in comparison'.[34] From the end of February district soviets also fed NKVD staff, on whose shoulders much of the ordinary administration of the city had fallen once the bulk of Party and Komsomol members departed for the front.[35]

At the bottom of Leningrad's food hierarchy came people who weren't Leningraders at all – refugees from the countryside. In September 1941, as peasant families streamed into the city in front of the advancing German and Finnish armies, the Military Council handed responsibility for them to outlying district soviets, who were instructed to check their identities, prevent them from boarding suburban trains into the centre, and house them in empty flats, schools and hostels.[36] 'Leningrad was encircled by a ring of peasant carts', wrote Likhachev, 'which weren't allowed into the city. The peasants lived in camps with their cattle and weeping children, who began to freeze to death on cold nights. To start with people went out to them to trade for milk and meat – they started slaughtering their cattle. But by the end of 1941 all these groups of peasants had frozen to death, as had the refugee women who had been packed into schools and other public buildings.'[37]

Likhachev exaggerated, but not by much. That the Leningrad authorities cruelly neglected refugees is confirmed by the NKVD, whose multifarious functions included inspecting the work of other government agencies. The living conditions of the 64,552 Karelian peasants (over a third of them children) housed in the city's north-eastern suburbs, a report of late November complained, were 'extremely unsatisfactory'. Their quarters were dark, dirty, unheated and lacked running water, and most had to sleep on the floor for lack of bedding. In the village of Toskovo, where eight hundred people had been put up in an unheated, broken-windowed school, they had started felling trees and demolishing farm buildings for fuel, despite which ten children had died of pneumonia in the past five days. The Toskovo peasants were also even worse fed than others, since the evacuation point's head of supply (since arrested) had been holding back their ration cards, using 'swindling combinations to obtain food for his own use'. No measures were being taken to prevent the spread of infectious disease: in one overflowing village a single doctor served five thousand people, and everywhere medical services were 'weak'. 'District organisations', the report summed up, 'ignore conditions at the evacuation points, and try to duck their responsibility to support the evacuee population. We consider it necessary to order district Party committees and soviet executive committees to sort out the evacuation points in their areas, and to improve evacuees' cultural and living standards.'[38]

By the time the NKVD reported again, two months later, refugees were dying in large numbers. In Vsevolozhsk, an evacuation point on the city's north-eastern perimeter, 130 corpses had been collected from homes and hostels. Another 170 had been found in the hospital, about a hundred lying unburied in the cemetery, and six on the streets. The NKVD's own contribution to improving 'cultural and living standards' was characteristic. Eleven peasants had been arrested for displaying 'anti-soviet attitudes', and a twelfth for having slaughtered cats and dogs to eat. Others were accused of 'attempting an organised uprising'. What they had actually tried to do was call a meeting to elect representatives to go to Moscow and ask Stalin for help.[39]

14

'Robinson Crusoe was a Lucky Man'

On 22 January 1942 Moscow's State Defence Committee did what it should have done six months earlier, and ordered the mass evacuation of Leningrad. The Ice Road having frozen to the requisite thickness several weeks earlier, it was to take place by lorry, across Lake Ladoga. Aleksei Kosygin, deputy chairman of the Council of People's Commissars (and later Brezhnev's number two), was sent to oversee the programme, which was to cover 500,000 civilians, prioritising women, children and the elderly.

Though the evacuation programme was compulsory, a substantial minority of Leningraders tried to evade it, fearing that they would not survive the journey, being loath to abandon relatives, or suspecting (often rightly) that once they left their flats they would never get them back again. One such was Aleksandr Boldyrev, pressured by his bosses into leaving with surviving Hermitage staff for Kislovodsk in the Caucasus: 'To go with dystrophy, in the cold . . . leaving the flat, Mama and everything, when here, maybe, we are on the eve of success. I can't do it . . . Apparently the Shtakelberg mother, sister and brother all died before they even set off, as did the bookkeeper Ponamarev. Their bodies were thrown off the evacuation train on to the platform of Finland Station.'[1] Vera Inber, unconsciously echoing Britain's Queen Elizabeth during London's Blitz, declared that her husband was staying with his students and she was staying with her husband.[2] Olga Grechina simply felt that to go would have been 'like abandoning the front'. A student friend of Georgi Knyazev's wanted to stay because she had only three more exams to go to complete her degree, and because she did not want to abandon her mother and aunts.[3]

With no choice whether to stay or go were thousands of ethnic German and Finnish peasants from the besieged villages around Leningrad, whose deportation had been ordered too late by Beria the previous summer. It was carried out, with customary brutality, by the military, under the direction of 'troikas' of local Party, soviet and NKVD bosses. Quotas were set for each district, deportees given only a few hours to pack, and their livestock and food stores confiscated amidst arson and looting.[4] The net effect was to strip the countryside around Leningrad of its farmworkers, with predictable effects on summer 1942's food production. In the 'Oranienbaum pocket', for example, the deportation of 4,775 peasants completely emptied twelve collective farms, and left another eight with only a handful of families.[5] Though some deportees feared they would be killed – 'taken across the bay and pushed under the ice' as a rumour went – in other cases ethnic Russians actually begged to be included. The Oranienbaum report also cites several instances of Red Army officers attempting to save Finns from deportation – taken as worrying proof that 'some military comrades have become so much part of the local population that they identify themselves with local interests, forgetting those of the state'. In total, from the start of the war to 1 October 1942, 128,748 people were forcibly deported out of the blockade ring, of whom slightly under half were ethnic Germans or Finns, and the rest 'criminals' or 'socially alien elements'.[6]

Within the city, however, the large majority of Leningraders were desperate to get out, forming frantic crowds outside evacuation offices and fiercely resenting superiors who jumped the queue. 'Why are they sending away all the factories, the institutes and the best cadres?' one man was overheard to complain. 'Apparently they're not so sure that the Germans aren't going to take Leningrad.' The Germans, said another, were preparing a big attack for the spring: 'The bosses take care of themselves and get out first, but we can be left behind.'[7] Even for those included in the programme, the practicalities involved were daunting. As well as being passed strong enough to travel and free from infectious disease, evacuees had to walk from office to office in search of stamps and paperwork, sell belongings so as to buy food for the journey, pack the permitted sixty pounds per person of luggage and drag it over the Liteiniy Bridge to Finland Station – all crippling tasks for the exhausted and emaciated. That the effort finished off many is demonstrated by the fatality figures for Finland Station's medical checkpoint: of the 2,564 people it processed from the beginning of February to 13 April, 230 died on the spot.[8]

Many evacuees also faced a dreadful sort of triage – should one stay behind and try to save the life of a family member too weak to travel, or leave the weak and save the strong? What famine experts call 'forced abandonment' was very common. Dmitri Likhachev cites three examples from among his friends, the first that of the Dostoyevsky scholar Vasili Komarovich. The day before their planned departure his wife and daughter dragged him by sled to the Writers' Union *statsionar*. On arrival they discovered that the clinic was not due to open for several days, but begged the doctor in charge to take him in. She refused but they left him there anyway, in a basement cloakroom. Fed by the doctor, Komarovich stayed alive just long enough to complete his doctoral thesis. Published after the war, it reads completely normally except that the footnotes are dated according to Church feast days. The second family Likhachev cites left behind a daughter who died in hospital, the third an elderly mother, who was abandoned, still tied to a sled, at Finland Station when she failed her medical.[9]

Yelena Skryabina was spared a similar choice by a timely death. 'Rumours about a possible evacuation', she wrote on 29 January, 'are becoming more and more persistent. My uncle . . . cannot stand these discussions. Even if he should be taken out of Leningrad, he wouldn't survive the trip. Here, sustained by his wife's care, he can still hang on.' He died the following day:

> My aunt, who always adored him, behaved as everyone does now – she didn't even cry. At six in the evening Lyudmila came home from work. I let her in and told her the sad news of her father's death. She wept bitterly and only then, somehow, did it really strike my aunt. She embraced her daughter and wept for a long time in her arms. It was easier to witness this outburst of grief than the terrible hardness one finds in everyone in Leningrad these days.[10]

One of the saddest siege stories is that of Yuri Ryabinkin, the fifteen-year-old who had been caught by the announcement of war on his way to a chess competition. A gauche, highly strung teenager cooped up with his family in terrifying circumstances, he is in many ways the Soviet equivalent of Anne Frank. His end, though, is far more ambiguous. Like his friends, he had initially greeted the war with childish excitement, using the unexpected time off school to play vingt-et-un and forfeits ('Lopatin crawled up a whole flight of the spiral staircase on all fours, Finkelshtein had to give Bron a piggyback') as well as standing fire duty on the roof of 34 Sadovaya Street, the sleek deco apartment building (today a bank) where he lived with his mother and younger sister.

In mid-October he began to 'fall down the funnel', first complaining of hunger ('it gives you an itchy sensation in the pit of the stomach, and your mouth waters all the time'), then beginning to hate a better-fed family that moved into their communal apartment. ('It's humiliating seeing Mother drinking water to fill herself up while A.N. stands there talking about the theatre . . . that Anfisa Nikolayevna is like a plump, well-fed cat . . .'[11]) By the end of the

month he found it difficult to climb the stairs, and had stopped
bothering to change his clothes. Though he had only one candle to
read by, he tried to escape into fiction – Dumas was 'most entertaining', Jack London's 'Love of Life' 'a wonderful piece'. A fortnight
later his face had swollen from dropsy and he had begun to obsess
about food ('Every night in my sleep I see bread, butter, *pirozhki*
and potatoes. And before I go to sleep the last thought in my head
is always that in twelve hours time the night will be over and I can
eat a piece of bread . . .'). His mother left each morning for work,
taking his younger sister with her; Yuri's job was to queue for rations:

> Mother and Ira come home hungry, frozen and tired . . . they can
> hardly drag their feet along. No food at home, no firewood for
> the stove . . . They start scolding and reproaching me because the
> neighbours downstairs have managed to get grains and meat, and
> I haven't . . . So it's back to the queues for me, to no avail . . . Oh
> if only I had a pair of felt boots![12]

In December his entries become almost hysterical, a mixture of
fantasising ('Mama will get a job as librarian in some newly organised hospital; I will be her assistant'), self-hatred at having filched a
few crumbs from the family food stock, and paranoia:

> What's this torture Mother and Ira arrange for me in the evenings?
> At table Ira eats deliberately slowly, so that she can feel that here
> she is, eating, while the rest of us, who have already eaten, sit
> watching her with hungry eyes. Mother eats hers first, then takes
> a little from each of us. When the bread's being divided Ira bursts
> into tears.[13]

At the end of the month the diary peters out into loose, wild scrib-
bles: 'I want to live, but I can't live like this! But how I want to live!'
and 'Where's Mama? Where is she?' The last is dated 6 January:

I can hardly walk or do anything. I have almost no strength left. Mama, too, can barely walk – I can't imagine how she manages it. Nowadays she hits me often, scolds and shouts. She has wild nervous fits because she can't stand my wretched appearance – that of a weak, hungry, tormented person who can barely move from one spot to another, is always in the way and 'pretends' to be ill and helpless. But I'm not pretending . . . Oh Lord, what's happening to me?[14]

What did happen to him, as the siege historians Ales Adamovich and Daniil Granin found out from his sister Ira forty years later, was that he was left behind. Having got evacuation slots for the whole family, traded belongings for food and warm clothing, and loaded a sled with necessaries and tradeable silver cutlery, Yuri's mother found that she could not lift her son downstairs. Leaving him lying on the sofa, mother and daughter set off, towing the sled, for Finland Station. 'Once we'd crossed the Neva', Ira remembered, 'Mother was desperate to go back for him. "Yura's back there, all on his own!" I was crying of course. But almost as soon as we boarded the train it started moving, and off we went.' What became of Yuri thereafter we do not know. He may have died in Leningrad or in evacuation, since the diary itself, handed in in response to a newspaper appeal in 1970, has been traced to Vologda province. He may even have survived the war but not wanted to re-establish contact with his family. Not much of it was left anyway. His father, who had been arrested during the 1936–7 Terror, perished somewhere in the Gulag. His mother died during the evacuation journey, on a bench at Vologda railway station. His sister Ira spent the rest of the war in a children's home and was later brought up by an aunt.[15]

It is another comforting siege myth that, once embarked on the Ice Road, evacuees enjoyed good care and security. Even Dmitri Pavlov, the supply chief whose 'Thaw'-era memoir is one of the more outspoken of the genre, claims that the evacuation was 'carefully thought out and well organised':

> A series of field messes was set up on the road for the evacuees. As soon as Leningraders crossed over the lake and reached land they were served hot cabbage soup, potatoes and meat, and other nourishment such as these exhausted people had dreamed of night after night. The fragrance of bread made from pure rye flour intoxicated the famished people. From their first step on land they were surrounded by loving care. Everyone felt in his heart the desire to help them in any way he could.[16]

Nothing could be further from the truth. The first endurance test evacuees faced was the train journey from Finland Station to Osinovets, which though only forty-five kilometres long could take several days. Having disembarked, they then had to bribe their way on to the lorries crossing the lake ice. Yelena Kochina only got through the violent, shouting crowds at the truck tailgates by slipping two litres of vodka to a driver; Igor Kruglaykov's mother bargained with a fat, drunk driver who wore a fur coat over his peasant tunic, first handing him a packet of cigarettes, then money, and finally her father's silver chiming pocket watch. The Ice Road itself resembled the North Pole, a blindingly white, featureless plain on fine days ('The poppy-red flag of the traffic controller', wrote Inber, 'is visible a kilometre away'), a howling maelstrom in blizzards and a black void at night. A lucky few crossed in buses sent from Moscow, but most in open or canvas-topped trucks, in which it was easy to die of exposure. Too weak to hold on as the trucks bumped over the ice, many passengers were simply jolted out. A woman soldier assigned to the route picked up the corpses of half a dozen babies and toddlers each morning, flung from their mothers' arms as the lorries raced to beat the dawn.[17]

On the opposite 'mainland' shore, reception facilities were worse than inadequate. Diarists describe queuing for hours for soup, being unable to find anywhere to sleep, and fighting for places on the trains onwards through unoccupied Russia. Nor, when food was available, were measures initially taken to prevent the starving from killing themselves by overeating. A doctor ordered to set up a medical station at Zhikharevo discovered that evacuees were immediately eating all the dry rations – smoked sausage and bread – given them for the three-day train journey onward to Tikhvin, and bursting their stomachs. Having pleaded in vain with the chief of the evacuation centre to change his arrangements, he eventually managed to get a meeting with visiting representatives of Moscow's State Defence Committee. Having described the results of his autopsies he persuaded them that evacuees should instead be fed in small quantities en route, with millet and semolina cooked in the train boilers.[18]

A typical account of the whole – resoundingly Soviet – evacuation experience comes from Vladimir Kulyabko, a widowed sixty-five-year-old refrigeration engineer. Having survived the first half of the winter on gifts from a neighbour who worked in a food shop, in February he was offered a place on one of the first convoys across the Ice Road. He accepted, hoping to reach his son, an army doctor stationed in Cherepovets, a town 400 kilometres east of Leningrad on the railway line to Vologda. Telling the manager of his apartment building that he was merely moving into another flat, he left the keys with a neighbour and paid another in kerosene, macaroni and nuts to help him get his luggage to Finland Station. Including stops to rest on sandboxes, the three-kilometre walk took two hours. Having been due to leave at 10.30 in the morning, the train did not appear until 6 p.m., at which point Kulyabko found his assigned carriage taken up by baggage-laden 'businessmen'. He managed to squeeze himself and his suitcase, basket and pillow into the draughty section at the end of the carriage where in normal times smokers gathered. The train finally got under way at 1 a.m., and food was handed out. To get any, Kulyabko soon realised, he would have to pay a bribe. A note – '400g of bread for Kulyabko, money enclosed, no need for change' – did the trick. 'In ten minutes I had my bread. Having learned from experience, I did the same thing for the soup.' On arrival at Osinovets six hours later he noticed fifteen corpses lying beside the tracks.

Getting on to a lorry to cross the lake, he took some time to work out, required more bribery:

> I waited, hungry and unfed like everyone else (despite the fact that in Leningrad we had been promised three meals a day and given the appropriate coupons). At about 5 p.m. I found the man in charge but he fobbed me off with some meaningless nonsense or other, and I realised I wouldn't be going anywhere soon. The lorries came and went, but the people in charge chose who to let on themselves, not following any sort of list or queue … I approached the boss once again, telling him that I was ill and that I was going to join my son, a decorated soldier.

Shortly afterwards he was approached by an overseer, who settled on 500 grams of tobacco in exchange for a place on the first closed lorry to come along. Four hours later Kulyabko was aboard, having cannily refused to hand over the bribe until he was actually seated inside with his luggage. 'The same system of bribery, but much pettier, pertained in the lorry itself. The driver constantly asked for cigarettes, which he was given. Otherwise the lorry went slowly, or things went wrong all the time. A cigarette given at just the right moment made all these problems disappear.' Having spent three hours stuck in a jam with food trucks heading the other way, the lorry finally arrived on the 'mainland' at five the next morning.

Though Kulyabko had now escaped the siege ring, this was far from the end of his difficulties. First he had to queue three hours for *kasha* and soup, for which evacuees were expected to produce their own plate and spoon – he got round the problem by giving the waitress fifty roubles and his passport as security for a bowl. When a train arrived, it was mobbed by the frantic crowd. Paying thirty roubles to a soldier to carry his luggage, Kulyabko managed to climb into a goods wagon with some emaciated engineering students, who refused him space round its hay-stoked stove. Five sleepless nights and days later, punctuated by long queues for food, petty thefts and the death of one of the students, whose friends pushed his corpse out of the train window, he reached Cherepovets:

> I crawl out of the wagon, fall over of course, drag down my three bundles and call out, 'Help me carry these to the station'. Nobody pays any attention. I try to drag them myself, but they are heavy and I fall over again. I stand there in despair. Finally I spot a street urchin and ask him to carry my things to the station. He says, 'Will you give me a smoke?' and I say that I will . . . We get to the station; I see a policeman and ask him, 'How do I get to this address?' He replies that there are horse-drawn cabs on the square. Stupidly, I go to the square, give the boy a cigarette and stand looking for the cabs. But there aren't any, and never have been. I appeal to this person and that for help, but nobody responds. So I start dragging my things to the left-luggage office, which thankfully isn't far. I push the suitcase over the snow with my feet, and carry everything else. I go for a metre, a metre and a half, and stop to rest. I stand there on the brink of tears. How will I get to Borya?

His saviour was a young soldier, who, refusing all thanks, picked up his bags and walked him to Borya's hospital, giving him an army ration rusk to eat on the way.[19] Kulyabko travelled when the mass-evacuation programme had been in progress for little more than a week, but conditions remained chaotic all the way through to mid-April, when the spring thaw brought the lorries – by now swishing axle-deep through meltwater – to a halt.[20]

How many people did the Ice Road save altogether? Officially 11,296 evacuees made it across in January 1942, 117,434 in February, 221,947 in March and 163,392 in April, making an impressive, plan-beating total of 514,069 in less than four months.[21] This takes no account, however, of those who died on the way, either during the crossing itself or in the trains that took evacuees onwards into unoccupied Russia. In the crowded, toiletless freight cars, as experienced by Kochina, stomach disorders raged:

> Whenever someone 'feels a need' the whole 'public' of the car usually takes part in its realisation. It works as follows: the door is opened by common effort and the cause of the commotion drops his trousers and sticks his rear into the wind. Several people hold him by the hands and under the arms. [During halts] we all crawl out of the train and squat next to the wagons, side by side – men, women and children. The locals crowd around, staring at us with horror . . . But we're indifferent to all that. We don't experience shame or any other feelings . . . The sick ride with us until they die. Then we simply throw them out of the moving train.[22]

That evacuees received inadequate care even after they had reached the 'mainland' is confirmed by an NKVD report of 5 March, which complains of 'irresponsible and heartless' treatment of evacuees by staff at a reception point, and 'inhuman' conditions on the trains. From one, seventeen corpses had been removed at Volkhov station, twenty at Babayevo, seven at Cherepovets and seven more at Vologda. From another, twenty-six had been removed at Volkhov, thirty-two at Tikhvin, four at Babayevo and six at Vologda.[23] A wartime mass grave at Vologda, filled mostly with fleeing Leningraders, is estimated to contain 20,000 dead.

For those who survived the initial evacuation journey there remained the problem, if not attached to an institution or within reach of relatives, of finding a local authority prepared to supply ration cards and accommodation. Since there were displaced people and chronic food shortages everywhere (even in Moscow, beggars died on the streets in the winter of 1941–2), this was extremely difficult. Skryabina, who crossed the Ice Road in February, first watched her mother die in a chaotic so-called hospital in Cherepovets, then spent weeks journeying with her emaciated sons from one railway town to another in search of a sympathetic official. When she eventually found one it was thanks to *svyazi*: her old family doctor had become a senior Party official in Gorky (now Nizhni Novgorod).

> His name worked like magic . . . The clerk pushed the people standing ahead of me aside and amiably invited us to follow him. He led us straight to the office of the Gorky Party Committee . . . In ten minutes I was out again with three documents in my hands – two for extra rations and one for a special transport headed for the Caucasus.

The rejections Skryabina had endured up to that point were predictable, as much a product of general wartime shortage and upheaval as of bureaucratic negligence. But she experienced them as malign and personal: 'I think', she wrote, 'that Robinson Crusoe was a lucky man. He knew quite well that he was on an uninhabited island and had to fend for himself. But I am among human beings.'[24]

Corpse-Eating and Person-Eating

Another aspect of the siege that has no place in the traditional Soviet story is crime. Leningraders, claims supply commissar Dmitri Pavlov, were too 'high-minded' to grab loaves that spilled from a bread truck hit by a shell, and 'jealously protected' the trees in the public parks from being cut down for firewood. Their example refuted the 'foreign writers who assert that man loses his morals and becomes a predatory beast when hunger affects him powerfully. If this were true, anarchy should have reigned in Leningrad.'[1]

Anarchy did not reign in Leningrad during the siege, but the city did suffer a crime wave, especially of theft and murder for food and food cards, and, most notoriously, of cannibalism. The commonest of violent crimes was simple mugging. Yelena Kochina, returning home from a bread shop in mid-December 1941, saw a teenage boy dressed in the uniform of one of the city's trade schools running towards her. She stood aside but he grabbed her bread and ran on, leaving her staring in horror at her empty hands. Back at home, a neighbour scolded her for not hiding the bread under her coat. Four days later Yelena's husband got in a fight with another trade-school boy over a spilled crust:

Today [Dima] ran into some sleds loaded with bread. An armed guard of five men accompanied them, and a crowd followed behind, staring spellbound at the loaves. Dima followed along with everyone else. Near the bread shop the sleds were unloaded, and the crowd fell on the empty boxes, picking out the crumbs. Dima found a large crust trampled in the snow. But a boy tore the crust out of his hands. He chewed it, this horrendous brat, smacking his lips and drooling saliva. Dima went mad. He grabbed the boy by his collar and began to shake him, not realizing what he was doing. The boy's head wobbled on his thin neck like a rag doll's. But he kept on hurriedly chewing with his eyes closed. 'It's gone, it's gone! Look!' he shouted suddenly and opened his mouth wide.[2]

Cited as thieves in dozens of similar accounts,[3] these trade-school boys, like the peasant refugees in the suburbs, were one of Leningrad's most vulnerable social groups. Greatly expanded just before the war, the trade schools – *remeslennye uchilishchya* – were low-prestige boarding institutions, designed to train up teenagers from the villages as factory hands. When the siege ring closed their pupils found themselves cut off from their families and at the mercy of often negligent or unscrupulous school managers. The commissar sent from Moscow to oversee mass evacuation over the Ice Road, Aleksei Kosygin, noticed their worse than average emaciation and was prompted personally to inspect Trade School no. 33. The boys, he discovered, were lice-ridden and sleeping two or three to a bed, without sheets or pillowcases or any isolation of sick from healthy. Even more shamefully, kitchen staff were systematically pilfering their food, leaving them with half or less of their proper ration. A pupils' representative, he wrote furiously to Zhdanov, should be allowed directly to oversee the kitchens, and managers and staff should be arrested and put on trial. The overall mortality rate in the trade schools is unknown, but has been estimated at a staggering 95 per cent.[4]

Theft by Leningrad's thousands of other abandoned children was reduced by the opening and subsequent evacuation of ninety-eight new orphanages, but these usually only took in children aged up to thirteen. 'The position of fourteen- and fifteen-year-olds left without parents', a report to Zhdanov noted, 'is especially difficult. They are not accepted into children's homes, and crowd near shops and bakeries, snatching bread and food from buyers' hands.' City education department staff, it went on, refused even to send younger children to orphanages unless they were clean, free of infection and in possession of all the correct papers.[5]

Of more concern to police was the threat that angry bread-shop crowds would get out of control, or descend into outright looting. Though food distribution was never seriously disrupted there were some near-riots, especially in January and February 1942, when Leningraders were queuing from the small hours, often to receive no bread at all. Late one January evening Dmitri Lazarev went to look for his wife, who had gone out to queue at seven that morning. He found her standing in line outside a bread shop on Bolshoi Prospekt:

> People were being allowed into the shop ten at a time. At one point, when the next ten were being allowed in, everyone behind rushed forward and started trying to break down the doors. A pair of policemen tried to hold back the crowd. Finally they began telling lies, promising that people would be let in as soon as the crowd took a few steps back. When the crowd did so they locked the doors and announced that the shop was closed and everyone could go home. There were shouts, complaints – some had not eaten for two days, others had starving children.

Order was only restored after Lazarev and some of the other men went round to the back of the shop and persuaded the manager to release rations for another seventy people.[6] Altogether, the NKVD lists seventy-two such 'attacks' by members of the public on food shops, carts and sleds in the first twenty-seven days of January. Though in one case looters threw bricks at shop staff, most consisted simply of queuers pushing their way behind the counter, or of small groups (sometimes of armed deserters, but more often of women or trade-school boys) knocking over delivery sleds or handcarts and making off with their loads.[7] 'In Bread Shop no. 318', states a typical report of early January,

> the crowd burst in, incited by a person unknown, and dragged away 100kg of bread. We managed to arrest a few people. At Bread Shop no. 399 about 50kg of bread were looted by the crowd, but not one looter was arrested. A group fell upon Bread Shop no. 318's cart, which had been bringing in the new delivery. On the night of 7 January two people were discovered hiding under the shop counter. They were found to be carrying knives. The same day Shop no. 20 on Gas Prospect was robbed. Similar incidents took place in the Smolniy and other districts.[8]

In response, more police were posted outside shops and delivery vehicles were instructed to vary their routes and provided with guards.[9]

One of very few diarists who admit to benefiting from food theft is Yelena Kochina. Her oedema-swollen husband Dima started stealing in mid-December, using a sharpened walking stick to spear loaves in a lightless bread shop. On one occasion a fellow queuer saw him steal, followed him out of the shop and threatened to report him:

> 'Give me half or I'll turn you in', she whispered, grabbing him by the sleeve . . . They went into a doorway, and Dima thrust the bread into the woman's face with the words, 'Here, stuff yourself!' The woman grabbed the bread, sat down on the step, and

began greedily to cram it into her mouth. For a short while Dima watched her in silence. Then he sat down beside her and began to eat his half. Thus they sat and ate, now and then cursing one another, until all the bread was gone.

A sackful of buckwheat, purloined from a factory food store in mid-January, enabled the Kochins to start regaining weight, which they hid from neighbours by deliberately not washing. Bread-shop staff, Yelena noted in self-justification, were no less dishonest, and 'round as buns': 'In return for bread they have everything they want. Almost all of them, without any shame at all, wear gold jewellery and expensive furs. Some even work behind the counter in luxurious sable and sealskin coats.'[10]

Murder for food or ration cards also became frequent, with 1,216 such arrests in the first half of 1942.[11] What Leningraders feared were attacks by strangers on a lonely street, but the cases detailed by the NKVD are of people killing family members, colleagues and neighbours. Again, both perpetrators and victims were often disadvantaged adolescents. A typical, pathetic, example is that of an eighteen-year-old who killed his two younger brothers with an axe, and was arrested while trying to kill his mother. Questioned, he explained that he had lost his job, and with it his worker's ration card, when caught in a petty theft, and that he wanted to use his brothers' coupons. Another two teenage boys, aged eighteen and fifteen, attacked and severely wounded their neighbours, a mother and her six-year-old daughter, and were arrested while trying to exchange their cards for bread. Yet another boy, a sixteen-year-old machinist, was murdered in his hostel by a workmate after he boasted of having managed to exchange several days' worth of coupons for food.[12]

More crime must have gone unrecorded, since in the depths of the winter the police themselves partially ceased to function. On 10 February the head of the Leningrad NKVD, P. N. Kubatkin, asked his superiors in Moscow for a thousand new men to guard the city's factories, since of the 2,800 men of his existing brigade, 152 had died of 'exhaustion', 1,080 were in hospital and at least a hundred reported in sick each day.[13] The Pavlovsk curator Anna Zelenova, one of whose jobs was to take privately owned antiques into official safekeeping, once emerged from a (reportedly grateful) collector's flat to find the policeman who had accompanied her dead on a chair on the landing.[14] Other anecdotal evidence is of widespread corruption and summary justice. 'If they discovered that bread had been stolen', a post-war émigré recalled, 'they would round up five people and shoot them for it, whether they had been involved or not.'[15]

But overall, the impression given by survivors of the first siege winter is less of fear of muggers and murderers, more of silence, emptiness and isolation. Eleven-year-old Anzhelina Kupaigorodskaya lived through it alone in her family's flat on the Fontanka, her chemical engineer parents having been forced to move into their workplaces. Seven decades later, she credits her survival to a list of rules written down for her on a piece of paper by her father: she was to wash and empty her slop bucket daily, never to collect more than one day's ration at a time, and regularly to visit the post office in case relatives had wired money. Going outdoors, she remembers, was frightening, but not because she feared crime – indeed, she only learned that there was any long after the war, by reading about it. At the time she felt 'alone in the city, absolutely alone. I would walk to the shop and back, enter our courtyard, climb the stairs and go in my door. If anybody had wanted to they could have pushed me over with their little finger. But I never met a soul.'[16] Kochina, waiting for her husband to return from his bread-thieving expeditions, used to go out on to the landing to listen for his arrival: 'From below silence rose like steam, condensing on the staircase. I spat into the stairwell and listened to how the spittle smacked resoundingly below. I stood in the darkness for a long time, spitting and listening.'[17]

Most notorious of the crimes that flourished during the siege –
and most symptomatic of Leningraders' desperation – was cannibalism. The poet Olga Berggolts first heard of it from a psychiatrist
friend:

> Not long ago Prendel told us that corpse-eating is on the rise. In
> May [1942] his hospital dealt with fifteen cases, compared with
> eleven in April. He had to – and still has to – give expert advice on
> whether cannibals are responsible for their actions. Cannibalism
> – a fact. He told us about a cannibal couple who first ate the
> small corpse of their child, then entrapped three more children
> – killed them and ate them . . . For some reason I found what he
> was saying funny – genuinely funny, especially when he tried to
> exonerate them. I said, 'But you didn't eat your grandmother!'
> And after that I just couldn't take his cannibal stories seriously. It's
> all so disgusting – cannibals, roofs with holes in them, blown-out
> windows, pointlessly destroyed cities. Oh yes, the heroism and
> romance of war![18]

Until the publication of police records in 2004, evidence as to
the use of human meat for food during the siege was anecdotal:
the rumours, believed by Leningraders at the time, of children
kidnapped on the street, and diary reports of corpses stripped of
thighs and buttocks as well as clothing. A lurid description of a
young couple lured into an apartment-turned-slaughterhouse,
related as fact by Harrison Salisbury in his *The 900 Days*, on closer
inspection turns out to have been drawn from a novel published,
presumably under the auspices of Nazi propagandists, in occupied
Ukraine.[19]

For most people at the time, cannibalism was similarly a matter
of second-hand horror stories rather than direct experience.
'On Pokrovskaya Square', wrote the geography teacher Aleksei
Vinokurov, 'I ran into a crowd of people silently staring at the

clumsily butchered corpse of a plump young woman. Who did this and why? Is this proof of the persistent rumours of cannibalism?'[20] When a 'rather healthy' acquaintance of Dmitri Likhachev's failed to return home after setting off to a strange address in search of a barter deal, he wondered if she had been murdered by the sinister traders who offered anonymous mince 'cutlets' for sale in the Haymarket.[21] Visiting her factory to collect her pay, Olga Grechina noticed that metal shavings had piled up around the lathes, and asked what had happened to an old cleaning lady, affectionately known as Auntie Nastya. Told that Nastya had been executed, she at first thought it must be a joke: 'But no, it's true! She ate her daughter – hid her under the bed and cut bits off her. The police shot her. These days you don't go before a court.'[22]

The city leadership was kept fully informed by the NKVD, which detailed its first nine cases of 'the use of human meat as food' in its situation report of 13 December 1941. A mother had smothered her eighteen-month-old daughter in order to feed herself and three older children; a twenty-six-year-old man, laid off from his tyre factory, had murdered and eaten his eighteen-year-old roommate; a metalworker (a member of the Party) and his son had killed two woman refugees with a hammer and hidden their body parts in a shed; an unemployed plumber had killed his wife in order to feed their teenage son and nieces, hiding her remains in the toilets of the Lenenergo workers' hostel.[23] Ten days later thirteen more cases were reported: an unemployed eighteen-year-old had murdered his grandmother with an axe, boiling and eating her liver and lungs; a seventeen-year-old had stolen an unburied corpse from a cemetery and put the flesh through a table-top mincer; a cleaner had killed her one-year-old daughter and fed her to her two-year-old.[24] Also among the first to resort to eating human meat were the criminally neglected pupils of the *remeslennye uchilishchya*. At Trade School no. 39 on Mokhovaya Street, the pupils were left to themselves. They had no supervision, and no ration cards were provided for them for December. Through December they ate the meat of slaughtered cats and dogs. On 24 December pupil Kh. died of malnutrition, and his corpse was partially used by the other pupils for food. On 27 December a second pupil, V., died, and his corpse was also used for food. Eleven people have been arrested for cannibalism, all of whom have admitted guilt. School director Leimer and commandant Plaksina, guilty of abandoning this group of pupils without provisions or supervision, have been subjected to criminal prosecution.[25]

Altogether, police only arrested twenty-six people for cannibalism in December, but the number shot up to 356 in January and 612 in February. It halved to 300 in March and April, then rose again slightly in May before falling off steeply through June and July.[26] By December 1942, when the phenomenon finally tailed off, 2,015 'cannibals' had been arrested in total.[27]

The Russian language makes the morally vital distinction between *trupoyedstvo* – 'corpse-eating' – and *lyudoyedstvo* – 'person-eating', or murder for cannibalism. The gruesome cases of intra-family killing highlighted by the police notwithstanding, the former was overwhelmingly more common (of the 300 'users of human meat for food' arrested in April 1942, for example, only forty-four were murderers).[28] Organised gangsterism was extremely rare: the NKVD reports mention only one such case – that of six young men, three of them railway workers, who lured a series of thirteen victims, mostly picked up outside bread shops, with offers of barter to a flat, where they were despatched with an axe-blow to the back of the head.[29] Cannibalism was also significantly less common in the city centre than in the suburbs, which were poorer, worse policed and hosted the overflowing cemeteries. (The largest numbers of arrests were made in the outlying Primorsky and

Krasno Gvardeisky districts and on the industrial Vyborg Side; the smallest in the Smolniy district, home to Party headquarters.[30]) On 22 December police patrolling the Serafimovskoye cemetery in Novaya Derevnya stopped two women carrying sacks, whch were found to contain the bodies of three infants. Questioning revealed that one woman was the wife of a soldier away at the front, the other that of a janitor, and that they had planned to feed the meat to their daughters, aged eighteen months and sixteen. Two more bodysnatchers – a factory worker and a carpenter – were arrested at the Serafimovskoye the following day; they too had planned to use the contents of their sacks to feed their children.[31] A forty-three-year-old unemployed man, his wife and thirteen-year-old son were caught 'systematically stealing' corpses from a hospital morgue, and a twenty-four-year-old nurse was arrested for scavenging amputated limbs from an operating room.[32]

Other easily accessible corpses were those of colleagues or relatives who had died of starvation. Typical of the kind of cooperative action this sort of *trupoyedstvo* often engendered were a clutch of cases in January and February. At the First of May Factory a group of nine men, all of whom lived in the same hostel, shared the corpse of a workmate.[33] At the Lenin Factory a woman worker shared the corpse of her eleven-year-old son with two female friends. A cleaner shared the body of her husband with her unemployed neighbour; the electrician and the deputy manager of a public bathhouse together ate its dead boilerman.[34] Three members of a civil defence team, one a Party member, shared a corpse they discovered while making safe a bomb-damaged building.[35]

The optical engineer Dmitri Lazarev gives a first-hand account of being invited to join such an enterprise:

Valentina Antonovna (a friend of Nina's [Lazarev's wife]) came round. Trembling with emotion, she recounted how yesterday a woman tried to drag her into a horrible business. Earlier in the day some civil defence workers had been crushed to death by falling beams, while dismantling a building on Krestovsky [Island]. Their bodies had been taken to an empty shed next to the flat in which this woman lives alone. She proposed to Valentina Antonovna that they take the corpse of one of the girls to her flat, prepare the meat, eat some and salt the rest for future use. She said she had firewood, but couldn't manage everything on her own. As an inducement she cited the example of her sister, who has been eating human meat for three weeks, has got back her strength and feels much better. Imperiously she said that she would brook no hesitation, that it was a question of life and death, and that the next morning she would call round and they would go to work together.

Valentina Antonovna didn't sleep all night. At one and the same time she refused, outraged, even to consider the suggestion, and convinced herself, looking at her sleeping grown-up son, that for his sake she ought to agree. But then she began imagining in detail what it would actually involve, and leapt up: 'No! Anything but that! I would lose my mind!' Before morning she had again convinced herself that it wasn't murder, that the girls were dead anyway, and that if she didn't do it her tall, broad-shouldered son would die of starvation. On this she went back to sleep, awoke this morning, and waited for her guest. But when the woman appeared Valentina Antonovna's reaction, quite unexpectedly, was a furious refusal. The woman left, viciously swearing and cursing.[36]

Overall, 64 per cent of those arrested for 'use of human meat as food' were female, 44 per cent unemployed or 'without fixed occupation' and over 90 per cent illiterate or in possession of only basic education. Only 15 per cent were 'rooted inhabitants' of Leningrad and only 2 per cent had a criminal record.[37] The typical Leningrad 'cannibal', therefore, was neither the Sweeney Todd of legend nor the bestial lowlife of Soviet history writing, but an honest, working-class housewife from the provinces, scavenging protein to save her family.

Remarkably, Leningrad's medical authorities made at least one attempt to have those driven to eating human meat classified as mentally ill. On 20 February 1942 the head of the Leningrad Front's medical services called a special meeting of seven senior psychiatrists – academics, the head of a psychiatric hospital, the chief court psychiatrist and a representative of the army medical service – to decide whether or not corpse-eaters should be held criminally responsible for their actions. The doctors' verdict, from the judicial point of view, was contradictory: corpse-eaters were sane, but also not incurably criminal. One dissenter argued that no mentally healthy person, by definition, could resort to cannibalism, but that they should nevertheless stand trial: 'These are inadequate and socially dangerous people! We need to deal with them strictly!' In conclusion it was decided that most cannibals were mentally healthy, but 'primitive, of a lower moral and intellectual level'. Though all were dangerous, 'periods of isolation' should be determined individually, taking into account the circumstances of the crime ('active or passive corpse-eating') and the offender's personality.[38]

In practice, however, all cannibals – sane, insane, murderers or harmless 'corpse-eaters' – were treated as criminals. Since no provision for cannibalism existed in the Criminal Code it was included under the catch-all clause of 'banditry' (the Code's article 59–3). By the time the psychiatrists convened, 554 'special category bandits' had already gone before military tribunals, and of these 329 had been shot and 53 given ten-year gaol sentences. At least another forty-five had died (presumably of starvation) in custody.[39] But although no official distinction was made between murderers and corpse-eaters, variations in sentencing suggests that in practice the latter got off relatively lightly. Of the 1,913 cannibals whose cases had been processed by early June, military tribunals sentenced 586 to execution and 668 to prison terms of five to ten years.[40] What happened to the remaining 659 is unclear. They may simply have awaited sentencing, but it is perhaps not wishful thinking to discern – in police reports' habitual observation that a particular 'user of human meat for food' was an unsupported woman with dependent children and no previous convictions – coded pleas for clemency. It would be good to know that they were answered.

Anton Ivanovich is Angry

An incongruous reminder of peacetime life, for people making their way down the Nevsky in the winter of 1941–2, was a series of flyers advertising a film comedy that had been due to open at the beginning of the war. Its title, pasted up on lamp-posts in large black letters, was *Anton Ivanovich is Angry*.

How angry were Leningraders, and why did their anger never break out into open revolt? On one level this is a frivolous question – Leningraders, like other Soviet citizens, felt loyalty to their country if not to Bolshevism, hated and feared the Germans and were too exhausted and emaciated to do more than strive for their own bare survival. On another, it is a conundrum. Hundreds of thousands had already directly experienced repression and impoverishment at the hands of their government before the war; now almost all were either close to death from starvation themselves, or watching helplessly as family and friends died around them. The hypocrisies and inequalities of Soviet life, moreover, were sharper than ever. People could see with their own eyes that the lights in government buildings stayed on, that corruption was rife, that their bosses' children ate while their own starved. Moscow was cut off, the rank-and-file police in almost as desperate a plight as themselves – what did they have left to lose? Bread shortages, a disastrous war and fury at government incompetence had sparked the February Rising in 1917. Why didn't they do the same a quarter of a century later?

That they would do so was certainly the expectation of the Nazis, whose pre-war confidence that invasion would immediately spark anti-Bolshevik revolt took a while to wear off. In particular, they vastly overestimated the importance of Russian anti-Semitism, every minor indication of which got top billing in SS and military intelligence reports. Their Russian-language propaganda was also startlingly inept, simultaneously denouncing the 'Jewish-Stalinist' Soviet government and boasting of the invincibility and ruthlessness of the Wehrmacht ('Finish your bread, you'll soon be dead' was one slogan; 'We bomb today, you die tomorrow' another).[1] Army intelligence began to correct itself in the autumn, admitting that though the 'Jewish question' was 'increasingly actively discussed' by Leningraders there was 'no evidence of organised or active resistance to the Communist authorities'. Leaflets air-dropped over the city, it was noted, were not being passed from hand to hand, but hidden away for future use in case Leningrad was abandoned. Another report twelve days later concluded that although the public mood was febrile and anxious, the 'Red government, with the help of terror and vigorous propaganda, holds the population strongly in hand, and at the present time an organised rising against the enemy cannot be counted on'.[2]

The SS's intelligence service, the Sicherheitsdienst (SD), persisted in its wishful thinking for longer, passing on every gloomy rumour and anti-Semitic *anekdot*. (One, according to the SD, had Russian prisoners of war refusing to obey German orders to bury Jewish POWs alive. 'Upon which, the German soldiers ordered the Jews to bury the Russians. The Jews took up their shovels without hesitation. Thus the Germans were able to demonstrate to the Russian POWs the true essence of Judaism.'[3]) By the middle of winter, however, both services had begun to realise that the brutality of the Nazi occupation was only stiffening Russian resistance. 'Earlier on,' the SD reported in February, 'deserters made the distinction between Nazis and Germans opposed to Hitlerism. But now they call all Germans "barbarians who must be destroyed".'[4] By May 1942, when intelligence on Leningrad was rolled into reports on the occupied territories in general, all hopes of a rising had been abandoned.

The Germans were not wrong, though, in thinking that Leningraders were angry. Gauging overall public opinion is hard, but the diaries show Leningraders raging as much against the incompetence, callousness, hypocrisy and dishonesty of their own officials as against the distant, impersonal enemy. Among the best evidence for what ordinary people thought of their government, paradoxically, is the records kept by the regime itself. Unlike other dictators, Stalin and his satraps never made the mistake of believing themselves beloved – on the contrary, they saw plots under every stone. Paranoia aside, the reports Zhdanov received every few days from the head of the 'instructors' department' of the city Party Committee were remarkably sophisticated, collating overheard snatches of conversation into quite rounded summaries of the issues preoccupying Leningraders at any one time. The age, sex, ethnicity and socio-economic status of each speaker were noted, but only if criticisms were overtly political were his or her details passed to the NKVD. Military censors, intercepting private letters to the front, tracked the percentage containing 'negative communications' (it rose from 6–9 per cent at the beginning of January 1942 to 20 per cent at the month's end[5]). Letters from members of the public direct to Zhdanov were similarly grouped by subject matter, and totals calculated monthly for each type.[6] Though the orders to sort out this or that problem that Zhdanov issued in response to this mass of data often went unfulfilled, he never went uninformed.

Support for the authorities rose and fell in line with ration levels and progress at the front. The wave of patriotism that engulfed Leningrad on news of the German invasion was short-lived, giving way to fear and contempt in the autumn, when the city seemed about to fall and the bosses fled by plane. 'We can't think of Napalkova', the archivist Georgi Knyazev wrote of a colleague on 29 November 1941,

> without loathing. It has come to light that the very day before she left she was haranguing some exhausted 'whining intellectual', saying that every Leningrader must be on the alert, prepared to repel the enemy, and so on. In the few hours before her flight she never even hinted to anyone that she was abandoning Leningrad, her colleagues and her fellow Party members. The case is especially painful because Napalkova joined the Academy's Party branch after so many people had unjustly been accused of disloyalty and expelled . . . That's how people who go around talking grandly about self-sacrifice, bravery and heroism fix themselves up.[7]

Though the problem was never as widespread as the Germans believed, autumn 1941 was also when scapegoating of Leningrad's sizeable Jewish minority (just over 6 per cent of its population pre-war) reached its height. On 1 September Irina Zelenskaya, a manager at the Lenenergo power station, was shocked by 'a flash of anti-Semitism' from a 'rude, vulgar girl' in the plant's canteen. Everywhere, she worried, there were 'mutterings in corners, sideways looks at Party members, distrust and animosity – it could all end in a terrible explosion'.[8] In the Russian Museum, according to (clearly anti-Semitic) Anna Ostroumova-Lebedeva, 'the staff were filled with indignation at the behaviour of the Jews . . . When there was an appeal for volunteers at a meeting, they spoke very fervently and patriotically, but in practice all without exception managed to find warm, safe berths for themselves.'[9] Instead of attacking the Germans, it was joked of the numerous Leningrad intelligentsia who evacuated to Central Asia, the Jews were storming Tashkent.

Support for the authorities rose in December, with victory at Moscow, but fell again in January 1942, when Soviet offensives failed to lift the siege and a promised ration increase failed to materialise. The announcement of the increase, on 25 December, had been greeted with wild rejoicing: 'They've increased our bread. Mama and I cried for joy . . . we're so happy I can't write!' a woman wrote to her husband at the front.[10] Vera Inber first heard of it from her maid, who had seen a man reeling out of a bread shop, laughing, crying and clutching his head.[11] The announcement, though, was a propaganda ploy; in reality, even less food was distributed than before. At 6 a.m. on 29 December Ivan Zhilinsky went to wait outside his loathed Shop no. 44 on Moskovskaya Street for a rumoured delivery of American canned meat. When the shop opened at first light three and a half hours later he discovered that it only had enough for two hundred people. Being number 233 in the queue he decided that the wait was no longer worth it, and returned home empty-handed. That day he and his wife's sole meal consisted of fifty grams of bread and a portion of 'soup' made from hot water, crumbs and cottonseed oil. Two days into the New Year queues were forming at one in the morning, and growing disorderly. 'Queue numbers', he wrote

are written down and handed out. When people have got theirs they hurry off to warm themselves up. But others, arriving later, sometimes weasel their way in, writing out new numbers . . . 6 a.m. arrives but still the shop is closed. It's still shut at seven, at eight. Then at nine, if she feels like it, the manager finally opens up, and everyone pushes inside, packing it full to bursting. All the glass in front of the cash desk has been smashed, the counters are pushed aside and so on.

The manager, a woman, used to sell vegetables out of a basket in the market . . . Her only worth, so far as I can see, lies in her Party card. Instead of trying to improve supplies, she spends her time serving friends through the back entrance. The whole 25th Section of the police get their rations at the back without queuing. There they fry up the newly-delivered meat, and wash it down

with wine . . . The shop is on a sidestreet, and no inspector ever
looks at it. But what could an inspector do? He's hungry himself,
and would sell his own father for a piece of meat.[12]

On this day, too, Zhilinsky failed to collect any food at all, despite
standing in line from five in the morning until seven in the evening.

The effect on public opinion of such experiences was predictable.
'If in the first days after the raising of bread norms the mood of the
city's population improved', a Party report of 9 January noted, 'more
recently a large section of the population have displayed despond-
ency and depression. This is due to the fact that no provisions have
yet been given out on the January cards, and many people haven't
yet received meat, sugar or grains for the last third or two-thirds
of December.' Cited as typical was the following exchange between
two women waiting outside a shop on International Prospect:

'On the radio we're always hearing that the population of
Leningrad bravely and heroically bears all hardships. But what
does this bravery cost? Every day more and more people die of
hunger! Death – that's the end of your bravery. Does the government know how many people are dying?'

'Obviously our government hasn't got anything to feed us with.
Ordinary people die, but nobody from the government does.
They're well fed, they don't care about us.'

Queuers standing within earshot, the report went on, failed to
contradict the women, listening instead in sympathetic silence.
Shortly afterwards the shop manager appeared and announced that
he had no food, whereupon the crowd began shouting angrily. He
told them to go to the district soviet, where there were 'people who
should do something'.

A fifty-gram increase in the non-manual worker's ration from

24 January also proved illusory. Although by this time flour was arriving fairly reliably via the Ice Road, the improvement coincided with a breakdown in water supply to the bakeries, with the result that for several days at the end of January and the beginning of February almost no bread was distributed at all. When the manager of a shop on Sovetsky Prospekt announced that he had only enough bread left for a few dozen people the crowd 'exploded in frenzied noise and shouting': 'They do what they want with us! Yesterday they gave us a ration increase, and today they take away all the bread!' 'They're taking away the last of our rations. What do they really want? They want us all to die like animals!' 'They plug our mouths with this fifty grams, but you have to queue for five hours in the cold to get it!' 'There's a war on, so they think civilians should die too!'[13] A book-keeper at the Comedy Theatre was overheard saying, 'The people are starving, but they bring Zhdanov cocoa in bed.' Ominously, his name is underlined in Zhdanov's copy of the report.[14]

On 13 January the chair of the city soviet, Petr Popkov, broadcast a speech in which he claimed that the worst was over, and that food supply was already beginning to improve. As an engineer rashly but rightly commented, these were 'empty words, intended to pacify the population'.[15] They had the opposite effect. Commentary from the crowd outside a shop on Dictatorship of the Proletariat (shortened, appropriately, to plain 'Dictatorship') Square was biting: 'Of course Popkov's got enough to eat – it's easy for him to speak. I'd like him to come out here and see how we're freezing.' 'They're always saying that things are getting better. But how are they getting better exactly? I've already been waiting for bread for four hours, and there's no sign of any.' 'Fine words from Popkov – he's full, and he's feeding us promises.' 'Soon they'll be evacuating us to Volkovo cemetery.'[16] The schoolgirl Klara Rakhman heard the speech on her family's radio: 'He says this whole story's only going to last another few more days, that soon things will get better. But when? Probably when we've already kicked the bucket.' Rumours circulated that Popkov had been arrested for sabotage, that Leningrad was about to be declared an 'open city', that Stalin was secretly negotiating peace or that he no longer cared about the city since it was to be handed over to Britain and America when the war was over.[17]

Popkov's hypocrisy stung some into threatening talk. 'He'll start talking sense', said a theatre employee, 'when we go and smash up the shops.' 'Look what our leaders have driven us to – people are killing and eating their children', a housewife declared. 'And we fools sit and say nothing. We need to rise up if we're not all to die of hunger. It's time to end this war.'[18] Nonetheless, only two accounts exist of anti-government demonstrations. The first, described in a German intelligence report, is said to have taken place at the Kirov Works in mid-October 1941. Hearing news that a Kirov-staffed regiment had been annihilated on the Finnish front, workers reportedly downed tools and demanded peace. NKVD troops fired into the crowd, killing many, and took the ringleaders away in lorries.[19]

The second account comes from a memoir written in emigration by Vasili Yershov, a former Red Army supply officer. He describes walking along Prospekt Stachek, the thoroughfare leading south towards the front line from the industrial Avtovo district, on the morning of Revolution Day, 7 November 1941, and seeing a crowd of several hundred ten- to fourteen-year-old children walking up to an army checkpoint. Reaching under their coats, they produced bundles of flyers bearing incitements to mutiny – 'Twenty-four years ago you destroyed Tsarism! Please destroy the hated Kremlin-Smolniy executioners now!' – and started handing them over the barrier to soldiers. A commissar ordered the soldiers to fire, and when they refused, fired himself. At the same moment a German artillery barrage began and the children scattered. Twenty children were arrested, together with the soldiers who had refused to shoot and several dozen of those soldiers' relatives.[20]

Since no reference to either incident has yet emerged from the (incompletely open) Party or security service archives, it is possible that they did not happen. The Germans' informant may have been aiming to please; Yershov may have been exaggerating so as to boost his chances of getting US citizenship, or reporting hearsay. Leaflets urging Leningraders to revolt, however, did undoubtedly circulate. One such, stuffed into the blue-painted metal mailboxes in the entrance of an apartment building on Vasilyevsky Island, summoned residents to a 'hunger demonstration' on Palace Square at 10 a.m. on 22 January, whence they were to 'proceed towards our fighters and ask them to give up this mindless resistance'. The troops would not fire since they were 'our fathers, brothers, sons', nor should the 'worthless NKVD' be feared since it had not the 'strength to restrain the hungry masses'. Readers were to write out another ten copies of the pamphlet each, and post them in the letterboxes of neighbouring buildings.[21] An engineer at a machine-tool factory was arrested for distributing a similar appeal:

> Working Leningraders! Death hangs over Leningrad. Two or three thousand people die daily. Who is to blame? Soviet power and the Bolsheviks. They assure us that the blockade will be lifted and food norms raised, but it turns out to be lies, as everything Soviet power promised proved to be lies. Seize the city leadership! Save yourselves and the Motherland, or death awaits![22]

Another pamphleteer, who signed himself *Buntovshchik* – 'Rebel' – regularly left bundles of Xeroxed leaflets in Moscow Station, as well as sending them direct to Popkov and Zhdanov. Despite extraordinary efforts to track him down, which included identifying all the sales outlets for a certain sort of envelope and handwriting checks on 13,000 people, he evaded the authorities' clutches for almost two years. When finally run to earth he turned out to be an ordinary fifty-year-old ethnic Russian worker in the Bolshevik Plant's steel foundry, his sole suspicious feature 'relatives in Poland'. 'What was Luzhkov's official position in the workshop?' Zhdanov's deputy Aleksei Kuznetsov wrote angrily on the case report. 'And what did the Party organisation know about him? Please check and inform me by word of mouth.'[23]

The Big House

Leaflets and two unverifiable demonstrations aside, public anger never turned into organised revolt. This was in part a case of better the devil you know: Leningraders might have feared and distrusted their own leaders, but they also learned, as shells rained around them and news came through of the utter devastation of newly liberated towns round Moscow, thoroughly to hate the Nazis. It was also an achievement of the Soviet regime, which was well informed, commanded genuine loyalty from many (especially the young), remained firmly in control of the army and police, and had long since destroyed all potential institutional sources of opposition. If, as the Cold War Sovietologist Merle Fainsod put it, catastrophe and crisis are the severest tests of a political system, the fact that Leningrad held out suggested that the Soviet apparatus was tough, durable, and capable of sustaining great shocks. The siege, he concluded, should teach the West not to underestimate Russian totalitarianism.[1]

Walk northwards up the Liteiniy, the broad Belle Epoque boulevard linking the Nevsky to Finland Station, and at the end of the street, just before the river, you reach a building known as the Big House – today the headquarters of the Federal Security Service and formerly those of its predecessors, the KGB and NKVD. Built in the 1920s, it is uncompromisingly modernist, its stark tiers of ox-blood marble a striking contrast to the florid grandeur of the preceding turn-of-the-century mansion blocks. When the air raids began, a siege survivor remembers, 'all Leningraders very much hoped that bombs would fall on the NKVD building on the Liteiniy, and destroy all its records. But the building, with its grand marble entrance, remained standing – enormous and terrible.'[2]

Terror, though particularly severe in the first twelve months of the war, continued throughout.[3] The large-scale deportations of July and August 1941 were followed by mini-purges in September, November and March, the last of which swept up around a hundred scholars at a variety of academic institutions.[4] By autumn 1942 more than 9,500 people had been arrested for political crimes, about a third of them intelligentsia or 'former kulaks, tradesmen, landowners, nobles and officials', the rest peasants and ordinary white- and blue-collar workers.[5] For those put in front of the military tribunals that supplemented the regular People's Courts, the chances of acquittal were extremely slim: only in 6 per cent of cases were not-guilty verdicts returned or the case dismissed. The civilian courts' comparative laxity (20 per cent dismissals or not-guilty verdicts) earned reprimands from the military prosecutor.[6]

Likhachev witnessed siege-time terror's workings at Pushkin House, where Grigori Gukovsky (the same professor whom Olga Grechina had criticised for avoiding the draft, and who had joked that if the Germans came he would pass himself off as Armenian) was arrested and forced to denounce three colleagues, one of whom subsequently died in prison. Likhachev – himself a veteran of five years on the Solovetsky Islands – was unjudgemental. 'At the time', he wrote later,

a conversation between two people about what they would do, where they would hide, if the Germans took the city, was considered little short of treason. I therefore didn't think of blaming Gukovsky in the least, nor the numerous others who under duress put their signatures to whatever the interrogator-torturer wanted . . . It was the first time Gukovsky had been arrested and he obviously didn't know that one should either refuse to answer the interrogator's questions or say as little as possible.[7]

Marksena Karpitskaya, another veteran of NKVD interrogation rooms as the daughter of 'enemies of the people', was called into the Big House and asked to join in the denunciation of a colleague at the Public Library, an elderly ex-officer in the tsarist army who helped out with small tasks in exchange for company and warmth. When she refused, the policeman sneered that this was only to be expected, given her parentage. Karpitskaya, to her own amazement

> exploded with rage. I said that nobody had yet proved that my parents were enemies of the people, and that what he was saying was itself a crime . . . Only the foolishness of youth could have possessed me to be so brave! He jumped up and lunged towards me, as if to hit me . . . I stood up and grabbed a stool . . . He came to his senses, sat down at his desk and asked for my papers.

Though ordered to leave Leningrad, Karpitskaya managed to evade deportation with the help of her boss at the Publichka, who put her up in her own office, hiding her whereabouts from the authorities for the rest of the war.[8]

The geography teacher Aleksei Vinokurov came to the attention of the security services when he posted up handwritten notices offering to buy landscape photographs of the Urals and Siberia. A scribbled response invited him to a flat on the Nevsky, where he was promptly handed over to a police lieutenant and escorted to the Big House. 'It was tedious at the NKVD', he confided to his diary. 'The staff at that establishment amaze with their dullness. The stupid interrogation procedure went on for about three hours. With difficulty the lieutenant wrote out the protocol, which I virtually had to dictate to him.' These were among the words underlined by Vinokurov's investigator a year later, when his flat was searched and his diary confiscated. Also underlined were mentions of seeing corpses fall out of the back of a truck, and emaciated soldiers, marching along the Nevsky, step out of line to trade tobacco for bread. So too were criticisms of Sovinformburo for its 'meaningless' reporting, and references to the Germans as Europeans. Combined with a hint that he wished to join relatives in the Nazi-occupied town of Staraya Russa this was more than enough to condemn him, and on 19 March 1943 he was shot, having been convicted of 'conducting counter-revolutionary agitation' at his school.[9] Cannier was Aleksandr Boldyrev, whose diary references to a 'stupid' English novel – title *Two Trips to the Big House* – were code for interrogation sessions.[10]

Execution may have been a merciful end, since memoir evidence suggests that the large majority of those imprisoned in Leningrad during the first siege winter died of starvation. An inmate of the Kresty ('Crosses') prison, a vast, red-brick neo-Byzantine edifice next to Finland Station, had the job of removing corpses from the cells. He counted 1,853 between 16 October and 2 February:

> Every day we removed between twenty-five and forty dead. The insides of their clothes were covered in a moving crust of lice. The bodies weren't marked or labelled in any way – these people were anonymous, nobody noted anything down. We carried them into the yard, where they were loaded on to lorries and taken away somewhere . . . And on 3 February I saw that the doors of all the cells in the prison corridor stood open. There was nobody left to lock up.[11]

The account tallies with a report from the city statistical service on total numbers of deaths in Leningrad prisons, which rose from zero in March 1941 to 1,172 in December, 3,739 in January 1942 and over two thousand in each of the next four months.[12] Prisoners were also put to work on the Ice Road and in Gulag enterprises within the siege ring, which included a logging camp, pig farm and power station as well as munitions, chemicals and cable-making factories. There, too, their chances of survival were slim: on 31 December the NKVD asked supply commissar Dmitri Pavlov to raise the bread ration for the 3,578 inmates of its labour camps from 250 grams a day to the manual workers' 350 grams, pointing out that the existing arrangements led rapidly to 'exhaustion' and 'unfitness for work'.[13]

Death in prison or a labour camp was probably the fate of the railway clerk Ivan Zhilinsky. Fifty-one years old; decent, intelligent, resourceful and patriotic, he is typical of the thousands of ordinary Leningraders who met their end during the siege at the hands not of the enemy, but of their own government. By midwinter he and his wife Olga were swollen with oedema and walked with sticks, surviving from day to day on the dependant's ration supplemented with cough drops, glycerine, castor oil, wallpaper paste and carpenter's glue, washed down with hot water flavoured with orange peel, mustard powder, blackcurrant twigs or salt. To light their freezing rooms they burned splints of wood. Zhilinsky's undoing, like Vinokurov's, may have been a connection with photography. Having left his pre-war job when the trams stopped running, and not received his pay (a promised delivery of firewood) at another, in mid-January he started advertising himself as a passport photographer for departing evacuees. The room in which he set up a makeshift studio was also occupied by his dead mother, who lay hidden, dressed in her best clothes with an icon at her head, behind a cupboard and a piano. The scheme worked, earning 100 grams of bread per photograph. But it came too late for Olga, who died in her sleep on 20 March. 'With Olya's death', wrote Zhilinsky, 'has come the spring thaw, of which she dreamt all winter.' She also died just too soon to receive a backlog of letters and money orders from relatives in evacuation, by whom the couple had mistakenly felt forgotten and deserted.

Zhilinsky was arrested without warning a week later, possibly at the instigation of hostile neighbours. Again, the police pounced on his diary, in which he had recorded his rather shrewd forecasts for the war. The Germans, he thought, had made a mistake in thinking they could 'take a stroll, as if in Poland, to the Urals', since the Russians, though not natural Bolsheviks, had a historic hatred of invaders and the advantages of boundless space, a 'special psychology – "he's a fool but he's our fool"', and the ability to do without. The Allies were drip-feeding the Soviet Union just enough aid to keep her fighting, but not enough to allow her to launch a major counter-offensive. After the war, they would turn Leningrad into an 'international port' and put pressure on the government to allow freedom of speech and religion, 'in the full sense of those words . . . Our lot, of course, will wriggle about just enough so that America and England back off and leave us to stew in our own juice . . . In the end, we'll find ourselves alone again with our Comintern, while the rest of the world remains democratic, parliamentary and capitalist, as we are accustomed to call the other side.'[14] On the basis of these comments Zhilinsky was accused of 'slandering Soviet reality' and sentenced to death, later commuted to ten years' imprisonment.

Most poignant, perhaps, of the yellowing papers in Zhilinsky's prosecution file is an inventory of the contents of his flat. 'The furnishings', typed a policeman, 'consist of two cupboards, two metal beds, a sofa upholstered in a checked fabric, a piano, a table, five chairs, a nickel-plated samovar, a hand-operated sewing machine, a lamp, a Red Guard gramophone and a circular wall clock.' The wooden building in which he and Olga lived is long gone; at one end of the street there now stands a shopping centre, at the other a car dealership, shiny bonnets ranged at the diagonal against smooth new asphalt. Less changed, a block to the north, is the Serafimovskoye cemetery, its leafy muddle of headstones washed by a quiet flow of strollers, flower sellers and old women with besoms. A lumpen

Brezhnev-era memorial inside the main gates commemorates the starvation dead, but the actual mass graves – a stretch of rough ground at the cemetery's boundary with a timber yard – have been left to themselves. To people like Zhilinsky – innocent victims not of the war, but of wartime terror – there is no monument at all.

PART 4

Waiting for Liberation: January 1942–January 1944

'Will trade for food', February 1942. On offer are gold cufflinks, a length of navy blue skirt material, patent leather boots, a samovar, a camera and a hand-drill.

Today I went to the clinic. Two topical notices had been posted up. The first – 'Report children left without care due to death of parents to room no. 4'. The second – 'The polyclinic does not issue exemption notes for labour duty'. And on the way home a notice pinned to a fence: 'Light coffin for sale' . . .

Dmitri Lazarev, April 1942

18

Meat Wood

For the rest of the world, Leningrad's agony took place out of sight and largely out of mind. Once the immediate threat to the city had receded, Allied eyes turned first to the battle for Moscow, then to an avalanche of losses in the Far East and elsewhere. The first month of Leningrad's mass death – December 1941 – coincided with the fall of Hong Kong; the second with heavy losses of Atlantic shipping to German U-boats; the third with Japan's capture of Singapore, together with 70,000 British and Commonwealth servicemen. As regards the Soviet Union, Britain and America's aim was simply to keep her from collapsing altogether or making a separate peace, while resisting Stalin's – and the British left's – increasingly importunate calls for a second front. The first of the Arctic convoys carrying tanks, Hurricanes and other military supplies diverted from Britain's Lend-Lease programme arrived in Archangel at the end of August, the prelude to four long years of acrimonious diplomacy. 'Surly, snarly and grasping', Churchill wrote later, 'the Soviet Government had the impression that they were conferring a great favour on us by fighting in their own country for their own lives.'[1]

All along the Eastern Front, in January 1942, the Wehrmacht ground to a halt. Analysts have made fun of the Nazi generals' postwar tendency to lay the blame for ultimate defeat in the East on the weather, the roads and Hitler's bullying – on anything, in fact, except for their own mistakes or superior Russian skill in the field. This is unfair: even by Russian standards, the winter of 1941–2 was punishingly cold, and hit the German armies hard, most of all those of Army Group North. The sudden plunge in temperature, Hitler stormed over dinner at the 'Wolf's Lair' on 12 January, was an 'unforeseen catastrophe, paralysing everything. On the Leningrad front, with a temperature of 42 degrees below zero, not a rifle, not a machine-gun nor a field-gun has been working on our side.'[2] Aircraft were grounded, tank and truck engines refused to start and horses waded in snow up to their bellies, so that to move from place to place troops had to shovel a path by day along the route their transports were to take at night. Soldiers stole clothes and bedding from local peasants (Soviet cartoons guyed them as comical 'Winter Fritzes', dressed in headscarves and frilly bloomers), or fell prey to frostbite and exposure. The Spanish 'Blue Division', despatched by Franco to aid the war on Communism, were so named, the press jeered, for the colour not of their shirts but of their faces.

Fritz Hockenjos's bicycle unit – now retraining as a ski unit – had been posted to the hamlet of Zvanka, on the west bank of the Volkhov River. Their quarters were an abandoned monastery, on what had once been the estate of Catherine the Great's court poet Gavriil Derzhavin. From the observation point at the top of its bell tower snow-covered heath and forest stretched to the horizon in every direction, broken only by the broad highway of the frozen river, a line of telegraph poles marking the Moscow–Leningrad railway line, and by the coming and going of planes to a distant Russian landing strip. In front, on the river's opposite bank, lay the Russians' newly formed Second Shock Army, expected to attack any day. Behind, in the frost-struck, crystalline woods, wandered the remnants of units destroyed in recent fighting. 'Daily', Hockenjos wrote,

we are spectators and actors in a gruesome drama that has been playing out in the white woods for the past few weeks – that of

a Russian regiment reaching bottom . . . The forest battle of 30
December seems to have been their last desperate throw, and the
dead included the regiment's commander. The survivors have
long since dropped their weapons and eaten their last pieces of
dried bread. Now they wander aimlessly here and there through
the woods, like animals cut off from their herd. Blind, apathetic
animals. They no longer even think of breaking out, though our
line is more than thin enough. Nor do they think of giving themselves up – they just walk and walk so as to still hunger and beat
off the cold. The forest is full of their tracks; not a day goes by
without one of our patrols meeting and shooting a few. One icy
moonlit night a patrol suddenly spotted them right there, thirty
paces to the side of the path – a long row of shadows trotting
silently along. They fired off everything they'd got; some fell in
the snow, the others continued to trot on in silence, just veering
off slightly towards the depths of the forest . . . Those that avoid
the bullet fall prey to hunger and cold, one after another. They
crawl into the undergrowth, curl up and that's the end. Some
stray mindlessly out into daylight at the edge of the forest, others
blunder in front of the sentry at our command post as if they
didn't see him. They can hardly lift their frozen black hands, or
move their lips. Blood seeps from their cracked faces. The bullet
is a mercy for them.

Sometimes this happens: the sentry, in his Swabian dialect, yells
down into the bunker, 'Here's another one!' In reply Obergefreite
K. asks everyone, 'Which of you new boys hasn't got any felt
boots yet?' A few hands go up and K. says, 'Karle, go and get
them!' Karle swings himself down from his wooden bunk, picks
up a rifle and goes outside. A shot is heard and Karle comes back
with a pair of felt boots under his arm.

The unit also stripped frozen Russian corpses: 'Their felt boots,
unfortunately, we have to cut from their feet, but they can be sewn

back together again. We're not yet as bad as the 2nd Battalion, who chop the dead Russians' legs off and thaw them out on top of the stove in their bunker.' By February, Hockenjos noted with a certain pride, he and his men had turned into proper *Frontschweine*. Dirty and bearded, they had learned to wear their padded cotton trousers outside their boots so as to keep the snow out, and their coats unbuttoned at the collar, so as to be able to reach inside quickly for hand grenades. Under their helmets their heads were wrapped in woollen shawls, and their noses with sticky medical gauze, to protect against frostbite. Armbands prevented confusion with the enemy. Hockenjos was touched to find, in a comfort parcel from the home front, an old-fashioned velvet muff. 'We definitely', he admitted, 'don't look like German soldiers at all any more.'[3]

The privations suffered by Leningrad's besiegers, though, were as nothing to those borne by its defenders. One of the archives' least-known revelations is the existence of starvation within the Red Army. Throughout the Red Army rations were poor: the bread 'similar to asphalt in colour and density', the *kasha* nicknamed 'shrapnel'.[4] But within Leningrad's blockade ring soldiers not only deserted, shot themselves in the hands or feet or committed suicide in substantial numbers, but actually died of hunger. To blame – aside from the blockade itself – were disorganisation, theft and corruption. Though the military ration – at its lowest 500 grams of bread and 125 grams of meat per day for a front-line soldier, 300 grams of bread and 50 grams of meat in the rear[5] – was theoretically enough to survive on, in practice many men received far less.[6]

One such was Semen Putyakov, a thirty-six-year-old infantryman stationed at an aerodrome on a quiet sector of the Finnish front, just to the north-west of Leningrad. From call-up onwards he confided to his diary a long series of grumbles – lack of training, 'museum exhibit' rifles, his lieutenant ('so dim that even the least educated soldiers are surprised at his orders'), senior officers' rudeness and use

of military vehicles to transport their girlfriends. In early December
he noticed for the first time that the officers were stealing the men's
food, ordering cookhouse staff to divide rations for six among eight
and taking the surplus for themselves. By the end of the month he
was permanently consumed by hunger, and getting into trouble for
making complaints:

> Yesterday, while collecting lunch, I asked one of the political
> workers why we weren't getting our full portions. I thought he
> was a fair man, and would want the full norm to reach our stom-
> achs. But he began to shout that it wasn't in the regulations for
> us to check the norms. So I asked where in the regulations it says
> that they can give us less than we're supposed to get. After that
> he went berserk. I must find out his surname. And his ugly mug
> looks healthier than it should.[7]

Putyakov celebrated New Year's Eve by shaving, looking at a photograph of his wife and children, and remembering meals from family
gatherings past. By 8 January he had difficulty walking: 'Gnawed
on horse-bones during wood-chopping. Hunger, hunger. My swollen face isn't going down. They say there'll be ration increases, but I
don't believe it . . . The devil knows what I'm writing, or what for.'
Furiously, he raved against his platoon's corrupt sergeant and junior
lieutenant – 'They're not men, they're beasts in human form.' Other
soldiers in the unit had already died of hunger – 'disgusting starvation deaths . . . it would be better to die in battle with the fascists'.
A few days after he tried to make an official complaint to an army
doctor he was arrested. Accused of 'expressing disappointment at the
food supply of the Red Army', he was executed on 13 March 1942.

Total mortality from starvation within the Leningrad armies is
impossible to estimate, but Putyakov's experience was no isolated
instance. Soldiers told similar stories in their letters home: 'We're
horribly hungry', wrote one. 'We don't want to perish from hunger.

Some comrades have already been sent to hospital. Some have died. What's going to happen? What good are deaths like these to the Motherland?' 'We get weaker every day', wrote another. 'We don't get any meat or fat, and 300 grams of bread. There's not a single grain in the soup, no potato, no cabbage – it's just muddy saltwater . . . We've lost a lot of weight – we look like shadows. We gnaw on oilseed cake, which is being fed to the horses in place of oats. We fill ourselves up with water.' A third had had 'enough of life. Either I'm going to die of hunger or shoot myself. I can't bear it any more.'[8] Vasili Churkin, on the front line just south of Ladoga with his artillery battery, complained that although his fellow soldiers were in some cases almost too weak to stand, a lazy *politruk* made them build him an extra-comfortable bunker at each new stop, while they slept outside on the snow. The man was 'good for nothing – just pointless extra weight'.[9] Inside the city, Leningraders were shocked at the extreme emaciation of the soldiers they saw in the hospitals or marching along the streets.[10]

Like Leningrad's starving civilians, some soldiers resorted to cannibalism. Hockenjos came across what he called a 'man-eaters' camp' in the woods behind Zvanka, the stripped limbs confirming the statements of two young Red Army nurses who had been taken prisoner and given jobs in his battalion's field hospital. Vasili Yershov (the same man who claimed to have seen children handing out anti-government leaflets at a checkpoint) was senior supply officer to the 56th Rifle Division of the 55th Army, stationed at Kolpino, just to Leningrad's south. Among his responsibilities was provisioning an army hospital. Housed in the former Izhorsky Works, its two to three thousand sick and wounded lay on straw in glass-roofed, cement-floored workshops, and the two hundred or more who died each day were buried in the factory yard. Medical personnel were numerous but unqualified and painfully thin, despite in theory receiving the military 'rear norm'. 'One day', Yershov relates,

Sergeant Lagun noticed that an army doctor, Captain Chepurniy, was digging in the snow in the yard. Covertly watching, the sergeant saw him cut a piece of flesh from an amputated leg, put it in his pocket, re-bury the leg in the snow and walk away. Half an hour later Lagun walked into Chepurniy's room as if he had something to ask him, and saw that he was eating meat out of a frying pan. The sergeant was convinced that it was human flesh . . . So he raised the alarm and in the course of the ensuing investigation it became clear that not only were the hospital's sick and wounded eating human flesh, but so too were about twenty medical personnel, from doctors and nurses to outdoor workers – systematically feeding on dead bodies and amputated legs. They were all shot on a special order of the Military Council.

Their executioner was a jolly, vulgar Captain Borisov of the Special Department, the army wing of the NKVD, to whom Yershov issued the special vodka ration handed out to firing squads (600 grams, a third before and two-thirds afterwards). 'I have to point out', Yershov adds, 'that Captain Borisov shot 50–60 per cent of people personally . . . He couldn't live without alcohol every day and so tried to carry out as many executions as possible himself.'[11]

Yershov also recorded the murder, by starving soldiers, of the carriers who twice daily toted insulated canisters of soup, strapped on to their backs with leather harnesses, from the field kitchens up to the front line:

In early January 1942 the divisional commander started getting urgent calls from regimental and battalion commanders, saying that this or that group of soldiers hadn't been fed, that the carrier hadn't appeared with his canteen, having apparently been killed by German snipers. Thorough checks revealed that something unbelievable was happening: soldiers were leaving their trenches early in the morning to meet the carriers, stabbing them to death, and taking the food. They would eat as much as they could, then bury the murdered carrier in the snow and hide the canteen before returning to their trenches. The murderer would go back to the place twice a day, first finishing off the contents of the canteen and then cutting off pieces of human flesh and eating those too. To give you some idea of the numbers I can tell you that in my division in the winter of 1941–2, on the front line alone – taking no account of units in the rear – there were about twenty such cases.[12]

Despite his Leningrad armies' dreadful state, Stalin included them in a general late winter offensive, planned while still in the midst of November and December's battle for Moscow. Vastly over-ambitious, it was designed to recapture Smolensk, the Ukrainian Donbass and the Crimea as well as to liberate Leningrad, and more broadly to deny the Germans breathing space in which to prepare for new assaults in the spring.[13]

Responsibility for breaking the German lines around Leningrad was to lie chiefly with General Meretskov's Volkhov Front, which faced Army Group North's Eighteenth Army along a line running south-east from Lake Ladoga, then south along the Volkhov River to Novgorod. While the armies within the siege ring did what they could to push south and east, those of the Volkhov front were to break westwards across the river, cutting off the German forces around Lyuban, Tosno and Mga. Altogether, 326,000 troops were initially to be committed to the operation, giving a theoretical 50 per cent advantage in manpower, 60 per cent in guns and mortars and 30 per cent in aircraft.

Ignoring Meretskov's pleas for more artillery, reserves and time in which to concentrate his troops and arrange his logistics, Stalin insisted that the offensive be launched in the first week of January. To keep (presumably terrified) Meretskov up to the mark, he despatched

to Leningrad the loathsome Lev Mekhlis, head of the Red Army's
Political Directorate and one of the organisers of the 1937–8 army
purges.[14] Things went badly from the outset: on the 4th and 5th
forty-eight hours of heavy fighting near Kirishi won a mere five kilometres of ground; on the 6th an assault across the Volkhov ice in the
face of machine guns lost over three thousand men in its first thirty
minutes. 'Continued enemy attacks', General Halder wrote dismiss-
ively in his diary, 'but nothing on a major scale.'[15] Uncoordinated
and intermittent, the offensive continued in piecemeal fashion on
into February. Hockenjos, returning to Zvanka on the twentieth,
found the monastery half destroyed by shelling from the opposite
bank of the Volkhov – the cloister full of craters, the chapel vault-
ing stove in, and the pines and oaks on the slopes leading down to
the river reduced to 'miserable broomsticks'. A week later a second
Soviet attack was beaten off with ease:

Ivan plastered the buildings and their surroundings with a pot-
pourri of greetings from artillery, anti-tank guns, bang-booms and
grenade-throwers. The high point came at bright midday, when
fifteen Russians in ski parkas, apparently fired up with vodka,
crept out into the open. Artillery Lieutenant Vogt and I watched
them from a communications trench on the forward slope. First
they approached a group of dark lumps which have been sitting
there in the middle of the Volkhov since the last Russian attack,
and searched them for something to eat. Through our binoculars
we could see them taking tin cans out of the dead men's back-
packs. Next they wandered over the snow towards our edge of
the woods, which sticks out from the northern side of the monastery hill towards the river. Two hundred metres short we hit them
with our big guns. Our aim was good – most of the fifteen stayed
lying down. I would have liked to let the fellows get closer to my
sentries, so as to pick them off with rifles, or even to the edge of
the forest where my men have been lying in wait for quite a while.

But the heavy weapons men didn't want to miss an easy meal.

In the evening two of the dead Russians tried to come to life, but my sentry was paying attention and shot them down. Another seven [sic] *Russ* the fewer.[16]

A few kilometres upstream, opposite the village of Myasnoi Bor ('Meat Wood') the Soviet offensive made better progress. Its striking force was the newly formed Second Shock Army, which despite being led by a militarily inept henchman of Beria's and manned by draftees from the treeless Volga steppe, broke through the German lines on 17 January and penetrated deep into the German rear. By the end of February 100,000 men held a 'pocket' roughly fifty kilometres square, its northern edge only ten kilometres away from one of the offensive's key objectives, the railway town of Lyuban.

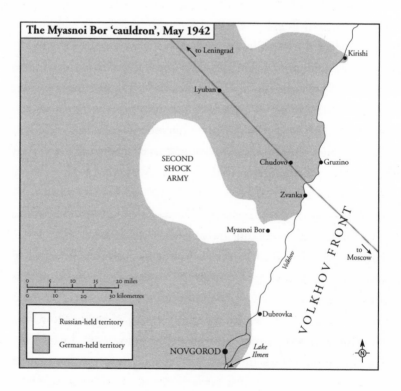

The Myasnoi Bor 'cauldron', May 1942

The gains, however, were more impressive on paper than in reality. Efforts to widen the gap in the enemy line foundered against swift reinforcement, Lyuban remained just out of reach, and the ground won consisted – a scattering of place names notwithstanding – of flat and virtually uninhabited forest, peat-workings and bog. Realising the Second Shock Army's vulnerability, on 2 March Hitler ordered Georg von Küchler (who had taken over command of Army Group North from von Leeb in January) to mount an Operation Predator to cut it off from the rest of the Volkhov front. 'Concentration of air force in that sector', Halder wrote in his diary, 'is requested for the period 7–14 March . . . After elimination of the Volkhov salient, no blood is to be wasted on reducing the enemy in the marshes; he can be left to starve to death.'[17] The ground attack was launched at daybreak on the fifteenth, and within five days had severed both roads – nicknamed 'Erika' and 'Dora' – into the pocket. By the end of the month, after desperate seesaw fighting round Myasnoi Bor, the Soviets held a corridor into the pocket only a kilometre and a half wide, along which supplies had to be hauled on sleds by night.

In April it began to thaw, glittering silence replaced by drizzle and the sound of running water. Still quartered at Zvanka, Hockenjos watched the landscape change, photographing the first small patch of earth – dark and strewn with wisps of straw – to emerge, and sitting for hours at the top of the monastery bell tower:

Reed beds, wide bodies of water between stretches of yellowed grass, black moorland and the sparse remains of the snow. Over it all a high spring sky with fine lamb's wool clouds: a sea of larks' jubilations and lapwings' cries. In the marshy forest to the right, goldfinches in every bush . . . Everywhere, the men sit in front of their bunkers with their shirts off, their torsos pale . . . They are whistling and singing. The cheerful noise must carry as far as the Russians, but I am not going to forbid it.[18]

For the trapped Second Shock Army, the thaw brought only new misery. The corridor connecting it to the rest of the Russian front became impassable, halting delivery of supplies and evacuation of the wounded. Horses died and were eaten; dugouts flooded and shells had to be carried by hand, the men wading up to their waists or jumping from tussock to tussock 'like rabbits', to derisive German shouts of *'Rus, kup-kup!'* For daytime cover they built 'breastworks' of branches, moss and dead leaves; at night they slept in the open around fires, scorching their sodden felt boots and quilted jackets. To reanimate the offensive, Stalin reshuffled his generals, recalling Meretskov and subordinating the Leningrad to the Volkhov Front under Zhukov's protégé Mikhail Khozin. Andrei Vlasov, a tall, spectacled professional soldier who had led the 37th Army out of encirclement at Kiev and spearheaded the December counter-attack in front of Moscow, was flown in to take over the Second Shock Army. On 12 May, having received intelligence that the Germans were bringing up reinforcements, Khozin ordered Vlasov to break out of encirclement and rejoin the rest of the Volkhov Front. Though five divisions and four brigades made it back through the Myasnoi Bor corridor, and at least two thousand men, according to German records, deserted, that left another seven divisions and six brigades – about 20,000 men in total – still trapped inside the German 'cauldron'.[19] 'The enemy would first surround a unit', a survivor remembered, 'wait for it to weaken for lack of supplies and then start pounding':

> We were completely helpless, since we had no ammunition, no petrol, no bread, no tobacco, not even salt. Worst of all was having no medical help. No medicine, no bandages. You want to help the wounded, but how? All our underwear has gone for bandages long ago; all we have left is moss and cotton wool. The field hospitals are overflowing, and the few medical staff in despair. Many hundreds of non-walking wounded simply

lie under bushes. Around them mosquitoes and flies buzz like bees in a hive. Come near and the whole swarm comes after you, covers you all over, gets into your mouth, eyes, ears – unbearable. Mosquitoes, flies and lice – our hated enemies . . . Nothing new about lice – but in *such* quantities . . . The grey devils eat us alive, with gusto, completely covering our clothes and bodies. You don't even try to squash them; all you can do, if you have a free moment, is shake them off on to the ground. You find six or seven on a single button . . .

The main problem, though, was hunger. Oppressive, never-ending hunger. Wherever you went, whatever you were doing, the thought of food never left you . . . Our food supply now depended on air deliveries by U2 [a type of small, one-engined biplane]. Each could carry five or six sacks of *sukhari*. But there were thousands of us – how could there possibly be enough for everyone? If a sack lands successfully, without bursting on impact, that means one piece of dried bread for two soldiers. Otherwise, you're on your own, you have to eat what you can find – bark, grass, leaves, harnesses . . . Once somebody found an old potato, buried among the ashes of a hut. We cut it up and each got a tiny piece. What a feast! Some men licked their piece, some sniffed it. The smell reminded me of home and family.[20]

Another reshuffle of the top brass, removing Khozin and separating the two northern commands again (the Volkhov Front was handed back to vindicated Meretskov, Leningrad to a taciturn, poker-faced artilleryman, Leonid Govorov), came far too late to make a difference.[21] By mid-June the remnants of the Second Shock Army had been pushed into a small stretch of swamp to the west of Myasnoi Bor:

White nights, so we had German planes overhead twenty-four hours a day, strafing and dropping bombs. The noise of shellfire was continuous and deafening, as was the sound of breaking and burning trees . . . We weren't an army any more – we were a market crowd. A complete mess – no communication between units, and lines of command had ceased to exist. No information on our own situation, but limitless amounts of German propaganda – flyers, newspapers, coloured proclamations – covering the ground and urging us to surrender . . . The forest burns, the peat smoulders. There are bomb craters everywhere and twisted, broken trees – piles of useless rifles, wrecked gun carriages. And corpses – corpses everywhere you looked. Thousands of them, stinking and covered in flies, decomposing under the June sun. You pass one and the flies rise off it into your face – you can't see anything, they're in your eyes, your nose, everywhere. Big fat buzzing flies – disgusting to remember. On every bit of dry ground there are wounded soldiers, screaming, moaning, pleading – some for water, some for somebody to finish them off. But nobody cares. People wander about the woods, indifferent, sullen, half-mad; in hats with the ear flaps tied under the chin so as to keep off the mosquitoes; eyes red and swollen from lack of sleep . . . Nobody has a watch, we lose track of time. What date is it? Is it day or night?[22]

The end came on the relentlessly sunlit nights of 21–24 June, in a series of suicidal breakouts through a gap in the German lines four kilometres long and only a few hundred metres wide. Those with enough strength carried rifles, and the emaciated and wounded nothing at all. The German fire, in the words of a survivor, was 'so fierce that everything was flung into the air – people, earth, trees. You couldn't see anything for smoke.' Stumbling over corpses old and new, he took shelter in a bomb crater, then slid down a bank past a German tank towards a stream. 'An astonishing silence fell, then suddenly, a voice: "Stop! Who goes there!" It was our soldiers; we had got through to the other side.'[23]

One soldier who did not get through to the other side was General

Vlasov, who had dropped all radio communication with front headquarters a few days previously. How exactly he spent the next three weeks is unclear, but on 12 July he was picked up by the Germans in a village on the western edge of the 'pocket' and flown to Vinnitsa in central Ukraine, site of Hitler's new forward headquarters and of a special camp for high-ranking Soviet prisoners. Here – perhaps in rush of anger at the Myasnoi Bor disaster, perhaps as the cumulation of years of suppressed doubt and frustration – Vlasov turned against Stalin, writing a letter to the Nazi authorities in which he argued that since many Soviet citizens were strongly anti-Bolshevik, civilians in occupied territory should be better treated and Soviet POWs recruited into a Russian Liberation Army. He had misjudged his audience: 'We will never build a Russian Army', Hitler sneered. 'It is a phantom of the first order.' Though the Nazis made good use of Vlasov for propaganda purposes, touring him round the occupied territories and putting his name to leaflets inciting the Red Army to surrender, he never met Hitler and was only given command of two POW-based divisions late in January 1945. Four months later he was captured by the Soviets amidst the confusion of the Prague Rising, and in July 1946 tried in a closed court and hanged.[24]

Vlasov's treason was also fatal to the reputation of the Second Shock Army, its demise transformed from heroic last stand into deliberate mass defection to the enemy. A Major General Afanasyev, Vlasov's chief of communications, was flown out from behind enemy lines in August, having spent the intervening weeks living off hedgehogs with partisans. His interrogation report, in which he describes Vlasov as lapsing into dumb indifference before wandering off into the woods alone, reeks of fear of accusation of treachery. On flying back over the Soviet lines, he claims, he could not help shouting, 'Hurrah! Long live our Great and Beloved Friend and Teacher Comrade Stalin!', although he was 'the only passenger, and the pilot could not hear'.[25]

*   *   *

Post-war, all mention of the Second Shock Army was taboo. No histories were written, ceremonies enacted or memorials erected, and the widows of its fallen were denied military pensions. Veterans were forced to treat their service as a shameful secret, on a par with having been the son of a kulak or priest. Rehabilitation did not begin until the late 1970s, when local volunteer groups began mounting expeditions into the backwoods to recover and decently inter tens of thousands of still unburied bodies.

Sasha Orlov is the son of one of the volunteer movement's founders. Wearing rubber waders and an army-issue jacket, he stands next to a decommissioned half-track in wilderness a few kilometres to the south-east of Myasnoi Bor. Snow and sky are a flat, dull grey; the oranges and golds of new willow and dead reeds muted. Just out of sight, where the ground dips, lies the Volkhov. Save for the twittering of finches in a nearby bush, it is completely silent. Here, Sasha explains, was a German bunker. Scraping at the snow with his foot, he rapidly uncovers a leather boot, a rusty saw, two earth-filled green wine bottles, a length of ammunition belt, a stovepipe, the spiral skeleton of a hose and dozens of pointy nosed 7.92mm rifle rounds, packed in neat rows inside a rotten wooden box. Ignoring nervous health and safety pleas, he breaks open one of the rounds against a stone and tips out a little heap of shiny slate-grey flakes. A lighter rasps and they flare and crackle, throwing off a miniature fountain of bright white sparks.

The group's finds are displayed in the gymnasium of a local school. There are hand-painted wall maps – the front lines carefully delineated in interlocking red and grey – a variety of guns (the police periodically take them away, Sasha says, but his group just goes out and gets more), and a litter of helmets, water bottles and tin spoons with Cyrillic initials scratched into the handles. Three fat ring binders are filled with the Red Army equivalent of dog tags: narrow paper forms, filled in by hand, which were rolled up and put inside small screw-top Bakelite cylinders. When found they are now almost always illegible, with the result that of the 29,000 bodies recovered from the Myasnoi Bor area to date, only 1,800 have been identified. Sasha's prize exhibit, unearthed at the site of Vlasov's last headquarters, hangs on the wall. It is a print matrix, lead type still gripped within a corroded metal frame, for the Second Shock Army's one-page 'newspaper'. The headlines read 'Death to the German occupiers', 'The enemy will not break our resistance' and 'Our victory is near'. The issue, almost certainly never produced, is dated Wednesday 24 June – the day on which what was left of the Second Shock Army rushed the Myasnoi Bor corridor for the last time.

Overall, the winter offensive of January to April 1942 lost the Leningrad and Volkhov fronts 308,000 out of a total 326,000 troops committed to combat. Of these 213,303 were 'medical losses' – i.e. the wounded and those who died in hospital – and 95,000 'irrecoverable losses' – i.e. the dead in battle, captured and missing. The operations of May and June lost the northern fronts another 94,000 men, of whom at least 48,000, according to German records, were taken prisoner at Myasnoi Bor.[26]

Ilya Frenklakh, survivor of the doomed People's Levy, had been transferred to a reconnaissance unit within the Volkhov Front's 52nd Army. His job was to lie motionless for hours at a time in no-man's-land, watching the enemy lines through binoculars. All around lay corpses, their relative states of decomposition indicating whether they had formed part of the autumn or spring 'call-ups to heaven'. 'As you lay there', he remembered,

you couldn't help thinking and comparing: why are the Germans so well-trained, while all we do is try to overwhelm them with numbers? Why do they use technology and brains, while all we've got is bayonets? Why is it that every time we attack, our blood flows in rivers and our dead pile up in mountains? Where are our tanks? Who needs this wretched village of Dubrovka? And lots more unanswered questions.

A feeling of nausea would descend – only people who fought at Leningrad or on the Volkhov in the first two years of the war will understand what I mean. If our generals and colonels had done their jobs properly we would have won with a quarter of the losses . . . Butchers and undertakers – we had plenty of those.[27]

The Gentle Joy of Living and Breathing

Through the spring and summer of 1942, for those with the mental energy to follow them, Sovinform's bulletins brought a torrent of bad news. The defeat of the Second Shock Army at Myasnoi Bor (inferred from the fact that it abruptly ceased to be mentioned) coincided with the encirclement and loss of 200,000 troops outside Kharkov, and with the abandonment of Crimea's Kerch Peninsula, its defence hopelessly bungled by Lev Mekhlis, the ignorant hatchetman who had helped to bring Leningrad's January offensive to disaster. The most cutting blow was the fall of Sevastopol, on 3 July. The naval base, historic home to Russia's Black Sea Fleet, had been surrounded since the previous November, 106,000 Soviet troops holding out against 203,000 Germans and Romanians under Erich von Manstein. Its civilians, like Leningrad's, had not been evacuated, but sheltered from intensive artillery bombardment in cellars, caves and catacombs, where they turned out clothing and munitions while feeding off cats and dogs.

Three days before Stalin finally ordered that Sevastopol be given up – the admiral in charge left by submarine – the press still boasted its invincibility: 'We have seen the capitulation,' thundered the *Red Star*, 'of celebrated fortresses, of states. But Sevastopol is not surrendering. Our soldiers do not play at war. They fight a life and death struggle. They do not say "I surrender" when they see a couple of enemy men on the chessboard.'[1]

This was a fling at Tobruk, the Libyan port, vital to the British Eighth Army's defence of Egypt, which Rommel had almost bloodlessly captured, together with 33,000 British and South African troops and large quantities of supplies, nine days earlier. Churchill got the news in the Oval Office, in the middle of a meeting with Roosevelt. 'It was', one of the generals present remembered, 'a hideous and totally unexpected shock. For the first time in my life I saw the Prime Minister wince.' In August Churchill flew, together with Roosevelt's envoy Averell Harriman, to Moscow for his first summit with Stalin. He had to break the news that a promised landing in northern France was now put off indefinitely in favour of Operation Torch, aimed at attacking Rommel in the rear via Vichy-held Morocco and Algeria. Stalin's reaction was so insulting that Churchill's interpreter thought his Russian counterpart must be mistranslating. In fact, he had the dictator's words perfectly – Stalin was telling his allies to their faces that they were frightened of the Germans.[2]

While the great powers wrangled, spring came to Leningrad. The ice rotted and broke on the canals, snow slid in water-heavy avalanches off roofs and balconies, and the straight-sided piles of fire-fighting sand, their retaining planks long gone for firewood, thawed and crumbled. At the Hermitage burst pipes flooded the cellar underneath the Hall of Athena, drowning a collection of eighteenth-century porcelain. Staff – by now nearly all women – waded into the murky water, awash with floating inventory labels, and delicately groped for Meissen goatherds and shepherdesses. Leaks sprang in the palace's bomb-shaken roof, and army cadets who helped move antique furniture into the dry were thanked with a tour of the galleries by a museum guide, who talked them through the absent masterpieces empty frame by empty frame.[3]

As the hours of daylight lengthened and ration levels increased,

Leningraders began to emerge from their 'small radii', reacquainting themselves with the outside world and with ordinary human feeling. Carrying basket and scissors, Olga Grechina combed the parks for the first dandelions and nettles – so many were doing the same that to find any she had to venture on to a firing range. When the trams started running again, on 15 April, people stumbled after them, laughing and crying.[4] 'In the dining room', wrote Dmitri Likhachev of Pushkin House, 'we met each other with the words "You're alive! I'm so glad!" One learned with alarm that so-and-so was dead, that so-and-so had left town. People counted each other, counted up those who were left, as at roll-call in prison camp.'[5]

On May Day (to mark which food shops dressed their windows with artificial fruit and vegetables*) the shipyard supervisor Vasili Chekrizov was pleased not only to see men going to work in ties and women in hats and lipstick, but also to see drunks. Normally they would have disgusted him, but this year they represented a welcome return to normality. A couple of weeks later he was amazed to wake up with an erection, and to hear, as he walked past a courtyard, a woman swearing and wailing. 'I don't know why she was weeping. All the same, tears are proof that the situation in Leningrad is improving. When every day hundreds of rag-wrapped corpses were being dragged along or thrown out onto the streets, there were no tears (or I didn't see them).'[6]

For Lidiya Ginzburg's starvation-numbed 'Siege Man' the first emotions to return were irritation – at leaking galoshes, broken spectacles, clumsiness in handling gloves and shopping bag in a crowded food shop – and impatience, the 'sense of lost time'. Next came grief, and its close companion, guilt:

Siege people forgot their sensations but they remembered facts. Facts crept slowly out from the dimness of memory into the light

---

* In Moscow, Alexander Werth noted 'cruel cardboard hams, cheeses and sausages, all covered in dust'.

of rules of behaviour which were now gravitating back to the accepted norm.

'She wanted a sweet so much. Why did I eat that sweet? I needn't have done. And everything would have been that little bit better.' . . . Thus Siege Man thinks about his wife or mother, whose death has made the eaten sweet irrevocable. He recalls the fact but cannot summon up the feeling: the feeling of that piece of bread, or sweet, which prompted him to cruel, dishonourable, humiliating acts.[7]

One such guilt-ridden survivor was Olga Berggolts, whose epileptic husband Kolya had died in hospital in February. She poured sorrow and remorse into her diaries – why hadn't she visited him every day? Why hadn't she been there at his death? Why hadn't she taken him some of the biscuits her sister sent from Moscow? How, most of all, should she feel about her colleague at the Radio House, Yuri (Yurka) Makogonenko, with whom she was still conducting a passionate affair?

Today, all day, I've had visions of Kolya, of how he was when I made my second visit to the hospital on Pesochnaya. His swollen hands, covered in cuts and ulcers. How he carefully gave them to the nurse so that she could change the bandages, all the time anxiously mumbling, making it hard for me to feed him, making me spill the precious food. I was in despair and in a fit of anger bit him on his poor swollen hand. Oh you bitch! . . . I was tired of him. I betrayed him. No, that's not right. I didn't betray, I just proved weak and callous. How Yurka calls me now! But this means cheating on Kolya! I DID NOT CHEAT. Never. But to give my heart to Yurka is to cheat on him . . . I'm unhappy in the full, absolute sense of the word . . . I hope that every terrible thing that can happen, happens to me.

This torrent of emotion coincided with the popular and official success of her long poem *February Diary*. In late March she was flown (chased by six Messerschmitts) to Moscow to attend a round of readings and receptions, including one at the headquarters of the NKVD ('I suppose there were some human beings among them. But what oafs, what louts they are.'). The event gave her the opportunity to petition on behalf of her father, at that moment on a prison train on his way to Minusinsk in southern Siberia.

> He writes 'Contact whoever you can – Beria etc. – but get me out of here'. He has been travelling since 17 March. They are fed once a day, and sometimes not even that. In his wagon six people have already died, and several more await their turn . . . My God, what are we fighting for? What did Kolya die for? Why do I walk around with a burning wound in my heart? For a system under which a wonderful person, a distinguished military doctor and a genuine Russian patriot, is insulted, crushed, sentenced to death, and nobody can do anything about it.[8]

Though she managed to get a meeting with the secretary of the NKVD Party organisation it achieved nothing: 'We had a "chat" (I can't even talk about this without shaking with hatred). He took my petition and promised to pass it on to the Narkom this evening. Will they do anything? Hard to believe.' The case was indeed shuffled back to Leningrad ('simply to rid themselves of the bother') and her father not allowed to return home until the war was over.

Berggolts's despair was compounded by Muscovites' ignorance of events in Leningrad. Like the military disasters of the war's first months, starvation had been kept out of the news. Though newspapers mentioned 'food shortage' they did so seldom and in passing, instead making ghoulish play of civilian deaths by German shelling and bombing.[9] Internally, euphemisms were coined to disguise the tragedy's stark simplicity: instead of 'hunger' or 'starvation' (the same word, *golod*, in Russian), government reports talked of 'exhaustion', 'avitaminosis', 'the cumulative effects of malnourishment', 'death due to difficulties with food supply', or most commonly of 'dystrophy', an invented pseudo-medical term which passed into common parlance and is still current today.[10] Though Berggolts was able to talk freely to her Moscow friends – and found herself doing so unstoppably, with the same 'dull, alienated sense of surprise' she had felt when released from prison in 1939 – her broadcasts were heavily censored. 'I've become convinced', she wrote,

> that they know nothing about Leningrad here. No one seems to have the remotest idea of what the city has gone through. They say that Leningraders are heroes, but they don't know what this heroism consists of. They don't know that we were starving, that people were dying of hunger, that there was no public transport, no electricity or water. They've never heard of such an illness as 'dystrophy'. People ask, 'Is it dangerous?' . . . I couldn't open my mouth on the radio, because I was told 'You can talk about anything, but no recollections of starvation. None, none. Leningraders' courage, their heroism, that's what we need . . . But not a word about hunger.'[11]

Bearing crates of lemons and tins of condensed milk, Berggolts returned to Leningrad on 20 April, to find that winter had ended and the air raids had resumed. She moved with Makogonenko out of his attic room with its view of shell-damaged roofs, down two floors into the flat of an actor recently killed at the front. Full of the actor's possessions – photographs, books, 'a mass of little saucers, two matching cups and a rusty mincer' – it increased her sense of disconnection, of having stepped into somebody else's life or into a life after death. Writing was impossible – 'like pulling ticker-tape out of my soul, bloodily and painfully'. A writers' conference held on

30 May should have been a magnificent occasion, a defiant celebration of the power of the word. But in reality it was 'organised hypocrisy' – dull, political and overcast by colleagues' dangerous envy of her sudden new fame.[12]

Six weeks later Makogonenko temporarily lost his job at the Radio House, for inadvertently allowing the broadcast of a banned poem, Zinaida Shishova's Sassoonesque *Road of Life*. With its reference to a corpse stored on a balcony, and deliberately trite, heavily sarcastic final couplet – 'Rest, son, you did all you had to/You were at the defence of Leningrad' – it had been deemed 'odd' and 'almost mocking' by the censors, and was taken off air mid-verse by a telephone call direct from the city Party Committee.[13] Berggolts's own *February Diary* was published but bowdlerised, a thrice-repeated line – 'In this dirt, darkness, hunger, sorrow' – made bland by the replacement of the words 'hunger' and 'dirt' with the safely abstract 'bondage' and 'suffering'.[14] Consolation came from ordinary members of the public, who wrote to Berggolts in their hundreds. Some of the letters were semi-official group efforts, from Red Army units or collective farms, but others were from private individuals, thanking her for putting their experiences and feelings into words. One woman described how Berggolts's broadcasts had helped her bear news of a son's death at the front, another how they calmed her as she tried to feed her dying husband in the darkness, the spoon often hitting his nose instead of his mouth. 'This is something truly splendid', wrote Berggolts:

> The people of Leningrad, masses of them, lay in their dark, damp corners, their beds shaking . . . (God, I know myself how I lay there without any will, any desire, just in empty space). And their only connection with the outside world was the radio . . . If I brought them a moment's happiness – even just the passing illusion of it – then my existence is justified.

Like others, she also found symbolism-freighted comfort in the coming of spring, in the greening of the city square limes (their buds stripped to the height of an upstretched hand), and in the sprouting of coltsfoot and camomile amid bomb-site rubble. One of her very few truly joyful diary entries was written on a warm June night while Makogonenko stood outside on the roof watching for incendiaries:

> Yesterday we had an amazing evening. At great expense Yurka bought a huge bundle of birch branches. We brought them indoors and put them in a vase. The window was wide open and you could see the great calm sky. A cool breeze wafted in, the city was very quiet and the scent of birch so sweet that my whole life, my best days, seemed reborn in me. Feeling poured through my soul – happiness, desire, content. Damp, fragrant childhood evenings in Glushina. My first evening with Kolya on the Island, when, young and handsome, he kissed me for the first time. I was wearing an embroidered smock and it smelled of birch then too . . . And now I have yesterday evening, when I lay next to a handsome, loving, present husband, and felt with my entire being that this is happiness – that he is here now, lying next to me, loving me, and that it's quiet and smells, smells of fresh birch. All this merged into one, painlessly – or to be more exact, with a pleasurable pain. Everything was wonderful, eternal, whole.[15]

The postal service started to work again towards the end of March, giving Leningraders what was often their first news for months of friends and relatives in evacuation. Since evacuees usually had only a vaguest idea of what those left behind had been through, the resumption of communication was often awkward. The classicist Olga Fridenberg, ridden with scurvy and walking with a stick, was insulted by a rather breezy letter from her cousin Boris Pasternak, describing life in the Urals town of Chistopol, where mud oozed from between the cobblestones and housewives collected water from the fire hydrant outside his window in buckets slung from wooden yokes. 'For some reason', he wrote apprehensively, 'I feel this letter is not turning out right, and I sense . . . that you are reading it with coldness and alienation.' He was right: Fridenberg expected more. 'No, I couldn't expect help from anywhere or anyone. The letter spoke of water buckets, and of a spirit worn smooth, like an old coin.'[16]

In February, the young curator Anna Zelenova had written to a colleague in Novosibirsk, candidly describing the tensions between museum staff cooped up together in St Isaac's. Now she back-tracked. Her first letter, she feared, might have given the wrong impression; though nobody was without his Achilles heel the trials of the winter had in fact bound the museum *kollektiv* more tightly together.[17] Bogdanov-Berezovsky, head of the Leningrad branch of the Composers' Union, started receiving requests from evacu-ated members that he check on their flats, an arduous task entail-ing bureaucratic battles with dishonest building managers as well as exhausting walks across the city. Anna Akhmatova, sick with typhus in intelligentsia-packed Tashkent, heard that a former neighbour, a small boy nicknamed Shakalik or 'Little Jackal', had been killed in an air raid. Once she had read him Lewis Carroll; now she wrote her own poem for him:

> Knock with your little fist – I will open.
> I always opened the door to you.
> I am beyond the high mountain now,
> Beyond the desert, beyond the wind and heat,
> But I will never abandon you . . .
> I didn't hear your groans
> You never asked me for bread.
> Bring me a twig from the maple tree
> Or simply a little green grass
> As you did last spring.

>Bring me in your cupped palms
>Some of our cool, pure Neva water
>And I will wash the bloody traces
>From your golden hair.[18]

The 'bloody traces', she later discovered, were misplaced, for it was Shakalik's older brother who had died, and not in an air raid but of starvation.

For Vera Inber a bundle of date-disordered letters from her daughter – in evacuation, like Pasternak, in Chistopol – brought news of the death from meningitis of her baby grandson. 'I read this letter to the end. Then I put it aside . . . then very quickly picked it up and read it again, vaguely hopeful that I had imagined it. No, it is all true . . . Our Mishenka is dead.' To mark his first birthday she had made him a rattle out of a pink celluloid cylinder, a dried pea and a piece of ribbon, and hung it at the end of her bed. By then, she now discovered, he had already been dead a month, and she hid the rattle away in a drawer.[19] At the front, Vasili Churkin received two letters. The first, from his father, told him that his older son, Zhenya, had been killed in battle three and a half months earlier. The second, from his younger son Tolya, described the death from starvation of his wife: 'They loaded her body, together with others, into a lorry in the court-yard of our building, just like firewood. She was taken away to the Piskarevskoye cemetery, to a communal grave . . . You and I, Papa, are all that's left of our family now. Take revenge on the two-legged beasts, Papa, for Mama and Zhenya!'[20] Tolya himself, just turned seventeen, looked forward to being called up, and hoped to join his father's unit.

For Vladimir Garshin – cultivated, fifty-four-year-old chief pathol-ogist at the Erisman Hospital and a conquest of Anna Akhmatova's – the way back to some sort of normality was work. In March he got undressed for the first time in three months: 'They put this strange bony body into the water and lifted it out again. The body couldn't get out of the heavenly water by itself. Warm! . . . It's somebody else's body, not mine. I don't know it; it works differently from how it did before. It produces different excreta; everything about it is new and unfamiliar.' His personality was new, too. By good luck he had not lapsed into indifference during the mass death, nor into hatred and rage. (This was true – a bag of oats he gave the family with whom Akhmatova stayed before evacuation saved their lives.[21]) Yet things were altered, he was 'not quite right'. He had to search inside himself, 'study this new body and this new soul, explore their hidden corners, as though I had moved into a new, unfamiliar flat'. He also literally dissected bodies in the Erisman's mortuary. As was to be expected, they carried no fat, but the most astonishing thing about them was their organs:

> Here's a liver – it has lost almost two-thirds of its weight. Here's a heart – it has lost more than a third, sometimes nearly half. The spleen has shrunk to a fraction of its normal size. We looked at the medical histories of these people. Some had been eating quite adequately for a while before they died, but they still didn't recover – they had already been damaged beyond repair. This is ghastly Stage 3 dystrophy, which is irreversible . . . Having used up its supplies of fat the body starts to destroy its own cells, like a ship which, having run out of fuel, is broken up to feed its own boilers. We knew all this in theory, but now we could see it with our own eyes, touch it with our hands, put it under the microscope.

Peering down through the lens at his specimens – 'the thinnest possible slices of human tissue – neat, colourful, prettily dyed' – he discovered within himself two contradictory emotions – the first that of greedy scientific enquiry, the second a burning desire to blame: 'These beautiful specimens scream of tragedy, of the fight the body puts up. They tell of destruction, of the crushing of the fundamental structures of living things . . . Because this "experiment" wasn't staged by life, not by life. Hatred for those who did stage it, that's what I feel.' Exactly who he thought those people were he did not specify.[22]

The government's first priority, when winter began to turn into spring, was to prevent outbreaks of disease. One urgent task was to collect the thousands of unburied corpses emerging from the snow or thawing out in basements and storage rooms; another to clear away the five months' worth of human waste – genteelly referred to as 'dirt' – clogging side streets and courtyards. While Garshin struggled to maintain detachment at his lab bench, outside his window pale, puffy-faced orderlies, their layers of coats bound tight with string, cleared the hospital grounds with picks and shovels. 'They can't work', Garshin wrote; 'All they're able to do is sit by a stove and drink tea. Yet they do work . . . It's a sort of survival instinct.' In mid-April 52 corpses were collected from the Erisman, 730 from the Kuibyshev Hospital, 114 from a children's hospital, 378 from a psychiatric hospital, 204 from Finland Station, 70 from the People's House and 103 from a cellar-turned-mortuary underneath the library at the Millionnaya Street end of the Hermitage. In the cemeteries, the winter's mass graves sank and stank, and had to be reworked.[23]

Efforts to stop people disposing of faeces outdoors, or relieving themselves in the common parts of their apartment blocks, had begun back in January, and got nowhere. 'At the entrance of no. 47 Sovetsky Prospekt', a policeman reported, 'a notice has been posted saying that anyone found disposing of human waste outside the building will be prosecuted. But in the courtyard there's not a single drain or cesspit into which waste could be poured away, and a latrine that was set up is so soiled that you can't get near it.' A woman who he caught emptying a slop bucket riposted: 'Prosecute away! Where else can I pour it? Over my head?' It was the yardman and building manager, she added, who ought to be prosecuted – thanks to them the pipes had frozen and she had to haul water from half a kilometre away. After several false starts, the clean-up campaign finally got going on 28 March. The first day was disappointing – people turned up late or not at all, transport was inadequate, there were not enough crowbars and 450 of the shovels distributed lacked handles. Though many labour-exempt – old people, war-wounded and children – voluntarily reported for duty, others tried to evade it. A housewife was heard to mutter, 'Let them feed us first, and then we'll work'; a female factory worker flatly declared, 'We don't want to, that's all'. A man who snapped 'I don't intend to work for the Soviet government' had his details passed to the NKVD.[24] Two days later, nonetheless, turnout had risen to 290,000. 'The entire population of the city', wrote Vera Inber,

> is out cleaning the streets. It's like putting a soiled North Pole in order. Everything's a mess – blocks of ice, frozen hills of dirt, stalactites of sewage . . . When we see a stretch of clean pavement we are moved. To us, it's as beautiful as a flower-strewn glade. A yellow-faced, bloated woman, wearing a soot-blackened fur coat – she can't have taken it off all winter – leant on a crowbar, gazing at a scrap of asphalt she had just cleared. Then she started digging again.[25]

To Olga Grechina, sent with her civil defence team to clear Lev Tolstoy Square, the scene resembled the 'excavation of some ancient city':

> In some places the snow had been cleared away down to the ground, in others work hadn't begun. There were crowds of people – more than we had seen together in one place for a long time. Those who couldn't work simply sat on stools, having been helped outdoors to enjoy the sun. Everyone worked happily and eagerly. Groups of the weakest dragged great boulders of snow and ice off to the Karpovka on huge sheets of plywood with ropes attached. All the dirt and snow was being dumped into the river.[26]

Aleksandr Boldyrev, still indefatigably doing the round of institutes in search of lunch passes and back pay, heard about the campaign two days in advance. It was sure, he thought, to finish off many, but officialdom's reasoning was 'better a few hundred housewives and dependants dead now, than several thousand in an epidemic in a month's time'. Summoned to help clear the grounds of the Hermitage, he put in two hours' work on the 28th ('slave-owner shouting from Ada and others') and another hour on the 29th before crying off with the excuse that he had hurt his knee ('The stench from the half-melted chocolate snow is disgusting. When you crack it with a pick thousands of droplets splash on to your clothes and face'). The next day he really did injure himself, slicing off the top of his thumb while chopping wood. A chit from a sympathetic doctor (thanked with a gift of art books) got him off further labour duty, but others were not so fortunate. 'Prushevskaya', he wrote on Easter Saturday, 'died in the Hermitage's recuperation clinic today. Though an extreme, text-book dystrophic, the day before yesterday she was still working clearing snow. Now Ada Vasilyevna comforts herself with the idea that [Prushevskaya] "was already mentally ill when she entered the clinic".'[27] Altogether, Hermitage staff cleared the complex of thirty-six tonnes of snow, ice, splintered wood, fallen plaster and broken glass.[28]

The March–April clean-up campaign is one of the set pieces of the siege, quoted as a turning point in almost every survivor interview, and credited with miraculously preventing epidemics of the three classic famine diseases – dysentery, typhoid fever and typhus. In reality, this was not quite true. Though the overall death rate fell from March onwards, in April numbers of dysentery and typhoid cases per thousand head of population were five to six times higher than a year earlier, and of typhus, twenty-five times higher. Quoting these numbers in a private letter to Zhdanov in mid-May, the head of the Leningrad garrison angrily blamed inadequate medical services and washing facilities. Half the city's public bathhouses, he pointed out, still weren't working; only 7 per cent of flats had running

water and 9 per cent sewerage, and up to a third of households still
suffered serious lice infection. Many courtyards were still covered
in human waste. Typhus 'hotspots' included recuperation clinics,
children's homes, railway stations and evacuation points, and unless
urgent measures were taken, would soon include army barracks.[29]
Dysentery – known as 'hunger diarrhoea' – also figures frequently in
diarists' accounts; it was often what finished off the already starving.
Boldyrev managed to joke about it. Forced, on his way to a meeting with Hermitage administrators, to 'do the unmentionable' in an
empty gallery – the one that normally housed Raphael's *Madonna
Conestabile* – he was delighted to find it conveniently provided with
a spade and large pile of fire-fighting sand.

As spring turned to summer and hopes that the siege would be lifted
faded, attention turned to avoiding a repeat of the mass-death winter.
Riding a tram again for the first time in months, Dmitri Lazarev
noticed that the previous year's public notices – 'Expose whisperers and spies!' 'Death to provocateurs!' – had now been replaced by
more practical exhortations:

> Fifteen hundredths of a hectare will produce 800kg of cabbage,
> 700kg of beets, 120kg of cucumbers, 130kg of carrots, 340kg of
> swedes, 50kg of tomatoes and 200kg of other vegetables! This is
> more than enough for an entire family for the whole year. Save
> ashes from the stove for your vegetable patch![30]

The gardening drive was enthusiastically taken up by Leningraders,
who with the help of government-organised distributions of seeds
and equipment – hoes and wheelbarrows were specially manufac-
tured – created thousands of vegetable patches in parks, squares
and on waste ground. At the Hermitage, staff grubbed up the lilacs
and honeysuckle of Catherine the Great's rooftop 'hanging garden'
in favour of carrots, beets, dill and spinach. The Boldyrevs planted

onions in a window box ('Oh I long for onion!'); the Likhachevs grew radishes in an upturned kitchen table. Altogether, according to *Pravda*, 25,000 tonnes of vegetables were grown on individual allotments in 1942, and 60,000 tonnes the year after. This made them twice as productive, in terms of weight per acre, as 633 new 'auxiliary farms' attached to institutes, schools and factories.[31]

The city also continued to requisition large quantities of food from collective farms within the siege ring. As well as making their usual deliveries, via their collectives, to the state, peasants were obliged to provide animals and seed corn to refugees in their areas, to subscribe funds to a tank column (dubbed the 'Leningrad Collective Farmer') and to 'donate' grain from their personal stores to the Red Army. District Party committees were instructed to rely on the Statistics Department rather than the farms themselves for harvest forecasts, and committees that failed to come up with their allotted quotas were accused of giving comfort to 'anti-collective elements'. In a rare concession to market forces, it was decided to offer underclothes, soap, thread, tobacco and vodka in exchange for deliveries of wild mushrooms and berries.[32]

An NKVD report on the public mood in villages around the town of Borovichi, east of Novgorod, illustrates the resentment these measures provoked. A series of public meetings had been held to raise funds for the 'Collective Farmer' tank column, duly raising three million roubles amidst patriotic speeches. 'We should help the Red Army chase these two-legged beasts from our land', a loyal *traktoristka* declared. 'My three sons have gone to the front. One has been killed, but our money will give the others the weapons they need to defeat the enemy.' Many, however, openly refused to donate – at least initially. 'I don't have any money so I'm not going to sign up', one forty-year-old woman said. 'There's nobody for me to borrow from, and if there were, they wouldn't have any money to lend me.' By the end of the meeting, however, she had been swayed, going home to fetch a subscription of 300 roubles. At the 'Red

Ploughman' collective a rash Estonian, having initially refused to subscribe, 'seeing the high spirits of the other members, signed up for 1,000 roubles and donated the sum in cash'.

Elsewhere villagers were more outspoken, emboldened by the sound of German guns actually to threaten their bosses. Scolded for bad work by the chairman of her village soviet, one woman spat back

> I can't wait for Soviet rule to end. It has bankrupted the peasants, left us hungry and barefoot, and now you're stripping us naked. But I'm not going to bow down before you fine gentlemen. Your reign's coming to an end. You sent all the good people out of the village, but just you wait, it'll be your turn next.

A fifty-year-old member of the 'Unity' collective was equally bold: 'Our time's coming, and we'll take what's ours. I may not be able to read or write but I'll be the first to turn the bosses in. I'll be believed. Then we'll repay you. And we won't just take a lamb from each of you; we'll flay a pair of belts off each of your backs.' (This 'counter-revolutionary activity', the report noted, had been documented in preparation for arrest.) There was also a widespread rumour that America and Britain, in exchange for opening a second front, were demanding that the collectives be broken up and the land given back to its peasant owners.[33]

In the city, new drives were launched against food theft and black-market trading. But although hundreds of food shop and food distribution agency staff were arrested (520 in July, 494 in August), and substantial amounts of ill-gotten property confiscated (sixty-two gold watches in September), both continued to flourish.[34] The outdoor markets, when shut down in one part of town, simply reappeared in another, and factory workers continued to complain that bosses and kitchen staff colluded to skim their rations. At the Sudomekh shipyard, the crackdown sparked a showdown between the factory's management and its Party organisation. 'The senior and junior managers are all drinking spirits', Party member Vasili Chekrizov confided to his diary.

> You see the bastards tipsy more and more often. If they're going to get drunk, I wish that at least they'd do it behind doors. They stuff their faces, give cover to all the thieving in the canteens, and have eliminated workers' control, since it gets in their way. There are lots of bosses like that – not just here, but everywhere . . . At meetings they declare their support for the gardening drive, and at weekends sometimes even go and inspect the allotments. But in private all they talk about is how to grab whatever they can for themselves. The inventory managers have got twenty ration cards each. Where are the NKVD? Can they really not catch them?

At a Party meeting at the end of August he (fruitlessly) stood up and made a public complaint: 'I was pleased with what I said, though I know that Kalinovsky [Sudomekh's director], Derevyanko and others will not forgive me. They can go to the devil. I said out loud what everyone in the hall was thinking . . . I won't sell myself for lentil soup, though I'm hungry every day.'

As well as trying to fulfil what was turning into a deluge of near-impossible production orders, Chekrizov was also put in charge of demolishing fourteen wooden buildings south of the Alexander Nevsky monastery, part of a government campaign to lay in supplies of firewood. Some were taken apart by hand, with saws and axes; others were slung round with a hawser attached to a tractor and pulled to the ground. Though Chekrizov accepted that the work was necessary he found it depressing, because the buildings were well constructed (with traditional cinders under the floorboards for insulation) and because their inhabitants had not yet been rehoused. To force one family to leave, he had to order his team to strip off their roof. Most, though, were resigned. 'We're wrecking their homes, which they've lived in for decades. They're not angry, they realise that the city needs firewood. They just sit there on their bundles and suitcases, waiting for transport.'[35]

An engineer to whom Vera Inber chatted on her way home from giving a talk at a factory told her that he had just been to see his family in Novaya Derevnya (the old working-class suburb, just north of Yelagin Island, where the Zhilinskys had lived). When he arrived his house had disappeared, nothing left of it except rubble and bits of broken furniture. Picking over the debris he found some family photographs. 'Now', he ruefully told Inber, 'my whole home fits in my pocket. I can carry it about with me.'[36] Olga Grechina, standing guard over a newly demolished house until a truck arrived, was timidly approached by an old woman who presented her with a small turnip and asked permission to drag away a plank. After an hour of standing watch Grechina had traded herself 'a whole dinner – several turnips and carrots'.[37] The demolition campaign, which continued all through the autumn, transformed the appearance of the city's village-like northern and eastern outskirts – doing more damage, Leningraders observed, than all the Germans' shelling and bombing.

The summer's gardening, food requisitioning, anti-corruption and demolition drives were accompanied by another mass evacuation over Lake Ladoga. Designed to remove all non-working Leningraders from the city, it was theoretically obligatory, though many – like Boldyrev and the painter Anna Ostroumova-Lebedeva – managed to evade it: Boldyrev because he calculated he was better off where he was, Ostroumova-Lebedeva (offered a flight out and lodgings with the sister of a friend) because she wanted to stay where she belonged:

To live and suffer in Leningrad for such a long time, and now, just before liberation, to leave! . . . I pictured myself in Kazan, in a warm room, safe from bombs and hunger – and I pictured myself in the role – not of sponger, but also not of tenant: an old woman who nobody needs. And I made the decision not to go anywhere. Nowhere![38]

The classicist Olga Fridenberg tried to leave with her blind, eighty-year-old mother, but gave up when their overcrowded train stopped without explanation for four days on the way to Osinovets. Bribing a guard with her last loaf of bread, she managed to disembark mother and luggage and get them back to their emptied, disordered flat, where they remained for the rest of the war.

Forced hastily to convert as many of their belongings as possible into cash or food, evacuees set up bric-a-brac tables on the pavements and inside the windows of ground-floor flats (it was astonishing, thought Grechina, how many old and beautiful things people had left to sell). Dmitri Likhachev, stripped of his residence permit and given three days' notice to depart following interrogation at the Big House, watched a stream of prospective purchasers go over the contents of his family flat: 'At bargain prices they bought chandeliers, carpets, the bronze writing set, malachite boxes, leather armchairs, the sofa, the standard lamp with the onyx base, books, postcards of town views – every single thing that my father and mother had gathered together before the Revolution.' Altogether the sale raised only 10,000 roubles, 2,000 of which went on six sacks of potatoes.[39]

The departures reduced Leningrad's civilian population to that of a small provincial city. Three and a half million before the war, it had fallen to about a million by April 1942, to 776,000 by the end of August and 637,000 by the end of the year.[40] Air raids and shelling fell off over the summer, leaving the atmosphere quiet and domestic, almost rural. In the parks, women in headscarves hoed rows of floppy-leaved cabbages. Boys fished along the embankments, sailors bicycled wildly down the middle of the streets, upturned iron bedsteads fenced off bomb craters and allotments. At the Hermitage, staff carried silk-upholstered furniture outside into the sunshine, brushing it clean of furry layers of sulphur-green mildew. The portico of St Isaac's, where Pavlovsk's treasures were stored, looked 'like a Naples backstreet', tapestries and carpets hanging from washing lines slung between polished granite pillars. In the courtyard of the Yusupov Palace scurvy-blotched hospital patients sunbathed in their underwear, oblivious to sexuality or embarrassment. Some found the quiet comforting, a reminder of holidays in grandparents' villages. Others, such as Vera Inber, newly returned from a trip to keyed-up Moscow, found it oppressive and desolate: 'The city is quiet and deserted to an extent that is shattering . . . How can one write in such a city! Even during the bombing it was easier.'[41] For Olga Fridenberg, writing to her cousin Boris Pasternak, it was 'cleaner than any city has ever been' – 'sterilised', 'holy' – but also 'without a germ of life in it. No pregnant women, no children's voices . . . A bell jar out of which all the air has been pumped.'[42]

Leningrad had also turned into a city of women, who now made up three-quarters of the population and the majority of workers in every manufacturing sector except weapons production and shipbuilding.[43] (The laying of a fuel pipe under Lake Ladoga, completed in June, allowed power stations and factories to resume limited production.) The Hermitage's head of security complained that whereas before the war he had had 650 guards, he now had 64, 'a mighty troop composed mostly of elderly ladies of fifty-five or more, plus some in their seventies. Many are cripples who used to serve as room attendants . . . at any one time at least a third of them are in hospital.'[44] Chekrizov unwillingly took on a batch of eighteen women, formerly clerks and bookkeepers, at his Sudomekh shipyard – they would be of no use, he grumbled, except to tidy up. A couple of months later he was eating his words, having successfully trained more than a hundred housewives as lathe operators, metalworkers and welders. They not only worked, he admitted, but 'worked well'.[45] The yard also employed over two hundred children under the age of eighteen, all either orphaned or without a parent in the city.

With more food available and fewer mouths to feed, most Leningraders now ate, by Soviet standards, almost normally ('A fairly well-organised system of under-nourishment', as Ginzburg sardonically put it). In addition to bread, meat, fats and sugar, coupons became exchangeable for tiny amounts of salt, wine, dried onion, dried mushrooms, cranberries, salted fish, coffee and matches. In works canteens, people no longer licked their plates, though they still ran a finger round the edge of the bowl and followed the waitresses with hungry eyes. The death rate, though still several times higher than before the war, fell steadily, and heart failure (an after-effect of severe malnutrition) took over from 'dystrophy' as the single biggest killer.[46]

The mental adjustment took longer. It was a continual surprise to encounter no queues at food shops – 'like a man who braces himself to pick up a heavy suitcase', wrote Ginzburg, 'and finds it empty'. The words 'I'm hungry', recently so charged with desperation and despair, only slowly reverted to their old function of expressing an ordinary desire for lunch. Most Leningraders were still extremely weak – their recovery as fragile, as Boldyrev put it of his family, as a spider's web that might at any moment be ripped apart by a passing tractor. When Anna Ostroumova-Lebedeva's surviving fifteen-year-old nephew came to visit her at the end of May she was shocked to see him 'corpse-pale, dragging his feet, unbelievably thin, using a walking stick, hair fallen out and head covered in a white fuzz'. (True to form, she set him to painting, and he completed 'a good study of trees, sky, and parts of the Anatomy Department'.)[47] The genuinely healthy still stood out, especially in the newly reopened public bathhouses. Berggolts saw a smooth-skinned, full-breasted young woman mobbed by blotched and bony fellow bathers, who slapped her bottom, hissing that she must be a canteen manager's mistress or thieving orphanage worker, until the girl dropped her water basin and fled.[48]

In the midst of recovery, also, a minority of people continued to die of starvation, either because their bodies had been pushed beyond recovery or because they fell outside the rationing system. From the spring, although ration levels gradually increased, getting a card was made harder. Another general re-registration in April reduced the number of cards in circulation, rules excluding those without residence permits were more harshly enforced and cards were withdrawn from the unemployed so as to push them into evacuation.[49] 'It's not medieval, like it was in the winter', wrote Berggolts in July,

> but almost every day you see someone lying propped up against a wall – either exhausted or already dying. Yesterday on the Nevsky, on the steps of the Gosbank, a woman lay in a puddle of her own urine. A pair of policemen were hauling her up by the armpits, and her legs, wet and reeking, dragged on the asphalt behind her.
>
> And the children, the children in the bakeries! Oh this pair – a mother and three-year-old daughter, with the brown motionless face of a monkey. Huge transparent blue eyes, frozen, staring straight ahead with accusation and contempt. Her taut little face was turned slightly upwards and to the side, her dirty, inhuman brown paw held out motionless in a begging gesture . . . What an accusation of us all – of our culture, our life! What a judgement – nothing could be more merciless.[50]

Lazarev was haunted by a starving teenage girl who approached him outside a food shop, begging for a piece of bread to go with a herring head and telling him that she 'lived without cards'. He gave her the makeweight from his family's ration and looked out for her the next day, but never saw her again. The editor of a factory newspaper picked up a starving child in the street:

In the morning on the way to work, I saw a little boy all on his own. Now and again he sobbed, and I was struck by his odd, uncertain gait. I approached him, and he disconnectedly muttered that his mother had gone, that he wouldn't have anything to eat until the evening. It was immediately obvious that he had lost his reason. His mind was wandering. He kept telling me about his father, and asked me to show him the way to the front. He was on his way to find him, but didn't know how to get there.[51]

Like the Gulag's 'goners', the still-starving acted as fearful reminders of mortality, objects of scornful mockery as much as of compassion. Lazarev's daughter and niece learned the following popular rhyme, adapted from the words of a pre-war children's song:

> A dystrophic walked along
> With a dull look
> In a basket he carried a corpse's arse.
> 'I'm having human flesh for lunch,
> This piece will do!
> Ugh, hungry sorrow!
> And for supper, clearly
> I'll need a little baby.
> I'll take the neighbours',
> Steal him out of his cradle.'[52]

To get rid of the physically useless, bosses used them to fill quotas of 'volunteers' for out-of-town logging camps and peat mines. Boldyrev, now enrolled at the Public Library, railed against the despatch to peatworks of a colleague, a 'second-degree dystrophic' and 'sorry, clumsy creature' quite incapable of digging for ten hours a day. 'Work!' he wrote angrily in his diary, 'after a day of it they fall off their feet. Tomorrow she has to go. Cruelty, pointless cruelty.' Four weeks later she returned and told him what it had been like:

For the strong it's fine there – extra bread, lunch. The barracks are warm and have electric light. Many gain weight and apply to stay for the winter – the camp regime, of course, doesn't bother them. But woe to the weak, because if you don't meet your norm they cut your rations. Our unfortunate librarian – who could hardly stand even before she left – was down to a single bowl of wheat soup a day. And this on a first-category card – in other words, she wasn't even being given the rations she was due. That's the system. Everywhere, all the time, the weak are now being trampled and repressed, on principle. 'Dystrophic' has turned into a swear word – in workplaces, on the streets, on the trams. Dystrophics are despised, persecuted, beaten into the ground. If you're applying for a job, the first requirement is not to look dystrophic. These are the morals of the second year of the siege.[53]

20

The Leningrad Symphony

For the American and especially the British governments, the Soviet partnership had always been fraught with difficulty. For the first two years of the war (as even the least nationalistic Russians prefer to forget), the Soviet Union had not only been publicly dedicated to world revolution, but in alliance with Hitler. There had also been intense public anger at its invasion of Finland, during which the British and French governments seriously considered sending a joint expeditionary force to the Finns' defence. Only when itself invaded by Germany did the Soviet Union abruptly turn from foe into friend.

Churchill, on hearing the news, immediately grasped that to sell this U-turn to the public he needed to draw a distinction between the Russian people and their government. He first did so in a speech broadcast on the very evening of Barbarossa, memorably declaring support for ordinary Russians – 'I see the ten thousand villages of Russia . . . where there are still primordial joys, where maidens laugh and children play' – while continuing to condemn the regime – 'No one has been a more consistent opponent of Communism than I . . . I will unsay no word I have spoken about it.'* Government information agencies were instructed to follow suit, but it was a hard

---

* In private he was more cynical: 'If Hitler invaded Hell', he famously told his private secretary later the same night, 'I would at least make a favourable reference to the Devil in the House of Commons.'

balance to strike. The BBC, obliged to broadcast a generous quota of Russian material but to steer clear of ideology, stuck mostly to the nineteenth-century classics (a radio adaptation of *War and Peace*, starring Celia Johnson as Natasha and Leslie Banks as Pierre, was a hit), folk songs and Rimsky-Korsakov. It took the corporation six months to get permission to broadcast the 'Internationale' ('we were asked not to overdo it'), and 'talkers' were restricted to distant historical topics, especially if left wing. Of Bernard Pares, distinguished founder of London University's School of Slavonic and East European Studies, it was decided that he couldn't 'do much harm on Peter the Great etc'.[1] Mass starvation in Leningrad – beyond the occasional observation that the city was 'in a bad way for food' – was not mentioned at all. Stressed instead were the city's cultural losses (Inber wrote a moralising article, for foreign consumption, about shell damage to a bust of Roentgen, inventor of the X-ray) and its stout defence. A Professor Ogorodnikov broadcast fraternal greetings – 'wearing an infantryman's greatcoat, with a rifle in my hands' – to the Astronomer Royal.[2] A proposal that the BBC broadcast its own Russian-language programmes direct to the Soviet Union got nowhere: when the suggestion was put to Maisky, according to Anthony Eden, the Soviet ambassador 'shied like a young colt'.[3]

In early 1942 news arrived of something that promised brilliantly to transcend all these difficulties – a new symphony, written in besieged Leningrad, by Dmitri Shostakovich. Though he looked younger with his cowlick and owlish spectacles, Shostakovich was thirty-four when the war broke out. A child prodigy, he had entered the Leningrad (then Petrograd) Conservatoire at the age of thirteen and joined the Soviet musical establishment six years later, when his First Symphony was taken up by the great German conductor Bruno Walter. In 1936 his career went dramatically into reverse, when his *Lady Macbeth of Mtsensk*, successfully premiered two years earlier, was suddenly denounced by *Pravda* as 'muddle instead of music'. Having spent the late 1930s in constant fear of arrest, he was (like Anna Akhmatova) brought back into the fold with the German invasion. As well as writing songs for the troops he very publicly joined in trench-digging, applied to join the People's Levy and was photographed, wearing an absurd, old-fashioned brass fireman's helmet, on the roof of the Conservatoire. On 17 September – just over a week after the siege began – he was summoned to the Radio House to make a national broadcast, from a text closely echoing *Leningradskaya Pravda*'s 'The Enemy is at the Gates' editorial of the previous day. He was speaking, he told listeners, from the front line. But though a battle to the death was joined outside the city walls, inside life went on as normal, as proven by the fact that two hours ago he had completed the first movement of a new symphony.

The first person to hear the symphony's outline, on a 'steel-grey, depressing sort of day' six weeks before, had been his secretary, Isaak Glikman:

He told me that he wanted me to hear the first pages of his new work. After a moment's hesitation he played the exposition and variation of the theme depicting the Fascist invasion. We were both extremely agitated; it was a rare event for Shostakovich to play with such manifest emotion. Afterwards we sat for a while in silence, which Shostakovich finally broke with the words (I wrote them down) 'I don't know what the fate of this piece will be.' After another pause he added, 'I suppose that critics with nothing better to do will damn me for copying Ravel's *Bolero*. Well, let them. That's how I hear war.'[4]

Equally moved was the composer Bogdanov-Berezovsky, who was among a group of musicians Shostakovich invited to his flat to hear a fuller run-through two days after his broadcast.

Unanimously we asked him to play it again. But the sirens rang
out – another air-raid alert. Shostakovich suggested that we take
a short break while he helped his wife and children, Galina and
Maksim, down to the air-raid shelter. Left to ourselves, we sat in
silence. No words seemed appropriate to what we had just heard.[5]

Realising the new work's propaganda value, in early October the
authorities evacuated Shostakovich and his family by air to Moscow.
From Moscow they travelled, in a chaotically overcrowded train (for
a horrible half-hour the symphony's manuscript was thought lost),
to the Volga town of Kuibyshev. There, despite shared living quarters
and desperate anxiety for his mother, sister and in-laws left behind
in Leningrad, Shostakovich finished the Seventh's orchestration.

Its various premieres – in Kuibyshev on 5 March 1942, in
Moscow (in the Kremlin's Hall of Columns) on the 29th, and in
London and New York in June and July – were sensations. 'The
Seventh Symphony', *Pravda* exulted after the Kuibyshev performance, 'is the creation of the conscience of the Russian people . . .
Hitler didn't scare Shostakovich; Shostakovich is a Russian man.'[6]
Attending the Moscow concert, Olga Berggolts passionately wished
that her dead husband could be there too – 'Oh what sorrow that I
can't tell Kolya about it. How terrible and unfair that he can't hear
it . . . Inside I was weeping all the time, listening to the first part,
and was so exhausted from the unbearable tension that the middle
section disappeared somehow. Did they hear it in Leningrad?'[7] For
Alexander Werth, also listening in Moscow, the symphony reflected
'infinite pity for the Russian people', and its sinister pipe and drum
march, repeated eleven times at ever-increasing volume, the feeling
that 'naked evil, in all its stupendous, arrogant, inhumanly terrifying
power', was overrunning the country.[8]

The symphony's London premiere – held on the first anniversary of Barbarossa – was broadcast across the Empire. Its opening
movement, the announcer intoned in what he was instructed should

be a 'sincere' and 'enthusiastic' voice, introduced two themes. The first was 'straightforward and sturdy, like the plain, tanned faces of the millions of Soviet men and women who gathered together on Sunday 22 June last year, in the midst of peaceful, joyous life'. The second symbolised the German invasion – 'the theme of the Fascists – brutal, senseless, implacable'. (References to its 'insidious' and 'sardonic' nature were cut from the script.) 'If you have ears to hear and heart to feel', the announcer sonorously concluded, 'I am sure you will agree that that music tells a story of sublime heroism, of unquenchable faith in victory.'[9] A proms performance followed under the baton of Sir Henry Wood, for which six thousand people packed the Albert Hall.

In New York the symphony sparked a tussle between the great conductors Leopold Stokowski and Arturo Toscanini, both of whom lobbied the Soviet embassy for the honour of directing its first performance. Toscanini and his NBC Orchestra won, and though Shostakovich privately loathed his interpretation ('He minces it up and pours a disgusting sauce all over it'), it glued millions of Americans to their radios. *Time* magazine celebrated the event by putting 'Fireman Shostakovich' on the cover, strapline 'Amid bombs bursting in Leningrad, he heard the chords of victory'. During the 1942–3 season the symphony was performed sixty-two times in the United States, many of the concerts turning into public demonstrations of support for a second front. Determined not to be outdone again by NBC, CBS paid the Soviet government $10,000 for whatever symphony Shostakovich composed next. Shostakovich himself, though praised to the skies in the Soviet press, was unnerved by it all – 'A new success', he later said, 'meant a new coffin nail.'[10]

The Seventh's final and most poignant premiere was that held in Leningrad itself, on 9 August 1942. The city's more prestigious orchestras having been evacuated as the siege ring closed, the performance fell to the Radio Committee Symphony, directed by Karl Eliasberg. Though severely depleted by the draft, the orchestra had continued to perform as the mass-death winter set in. It had given its last public concert (of Tchaikovsky) on 14 December, in the Philharmonia's freezing blue and white Great Hall, and its last live broadcast on New Year's Day 1942, of excerpts from Rimsky-Korsakov's *Snow Maiden* (the lead tenor, I. A. Lapshenkov, barely made it through his aria and died the same evening). A few weeks later Berggolts overheard Makogonenko dictating a memo: 'Leader, first violins – dead. Bassoon – near death. Senior percussionist – dead.'[11] Twenty-seven members of the orchestra had perished altogether.

At the end of February 1942 the Radio Committee announced that the orchestra was being reconstituted, and broadcast an appeal requesting all musicians left in the city to report for registration. When only sixteen did so, Eliasberg hauled himself out of the *statsionar* in the Hotel Astoria and hobbled from apartment to apartment urging the bedridden on to their feet. The first rehearsals, an oboist remembers, were only forty minutes long, and she was embarrassed to see friends' faces dirty with soot, and lice crawling over their collars. Meals were provided, though most took the extra food home to their families. A first concert – of waltzes, and extracts from *The Nutcracker* and *Swan Lake* – was held on 5 April, in the vast Aleksandrinsky Theatre. The oboist watched Eliasberg mount the podium:

> Karl Ilyich came out all starched, in tails. But when he raised his arms his hands shook. I had this feeling that he was a bird that had just been shot, that at any moment he would plummet to the ground . . . After a while his hands stopped shaking, and he began to conduct.
>
> When we finished the first piece the audience started to applaud, but there was no sound because everyone was wearing mittens. Looking out at the crowd, you couldn't tell who was a man and who was a woman – the women were all wrapped up, and the men were wearing scarves and shawls, or even women's

fur coats. Afterwards we were all so inspired, because we knew that we had done our job and that our work would continue.[12]

Rehearsals for the Shostakovich began in mid-July, only a few weeks before the premiere. Scored for eight horns, six trombones, five timpanists, two harps and a minimum of sixty-two strings, the symphony far outran the Radio Committee's resources, though extra brass players were drafted in from military bands, and given manual workers' ration cards. Microfilm of the score arrived by air from Sweden, and each musician copied out his own part by hand. The male players were provided with jackets and the females with dark dresses – though they looked, the oboist remembered, as if they were hanging on coathangers. On the morning of the concert – its date the first anniversary of that on which Hitler was said to have planned to hold a victory banquet at the Astoria – General Govorov mounted a special Operation Squall, so as to prevent disruption from air raids or barrages. Inside the grandee-packed auditorium the performance itself was ragged, but the atmosphere overwhelming. 'Some wept', remembered a woman in the audience,

> because that was the only way in which they could express their excitement, others because they had lived through what the music was now expressing with such force, many because they were grieving for those they had lost, many because they were overcome with the mere fact of being present here in the Philharmonia.

During the finale everyone stood: 'It was impossible to listen sitting down. Impossible.'[13] The besieging Germans, hearing the music ring out from loudspeakers across no-man's-land, are said to have realised at that moment that the war in the East would never be won – Leningrad was invincible, and so was Mother Russia.

It is a wonderful story, but seems to resonate more in retrospect than it did among Leningraders at the time. Few diarists mention the concert, and then only in passing. The chameleon Seventh – by turns menacing, nervy, terrifying and transcendent – perhaps better suited the summer of 1941, when Shostakovich wrote it, than numbed, emptied 1942. As Vera Inber, who attended the Leningrad premiere, wrote in her diary when she got home, 'The rumbling approach of the German tanks – there it was. But the shining conclusion is yet to come.'[14] Later the symphony became a pawn of the Cold War, played to death in the Soviet Union and written off as a bombastic slice of Stalinism in the West. Shostakovich was able to clear its name only posthumously, via memoirs written by friends. Composing the famous 'Fascist' pipe and drum march, he explained, he had had in mind not only the Nazis but 'other enemies of humanity . . . I feel eternal pain for those who were killed by Hitler, but no less pain for those killed on Stalin's orders. I suffer for everyone who was tortured, shot or starved to death. There were millions of them in our country before the war with Hitler began.'[15]

The other great recovery story of 1942 is that of Leningrad's children. At the beginning of the siege children aged twelve and under made up just under 20 per cent of Leningrad's civilian population of 2.4 million. By May, 170,000 had either died or been evacuated over the Ice Road, and thousands more had been orphaned or left without care.[16] One of the most oft-quoted records of the siege, scribbled in pencil over the pages of a pocket address book, is that kept by twelve-year-old Tanya Savicheva:

28 December 1941 at 12.30 a.m. – Zhenya died. 25 January 1942 at 3 p.m. – Granny died. 17 March at 5 a.m. – Lyoka died. 13 April at 2 a.m. – Uncle Vasya died. 10 May at 4 p.m. – Uncle Lyosha died. 13 May at 7.30 a.m. – Mama died. The Savichevs are dead. Everyone is dead. Only Tanya is left.

From January onwards teams of civil defence workers, mostly young women in their late teens or twenties, did the rounds of 'dead' flats picking up children like Tanya. They were handed in to police-run reception centres, similar to those opened five years earlier to process the offspring of purge victims. From the centres younger children, aged three to thirteen, were transferred to 130 new children's homes (ninety-eight in the city, thirty-two in surrounding towns and villages) which opened from January to March. By the end of the year 26,250 children had been taken in, 54 per cent of them orphaned, 30 per cent with a single parent serving in the forces.[17]

Older children were enrolled with civil defence teams or factories, either directly or via trade schools. Fourteen-year-old Galina Vishnevskaya, abandoned in Kronshtadt by her father and stepmother, joined an all-women civil defence brigade. She lived in barracks, wore a boiler suit and learned how to shoulder planks, dig up broken pipes, drink vodka, smoke *makhorka* and sing jazz to sailors. 'It was', as she put it in her memoirs, 'no institute for aristocratic young ladies . . . I came to know life as it really is – life as I would never have known it under other conditions.'[18]

Another sole survivor child, aged eight at the time, was Irina Bogdanova. Her family had already been half-destroyed by the Terror, during which her paternal grandparents were exiled to Archangel and her father, a journalist on *Leningradskaya Pravda*, committed suicide. Irina – a plump, pretty girl in white socks with blonde pigtails – was brought up by her mother (a frequently absent geologist), aunt and grandmother in a flat on Barmaleyev Street, on the Petrograd Side. Come February 1942, the adults succumbed one by one to dysentery, leaving Irina alone with the corpses of her mother and grandmother. She was picked up ten days later by a twenty-one-year-old civil defence worker, who handed her in to the police together with her clothes, shoes and unused ration card ('Just think, in those conditions, how honest she was not to take it!' Irina exclaims now). On her registration form someone first wrote 'boy' and then corrected it to 'girl'. The days Irina spent alone are a blank: the first thing she remembers is waking in a large, light room and realising that the girl with whom she was sharing a bed was dead. This was not unusual: of the 4,508 children received into ten suburban orphanages, 682 died, mostly within a few days of admission.[19]

Through the spring and summer of 1942 the orphanages – 38,080 children in total – were evacuated to the 'mainland'.[20] Shuffled between overburdened local administrations, they often travelled for weeks, ending up in deep countryside far from medical services or communications. An extreme case was Children's Home no. 82, whose 135 orphans ended up quartered in two small, unlit huts in a tiny settlement in western Siberia, twenty-five kilometres from the nearest telegraph and 800 kilometres from a railway line.[21] Irina was evacuated with her Children's Home no. 57 to a village in Yaroslavl province. Life there she remembers as 'hard but good'. The children slept on hay-filled mattresses, were put to serious work collecting mushrooms and berries – none could be eaten until one had fulfilled one's norm – and ostracised if caught filching food. Irina had to apologise in front of the whole school after she was caught digging the crumb out of a loaf on the way home from the village bakery, squishing it together with buds pulled off overhanging lime trees: 'They were sweet and sticky, and so good with the bread – I remember the taste even now.'[22]

For children as for adults, of course, recovery entailed much more than better rations. Survivors remember persistent anxiety, dullwittedness, distrust of adults and obsession with food. Asked if she liked gingerbread, a girl in evacuation in the Urals didn't understand the question: 'I remember sitting there and wondering – What does it mean this "nice" or "not nice"? . . . What is this phrase "I don't want to eat"?' At night she sneaked outdoors and dug in a nearby field for bread, which she believed grew underground like potatoes. 'I thought that all I had to do was dig a small hole and there I'd find a fresh loaf. I'd take it and eat my fill.'[23] A paediatrician gave the children on her ward drawing materials: one drew a clock face, captioned 'This is our watch. It tells us when we can eat the next little piece of bread'; another, a nine-year-old boy, drew a large black square.[24] An entrant in a story competition imagined the vegetables she was cultivating in her school allotment as tiny people with green legs and heads, who ran up the stairs of an apartment building to save a thin, golden-haired girl, or raced through shellfire to a Red Army dugout.[25] Other children hoarded obsessively, collecting crumbs in matchboxes, developed stammers or would not speak at all.[26] For teachers, one of the most cheering signs of recovery was when their pupils started misbehaving again. One girl, told to report to her headmistress for running out on to the street, was amazed when the usually stern woman burst into tears: 'It was our first childish prank; it meant that we were returning to life and that made them very happy.'[27]

Saved by a school, in the role of teacher rather than pupil, was Olga Grechina. Since the beginning of the war she had dug trenches, worked in factories, cleared snow, had several close shaves during air raids and lost her mother to starvation. Her sixteen-year-old brother Vovka had turned into a stranger, appearing at their flat only rarely and with odd new possessions – clothes, a bicycle and jars of half-rotten salted tomatoes – which he fantastically claimed had been lent by relatives or turned out of the Smolniy's cellars. 'Already', she wrote, 'he wasn't the same happy little elephant who all my schoolfriends adored, a bit of a coward and none too keen on his lessons.' In May 1942 all became clear, when she heard that he had been arrested for stealing – not only from bread shops, she discovered, but from neighbours and relatives, including two spinster aunts whose cards he had taken, promising to return with their rations; they had subsequently died of starvation. Despite doing the rounds of the police stations and joining the long, silent queues outside the Kresty, Olga had no further news of her brother until the summer of the following year, when she received official notification that he had died of 'dystrophy' in a camp in Yaroslavl province.

After Vovka's arrest, Olga suffered a nervous breakdown. Forced to sell remaining family valuables to an avaricious schoolfriend (her parents' silver wedding anniversary tea set went for a few roubles, an oak table for two kilos of millet), she felt surrounded on all sides by loss and betrayal, started to suffer hallucinations and fell into deep depression. Attending teacher training in response to a radio appeal for nursery school staff, she sat at the back and slept:

> I woke rarely and couldn't write or remember anything. Luckily there were no exams – I would have failed them. There were a couple of nice girls there but I spoke to them robotically – I think they thought that I was mentally handicapped. And this was actually true, since I remember nothing from June. I don't remember what I ate, who I saw, or any other details of my life then. I didn't feel that I was dying, but that I was already dead.[28]

Her salvation was Boarding School no. 43, a tightly run, well-connected institution housed in a handsome nineteenth-century building one block down from the Hermitage on the Neva (and still there today). The headmistress, presented with a skinny, spectacled twenty-year-old with a plait pinned round the top of her head and darned socks, immediately despatched her to dig potatoes at the school's affiliated collective farm, where she was fed cabbage soup, dozed through the days with her 'nose in the earth', and opened up to fellow staff, mostly newly widowed university lecturers, through the long pale evenings. In September they returned to the city and Olga was put to mending schoolbooks ('It was very hard not to eat the paste, made from pure white flour') before being given charge of a class of thirty-five 'no longer starving, and quite lively' four-year-olds. 'You are not herding children', she was told, 'you are bringing them up.'

The job was an extraordinary one. The teachers lived full-time at the school, together with 120 four- to seven-year-olds. At night – when not taking the children down to the air-raid shelter – they slept on pushed-together tables, and during the day not only taught, but stoked stoves, hauled water up two flights of stairs from the unlit basement of a neighbouring building, washed and dried sheets (six of Olga's group were bed-wetters), flushed out lavatories, folded and unfolded camp beds (four times a day, taking into account after-noon naps) and shaved the children's heads to rid them of lice. In the evenings they repaired the children's clothes, reusing buttons and elastic. There was no soap, no toothpaste and so little crockery that everyone drank from saucers. Staff were also drafted to outside 'voluntary' work, demolishing buildings for firewood and emptying bedpans in a nearby military hospital. Though it was forbidden to talk in front of children about the war – they were to be 'transported to a world of fantasy, fairy tales and art' – reality inevitably intruded. On walks they competed for spent shot from the anti-aircraft guns on the *Kirov*, moored nearby on the Neva embankment, and at break-time distressed Olga with their games:

> Today the children found some sort of hole in the yard, and began to dig, chanting, 'Come on, come on, dig quicker. Our little ones are in there. The Germans have killed them all!'
>   Lida: 'My Vovochka's in there!'
>   Rufa: 'And my Lilenka and Granny!' . . .
>   Tearing the girls away from this game was very difficult. It fascinated them and they came back to it again and again. It was always Rufa, five years old and the oldest in my class, who started it. She hadn't been to kindergarten before and had been living with a Granny who fell asleep and didn't want to wake up any more. Before that there had been a Lilenka – probably a younger sister – who also fell asleep forever.[29]

Never having had much to do with small children before, Olga initially found controlling her 'collective' almost impossible, but quickly learned the tricks of the trade. At mealtimes she quietened them with the help of a floppy-eared dog glove-puppet that had been her own childhood toy. During air-raids she repeated again and again a tale from the Brothers Grimm, of a magic pot that produces a non-stop flow of sweet golden *kasha*, so much of it that it pours out of the house and floods the whole town. 'A mass of energy, time and starch' went into preparations for New Year's Day 1943. Besides having to recite crass poems in praise of Voroshilov, distributed by the city education department, the children dressed up as snowflakes, rabbits and bears, and a teacher as Snegurochka – Russia's Little Snow Girl, grand-daughter of Grandfather Frost – juggling snowballs made of cotton wool. Aunt Motya, the incorruptible eighty-year-old School cook, made *pirozhki* out of carefully hoarded flour. Olga stayed with School no. 43 all the way through to the autumn of 1944, before resuming her university degree. It had not only saved her from despair but given her 'a place in the world'. 'I felt that I needed people', she wrote later, 'and that they might need me.'

The Last Year

Hitler's objectives for 1942 included Leningrad. It was to be stormed, a Führer Directive of 5 April instructed, as soon as victory in the Crimea had freed up the necessary armour and artillery, in an operation to be code-named *Nordlicht*, or 'Northern Light'.[1] Ignoring his generals' pleas for another attempt on Moscow, Hitler reiterated his intention after Sevastopol's capture, ordering Manstein to lead five divisions and a giant railway gun, the 'Heavy Gustav', north.[2] 'St Petersburg', he mused over lunch a few days later, 'must disappear utterly from the surface of the earth. Moscow, too. Then the Russians will retire into Siberia.'[3] Far from retiring to Siberia, in mid-August the Red Army launched its fourth attempt to break the Germans' hold on the southern shores of Lake Ladoga, concentrating on the already blood-soaked Sinyavino ridge south of Shlisselburg. Manstein's new divisions were able to prevent a breakthrough, but not to embark on *Nordlicht*. Meanwhile, Hitler also launched Operation *Blau* ('Blue'), his mighty southward push towards rhe Caucasus and Central Asia. Rostov-on-Don fell in the last week of July, and by mid-August panzers were pushing into the foothills of the Caucasus, within tantalising reach of the Baku oilfields.

Beneath the surface, though, the war was beginning to tip in Russia's favour. By autumn the Wehrmacht was grossly overstretched: its supply lines thin, its recruits ever younger and rawer, and its generals increasingly yes-men – 'nodding donkeys', as Speer called them[4] – of the Führer. (Halder resigned in September, bewailing Hitler's 'fits of insane rage' and 'chronic tendency to underrate the enemy'.) The Red Army, in contrast, was beginning to pull itself together. Unlike Hitler, Stalin had begun to realise that military decisions were better left to the professionals. Increasingly, he listened to his generals, and in October stripped the political commissars who dogged regular officers' footsteps of most of their powers. Lend-Lease supplies were beginning to arrive overland via Vladivostok and Tehran, instead of on the precarious Arctic convoys, and weapons production was increasing, especially of the robust, reliable T-34 tank and PPSh-41 sub-machine gun.

The sheer size of the Soviet population was also beginning to tell, as was the Red Army's willingness to use women, who were drafted in large numbers from the spring of 1942 onwards. Used in ancillary roles from the start of the war, women – mostly, like their male counterparts, in their late teens or early twenties – were now trained as fighter and bomber pilots, anti-aircraft gunners, observers, snipers, mine-clearers and ordinary infantrymen. 'This morning', wrote a disconcerted Fritz Hockenjos, 'one of my sentries spotted a riflewoman. For fun he shot at her. She dived for cover, ran, turned around, shot back and ran on – as good as any well-drilled soldier. Let's hope I never have to deal with women like that.' Later, during a Russian attack near Pskov, his men reported seeing female soldiers running forward with mats, which they threw over barbed-wire entanglements for the infantrymen following behind. 'We shot them and the infantry down. The men told me about it later, using bawdy jokes to hide their discomfort. When I asked how they knew they weren't men they said "When they jumped, everything jiggled."'[5] By the end of the war, some 800,000 such women had served in the Red Army altogether.

That the war in the East was turning became apparent to the world at Stalingrad, the small city on the Volga – less than 200 kilometres from the present-day Russian border with Kazakhstan – which is still synonymous with Soviet stubbornness and Nazi overreach. Besieged from August 1942, it seemed permanently about to fall until mid-November, when Zhukov launched an ambitious counter-encircle-ment of Paulus's Sixth Army. A mid-December attempt to relieve the Sixth Army, led by Manstein, failed, and seven more weeks of terrible slaughter later Paulus surrendered, together with more than 90,000 troops. What hurt most, Hitler raged in his 'Wolf's Lair', was that Paulus had not committed suicide: 'What is Life? Life is the Nation . . . He could have freed himself from all sorrow, ascended into eternity and national immortality, but he prefers to go to Moscow.'[6] The same less-than-cheering sentiment was pre-printed on the *Feldpost* cards on which Hockejos wrote notes home to his wife: 'It's completely unimportant whether or not we live; what's necessary is that our *Volk* lives, that Germany lives.'

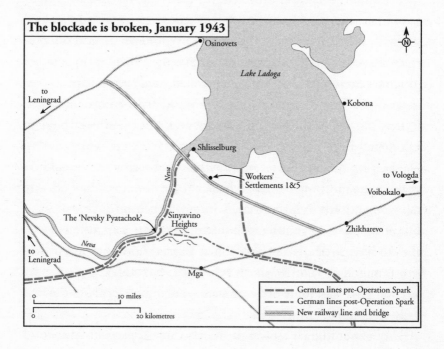

The blockade is broken, January 1943

For Leningrad – now down to a fifth of its pre-war population – the second winter of the siege was nothing like the first. Again, households retreated into single rooms heated by smoky *burzhuiki*; again, they sealed up their windows and laid in stocks of food and firewood. But the winter was a mild one, more flats now had electricity and water, and ration levels were the same as Moscow's: there was no repeat of 1941–2's mass death.

While the battle of Stalingrad was still at its height, Stalin ordered another push to liberate Leningrad. Code-named Operation *Iskra*, or 'Spark', it was essentially a better planned, better equipped repeat of the previous August's Sinyavino offensive. The Leningrad armies would force the Neva at three points along the river south of Shlisselburg; the Volkhov armies would thrust westwards, meeting up with them south of Ladoga. A preliminary attempt to drive tanks across the Neva failed, the ice proving not yet thick enough to bear their weight, and the operation was put off to 12 January, by which time the temperature had fallen to -15°C. Overseen by Zhukov, it began at first light, with a two-hour barrage from more than 4,500 guns. This time the tanks got across, on ingeniously designed pontoons that had been moved into place under cover of darkness and frozen into position with water sucked from under the ice. By the end of the day a bridgehead five kilometres long and one kilometre deep had been established on the Neva's southern bank. By the 14th the two Soviet fronts were only three miles apart, and at 9.30 in the morning of the 18th they finally met, at peatworks that have gone down in history as 'Workers' Settlements nos 1 and 5', but which were in reality outposts of the Gulag. Later the same day the Red Army liberated Shlisselburg. It was almost empty, all but a few hundred of its inhabitants having died of starvation, been sent away as slave labourers or fled together with the Germans.

In Leningrad, crowds gathered round the street-corner loudspeakers. 'An extraordinary day', wote Vera Inber on the 16th:

The entire city is waiting . . . Any moment now! People are saying that our fronts – the Leningrad and the Volkhov – have joined up. Officially nothing is known . . .

Somewhere guns are booming. The all-clear has just sounded. Ordinary siege life goes on, but everyone is waiting. Nobody says anything – nobody dares to, in case a wrong word gets to wherever our fate is being decided, and changes it all. I'm perplexed and bewildered. I can't find a place for myself. I try to write and can't.[7]

The official announcement came two days later, pasted up in massive lettering on posters all over the city. 'The blockade is broken! The blockade is broken!' exulted Anna Ostroumova-Lebedeva. 'What happiness, what joy! All night nobody slept. Some wept for joy, some celebrated, some just shouted . . . We're no longer cut off from the Motherland! We share a pulse!'[8] 'Everybody congratulates each other', wrote Dmitri Lazarev, 'recounts how and from whom they heard the news – how women ran out of the building managers' offices, who kissed who, who crossed themselves . . . Never mind the raids and the bombardments, however hard or frequent. The blockade is broken – it's the beginning of the end!'[9]

It was the beginning of the end, but only that. The victory was cheap by Soviet standards (34,000 killed, missing or captured) but far from complete.[10] The Red Army had broken the German hold on Lake Ladoga, but had cleared only a fragile corridor to the 'mainland', just five miles wide at its narrowest point. South and west of Leningrad, the German armies still crouched in the outer suburbs. (Fritz Hockenjos, peering from his new observation post – another monastery bell tower – on the Gulf of Finland, could see cars and pedestrians moving along the streets, and count the windows in a government building.[11]) In February 1943 a second operation, 'Polar Star', aimed to lift the siege completely by encircling Germany's Eighteenth Army to the west, cutting its railway connection to the rear at Pskov. It failed thanks to rain, Hitler's belated caution after Stalingrad, and to the Spanish Blue Division, which successfully defended its positions in vicious hand-to-hand trench fighting. (Hockenjos, who had earlier dismissed the Spaniards as 'a great bunch of *caballeros*, dagger-wielders and operetta tenors', presumably had to eat his words.)

The corridor did, however, allow the construction of a new thirty-four-kilometre temporary railway line into Leningrad, via a pontoon bridge over the Neva. The first train direct from the 'mainland' rolled into Finland Station on 7 February, to speeches, bunting and a brass band. Decorated with oak-leaf-wreathed portraits of Stalin and Molotov and a banner proclaiming 'Death to the Fascist German Usurpers!', it is said to have carried butter ('for Leningrad's children') and kittens, the latter in great demand thanks to a plague of rats. Vulnerable to shelling until the Germans were finally pushed off the Sinyavino ridge in September, the line supplemented what were now well-organised ice and barge routes over Lake Ladoga.

Inside the city, the mood of 1943 became one of strained, wrung-out waiting – for a second front, for shelling and air raids to stop, for the war to end and normal life to resume. Everyone still suffered nagging hunger. The librarian Mariya Mashkova was overwhelmed by waves of depression, unable to take an interest in anything and exhausted by unshakeable thoughts of bread and *kasha*. Though her flat was now clean and warm, with working electricity, lavatory, telephone and radio, she felt constant exhaustion and irritation. At work tasks 'slipped through her hands', at home she felt guilty at her inability to take pleasure in her children. Her emaciated, rheumatic husband had closed in on himself, speaking little and sleeping 'like a marmot' in the evenings, while she resentfully darned socks or read *The Brothers Karamazov*. Her friend Olga Berggolts's gossip about flirtations and jealousies at the Radio House she found incomprehensible, and the sight of a woman breast-feeding in a doctor's waiting room almost repulsive. The baby would have been conceived, she calculated, in February or March of the previous year – 'the months when people were collapsing in hundreds of thousands, dying of hunger, the morgues full, bodies everywhere, black wrinkled faces. And together with that, the start of a new life! Where did they find the strength, the desire?'

Shades of the mass death were still everywhere, most of all in the wrecked and filthy 'dead' flats from which it was Mashkova's job to rescue books for the Public Library. Each had its tale of death, looting, suicide; of children arrested, gone to orphanages or simply missing. On 7 April 1943 she visited three such, one in particular 'typical for Leningrad':

> Once there was a family of six. The father and eldest daughter leave for the Red Army and no more is heard of them. Nobody knows if they are alive or dead. The mother stays on in Leningrad with three children – mentally handicapped Boris, aged eight, Lida, aged thirteen, and Lyusya, fifteen. Bravely she tries to save them from death's clutches, but can't do it. In December Boris dies, in January Lida, and then, of hunger diarrhoea, the mother herself. The only one left is Lyusya – on a dependant's card in a dark, cold, wrecked flat, covered in muck and soot. She drags herself to the market, sells things, then as a last resort, starts stealing from the neighbours. She was caught with stolen food cards and arrested; there's been no news of her since March of last year. Perhaps she's dead too. And what remains is a frightening, dystrophic room, full of filth and rubbish. No family – just two empty beds amid the chaos – all that's left of a once-cosy home. Oh how familiar this is!

There were shades, too, of terror: Mashkova was summoned to the Big House four times, always late at night, in February and March. One meeting lasted an exhausting nine hours. Though she refers to the encounters only briefly and vaguely in her diary ('I came home angry; I'm sick of complicated relationships') she was almost certainly being asked to inform on friends and colleagues.

As winter turned to spring her life became superficially more cheerful. On Easter Sunday she and her husband got tipsy on five litres of beer and went shopping for clothes; on May Day they spring-cleaned their flat, had friends round to eat *pirozhki* and watched the children perform in a school concert. But her depression and self-disgust failed to lift.

> Where can we find the strength to live happily, joyously, without endless worry? Why can't the children be the basis for happiness? They are good children after all, and we should be living just for them. Why can't we suppress the fear that the rest of our lives will be nothing but strain and effort? . . . Is it really just the lack of a piece of bread and a bowl of soup? Are our inner resources really so meagre that this defines everything around us?[12]

Frequent air raids added to the strain, alerts averaging slightly over one per night from January through to May.[13] Shelling – worse in the first half of the year – became so accurate that tram-stops had to be moved and the newly reopened Aurora and Youth cinemas closed again.[14] Barrages now fell into an established pattern, coinciding with morning and evening journeys to work. They were extra heavy on public holidays (on 1 May 1943 Vera Inber's building 'swayed and rocked like a swing'), and when news came through of (now frequent) Soviet victories. Well-established 'lucky' spots included Aleksandrinskaya Square, with its statue of Catherine the Great surrounded by her generals and courtiers, and the Radio House, said to have lead foundations dating from its days as the Japanese consulate. Unlucky ones were the Liteiniy or 'Devil's' Bridge, the square in front of Finland Station, nicknamed 'the valley of death', and the corner of the Nevsky and Sadovaya, opposite the Public Library. On 8 August Mashkova's children narrowly missed being killed there on their way home from a fishing expedition: 'Suddenly they appeared, words tumbling out about severed limbs, blood, a crushed lorry – then all in the same breath about the three little fish they had caught, still flapping in their net. I kissed them, hugged them, was overjoyed and at the same time felt completely broken.'[15]

Anna Ostroumova-Lebedeva still lived on the Vyborg Side with her maid Nyusha, whose only son had been killed at the front the previous year. During air raids they slept in the hallway, Ostroumova-Lebedeva on a folding chair, Nyusha on a trunk. With each impact the building 'jumped'; pans fell off the shelves, spent shot from anti-aircraft guns pattered like dried peas on the roof and new cracks appeared in the ceiling. Once a bomb splinter flew in at the window and lodged in a chair, and they knew that if an incendiary landed in the attic the building would almost certainly burn down, since there were no other residents left to stand guard duty. In the mornings the pavements were covered with broken glass, crunchy and glittering. Ostroumova-Lebedeva was kept going by work – her first post-starvation woodcut was a special moment, tools slicing as surely as ever into smooth, golden board – and by the kindness of a loyal circle of friends, mostly younger women artists. For her seventy-second birthday, on 15 February 1943, they brought her a candle, half a litre of milk (for which the giver had walked five kilometres each way to a hospital), a small packet of tea, three sweets and two tablespoons of coffee. Nyusha presented her with a bar of kitchen soap. 'All welcome and useful presents ... [We] didn't talk about food, rations, bread, dystrophy and so on, but about books, creativity, art – about the things close to my heart, by which I live.' In the summer she started going for walks, mourning damage to favourite buildings and picking the clover and buttercups that grew amidst tall grass along the edges of the pavements. The weeds made her feel as though she were walking on 'free earth, in a field somewhere ... These humble flowers, so delicate and fleeting, bring my soul instant peace and happiness.'

There was more escapism in going over her girlhood diaries, with their notes on turn-of-the-century trips to Italy and watercolour sketches of Lugano and the Simplon Pass. On quiet days she wrote them up in the hospital gardens, amidst slit trenches and vegetable plots. During raids she sheltered in her windowless bathroom, writing on a board balanced across the washbasin. In the midst of a barrage on a hot night in late July a friend telephoned to ask if she was all right:

> In between the whistles and bangs of the shells I shouted, 'We're still here! We're still here!' And remembering that she'd been abroad I added, 'For God's sake, tell me what those flowers are called, that grow high up in the snow, in the Alps. I've been trying to remember all day!'
> 'Cyclamen!'
> 'Yes, yes, cyclamen!'

A few days later she and Nyusha had a near miss when a shell hit the roof two rooms away and penetrated down to the bottom floor. Thereafter they went to a shelter during raids, but did not move out.

Barrages also disrupted work at the Sudomekh shipyard. On 18 April thirty-one shells hit Vasili Chekrizov's workshop, forcing it to relocate. 'My girls were in there when it started', he noted approvingly, 'but before they left they locked up. Good girls . . . By evening everyone had turned glazier, boarding up the windows with plywood.'[16] When not repairing bomb damage, much of his time was spent battling on behalf of his staff with bureaucracy:

> Interesting fact. A girl came out of hospital, went to her hostel. It had moved. Where to, nobody knew. No belongings, money or cards. The district soviet sent her to us. Processing will take six days. She spent last night outdoors in a courtyard. Today is a

Sunday, so we can't register her, and without registration we can't give her a place in our hostel. Nor can she get new cards . . . I decided to send her to the allotment organisers, but even there she can't get cards before Tuesday. Without cards she'll go hungry, and in three days she'll be back in hospital as before . . . So I arranged with the canteen that they'll feed her today and tomorrow, but will they actually do it? That's an example of the kind of work I've been caught up in for the last ten days. Everywhere there's a shortage of hands, and the ones we do have, we use unproductively.[17]

Alongside these routine concerns, Chekrizov also continued to play his part in the virtual reality of workplace politics. At a meeting in July, the shipyard's Party organisation staged a mini-purge. One man was sentenced to death and seven to lengthy prison terms, for colluding in food theft with senior management and for 'preparing to welcome the Germans'. Despite having been unjustly expelled from the Party himself in the 1930s, Chekrizov seems to have no doubts about the latter charge, asking his diary 'How did the Partorg miss it?'

In other institutions too, repression ground on. Yakov Babushkin, the lively and outspoken radio producer who had organised the Shostakovich premiere, was sacked from the Radio House in April; he thus lost his exemption from the draft, and was killed at the front a few weeks later.[18] At the Yevropa hotel-turned-hospital, Marina Yerukhmanova, the twenty-one-year-old who had survived the mass death working as an orderly, was called to give evidence in the trial of its senior administrator, a man adored by the staff for his fairness, openness and charm. Defended only by Marina – who had naively assumed that others would speak up for him too – he was found guilty of 'counter-revolutionary activity' under Article 58 of the Criminal Code, 'plus endless other numbers and letters. The whole alphabet, apparently, did not suffice to enumerate his crimes.' Marina – stunned by the sight of her boss unshaven, beltless and with a look of bitter resignation on his face – was given the sack, together with her mother and sister.[19]

Following the partial breakthrough of January 1943 the north saw little serious fighting for several months. An early spring thaw hindered troop movements, and save for another unsuccessful attempt to widen the land corridor to the 'mainland' in July, attention turned to the centre and south, where the Red Army's great post-Stalingrad counter-offensives were gathering speed. Rostov-on-Don was liberated in February; Kharkov, following July's great tank battles outside Kursk, at the end of August. On 3 September Stalin finally got his second front, when the Allies landed in mainland Italy.

Outside Leningrad, meanwhile, trench life fell into a quiet routine. South of the Kirov Works soldiers treated visitors to home-made pickled cabbage and salted cucumbers. On the Volkhov, Vasili Churkin slept a lot, collected wild raspberries, watched his general exercising with dumbbells in the mornings and wrote his diary at a desk equipped with a kerosene lamp, inkwell, box for nibs and glass filled with wild flowers. Elsewhere soldiers used dynamite to fish for bream and pike, distilled *samogon*, used tethered geese as sentries and whittled knives out of the Plexiglas windscreens of downed planes. On the other side of no-man's-land Fritz Hockenjos passed the time birdwatching (the soldier who brought him news of the first lark earned a schnapps), taking photographs – favourite subjects churches (ruined) or trees (charred) silhouetted against dramatic sunsets – and making a pet of a stray cat, which he named Minka and allowed to sleep next to his head on his rolled-up coat. His men put up comic signs – 'Berlin 1,400km, Leningrad 3km'; *Kein Trinkwasser* when their trenches flooded – and named the sheltered corners in which they played cards the *am Wilden Mann* and the *am Alten Fritz*, after Swabian pubs. Separated by only a few hundred yards of wire-entangled mud, the two sides developed a sort of intimacy, ogling the girls that visited each other's dugouts, shouting badinage – 'You give us one of your Uzbeks, and we'll give you one of our Romanians' – and coming to unspoken agreements about when and where to shoot. 'One night the Russians are all over no-man's-land and we lie in front of the wire waiting to take prisoners', Hockenjos observed, 'and the next night we change roles.'[20] He noted the tune of 'Kalinka' – picked up from Russian soldiers' singing – in neat manuscript on the back of a range-finding form.

In September 1943, by which time the Wehrmacht was in general retreat along its whole central and southern front, Hitler's generals began to argue for withdrawal from Leningrad. With armour and guns committed to defending Smolensk and Kiev, they no longer had any hope of reinstating a full blockade, and the retreat in the south left the northern armies dangerously exposed, especially since swelling numbers of partisans now regularly blew up railway lines and supply convoys that ventured off the major roads. (The head of the regional partisan organisation claimed, in a memo to Stalin of 25 September, that his five thousand-odd men had blown up 673 road and railway bridges, destroyed 7,992 freight wagons and flatbeds and burned 220 warehouses, 2,307 lorries and cars, 91 planes and 152 tanks. 'The partisans let me through again', Hockenjos wrote sarcastically in his diary on his return from a brief spell in hospital in Narva.[21]) Soviet intelligence recorded the doubts spreading among the lower ranks: 'We shouldn't be bothering with these marshes', one captured German soldier told his interrogators, 'they should send us to defend Ukraine.'[22] Another, a deserter from the German garrison at Novgorod, claimed that his officers spent all their time drinking and gambling, while the rank and file put their faith in 'some destructive weapon that has so far been kept a great secret'. He himself had decided to swap sides before he got killed.[23] A third explained that he had always got his news from the cook in his field kitchen, 'but now he knows no more than we do. If we're being kept out of the picture on events at the front it's because things aren't going so well. Russia is too big for us to defeat her.'[24]

Though unwilling to give the Finns (now putting out diplomatic feelers to America) an excuse to drop out of the war by abandoning Leningrad, Hitler allowed himself to be partially persuaded, giving von Küchler permission to build a new defensive 'Panther Line' behind the River Narva and lakes Peipus and Pskov. Fifty thousand labourers, mostly drafted from the local population, constructed 6,000 bunkers, laid 125 miles of barbed wire and dug 25 miles of trenches and tank traps. Army Group North's lines were shortened by a quarter, the retreat including at least a quarter of a million Soviet civilians – some willing, others rounded up so as to prevent their recruitment into the advancing Red Army. (A peasant woman with whom Hockenjos was briefly quartered was busy packing – less, he thought, in compliment to the Germans, more because she feared the Bolsheviks even more.) The ring round Leningrad, however, remained as tight as ever. From Pushkin and the Pulkovo hills, the bombardment of the city continued with futile malice – the deaths caused (like those of two girl students at the Erisman in December) all the crueller since the end of the siege was now so obviously near.

At the end of September the Red Army recaptured Smolensk; on 6 November, having made a brilliant unobserved crossing of the Dnieper, it liberated Kiev, just in time for Revolution Day. In the north, General Govorov's planning for the final liberation of Leningrad was now almost complete. The offensive was to be three-pronged – east from the 'Oranienbaum pocket', into which 52,000 troops had secretly been moved, towards Peterhof and Uritsk; south from the city itself towards Pushkin and Pulkovo; and west from the Volkhov towards Novgorod. Pleading by Zhdanov secured an extra 21,600 guns, 1,475 tanks, 1,500 of the multiple rocket launchers called 'Katyushas' and 1,500 aircraft. With nearly twice as many men as Army Group North (1.24 million compared to von Küchler's 741,000), more than twice as many guns, and more than four times as many tanks and planes, Govorov now had overwhelming superiority of numbers, and controlled the air so thoroughly that Red

Army lorries no longer bothered to shade their headlights at night.

The attack itself began on the morning of 14 January 1944, with a massive bombardment from Oranienbaum. In thick fog, 104,000 shells were fired in an hour and five minutes. 'We can forget about my leave', a German officer wrote to his wife that evening. 'Here a battle is boiling which outdoes everything we've seen up to now. The Russians are advancing on three sides. We're living through hell. I can't describe it. If I survive, I'll tell you about it when we see each other. At the moment all I can say is one thing – wish me luck.'[25] The bombardment was followed the next morning by an hour-and-forty-minute, 220,000-shell onslaught on Pulkovo. Barrage and counter-barrage stunned Leningraders, shivering plaster from ceilings, setting light fittings swaying and shaking one of the workshops at Chekrizov's shipyard to the ground. Huddled in shelters and stairwells, they prayed that this really was the end. 'I sat on the edge of Mama's bed', wrote Olga Fridenberg on the 17th:

Thunderous shelling. I looked at the clock to check the intervals [between hits]. Another crash, but this time no explosion – a dud must have hit a neighbouring building. Yet another crash, and the world reeled. We were hit. I looked up to see all the windowpanes fly out at once. And in flew the freezing January air.

Superhuman powers were born within me. I seized a winter coat, wrapped Mama up in it, and dragged her heavy bed out into the corridor, then into my own room. One of my windows was miraculously intact, and I stuffed the other with rags.[26]

Anna Ostroumova-Lebedeva spent the whole of the 18th and 19th in her bathroom, braced against the whistling and crashing outdoors. 'I have to admit that the shelling throws my thoughts completely off track. In my head everything is twisted into a tight knot. Nobody can get used to this. Uncontrollable shaking overtakes me; my heart contracts. Every second you expect the shell that will end your life.' That evening's news bulletin made her weep for joy: Peterhof, Krasnoye Selo, Ropsha and eighty villages along the Volkhov had been freed.

Vera Inber, trying as usual to work in her room at the Erisman ('Dear God, what a din!'), watched Red Cross buses driving back and forth from the railway stations, collecting wounded soldiers. How many, she wondered, were there in all the city hospitals put together? Surely, surely, their sacrifice could not be in vain? On the Sunday morning of 22 January – the day after Mga was liberated and von Küchler flew to the 'Wolf's Lair' to demand permission to abandon Pushkin – she got a telephone call from the Writers' Union telling her to be ready in an hour for a press tour of newly liberated Peterhof. The drive there took her through the recent battlefields. To the sides of the road, banks of rubble marked what had been villages; the fields, churned by artillery fire, were as brown as if new-ploughed. Sappers worked along a ditch with their dogs, and defused shells lay, finned and silvery, in rows on the verges, like displays of newly caught fish. Peterhof town itself was unrecognisable, a 'strange, white, lunar' landscape punctuated by a few fantastically shaped fragments of brick wall and a single ruined church. Rastrelli's great baroque palace had been completely gutted by fire – it would 'beyond human effort', Inber immediately assumed, to restore it. On the drive home in the dark, by the light of a burning house, she saw a column of POWs. Dirty and unshaven, they were the first Germans she had seen for the whole of the war.

At eight o'clock on the evening of 27 January 1944 – four days after the last German shell fell on Leningrad – Inber made it from a Party meeting to the old riverside parade ground known as the Field of Mars just in time for the official victory salute. Parks, bridges and embankments were packed with people, mixed up with tanks and military motorbikes. From the dockyards in the west to the Smolniy in the east 324 guns fired twenty-four salvoes, flames shooting from their muzzles 'like hellfire in old pictures'. Flares arched above the

Neva, their crimson, green, blue and white reflected on the ice and on a sea of upturned faces. A searchlight picked out the gilded angel on top of the Peter and Paul spire, the beam so sharp that it seemed solid, a bridge up which one could walk to heaven. 'The greatest event in the life of Leningrad', Inber wrote in her diary later that night. 'Complete liberation from the Blockade. And here, though I'm a professional writer, words fail me. I simply state that Leningrad is free.'[27]

PART 5

Aftermath

Sketch for a proposed memorial to the liberation of Leningrad
(Aleksandr Vasilyev, February 1943)

I don't often visit memory
And it always surprises me.
When I descend with a lamp to the cellar,
It seems to me that a landslide
Rumbles again on the narrow stairs.
The lamp smokes, I can't turn back
And I know that I am advancing on the enemy.

Anna Akhmatova, 1940

Coming Home

The end, like the end of all great conflicts, left a vast silence – the silence of hushed sirens and guns, of the never-to-return missing and dead, and in Leningrad's case, of grief and horror unexpressed, of facts falsified or left unsaid. It also meant new beginnings – militarily, of the great Soviet push to Berlin; privately, of facing up to loss and rebuilding lives; publicly, of repopulating and repairing an emptied and damaged city; politically, of new rounds of repression.

The end of the siege was not the end of the fighting. It took the Red Army only three weeks to push von Küchler's Sixteenth and Eighteenth Armies back to the Estonian border, but until July 1944 to break the Panther Line and to expel them from the border citadel of Narva, dogged German resistance exacting a massive military death toll to book-end that of the opening months of the war. One of the fallen was Vasili Churkin's seventeen-year-old son Tolya. In his free time, Churkin searched for his corpse, until he realised that 'if I wanted to turn over every dead body on this little piece of ground it would take months and months. They were everywhere – along both sides of the roads, in the woods, in clearings. The Narva bridgehead was swallowing division after division.'[1] In the six months from the start of Leningrad's liberation offensive, more than 150,000 Soviet troops were killed, captured or went missing – often in the same sort of clumsy infantry charges that had cost so many lives two years earlier.[2] Rejoining his men at Gatchina after Christmas home leave, Hockenjos was told 'over and over how they had shot the Russians to bits and sent them packing – the Leningrad Guards, who attacked in large, unmissable groups, waving red flags'. Was it 'Russian stubbornness', he wondered, that made 'fifty men come out of the forest in the middle of the day and march towards us through the snow across an open field', or was it 'the ice-cold devilry of some Commissar, sitting at the edge of the trees and sending out a company just so as to test our defences? Either way, we picked them all off easily with rifles, and didn't even have to bother with our guns.'[3]

Commissar or no, the Red Army was advancing and the Wehrmacht retreating, scorching earth as it went. ('I could shoot those *Brandkommando* lads', Hockenjos worte in disgust, 'running from house to house with their bundles of burning straw. Of course they're following orders but they're enjoying themselves too.'[4]) Fittingly, Army Group North met its end under siege itself, trapped on Latvia's Courland Peninsula. Unable to admit that the war with Bolshevism was lost, Hitler did not allow it to start evacuating by sea until January 1945, by which time the Red Army was already entering Germany. More than 200,000 German troops were still defending the peninsula on VE Day – 9 May rather than 8 May to Russians – when they surrendered to General Govorov. A separate Soviet drive northwards through the Karelian Isthmus, led by Meretskov, ended with the Finnish armistice of 19 September 1944. (Churkin, quartered in an astoundingly neat Finnish farmhouse, saw Mannerheim's plane flying overhead to Berlin, escorted by three Soviet fighters.) The border was redrawn as at the end of the Winter War, leaving Finland's second city of Viipuri to Russia – where it remains, lovely but dismally neglected, to this day.

Leningrad's liberation found now twelve-year-old Irina Bogdanova still with her children's home in the Yaroslavl countryside. The announcement, she remembers, was greeted with shrieks of joy and flying pillows:

> Then after a few minutes, in a corner of the dormitory, someone started crying. Then in another corner, another child, until we were all crying. And none of us wanted any breakfast or any lunch. Not until suppertime were the teachers able to coax us into the dining room. It was because we suddenly realised that nobody was waiting for us. Living in the children's home we hadn't thought about this, we'd just been waiting for the war to be over. Only with victory did we have to come to terms with life again, with all that we had lost.[5]

Olga Grechina, serving out her last months at Boarding School no. 43, celebrated with her colleagues:

> The staff gathered together in the evening, instead of eating in their separate corners as usual. People brought out vodka; we sang, cried, laughed; but it was sad all the same – the losses were just too large. A great work had ended, impossible deeds had been done, we all felt that . . . But we also felt confusion. How should we live now? For what purpose?[6]

Olga Fridenberg mourned her mother, spending long hours curled up in bed with her face to the wall, or mechanically tidying and sweeping:

> Now I have so much time, I feel cast away in it. All around me it stretches away into infinity. I want to fill it by doing things, by moving about in space, but nothing helps . . . Only late in the evening do my spirits revive somewhat – another day is over. Relieved, I lie down and for seven hours am blissfully unaware of time . . . Waking up in the morning is frightful – that first moment of consciousness after the night. I am here. I am in time again.[7]

Evacuees started returning in large numbers in the summer of 1944, more than doubling Leningrad's population in twelve months and bringing with them breaths of Central Asia and the deep Russian countryside. One girl, fresh from a farm on the southern steppe, missed riding horses bareback out to pasture and instead took to climbing the city rooftops – 'five floors or higher, and the steeper the better'. A friend of Vera Inber's brought home a spinning wheel, which she plied in between playing Beethoven sonatas.[8] Soldiers started coming home a year later, in the summer of 1945. Brought up to believe in the backwardness of capitalism, they had been astonished by their glimpse of German living standards, even in wartime. Why, many wondered, had the Germans bothered to invade, when they already had so much themselves?

Slowest to return were surviving POWs. Of the approximately 4.5 million Soviet servicemen taken prisoner in total during the war, about 1.8 million were still alive at its end, the remainder having been executed (if Jewish or Party members), or killed by starvation and disease. Many died on forced marches westward as the Wehrmacht retreated. The Red Army, when it reached their camps, promptly reinterned the survivors and subjected them to 'filtration'. Standard questions were 'Why didn't you shoot yourself instead of surrendering?' 'Why didn't you die in the prisoner-of-war camp?' and 'What assignments were you given by the Gestapo and the Abwehr?' – plus, for those liberated by the Allies, 'What assignments were you given by Anglo-American intelligence?' Lev Kopelev, a *politruk* arrested for protesting at the Red Army's mass rape of German and Polish women, found himself sharing a cell with two young Leningraders. Captured at the age of twelve, when the Wehrmacht overran their Pioneer camp near Luga, they had been sent as slave labourers to Germany, then back to the Russian front to work as spies, at which point they immediately crossed to the Russian lines and gave themselves up to the first Red Army unit they found. Though Kopelev assured the boys that they would soon be freed and allowed home, what in fact happened to them he never knew. He himself was convicted of the usual 'anti-Soviet activity' and sent to the Gulag, where he remained until 1954.[9]

Reunions (for those lucky enough to have them) were often difficult. Children failed to recognise their parents, parents no longer knew their children, spouses found each other changed and alien. Even the city looked different – lean and hard, hollow-eyed, gap-toothed, shrapnel-pocked. Elated to be home again, Anna Akhmatova was met at the railway station by her pre-war lover, the pathologist Vladimir Garshin. They had agreed, via letters, to marry, and that Akhmatova would take his name. Now she discovered that he had changed his mind. Akhmatova pretended to herself that Garshin had lost his reason ('The man who means/Nothing to me now . . . Wanders like a ghost on the outskirts/The back streets and backyards of life') but in fact he had simply fallen in love with someone else. Humiliated, Akhmatova cut all dedications to him from her poems, and moved back into her old room next to Nikolai Punin's in an annexe to the Sheremetyev Palace. Its windows were repaired thanks to Olga Berggolts, who begged help from a conservator at the Public Library. When she stressed Akhmatova's importance, the man told her not to insult his intelligence – 'I am literate!' – and removed the necessary glass – 'I think they will forgive us' – from some framed prints of great nineteenth-century writers.

Churkin, both of his sons having died at the front and his wife of starvation, had nobody to come home to at all. Put up by friends, it was three days before he could bring himself to visit his own flat. It had been broken into:

An awful mess; the thieves had turned everything upside down. All the clothes – suits and coats – and valuables gone. Everything that didn't interest them strewn about the floor . . . All I took was our photo album. Here they are, my darlings, looking silently up at me. I'll never see them again. I felt such pain that I burst into tears.[10]

Out in Yaroslavl, Irina Bogdanova was luckier. Though she too had lost her whole immediate family, she remembered the address of some family friends – four spinster sisters, of aristocratic Polish background, in whose tar-paper cottage in a dacha village east of Leningrad she had once stayed for the summer. On receiving Irina's letter – written in a childish hand, with polite enquiries as to the health of their cat and dog – the two surviving sisters (the others had died of starvation) immediately made the journey to Yaroslavl and took Irina home, subsequently bringing her up as their own. As they saved her so she now preserves the memory of them – a clutch of turn-of-the-century studio photographs, printed on gilt-edged board, of handsome young women with tiny waists and thick, upswept hair. Their hats, wide and white, are topped with doves' wings.

Leningrad also, of course, needed physical repair. Though nothing like flattened Kharkov, Minsk or Stalingrad – or even, according to people who saw both, London – it had been hit by over 150,000 heavy artillery shells and over 10,000 bombs and incendiaries during the siege.[11] Few were the unbroken windows, uncracked walls, roofs that did not leak. The Hermitage, miraculously only directly hit twice during the siege, put in a bill for sixty-five tonnes of plaster, a hundred tonnes of cement, six thousand square metres of glass, eighty tonnes of alabaster and six kilos of gold leaf.

As the city refilled, demand for undamaged housing increased, sharpening disputes between returnees and the new occupants, legal or otherwise, of their vacated flats. Ex-servicemen, and civilians who had been evacuated individually (the political and cultural elite), in theory got back their pre-war accommodation automatically, but civilians who had been evacuated with their workplaces (the rank and file) did not. In practice, even for the first two categories restitution often required bribery and pull. A law forcing the return of valuables bartered away at knockdown prices was not properly enforced either, and it was a common post-war experience to see a familiar picture hanging on the wall of a hard-currency shop, or a mother's brooch on the lapel of a stranger.[12]

The worst architectural losses were the imperial summer palaces. One of the first to see Pavlovsk, eight days after its liberation, was Anna Zelenova. Given permission, but no transport, to go and find out what had become of it, she set out on foot. It wasn't a lonely walk, she gleefully wrote to a colleague in evacuation, because she was kept company by flocks of crows, circling above all the unburied German corpses. One had been propped up against a fence and a note attached: 'Wanted to get to Leningrad. Didn't make it'. At the entrance to Pavlovsk park she saw that the central pillar of its double gates had been demolished to make way for tanks. The park itself was cut about with shell craters, tree stumps, dugouts and firing points. In one bunker she found tapestries with swastikas cut out of them, in another oil paintings and a grand piano. Inlaid doors had been used to make footbridges across ditches, mahogany wardrobes turned into latrines. The palace itself – torched, like Peterhof, by the Germans on departure – had been burning for ten days:

> The dome has gone, and the clock towers, and the Rossi library has burned to the ground, including its walls. There's no right wing or throne room, no trellised gallery above the colonnades. The picture gallery has gone, the chapel, the whole Palace . . . Looking in through the ground-floor windows you can see the sky, and the only way you can tell which room is which is by the remaining fragments of plasterwork on the walls.

Inside, Zelenova found graffiti, remnants of parquet flooring like half-done puzzles, and piles of empty wine bottles. Charred beams still smoked and molten lead dripped from what was left of the roof on to her camera. The statue of Tsar Paul in front of the main entrance had been turned into a telegraph pole, his bicorne hat draped with cables. ('I'm so glad that Pavel stands with his back to the palace.')

In flattened Pushkin, the Catherine and Alexander Palaces stood equally in ruins, the Catherine in part because the Red Army had failed to defuse two sets of delayed action bombs, the second of which exploded on 3 February, more than a week after liberation: 'A shameful disgrace – people should have been at their posts in the first few hours', Zelenova's colleague wrote back when she told him the news.[13] For years after the war his own job would be to scour the roads to Berlin for looted imperial treasures. Among those never found were the delicately carved panels of the Catherine Palace's fabled Amber Room, given to Peter the Great by Friedrich Wilhelm of Prussia. Hidden behind fake walls, they had quickly been discovered by the occupying Nazis, who packed them into crates and sent them to Königsberg (now Kaliningrad) in Eastern Prussia. Last seen in Königsberg's castle, what happened to them next is a mystery. Treasure-hunters notwithstanding, today's best guess is that they were destroyed by a fire which swept through the building a few days after it fell to the Red Army in April 1945.[14]

The palaces' deliberate destruction, according to the journalist Alexander Werth, 'aroused among the Russians as great a fury as the worst German atrocities against human beings'. Like most, he initially assumed them to be unrestorable. Standing at the top of Peterhof's grand cascade, soviet chairman Petr Popkov is said to have waved a hand at the blackened shell in front of him and declared 'This will all be razed!'[15] Others thought the ruins should be left as a monument to Nazi brutality, or replaced by workers' housing.

The decision to rebuild, taken by Stalin himself, was in tune with a new public mood that swept over the whole Soviet Union at the end of the war. First, everyone simply yearned for an easier, pleasanter, 'normal' life. Olga Grechina, scratching around for a respectable wardrobe for her new start at university, acquired new boots by taking the blades off a pair of skates. Marina Yerukhmanova, sacked from the Yevropa, adopted a stray St Bernard – the same breed her grandparents had owned – which she fed Eskimo ice creams and hoisted on to pavement weighing machines. (It had been rescued, she liked to think, by victorious *tankisti* from some abandoned German *Schloss*.) Nikolai Ribkovsky, the apparatchik who dined off ham and turkey at a Party rest-house in the middle of the mass death, looked forward to the day when he could afford to take a girl to the Mariinsky and treat her to coffee and cake in the interval. Botanists at the Botanical Gardens drew up a wish list of sunny countries to which they wanted to launch new plant-collecting expeditions – India, Madagascar, Java, Australia and Ceylon.[16]

Second, people realised that Communism was here to stay. Before the war, it had been possible to regard the regime as something temporary. The conversational code for tsarism had been 'the peaceful time', implying the possibility of return to a natural order. Now the phrase fell out of use: Leningrad had permanently replaced Petersburg. But third, people wanted this Communism to be of a different sort. Having fought, worked and suffered for their country for four years, they felt that they had earned the right to be trusted by its government. They longed for the ordinary decencies of civilised life – security, comfort, entertainment – but also for freedom to express their opinions, explore the outside world, and genuinely to participate in public life. In the first post-war elections to the Supreme Soviet Leningraders defaced their ballots, scribbling 'When are you going to abolish Communist serfdom?' 'Give us bread and then hold elections'; 'Down with hard labour in the factories and collective farms', or even crossing out the candidate's name and writing 'For Adolf Hitler'. 'It's humiliating', an actor at the Aleksandrinka was overheard to exclaim. 'You feel like a machine, a pawn. How can you vote when there's only one name on the list?'[17]

Alexander Werth, allowed briefly to report from Leningrad in September 1943, had sensed the yearning for change. A banquet in his

honour at the Writers' Union featured the usual toasts to Churchill and
Eden, but he detected behind them 'more even than in Moscow . . .
a real thirst for close future contacts with the West. They thought in
terms of harbours and ships – ships carrying passengers to and fro,
and goods, and books and music, and paintings and gramophone
records.' Interviewing Popkov, he was struck by the fact that he called
himself Leningrad's 'mayor' rather than chairman of its soviet, and,
visiting an airbase, by the mottoes pinned up in the mess, which were
drawn not from Lenin but from an etiquette manual of the pre-revolutionary Corps des Pages ('Avoid gesticulating and raising your voice',
and 'An officer's strength lies not in impulsive acts, but in his imper-
turbable calm'). His elderly chambermaid at the Astoria, accepting a
Lucky Strike, reminisced about the Egyptian Tanagras she had smoked
when in service with a Princess Borghese, and of annual trips to Paris
to buy lingerie at Paquin and Worth. On his final evening, Werth was
taken to see a packed-out stage adaptation of Frank Capra's comedy *It
Happened One Night*, complete with show tunes, millionaire, detectives
and gangsters – 'all dressed like "real" Americans in the brightest light-
blue and purple suits'. Everywhere, he noticed, pictures of Zhdanov
outnumbered those of Lenin and Stalin. All in all, he came away with
'the curious impression that Leningrad was a little different from the
rest of the Soviet Union', its traditional superiority complex heightened
by awareness of having fought its 'own show', without Moscow's help.
There was even a rumour that it might become the capital again – if
not of the whole Soviet Union, then of the Russian Republic.[18]

These hopes – for comfort, a degree of political pluralism, contact
with the outside world and a special role for Leningrad – were almost
entirely disappointed after the war. Living standards did – agonisingly slowly – improve, but for Leningraders, as for other Russians,
the early Cold War years brought only renewed repression, reaching
a climax in the late 1940s and early 1950s before falling sharply off
with Stalin's death in 1953.

With hindsight, that this would be so had always been obvious. No longer constrained by the war effort to pay heed to public opinion, and aware that soldiers returning victorious from Europe had a history of fomenting revolt, Stalin had no intention of loosening his grip. Though the Leningrad NKVD arrested fewer people than usual for political crimes in 1944 (373 in total), this was only because it was busy hunting down collaborators in the newly liberated towns round about. Arrests rose again in 1945.[19] Censorship, having slackened slightly during the war, became stricter, especially in regard to 1941–2's mass death. A handicapped twenty-year-old's diary recorded, alongside her father's death from starvation, the discovery of dismembered bodies in a musician neighbour's flat. She read it aloud to friends; one of them informed on her and she was sent to the Gulag for six years. Violinists, in the official version, hadn't spent the siege eating children, but playing Shostakovich in fingerless gloves.[20] Inber criticised Berggolts for continuing to produce 'sad, old-fashioned' poetry, only to find that a Writers' Union meeting damned her own work as 'repulsive', 'clinical' and 'torture to read'.[21] At the Radio House, staff were ordered to destroy wartime recordings of unscripted interviews with ordinary members of the public; instead, they took the reels home hidden under their coats, or filed them in boxes labelled 'folk music'. Fridenberg, commissioned (by, she was appalled to discover, the NKVD) to collect accounts of 'Leningrad heroines', was steered towards 'favourites and pets of the authorities . . . Everything living, everything genuine was inadmissible . . . Though much that was unbelievably tragic was conveyed to me orally, nobody dared write down the truth.'[22]

Remaining hopes for a 'Leningrad Spring' were dashed, very publicly and deliberately, in the summer of 1946, by a crackdown on the Leningrad intelligentsia. Initiated by Stalin, it was deputised to Zhdanov, by now back in Moscow and widely touted as Stalin's successor. He chose as his victims Anna Akhmatova and the satirist Mikhail Zoshchenko, picking them out for their popularity ('I

knew I was doomed the moment a girl ran up to me and dropped
on her knees', Akhmatova said of a triumphant public poetry reading) and because they embodied the clever, sceptical, Europhile
Leningrad spirit. As the writer Konstantin Simonov put it in his
memoirs:

> I think the attack against Akhmatova and Zoshchenko was not
> concerned so much with them in particular . . . Stalin was always
> suspicious of Leningrad, a feeling that he had retained since the
> '20s . . . I thought then 'Why Akhmatova, who hadn't emigrated,
> who gave so many poetry readings during the war?' . . . It was a
> way of putting the intelligentsia in their place, of showing them
> that the tasks before them were just as clear as ever.[23]

The blow fell on 15 August, in the form of a resolution by the
Party's Central Committee. Akhmatova's work was condemned
as 'empty and frivolous . . . permeated by the scent of pessimism
and decay', Zoshchenko's as 'putrid, vulgar nonsense', liable to lead
astray Soviet youth. Both displayed 'cringing servility towards the
bourgeois culture of the West'. One of two Leningrad magazines
that published them was closed down, and the other put under the
editorship of a Central Committee propaganda chief. A week later
Zhdanov flew to Leningrad to anathematise the pair in person, in
a speech to the Writers' Union. As the significance of his words (he
described Akhmatova as 'half whore, half nun' and Zoshchenko as
'a trivial petit-bourgeois . . . oozing anti-Soviet poison') sank in, the
audience froze into silence – 'congealing', as one of its members
put it, 'over the course of three hours into a solid white lump'.[24]
One woman tried to leave the hall, but was prevented from doing
so and sat down again at the back. There were no other protesters
and a vote to expel Akhmatova and Zoshchenko from the Union
was passed unanimously. The meeting ended at one o'clock in the
morning, the assembled writers filing silently out into the warm

summer's night. 'Just as silently', remembered one, 'we passed along the straight avenue to the empty square, and silently went off in late trolley-buses. Everything was unexpected and incomprehensible.'[25] Akhmatova herself, magnificently contemptuous, claimed to have been unaware of the resolution's existence until she saw it printed on a sheet of slimy newspaper from which she had just unwrapped some fish. Simonov's interpretation of the affair is borne out by the fact that despite Zhdanov's blood-curdling rhetoric neither she nor Zoshchenko was arrested, but both were reduced instead to their old pre-war existence of secrecy and penury, burning notebooks and living off the kindness of friends. One of the few brave enough not to drop Akhmatova was the much younger Olga Berggolts, who in consequence lost her position on the board of the Writers' Union.

In August 1948 Kremlin politics were upended by Zhdanov's death (without outside help) from a heart attack. Malenkov and Beria immediately began to reassert themselves, broadening the highly publicised crackdown on the Leningrad intelligentsia into a secret purge of Zhdanov's protégés at the Kremlin and the whole Leningrad Party.

What became known as the 'Leningrad Affair' began in February 1948, with the dismissals from their posts of Zhdanov's wartime deputy Aleksei Kuznetsov, who had followed him to Moscow and been given oversight of the NKVD, of 'Mayor' Popkov, who had taken over as Leningrad's First Party Secretary, and of Nikolai Voznesensky, a clever young economist who had ridden on Zhdanov's coat-tails to become head of the State Planning Commission. 'The Politburo considers', ran a secret resolution, that 'Comrades Kuznetsov . . . and Popkov have [demonstrated] a sick, un-Bolshevik deviation, expressed in demagogic overtures to the Leningrad organisation, unfair criticism of the Central Committee . . . and in attempts to present themselves as the special defenders of Leningrad's interests.'[26]

Though 'the hunt was on', as Khrushchev later put it, the

Leningraders were initially left at liberty; Voznesensky was even still invited to Stalin's drunken midnight dinners. Finally, on 13 August, Kuznetsov, Popkov and three others were invited to Malenkov's office and arrested on arrival by his bodyguard. Though Voznesensky wrote a grovelling letter to Stalin – 'Please give me work, whatever's available, so I can do my share for Party and country . . . I assure you that I have absolutely learned my lesson on party-mindedness' – it did him no good.[27] He was arrested in turn on 27 October and joined Popkov and Kuznetsov in a special prison. In September 1950 they were put on closed trial in Leningrad, in the old Officers' Club building on the Liteiniy. Kuznetsov refused to confess and was immediately executed – according to Khrushchev 'horribly, with a hook in the back of his neck'.[28] Voznesensky may have been kept alive for a little longer. There is a story that a few months after the trial Stalin asked Malenkov what had become of the famously workaholic Planning Commission head, and suggested that he be given something to do. Malenkov replied that this would not be possible, since he had frozen to death in the back of a prison truck.[29] Altogether, sixty-nine Leningrad-connected Party officials were executed, imprisoned or exiled between 1949 and 1951, plus 145 of their relatives. Least deserving of pity was P. N. Kubatkin, head of the Leningrad NKVD. The standard mugshots taken at his arrest – facing the camera and in right profile – show him haggard and dishevelled, just like his thousands of wartime victims.

Conducted in great secrecy, the 'Leningrad Affair' remains something of a mystery today. The pretexts for it, whispered in Stalin's ear by Malenkov, were that Voznesensky had massaged production figures, and that the Leningrad Party had set up an agricultural trade fair without Moscow's permission. In reality, it seems to have been the product of Cold War tension – 1949 was the year of the Berlin airlift, the founding of NATO and the Soviet Union's first atom bomb – combined with Stalin's fear of rivals. He may have been

rattled by talk of a Leningrad-headquartered Russian (as opposed
to all-Union) Communist Party, and by a friendly visit to the city
by a delegation from Tito's independent-minded Yugoslavia.[30]
Revisionists argue that the purge was a shrewd power play, reas-
serting Stalin's supremacy and balancing the Kremlin factions.
Conventionally, and more convincingly, it was simply one of the last
spasms of an ageing, paranoid mind.

In parallel with the 'Leningrad Affair', Stalin also launched, again
with Malenkov's and Beria's encouragement, a Union-wide 'war on
cosmopolitanism'. Wartime harnessing of traditional values – the
return of military ranks and insignia, honours named for Suvorov
and Nevsky – now curdled into virulent anti-Westernism. It was the
era of crackpot pseudo-genetics, of 'city' instead of 'French' bread,
and of boasts that Russians had invented the radio, the aeroplane and
the light bulb. People with foreign connections or Jewish surnames
began to vanish daily ('It used to be a lottery', quipped one, 'now it's
a queue'),[31] and at Leningrad University colleagues gathered once
again to accuse each other of 'formalism', 'bourgeois subjectivism' or
'bowing to the West'. 'All the professors', Olga Fridenberg wrote of
her classics department,

> were ritually humiliated. Some, like Zhirmunsky, endured it
> elegantly and with flair . . . but Professor Tomashevsky, a man
> not yet old, of cool temperament and caustic wit, very calm and
> unsentimental, walked out into the corridor of the Academy
> of Sciences after his examination and fell into a dead faint.
> The folklorist Professor Azadovsky, already weakened by heart
> disease, lost consciousness during the meeting itself and had to
> be carried out.

It has been calculated that Union-wide, so many Jews lost their jobs
that by 1951 they held less than 4 per cent of senior government,
economic, media and university posts, down from 12 per cent in

1945.[32] The highest-profile victim was Molotov's luxury-loving fifty-three-year-old wife Polina, formerly People's Commissar for fisheries. A grotesque pseudo-prosecution, involving accusations of Zionist espionage and group sex, ended with her divorce from Molotov and a five-year sentence to the camps. For all the ugliness Fridenberg found an ugly new word – '*skloka*' – standing for 'base, trivial hostility; spite, petty intrigues. It thrives on calumny, informing, spying, scheming, slander . . . *Skloka* is the alpha and omega of our politics. *Skloka* is our method.'[33]

Akhmatova, though left at large, was made to suffer by proxy. One of the thousands arrested was her thirty-seven-year-old son Lev Gumilev, not long demobilised having fought all the way to Berlin. He had spent several years in the Gulag before the war, now he was sentenced to another ten, and, despite his mother's petitions and obedient hackwork (a cycle of patriotic poems titled *In Praise of Peace*), not released until Khrushchev's general amnesty of 1956. Also arrested was her ex-husband Nikolai Punin, who, having publicly observed of the disappearance of eighteen colleagues that 'we lived through the Tartar invasion and we'll live through this', was charged with being 'an advocate of the reactionary idea of "art for art's sake"' and sent to the Arctic Komi Peninsula. From camp he wrote his granddaughter jokey letters about sandcastles, hedgehogs and mushrooms, before dying there four years later at the age of sixty-five.[34]

The same year another old man died alone – Josef Stalin. The news was met with a mixture of stunned silence and intense, cathartic emotion. In schools, teachers led their pupils in mass lamentation; in communal apartments, people struggled to look solemn or burst into tears; in the camps, guards gathered in nervous huddles as prisoners yelled and threw their hats in the air. Hysterical crowds followed the great dictator's funeral cortege in Moscow, but in Leningrad a man lost his Party card for twice turning off the radio during the orations and quietly carrying on with his work. 'We were doubly besieged', Likhachev had written, 'from within and with-out.'[35] The 'siege within' was not yet over: the Soviet Union would remain, and remain greyly repressive, for almost another forty years. But it would never be as bad again.

The Cellar of Memory

The chief memorial to the siege of Leningrad is the Piskarevskoye cemetery, in the city's housing project and ring road-busy north-east. Opened in 1960, it is by Soviet standards a rather self-effacing complex, emphatically a place for mourning rather than victory celebration. The mass graves – big, grass-covered barrows, each marked (symbolically, since the burials were never so tidy) to a particular year – line a long central avenue. At one end an eternal flame wavers, transparent in the sunshine; at the other a statue of a broad-hipped woman in a long dress stands outlined against clouds and sky. The frieze behind her is carved with famous, untrue words from Berggolts: 'No one is forgotten, nothing is forgotten'.

Away from the central avenue, the mounds go on, shaded by limes and birches. Here they are less closely mown, and the dips between them soft with buttercups and cow parsley. One has a rabbit hole in its side. There are individual graves, too – nineteenth-century ones left over from the site's days as an ordinary cemetery, and hundreds upon hundreds belonging to soldiers who died in Leningrad's military hospitals, their young faces – handsome, jug-eared, freckled, Asian, with spectacles and without – gazing in fuzzy black and white from oval ceramic medallions. A loudspeaker system hisses into life – Beethoven's Funeral March, the solemn chords distorted by the breeze and long use. When it snaps off again, the sounds are of bird-song and distant traffic.

Like all such places, the Piskarevskoye fails. Statues, landscaping, poetry – nothing can say all that should be said and felt about a tragedy on the scale of Leningrad. Perhaps, for a modern visitor, no adequate response is possible anyway. All one can do is take time, bring to mind, pay respect. Memorialising the siege has been problematic for the Soviet – now the Russian – state, too. Until Stalin's death it was pushed into the background, an embarrassing reminder of the disastrous opening stages of the war. No memorial to the starvation dead was erected, they were cited but substantially undercounted at Nuremberg, and anti-begging decrees swept thousands of disabled ex-servicemen off the streets to the old monastery islands of Valaam in the far north of Lake Ladoga. The mass graves were fenced off and left to sprout nettles and brambles.

Some of the undergrowth was cleared under Khrushchev, who allowed the construction, following lively public debate as to a suitable site, of the Piskarevskoye complex, and the publication of Dmitri Pavlov's outspoken (for the time) account of wartime food supply. It grew back again, in different form, under Brezhnev, who conscripted the siege into his cult of the Great Patriotic War, designed to substitute for the fading charms of Marxism-Leninism. In this version civilian suffering took the foreground again, but in abstracted, sanitised form. Extremes of horror were reduced to easy shorthand – cold, dark, a child's sledge, a *burzhuika* – and heartbreaking moral and social breakdown was transformed into an uplifting redemption story. Leningraders had been selfless, disciplined heroes, unwavering in their faith in ultimate victory. Simply by surviving in the city they had helped to defend it, and when they died of hunger they did so nobly, in a sort of ecstatic trance. From this martyrdom they had emerged tempered, purified, a special race. Leningrad boys and girls, the cult's most extravagant rhetoricians urged, should only marry each other.[1]

Attempts to restore some reality to the siege story met determined resistance. When Harrison Salisbury published his classic (but itself romanticised, particularly as regards Voroshilov and Zhdanov) *The 900 Days* in 1969, it was attacked not only by *Pravda*, in an article signed by Zhukov, but by the Western left.[2] It was not published in Russian until 1994, six months after Salisbury's death. The ground-breaking oral history *A Book of the Blockade*, compiled by the historian Ales Adamovich and the novelist Daniil Granin, similarly came under fire when first published in 1979, despite over sixty excisions by the censors. The gag applied not only to the siege, but to particularist 'Petersburg' history writing in general. Shostakovich's amanuensis Solomon Volkov, trying to get a book on Leningrad composers published in the early seventies, was faced with this 'over and over. The very concept of Petersburg or Leningrad culture was being quashed. "What's so special about this culture? We have only one culture – the Soviet one!"'[3]

The floodgates opened in the late 1980s, with Gorbachev's policy of *glasnost* or 'openness', precursor to the collapse of Communism and the entire Soviet Union. Suddenly it became possible to subject the siege to genuine analysis. Wartime terror could openly be criticised for the first time; so could the senseless waste of the People's Levy and the tragic inadequacies of the evacuation and rationing programmes. Uncensored personal accounts streamed into newspapers and journals, their unadorned fact-telling and often bitter tone acting like paint-stripper on the Brezhnevite myth of universal staunchness and self-sacrifice. Adamovich and Granin were able to fill out their *Book of the Blockade* with sharper diary extracts (such as those of Yuri Ryabinkin, the teenage boy abandoned by his mother), and with material on cannibalism and the 'Leningrad Affair'. Several revelatory document collections appeared, most startlingly from the archives of the Federal Security Service, the successor to the NKVD.

Zhdanov's reputation – hitherto that of a wise and beloved war leader – took a plunge, and his name was removed from schools, factories, a battleship and the Black Sea port of Mariupol. The biggest renaming was that of Leningrad itself, which on 1 October 1991, after a closely fought referendum, became again Sankt-Peterburg – to English-speakers, St Petersburg.[4]

Still important guardians of the siege story are the dwindling band of *blokadniki* themselves. For them the siege is not history but acute, lived experience, and their memories of it, as Olga Grechina puts it, 'a minefield of the mind. You only have to step on them, and you explode. Everything flies to hell – quiet, comfort, present-day happiness.'[5] Memory triggers lurk in wait all around – a particular outdoor tap or fire hydrant, the drone of an aeroplane or the squeak of sled runners, the smell of joiner's glue or just the sight of untrodden snow on a city pavement. One man never puts up a New Year's tree, because it reminds him of the one underneath which his father lay dying of hunger; others always detour round particular streets or bridges. For Grechina, one day in 1978, it was the smell of a bonfire, drifting in at her window. Having for years given the conventional version of the siege in talks to students, she sat down at her desk and wept and wrote for two days and nights, releasing a torrent of long-pent-up grief and anger. Siege-time behaviours have stuck, too – *blokadniki* say they cannot leave food on their plates, throw away even the stalest bread, or pass a discarded piece of wood without wanting to take it home to feed a non-existent *burzhuika*. Survivors' guilt, though never given this name, is common, expressed in many cases as distress at not having secured a relative a proper burial. One woman, not knowing where her father is buried, visits the Piskarevskoye each year on his birthday, and lays flowers on every individual grave she can find whose occupant had the same Christian name or date of birth. She never, she remarks, has flowers enough.[6]

Many survivors have blocked out the siege entirely, never talking about it even to close friends and family. Others – as Grechina once did – have adopted the possible-to-live-with Brezhnevite version, subsuming their own acutely painful memories into a larger, safer story. But even for those who wanted to talk frankly, making themselves heard could be difficult. 'Inside', wrote Marina Yerukhmanova,

> there was always this question – Can't I just talk about it how it was? Sometimes I wonder why we kept quiet. Probably because it was somehow not done to talk about it . . . Every time conversation touched on the blockade, it seemed that everybody knew everything already – they'd read about it, heard about it, seen the films – and repetition of the details would give neither satisfaction to the teller nor understanding to the listener.
>
> We too watched the films, read what was written about those times. But though your stomach turned upside down, somehow none of it put across the feeling of those days.

Blokadniki often complain that nobody is interested in the siege any more. 'Each generation has its own wars – Afghanistan, Chechnya', says one. Another describes giving a talk about the siege to young offenders, and getting no reaction except when she showed them how scurvy had left her with only six teeth.[7] Grechina stresses the tension between siege veterans and post-war incomers to Leningrad, who she claims used rudely to grab *blokadnik*-reserved seats on public transport, justifying themselves on the grounds that in their villages 'everyone starved too'.[8]

That the siege took a back seat was true in the 1990s, when the fashionable subjects were the Terror and the Gulag, but is not so now. The last decade has seen the publication of dozens of memoirs and diaries, albeit usually in tiny print runs or in academic journals. The flood continues: just in the time it has taken to research this book several important new accounts have appeared, and more will doubtless continue to emerge from dusty files and top-of-the-wardrobe suitcases.

There has also been a last-minute effort to collect oral testimonies from the remaining siege survivors. Though interviewing *blokadniki* often tells one more about the strategies the mind employs to make the unbearable bearable than about the siege itself, it is nonetheless a compelling exercise. Sitting at a *zakuski*-covered kitchen table, in a mahogany-panelled backroom of the Public Library or in a shiny new café, these women – they mostly are women – were actually there. They were the muffled black and white figures shuffling along a snowy street, they themselves queued outside the bread shops, hoisted buckets of water up ice-covered stairs, watched their own flesh fall away and discolour, their parents and siblings fade and die. The events of the siege are distant and strange, but they happened not so very long ago, to that woman sitting right in front of me, insisting that I take another slice of bread and butter and a fresh cup of tea.

Blokadnik interviewees are, by definition, psychological survivors, people who have adapted or come to terms with tragedy to the extent of being able to relate it on demand to a stranger with a notebook. It is nonetheless immensely touching how they tend to stress the positive – the bits of luck that came their way, the self-denial of mothers, the kindnesses of strangers. They dislike being labelled heroes – they were just children, they point out; the heroes were the adults who saved them. Irina Bogdanova, rescued from her corpse-filled flat seventy years ago, keeps saying 'I was lucky' and 'I was blessed' – blessed to have been picked up by conscientious Komsomol girls, blessed to have been adopted by the spinster sisters who became her new family. The only time tears come to her eyes is when she tells of a petty cruelty – that of the new occupants of her family's flat, who, when she called round at the end of the war, refused to let her in. The sole personal possession she retains from childhood is a brass crucifix of her mother's, which they handed her, wrapped in newspaper, through a crack in the door.

This reluctance to judge, this magnificent determination to focus on scant human kindness rather than abundant human callousness, is a different thing from Soviet-era pasteurisation. Ironically, it is not the siege survivors themselves but their sons and daughters – the generation currently in their sixties and seventies rather than eighties and nineties – who are most protective of the conventional Soviet narrative. Actual *blokadniki* are anxious to stress the siege experience's closed, stony quality; its complete lack of redemptive value and the depth of damage done. I interviewed the historian Anzhelina Kupaigorodskaya, who lived through the first siege winter entirely alone save for occasional visits from her factory-tied father, sitting rather awkwardly on a sofa in a corridor in the Academy of Sciences. 'All those stories', she said, 'of girls too weak to stand roped to lathes, clutching their dolls – they're just post-war sentimentality.' In reality the siege was drab, hard and horrible. No human being should have to live through such a time. As we parted she struggled to her feet, gripping my arm. Now that my questions were over this was the important thing, the point she was determined to get across.

Russians' attitude to the Second World War in general is uncomplicated: fierce pride in having won a just war; fierce hatred of an enemy who wanted to destroy them. Other considerations – the pre-war purge of army officers, the Nazi–Soviet pact, the military blunders, the massacre of Polish POWs at Katyn, the wartime arrests and deportations – are (sometimes reluctantly) acknowledged, but beside the point.

The fact remains that Russia's Great Patriotic War – as it is still mostly called – was won at unnecessarily huge cost. Of this the blockade of Leningrad is perhaps the most extreme example. Nazi Germany initiated the siege, with purposive and inhuman deliberation, but it was the Soviet regime that failed to evacuate the civilian population in time, to lay in food stocks, to stamp out food theft or to organise the Ice Road properly. It was also the Soviet regime that threw away thousands of young lives in the People's Levy, and continued to imprison and execute its own humblest and most patriotic citizens even as they died of hunger. Had Russia had different leaders she might have prepared for the siege better, prevented the Germans from surrounding the city at all, or, indeed, never have been invaded in the first place.

Counter-factual history only takes one so far. This book is designed in part to correct Soviet myths, and as such, dwells on the negative. What it does not argue is that Leningrad should have been surrendered. The Nazis, too, would have let civilians starve to death, as they did in other Russian cities they occupied. All the city's remaining Jews would have been rounded up and murdered. The 300,000 Axis troops pinned down outside Leningrad (15–20 per cent of the Eastern Front total) would have pushed further east, meaning a longer war, even greater swathes of Russia fought over and occupied, and a heavier burden on the other Allies. Finally, Leningrad would almost certainly have been physically destroyed, first by the Soviets as they abandoned it, again by the Germans as they finally retreated west. One of Europe's most ravishing cities would today be either a Stalinist megalopolis, like Kharkov and Kaliningrad, or a patchy, artificial reconstruction, like Warsaw and Dresden.

None of the diarists most extensively quoted here is still alive. Dmitri Likhachev, the young medievalist who heard of the invasion while sunbathing on the bank of a river, enjoyed a distinguished academic career, becoming head of the university's Ancient Russian Literature department and a leading pro-democracy activist of the *glasnost* era. He died in 1999, at the age of ninety-two.

Yelena Skryabina, the young mother who initially half-welcomed the news of invasion, emigrated with her sons to America after the war, becoming Professor of Russian at the University of Iowa. Her husband, left behind in Leningrad, assumed that she had died during evacuation and married her widowed best friend.

Anna Ostroumova-Lebedeva continued to paint and to enjoy official favour, publishing three volumes of heavily censored diaries before her death in 1957.

Mariya Mashkova was sacked by the Public Library during the 'anti-cosmopolitanism' campaign, but rehired three years later and worked there until retirement.

Olga Fridenberg lost her directorship of the University's classics department during the 'anti-cosmopolitanism' campaign, and with it her appetite for life, but lived just long enough to see Stalin dead and her cousin Boris Pasternak awarded the Nobel Prize for Literature.

Anna Zelenova saw her beloved Pavlovsk Palace fully restored, dying in 1980 while delivering a lecture at a Party meeting.

Aleksandr Boldyrev divorced and remarried shortly after the war. Though he became estranged from his daughter he never lost his attachment to the Hermitage, from which he retired having published over a hundred studies of ancient Persian literature. He died in 1993.

Olga Grechina became an assistant professor at the Herzen Pedagogical Institute, her specialism Pushkin's use of folklore. She married and had two daughters, and died in 2000 at the age of seventy-eight.

Vera Inber joined the Party and returned with her husband to Moscow. Despite her Trotsky connection she was untouched by the post-war purges and remained a loyal member of the literary establishment until her death in 1972.

Olga Berggolts buckled under the strain, taking to drink and feeling paradoxical nostalgia for the intensity and sense of purpose of siege-time life. A chance meeting at the theatre with her former NKVD interrogator ('Do you recognise me, Olga Fyodorovna? Can I be of service?') helped free her exiled doctor father, who returned to Leningrad in 1948 but died less than a year later.[9] Though her own death in 1975 got little official notice, news of it spread by word of mouth, and her funeral in Volkovo cemetery turned into a spontaneous public event, attended by thousands of ordinary Leningraders.

Vasili Chekrizov continued to work in shipbuilding and lived to the age of ninety-seven, cursing 'Bloody Boris [Yeltsin]' for Communism's collapse in a postscript to his wartime diary.

Oberleutnant Fritz Hockenjos left his bicycle unit to join an SS infantry division on the Rhine, where he was captured by the Americans. Having spent two years in a prisoner of war camp he returned to his career as a forestry manager, and wrote a popular series of walking guides to the Schwarzwald.

Leningrad – Petersburg – is still a melancholy city. Twenty years after the end of Communism, its reintegration into the West still feels partial and provisional, a bright new patina of illuminated signs and PVC windows failing to disguise the dripping gutters and vagrant sycamore seedlings of the dank courtyards behind. Like other former capitals, it also has a Marie Celeste quality, its once-bustling palaces and government buildings now sleepy academic institutes or quiet museums. The melancholy, though, is of the pleasant autumn-leaf, peeling-stucco kind; nostalgic rather than tragic, its attendant ghosts the vivid characters of fiction – white-shouldered Princess Hélène, Raskolnikov with his axe – rather than the shadowy multi-tudes of the siege. In contrast with brash Moscow, the new rich do not dominate. Bookshops outnumber Versace boutiques; elderly women, shabby of cardigan and splendid of face, fill the stalls of the Philharmonia, and the students flocking out of their lectures on to the Moika flirt with each other, not with the snaky men in fine Italian knits sipping eight-dollar espressos at the bar of the Yevropa. Changing but unchanged is what Akhmatova called the operatic weather: restless skies give their colour to the moving river; snow falls endlessly, in thick disorienting whirls; sea winds bruise the eyes and sweep the streets fiercely clean.

The last word goes to Lidiya Ginzburg, most analytical and perhaps also most accepting of all the blockade memoirists. After even the greatest tragedies, she obliquely reminds us, life flows on.

New replaces old; absences are filled; the past is overlaid and forgotten. It is June, the time of the White Nights, and her anonymous Siege Man has been working into the small hours. Emerging from his shuttered office onto the Nevsky, he feels 'the usual astonishment' at finding the sun still shining, light bouncing off the wet pavements. 'It is this inexhaustibility', he thinks, 'that real Leningraders love so much. The feeling of untouched reserves of life, waiting to be released each day.'

Appendix I

How Many?*

Two approaches have been used to estimate the total number of civilian deaths during the siege of Leningrad.

The first is based on official death registrations. Using data from the city's central labour agency, the fifteen municipal districts and from local authorities in outlying Kronshtadt and Kolpino, a 'Commission to Investigate Atrocities Committed by the Fascist Occupiers', set up in 1943, arrived at a total of 649,000 civilian deaths during the siege, 632,253 of them from starvation and associated illnesses, the remaining 16,747 caused by bombing and shelling. These numbers were cited by the Soviet government at the Nuremberg war crimes trials, and have been widely quoted since. They are also within the same order of magnitude as figures from Leningrad's Burial Trust, the government agency responsible for cemeteries. The Trust's records show it disposing of around 460,000 corpses in the fourteen months from the beginning of November 1941, to which should be added another 228,263 buried by the civil defence organisation (MPVO) making 688,263 burials in total.

This 650,000-690,000 range for the death toll is, however, almost certainly a substantial under-estimate. Many siege deaths were never registered ('a negligible proportion of the population went to the registry

---

*   V.M. Kovalchuk and G.L. Sobelev 'Leningradsky "Rekviyem": o zhertvakh naseleniya v Leningrade v gody voiny i blokady' *Voprosy istorii* 12 (1965) p191.
Nadezhda Cherepenina 'Assessing the Scale of Famine and Death in the Besieged City' in John Barber and Andrei Dzeniskevich (Eds.) *Life and Death in Besieged Leningrad, 1941-44* London 2005, p28. See also Eleanor Martineau 'Blokada mezhdu geroizmom i tragediyei (k metodike voprosa)' *Trudy Gosudarstvennogo Muzeya Istorii Sankt Peterburga* 5 (2000) p253.

offices', according to the Leningrad Municipal Services Department) or registered long after they occurred. The Commission was still receiving new wartime registrations as late as 1959. The Burial Trust numbers are similarly dubious, as evidenced by chaotic scenes in cemeteries and mortuaries, and by the fact that the Trust could not produce daily figures for deliveries and burials when ordered to do so by the city soviet at the end of December 1941.

Historians have also tried to calculate the death toll from the top down, by looking at the drop in Leningrad's population from the beginning of the siege to its end, and assuming that all absences not otherwise accounted for were due to starvation or bombardment. When the siege ring closed in early September 1941 the city's civilian population was about 2.5m, including roughly 100,000 newly-arrived refugees. By the end of 1943, on the eve of liberation, it had decreased by at least 1.9m, to no more than 600,000. In that time about one million Leningraders had been evacuated across Ladoga, and another 100,000 been sent to the front, which leaves assumed deaths from starvation at no less than 800,000.

The demographer Nadezhda Cherepenina recently reworked this calculation, based on the number of Leningrad residency permits extant over time. Her death-toll estimate – of 700,000 – is lower in part because it excludes the city's illegal, unregistered underclass, as well as unregistered peasant refugees. Lastly, none of the above calculations includes deaths in rural areas within the siege ring, nor the tens of thousands who perished on the Ice Road and beyond. The best, therefore, that one can safely say is that the siege's civilian death-toll was not less than 650,000 and not much more than 800,000. If a single figure must be given it should probably be about 750,000, or between one in three and one in four of Leningrad's immediate pre-siege population.

Appendix II

Civilian deaths, July 1941 to December 1942

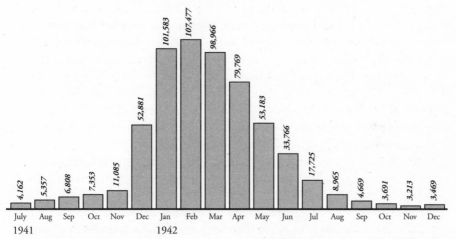

4,162	5,357	6,808	7,353	11,085	52,881	101,583	107,477	98,966	79,769	53,183	33,766	17,725	8,965	4,669	3,691	3,213	3,469

July	Aug	Sep	Oct	Nov	Dec	Jan	Feb	Mar	Apr	May	Jun	Jul	Aug	Sep	Oct	Nov	Dec
1941						1942											

Source: City Statistics Office, reports of 31 October 1942 and 15 February 1943. Given in Dzeniskevich *Leningrad v Osade* docs. 149 and 151, pp. 314 and 316. The figures are based on registry office returns from Leningrad's fifteen municipal districts. They do not include deaths in Kronshtadt, Kolpino or other towns and villages within the siege ring.

Daily bread ration, in grams

From:	1941 18 July	2 Sep	12 Sep	1 Oct	13 Nov	20 Nov	25 Dec	1942 24 Jan	11 Feb
Manual workers	800	600	500	400	300	250	350	400	500
Office workers	600	400	300	200	150	125	200	300	400
Dependants	400	300	250	200	150	125	200	250	300
Children under 12	400	300	300	200	150	125	200	250	300

Source: Pavlov, *Leningrad 1941*, p. 79

Notes

INTRODUCTION

1 Olga Berggolts, 'Tragediya moego pokoleniya', *Literaturnaya gazeta*, 18 July 1990, p. 5.

2 Evan Mawdsley, *Thunder in the East: The Nazi-Soviet War 1941–1945*, p. 238. The death rate among Soviet soldiers taken prisoner by the Nazis is reckoned to be even higher, at 55 per cent.

3 Professor Ulrich Herbert, interview with the author, Freiburg, April 2008.

4 *The Times*, 19 January 1943.

5 Commander Geoffrey Palmer; interview with the author, Sherborne, July 2007. Commander Palmer, who sadly passed away before this book was completed, was probably the last Englishman to have met Stalin. He described him as resembling 'a benevolent grocer; someone who would make a good godfather to one's children. He looked you straight in the eye, but then you realised that he was looking right through you and out the other side. It was rather uncanny.'

6 The diarist Vera Inber describes visiting the museum on D-Day: see her *Leningrad Diary*, p. 204. For an interview with the curator at the reopened museum see Cynthia Simmons and Nina Perlina, eds, *Writing the Siege of Leningrad: Women's Diaries, Memoirs and Documentary Prose*, p. 170. See also Lisa Kirschenbaum, *The Legacy of the Siege of Leningrad, 1941–1995: Myth, Memories, and Monuments*, p. 144. The book is a fascinating analysis of siege memorialisation up to the present – the 'story of the story of the siege', as Kirschenbaum calls it.

7 Anne Applebaum, *Gulag: A History of the Soviet Camps*, p. 14.

8 See Sergei Yarov, 'Rasskazy o blokade: struktura, ritorika i stil'', *Nestor*, 6, 2003, p. 422.

PART I. INVASION: JUNE–SEPTEMBER 1941

CHAPTER 1: 22 JUNE 1941

1 Dmitry Likhachev, *Reflections on the Russian Soul: A Memoir*, p. 215.
2 Yelena Skrjabina, *Siege and Survival: The Odyssey of a Leningrader*, p. 3.
3 Ales Adamovich and Daniil Granin, *A Book of the Blockade*, p. 236.
4 Edward Crankshaw, ed., *Khrushchev Remembers*, London, 1971, p. 135.
5 Harold Shukman, ed., *Stalin's Generals*, pp. 2, 319–20.
6 Solomon Volkov, *St Petersburg: A Cultural History*, p. 425.
7 G. Kulagin, *Dnevnik i pamyat: o perezhitom v gody blokady*, Leningrad, 1978, p. 17.
8 Elliott Mossman, ed., *The Correspondence of Boris Pasternak and Olga Freidenberg, 1910–1954*, p. 203.
9 Evan Mawdsley, *Thunder in the East: The Nazi-Soviet War 1941–1945*, p. 8.
10 John Erickson, *The Road to Stalingrad: Stalin's War with Germany*, vol. 1, p. 105.
11 Dmitri Volkogonov, *Stalin: Triumph and Tragedy*, pp. 401–2; Mawdsley, *Thunder in the East*, p. 37.
12 Hugh Trevor-Roper, ed., *Hitler's Table Talk 1941–1944*, p. 24.
13 Charles Burdick and Hans-Adolf Jacobsen, eds, *The Halder War Diary, 1939–1942*, p. 313.
14 Mawdsley, *Thunder in the East*, p. 11; Antony Beevor, *Stalingrad*, pp. 14–15; Mark Mazower, *Hitler's Empire: Nazi Rule in Occupied Europe*, pp. 142, 147.
15 Field Marshal von Kleist, in Basil Liddell Hart, *The Other Side of the Hill: Germany's Generals, Their Rise and Fall*, p. 182.

CHAPTER 2: BARBAROSSA

1 Yelena Skrjabina, *Siege and Survival: The Odyssey of a Leningrader*, p. 4.
2 Andrei Dzeniskevich, ed., *Leningrad v osade: sbornik dokumentov*, doc. 197, p. 466.
3 Richard Bidlack, 'The Political Mood in Leningrad during the First Year of the Soviet-German War', *The Russian Review*, 59, January 2000, p. 99.
4 Dzeniskevich, ed., *Leningrad v osade*, doc. 197, p. 466.
5 Interview with Dr Lyuba Vinogradova, Moscow 2007.
6 Andrei Dzeniskevich, 'The Social and Political Situation in Leningrad in the First Months of the German Invasion: The Social Psychology of the Workers', in Robert Thurston and Bernd Bonwetsch, eds, *The People's War: Responses to World War II in the Soviet Union*, p. 78.

7 Lidiya Ginzburg, *Chelovek za pismennym stolom*, p. 579.

8 Ibid., p. 91.

9 Katherine Hodgson, *Voicing the Soviet Experience: The Poetry of Olga Berggolts*, p. 67; Harrison Salisbury, *The 900 Days: The Siege of Leningrad*, pp. 121–2.

10 Leon Gouré, *The Siege of Leningrad*, p. 59.

11 Dzeniskevich, ed., *Leningrad v osade*, p. 151.

12 Skrjabina, *Siege and Survival*, pp. 10–11 (1 July 1941).

13 O. I. Molkina, 'Nemtsy v koltse blokady', *Istoriya Peterburga*, 3, 2006, pp. 62–4.

14 These numbers are derived from two NKVD documents. The first, in Dzeniskevich's document collection *Leningrad v osade*, p. 442, of 1 October 1942, gives a total of 58,210 Finns and Germans deported to date. The second, in Nikita Lomagin's document collection *Neizvestnaya blokada*, vol. 2, p. 37, of 4 April 1942, gives a total of 35,162 Finns and Germans deported during the second half of the previous month. The March 1942 deportations were mostly from towns and villages around the city.

15 Cynthia Simmons and Nina Perlina, eds, *Writing the Siege of Leningrad: Women's Diaries, Memoirs and Documentary Prose*, pp. 37–9.

16 Dzeniskevich, ed., *Leningrad v osade*, pp. 441–2; John Barber and M. Harrison, eds, *The Soviet Home Front 1941–1945*, London, 1991, p. 66; Orlando Figes, *The Whisperers: Private Life in Stalin's Russia*, pp. 385–6.

17 The Council of People's Commissars only ordered mass mobilisation on 2 July (Gouré, *The Siege of Leningrad*, p. 38).

18 Gouré, *The Siege of Leningrad*, p. 22; Salisbury, *The 900 Days*, p. 168.

19 Adamovich and Granin, *A Book of the Blockade*, pp. 237–8.

20 Dmitri Likhachev, *Reflections on the Russian Soul: A Memoir*, p. 220.

21 Adamovich and Granin, *A Book of the Blockade*, p. 229.

22 Throughout the Stalin period, temporarily moving elsewhere was a surprisingly effective way of avoiding the local security services, who were often more concerned with filling their quotas than with exactly who they put behind bars. Lidiya Chukovskaya, friend and amanuensis of Anna Akhmatova, escaped the purges of 1937 simply by moving to Kiev to live with her parents-in-law. 'You are like a glass which has rolled under a bench during an explosion in a china shop,' said Akhmatova.

23 Alexander Werth, *Russia at War, 1941–1945*, pp. 162–7.

24 Ibid., p. 184.

25 Anna Ostroumova-Lebedeva, *Avtobiograficheskiye zapiski: Leningrad v blokade*, p. 250.

26 David Glantz, *The Battle for Leningrad 1941–1944*, pp. 30–31.

27 Eino Luukkanen, *Fighter over Finland*, p. 116; Salisbury, *The 900 Days*, p. 106.

28 RGVA: Fond 32904, op. 1, delo 81, p. 28.

29 Glantz, *The Battle for Leningrad*, pp. 35, 37.

30 Yelena Kochina, *Blockade Diary*, pp. 35–6, 3 and 9 July 1941; Ginzburg, *Chelovek na pismennym stolom*, p. 4.

31 Antony Beevor and Lyuba Vinogradova, eds, *A Writer at War: Vasily Grossman with the Red Army 1941–1945*, p. 9; Gouré, *The Siege of Leningrad*, p. 68.

32 Skrjabina, *Siege and Survival*, pp. 13–15.

33 Interviewed by the author, St Petersburg, September 2008.

34 RGVA: Fond 32904, op. 1, delo 79, pp. 58, 86.

35 Beevor and Vinogradova, eds, *A Writer at War*, p. 41.

36 RGASPI: Fond 77, op. 4, delo 48, pp. 11–20.

37 Charles Burdick and Hans-Adolf Jacobsen, eds, Franz Halder, *The Halder War Diary, 1939–1942*, pp. 445–6, 3 July 1941.

38 Simon Sebag Montefiore, *Stalin: The Court of the Red Tsar*, p. 328; Richard Overy, *Russia's War*, p. 81; Salisbury, *The 900 Days*, p. 105.

39 TsAMO: Fond 96a, op. 1711, delo 24, pp. 24–5. Also quoted by Glantz, *The Battle for Leningrad*, pp. 42–3.

40 See for example the 9th Pskov NKVD Border Detachment on 3 July 1941. RGVA: Fond 32904, op. 1, delo 79, p. 88.

41 Sebag Montefiore, *Stalin*, p. 338; Geoffrey Jukes in Harold Shukman, ed., *Stalin's Generals*, p. 129.

42 Shukman, ed., *Stalin's Generals*, pp. 313, 320. General Alan Brooke, Britain's Chief of Imperial General Staff, sat next to Voroshilov at dinner during the Moscow Conference of August 1942. He reckoned him 'a fine hearty old soul, willing to talk about anything with great vivacity', but with the military expertise of a 'child'.

43 Salisbury, *The 900 Days*, pp. 112, 282, 322, 404. See also Evan Mawdsley, *Thunder in the East: The Nazi-Soviet War 1941–1945*, p. 450.

44 Burdick and Jacobsen, eds, Franz Halder, *The Halder War Diary*, pp. 458–9, 446–7.

Chapter 3: 'We're winning, but the Germans are advancing'

1 Nikita Lomagin, *Neizvestnaya blokada*, vol. 2, doc. 30, p. 161; Alexander Werth, *Russia at War, 1941–1945*, pp. 179, 241, 399; Leon Gouré, *The Siege of Leningrad*, pp. 68–70.

2 Lidiya Osipova, 15 July and 13 August 1941, in Lomagin, *Neizvestnaya blokada*, vol. 2, pp. 442–3.

3 Georgi Knyazev, in Ales Adamovich and Daniil Granin, A *Book of the Blockade*, p. 261; Andrei Dzeniskevich, 'The Social and Political Situation in Leningrad in the First Months of the German Invasion: The Psychology of the Workers', in Robert Thurston and Bernd Bonwetsch, eds, *The People's War: Responses to World War II in the Soviet Union*, p. 73; Igor Kruglyakov, interviewed by Dr Lyuba Vinogradova, Moscow, January 2007.

4 Irina Reznikova (Flige), 'Repressii v period blokady Leningrada', *Vestnik 'Memoriala'* 4/5 (10/11), p. 96; Gouré, *The Siege of Leningrad*, p. 71.

5 Dmitri Likhachev, *Reflections on the Russian Soul: A Memoir*, p. 222; Yelena Skrjabina, *Siege and Survival: The Odyssey of a Leningrader*, p. 21. See also Dmitri Lazarev, in *Trudy Gosudarstvennogo Muzeya Istorii Sankt-Peterburga*, vol. 5, p. 195.

6 Yelena Kochina, *Blockade Diary*, p. 33 (June 1941).

7 Georgi Knyazev, 20 July 1941, in Adamovich and Granin, *A Book of the Blockade*, p. 256.

8 Anna Ostroumova-Lebedeva, *Avtobiograficheskiye zapiski: Leningrad v blokade*, pp. 250–51.

9 Gatchina had officially been renamed Krasnogvardeisk, or 'Red Guard-ville', but the old name was more commonly used.

10 David Glantz, *The Battle for Leningrad 1941–1944*, p. 38.

11 Olga Grechina, in Cynthia Simmons and Nina Perlina, *Writing the Siege of Leningrad: Women's Diaries, Memoirs and Documentary Prose*, p. 107.

12 Olga Grechina, 'Spasayus spasaya chast 1: pogibelnaya zima (1941–1942 gg.)', *Neva*, 1, 1994, pp. 220–21.

13 Kochina, *Blockade Diary*, p. 34.

14 Skrjabina, *Siege and Survival*, pp. 12–13, 21 (8 July and 12 August 1941).

15 Rimma Neratova, 'Zhizn v Leningradskoi blokade', *Zvezda* (1996), pp. 18–28.

16 Charles von Luttichau, quoted in Glantz, *The Battle for Leningrad 1941–1944*, p. 41; General Blumentritt, quoted in Basil Liddell Hart, *The Other Side of the Hill: Germany's Generals, Their Rise and Fall*, p. 187.

17 Glantz, *The Battle for Leningrad 1941–1944*, pp. 44–7; Harrison Salisbury, *The 900 Days: The Siege of Leningrad*, pp. 189–90.

18 Yevgeniya Baikova, www.hermitagemuseum.org

19 Militsa Matye, www.hermitagemuseum.org

20 Knyazev, 7 and 15 July, in Adamovich and Granin, *A Book of the Blockade*, pp. 244–5.

21 Skrjabina, *Siege and Survival*, pp. 8–9 (28 June 1941).

22 Ibid., p. 15 (18 July 1941).

23 Kochina, *Blockade Diary*, p. 36 (10 July 1941).

24 Vasili Churkin, in *Voyennaya literatura: dnevniki i pisma* http://militera.lib.ru/ db/churkin part 1, p. 2 (15 August 1941).

25 Glantz, *The Battle for Leningrad 1941–1944*, p. 58; TsAMO: Fond 217, op. 1217, dela 32, 33; Nikita Lomagin, *Soldiers at War: German Propaganda and Soviet Army Morale during the Battle of Leningrad, 1941–44*, Carl Beck Papers, 1306, p. 11.

26 17 August 1941; RGASPI: Fond 558, op. 11, yed. khr. 492, p. 1.

27 RGASPI: Fond 558, op. 11, yed. khr. 492, p. 13.

28 Ibid., p. 20.

29 Salisbury, *The 900 Days*, p. 228.

30 People and freight numbers from Panteleyev, quoted in Salisbury, *The 900 Days*, p. 232.

31 Death-toll estimates are very approximate. The rumour at the time was of 17,000 lives lost; the official Soviet version was 5,000. A post-Soviet Russian naval historian puts it at 'over 12,000'. See Salisbury, *The 900 Days*, p. 238, and Evan Mawdsley, *Thunder in the East: The Nazi-Soviet War 1941–1945*, p. 83.

32 Glantz, *The Battle for Leningrad 1941–1944*, p. 46.

33 On 29 September 1941 the head of the Baltic Fleet's Political Directorate instructed his staff to inform all naval personnel that family members of sailors who surrendered to the Germans would immediately be executed as 'traitors to the Motherland'. In January 1942 the directive was rescinded and branded as illegal; there is no record of it having been put into force (see Lomagin, *Soldiers at War*, p. 15).

CHAPTER 4: THE PEOPLE'S LEVY

1 Ilya Frenklakh, www.iremember.ru, pp. 2–3.

2 TsGAIPD SPb: Fond 2281, op. 1, delo 22.

3 Interviewed by the author, St Petersburg, March 2008.

4 Report by Nikita Karpov, Partorg at the Kirov plant and member of the First Division of LANO, 30 September 1943. TsGAIPD SPb: Fond 4000, op. 10, delo 1320, p. 14.

5 TsGAIPD SPb: Fond 25, op. 12, svyazkha 3, 1118, ed. kr. 13. Harrison Salisbury, *The 900 Days: The Siege of Leningrad*, p. 220.

6 David Glantz, *The Battle for Leningrad 1941–1944*, pp. 126–7; Richard Bidlack, *Workers at War: Factory Workers and Labor Policy in the Siege of Leningrad*, Carl Beck Papers, 902, p. 8.

7 TsGAIPD SPb: Fond 25, op. 12, svyazkha 13.

8 Nikita Karpov. TsGAIPD SPb: Fond 4000, op. 10, delo 1320, p. 15.

9 TsGAIPD SPb: Fond 2281, op. 1, delo 15, p. 9.

10 TsGAIPD SPb: Fond 2281, op. 1, delo 2, p. 35.

11 Leon Gouré, *The Siege of Leningrad*, p. 31; Dmitri Likhachev, *Reflections on the Russian Soul: A Memoir*, p. 226.

12 TsGAIPD SPb: Fond 2201, op. 1, delo 23.

13 Ibid., political report of 10 July 1941.

14 Ibid., political report from the Moskovsky district LANO division, 9 July 1941.

15 Lidiya Ginzburg, *Blockade Diary*, p. 79.

16 See for example TsGAIPD SPb: Fond 2281, op. 1, delo 28, p. 20.

17 TsGAIPD SPb: Fond 2281, op. 1, delo 15, p. 12.

18 TsGAIPD SPb: Fond 2201, op. 1, delo 23.

19 Andrei Dzeniskevich, *Leningrad v osade: sbornik dokumentov*, doc. 49, p. 131.

20 TsGAIPD SPb: Fond 2281, op. 1, delo 29, pp. 2–4.

21 Iosif Altman, workshop supervisor at the Red Chemist Factory and member of the First Division. TsGAIPD SPb: Fond 4000, op. 10, delo 1305.

22 From Subbotin to the Defence Council of the Northern Front, July 1941. TsGAIPD SPb: Fond 2281, op. 1, delo 11; Gouré, *The Siege of Leningrad*, pp. 33–4.

23 Political Department meeting of 8 July 1941. TsGAIPD SPb: Fond 2281, op. 1, delo 15, pp. 7–8.

24 TsGAIPD SPb: Fond 2281, op. 1, delo 15, p. 13.

25 Charles Burdick and Hans-Adolf Jacobsen, eds, Franz Halder, *The Halder War Diary, 1939–1942*, p. 452 (6 July 1941).

26 Meeting of 29 July 1941. TsGAIPD SPb: Fond 2281, op. 1, delo 46.

27 TsGAIPD SPb: Fond 2281, op. 1, delo 26, p. 2.

28 Dobrzhinsky, First Division, TsGAIPD SPb: Fond 2281, op. 1, delo 15, pp. 10–11.

29 TsGAIPD SPb: Fond 2281, op. 1, delo 22, pp. 132–4.

30 Ibid., p. 137.

31 Political dept report of 29 August 1941. TsGAIPD SPb: Fond 2281, op. 1, delo 202. Salisbury, *The 900 Days*, p. 191.

32 Report to Zhdanov from LANO political department head Kononchuk, mid-August 1941. TsGAIPD SPb: Fond 2281, op. 1, delo 18.

33 TsGAIPD SPb: Fond 2281, op. 1, delo 18.

34 Dzeniskevich, *Leningrad v osade*, doc. 49, pp. 132–3.

35 Gouré, *The Siege of Leningrad*, p. 35.

36 Alexander Werth, *Leningrad*, pp. 110–11.

37 TsAMO: Fond 96a, op. 2011, delo 5, pp. 133–7.

38 Frenklakh, www.iremember.ru, p. 6.

39 Given in Dmitri Volkogonov, 'Voroshilov', in Harold Shukman, ed., *Stalin's Generals*, p. 318.

Chapter 5: 'Caught in a Mousetrap'

1 Vera Inber, *Leningrad Diary*, p. 10.

2 Dmitri Pavlov, *Leningrad 1941: The Blockade*, p. 9. This is often wrongly referred to as the 'Enemy at the Gates' announcement. In fact the *Leningradskaya Pravda* article headlined 'The Enemy is at the Gates' did not appear until 16 September.

3 Inber, *Leningrad Diary*, pp. 11, 13, 15 (24 and 26 August, 1 and 8 September 1941).

4 Ales Adamovich and Daniil Granin, *A Book of the Blockade*, pp. 271–2.

5 Anna Ostroumova-Lebedeva, *Avtobiograficheskiye zapiski: Leningrad v blokade*, pp. 252–3 (4 and 16 August).

6 Pavlov, *Leningrad 1941*, pp. 47–8; Ivan Andreyenko, deputy chairman of the wartime Leningrad City Soviet, quoted in Adamovich and Granin, *A Book of the Blockade*, p. 122.

7 Leon Gouré, *The Siege of Leningrad*, pp. 51–2.

8 Yelena Skrjabina, *Siege and Survival: The Odyssey of a Leningrader*, p. 7 (June 26 1941).

9 Yelena Kochina, *Blockade Diary*, p. 35 (2 July 1941).

10 Klara Rakhman, unpublished manuscript, held by the diarist's family.

11 Georgi Knyazev, 17 July 1941, in Adamovich and Granin, *A Book of the Blockade*, p. 246.

12 Adamovich and Granin, *A Book of the Blockade*, pp. 250–52.

13 Order to district Party secretaries, 11 August 1941. RGASPI: Fond 17, op. 22, delo 1644, p. 41.

14 Skrjabina, *Siege and Survival*, pp. 17–18 (2 August 1941).

15 Nina Malakova, in Michael Jones, *Leningrad: State of Siege*, p. 98. Jones interviewed survivors of the Lychkovo bombing in 2007.

16 Mariya Motovskaya, in Adamovich and Granin, *A Book of the Blockade*, p. 247.

17 Ibid., pp. 248–9. Dmitri Likhachev, *Reflections on the Russian Soul: A Memoir*, p. 218.

18 William Moskoff, *The Bread of Affliction: The Food Supply in the USSR during World War II*, p. 34.

19 Interviewed by the author, Vsevolozhsk, November 2006.

20 Skrjabina, *Siege and Survival*, p. 10.

21 Ibid., p. 24; Likhachev, *Reflections on the Russian Soul*, p. 227.

22 Sidney Monas and Jennifer Greene Krupala, eds, *The Diaries of Nikolay Punin, 1904–53*, pp. 182–3.

23 Cynthia Simmons and Nina Perlina, eds, *Writing the Siege: Women's Diaries, Memoirs and Documentary Prose*, pp. 107–8.

24 Pavlov, *Leningrad 1941*, p. 47.

25 Aleksandr Barbovsky, 30 August 1941. RGALI: Fond 2733, op. 1, yed. khr. 872, pp. 15–16.

26 The commission's visit is hard to date exactly. Salisbury infers from Admiral Kuznetsov's memoirs that it set out on 27 August and arrived on the 28th. However, Stalin ordered the mission on the 21st, included Molotov among the addressees of a communication of 27 August and ordered its return on 29 August, suggesting that it arrived several days earlier.

27 RGASPI: Fond 558, op. 11, yed. khr. 492, p. 27.

28 Ibid., p. 35.

29 Ibid., p. 39.

30 Simon Sebag Montefiore, *Stalin: The Court of the Red Tsar*, p. 627.

31 Nikita Lomagin, *Neizvestnaya blokada*, vol. 2, doc. 4, p. 29.

32 Lyubov Shaporina, 4 September 1941, in Simmons and Perlina, eds, *Writing the Siege*, p. 22.

33 Olga Berggolts, 2 September 1941; *Zvezda*, 3, April 1991, p. 128.

34 TsAMO: Fond 148a, op. 3763, delo 97, p. 29.

35 Skrjabina, *Siege and Survival*, p. 23 (23 August 1941).

36 Adamovich and Granin, *A Book of the Blockade*, p. 269.

PART 2. THE SIEGE BEGINS: SEPTEMBER–DECEMBER 1941

CHAPTER 6: 'NO SENTIMENTALITY'

1 Sonia Orwell and Ian Angus, eds, *The Collected Essays, Journalism and Letters of George Orwell*, vol. 2, *My Country Right or Left*, London, 1970, p. 460.

2 Winston Churchill, *The Second World War*, pp. 467–8.

3 RGASPI: Fond 558, op. 11, yed. khr. 492, p. 49.

4 The exact date of Zhukov's arrival in Leningrad has only recently been firmly established. Though in practice he took over command immediately on arrival, the relevant Stavka order was not formally issued until 11 September.

5 *The Memoirs of Marshal Zhukov*, London, 1971, pp. 300, 314–16.

6 Viktor Anfilov, *Zhukov*, in Harold Shukman, ed., *Stalin's Generals*, p. 350; David Glantz, *The Battle for Leningrad 1941–1944*, p. 78.

7 V. F. Chekrizov, 'Dnevnik blokadnogo vremeni', in *Trudy Gosudarstvennogo Muzeya Istorii Sankt-Peterburga*, vol. 8.

8 Anna Zelenova, *Stati, vospominaniya, pisma: Pavlovsky dvorets, istoriya i sudba*, pp. 83–90. See also Susan Massie, *Pavlovsk: The Life of a Russian Palace*, pp. 195–202.

9 Lidiya Osipova, 'Iz dnevnika o zhizni v prigorodakh Leningrada', in Lomagin, ed, *Neizvestnaya blokada*, vol. 2, p. 441. The full diary is held by the Hoover Institution.

10 Valerian Bogdanov-Berezovsky, *Iz dnevnikov blokanikh let* (typescript), pp. 9–10; RGALI: Fond 1817, op. 2, yed. khr. 185.

11 Konstantin Plotkin, *Kholokost u sten Leningrada*, pp. 33–56.

12 Glantz, *The Battle for Leningrad*, pp. 81–2.

13 Dmitri Pavlov, *Leningrad 1941: The Blockade*, p. 21.

14 G. F. Krivosheyev, ed., *Rossiya i SSSR v voinakh XX veka: poteri vooruzhyonnykh sil*, p. 271; Evan Mawdsley, *Thunder in the East: The Nazi-Soviet War 1941–1945*, pp. 86–7.

15 Charles Burdick and Hans-Adolf Jacobsen, eds, Franz Halder, *The Halder War Diary, 1939–1942*, pp. 487, 498–500 (26 July and 6, 7 August 1941).

16 Ibid., pp. 511, 514–15 (18 and 22 August 1941).

17 See Führer Directive no. 35, 6 September 1941.

18 Burdick and Jacobsen, eds, Franz Halder, *The Halder War Diary*, 18 September 1941, p. 536.

19 Bundesarchiv/Militärarchiv: RM7/1014. Given in *Verbrechen der Wehrmacht: Dimensionen des Vernichtungskrieges 1941–1944*, p. 310.

20 Hugh Trevor-Roper, ed., *Hitler's Table Talk, 1941–44*, pp. 39–40.

21 Burdick and Jacobsen, eds, Franz Halder, *The Halder War Diary*, p. 458.

22 Bundesarchiv/Militärarchiv: RW4/v. 578, bl. 144–146. Given in *Verbrechen der Wehrmacht*, pp. 312–14.

23 Bundesarchiv/Militärarchiv: RM7/1014, bl. 39–41. Given in *Verbrechen der Wehrmacht*, pp. 315–17.

24 Trevor-Roper, ed., *Table Talk*, p. 44.

25 'The Führer's Decision on Leningrad', transmitted by naval command to Army Group North, 29 September 1941. *Tagebuch der Seekriegsleitung*, quoted in Max Domarus, *Hitler Reden und Proklamationen 1932–1945*, vol. 4, Mundelein, 2000, p. 1755.

26 Wilhelm Ritter von Leeb, *Tagebuchaufzeichnungen und Lagebeurteilungen aus zwei Weltkriegen*, Stuttgart, 1976, p. 373 (12 October 1941), in *Verbrechen der Wehrmacht*, p. 318.

27 Army Group North war diary 27 October 1941, *Verbrechen der Wehrmacht*, p. 12.

28 Führer Directive no. 35, 6 September 1941. In Hugh Trevor-Roper, ed., *Hitler's War Directives, 1938–1945*.

29 Michael Jones, *Leningrad: State of Siege*, p. 33.

30 For more on Halder's post-war career see Ronald Smelser and Edward Davies, *The Myth of the Eastern Front: The Nazi-Soviet War in American Popular Culture*.

CHAPTER 7: 'TO OUR LAST HEARTBEAT'

1 Lyubov Shaporina, 8 September 1941, in Cynthia Simmons and Nina Perlina, eds, *Writing the Siege of Leningrad: Women's Diaries, Memoirs and Documentary Prose*, p. 23.

2 MPVO report of 9 September 1941, in Andrei Dzeniskevich, ed., *Leningrad v osade: sbornik dokumentov*, p. 364.

3 The first artillery shells reached the suburbs on 4 September, and the first bomb on the 6th, unnoticed by most Leningraders. The date of the first full-scale raid was 8 September.

4 Nikolai Sokolov, 'Tyoplaya vanna dlya begemota: zoosad v gody voiny', *Rodina*, 1, 2003, p. 153.

5 Olga Berggolts, 'Blokadniy dnevnik', *Zvezda*, 4, April 1991, p. 130 (8–9 September 1941).

6 Leon Gouré, *The Siege of Leningrad*, pp. 101–2.

7 Unpublished manuscript, in possession of the diarist's family.

8 Vladimir Garshin, 'Tam, gde smert pomogayet zhizni', *Arkhiv Patologii*, vol. 46, no. 5, 1984, p. 84.

9 Berggolts, 'Blokadniy dnevnik', *Zvezda*, 4, April 1991, p. 131 (12 September 1941).

10 Lidiya Ginzburg, *Blockade Diary*, p. 24.

11 Vera Inber, *The Siege of Leningrad*, pp. 23–4, 27 (20 and 26 September 1941).

12 Olga Grechina, 'Spasayus spasaya chast 1; pogibelnaya zima (1941–1942 gg.)', *Neva*, 1, 1994, pp. 227–31.

13 Harrison Salisbury, *The 900 Days: The Siege of Leningrad*, pp. 304, 336.

14 TsGAIPD SPb: Fond 2281, op. 1, delo 27, pp. 2–4.

15 Ales Adamovich and Daniil Granin, *A Book of the Blockade*, p. 282.

16 Stanislav Bernev and Nikita Lomagin, eds, *Arkhiv Bolshogo Doma: Plan 'D'*. The book contains facsimiles of relevant documents from the FSB archive.

17 Gouré, *The Siege of Leningrad*, p. 99.

18 For the dismissal of A. P. Rovinsky of the Red Chemist plant, see RGASPI:

Fond 17, op. 22, delo 1643, p. 97. For that of A. I. Volkov, director of the 'Forward' plant, see ibid., p. 101.

19 RGASPI: Fond 17, op. 43, delo 1137, p. 68.

20 TsGAIPD SPb: Fond 24, op. 26, delo 5760.

21 Inber, *The Siege of Leningrad*, p. 19 (16 September 1941).

22 Nikita Lomagin, *Soldiers at War: German Propaganda and Soviet Army Morale during the Battle of Leningrad 1941–44*, Carl Beck Papers, 1306, p. 14.

23 Irina Reznikova (Flige), 'Repressii v period blokady Leningrada', *Vestnik 'Memoriala'* 4/5 (10/11), 1995, p. 102.

24 Richard Bidlack, 'The Political Mood in Leningrad during the First Year of the Soviet-German War', *The Russian Review*, 59 (January 2000), pp. 102–3.

25 For a vivid description of Moscow's *bolshoi drap*, see Rodric Braithwaite, *Moscow 1941: A City and its People at War*, pp. 244–55.

26 Salisbury, *900 Days*, p. 352, and Michael Jones, *Leningrad: State of Siege*, p. 135.

27 Gouré, *The Siege of Leningrad*, p. 183; RGASPI: Fond 558, op. 11, yed. khr. 492, p. 55.

28 RGASPI: Fond 558, op.11, yed. khr. 492, p. 60.

29 N. Voronov, 'V trudnye vremena', *Voyenno-istoricheskiy zhurnal* no. 9, 1961, pp. 71–2.

30 RGASPI: Fond 558, op. 11, yed. khr. 492, p. 64.

31 RGASPI: Fond 77, op. 3, delo 126, p. 9. Also TsAMO: Fond 96a, op. 2011, delo 5, pp. 138–40.

32 TsAMO: Fond 96a, op. 2011, delo 5, pp. 138–40.

33 RGASPI: Fond 77, op. 4, delo 48, p. 51.

34 See for example a letter from Kuznetsov to Stalin of 8 November 1941. RGASPI: Fond 77, op. 4, delo 48, pp. 51, 54.

35 RGASPI: Fond 77, op. 3, delo 126, p. 24. Also TsAMO: Fond 113a, op. 3272, delo 3, pp. 166–71.

Chapter 8: 125 Grams

1 Marina Starodubtseva (née Yerukhmanova), *Krugovorot vremeni i sudby: vospominaniya*. The manuscript was written in the late 1970s and is held by the Starodubtsev family. Chapter 7, pp. 506–17, covers the author's siege experiences.

2 See Nikita Lomagin, *Neizvestnaya blokada*, vol. 2, doc. 7, p. 34, and Dmitri Pavlov, *Leningrad 1941: The Blockade*, p. 48.

3 Lomagin, *Neizvestnaya blokada*, vol. 2, p. 191.

4 Pavlov, *Leningrad 1941*, p. 49.

5 Ibid., p. 31.

6 Ales Adamovich and Daniil Granin, *A Book of the Blockade*, p. 348.

7 Pavlov, *Leningrad 1941*, pp. 51–3.

8 Starodubtseva, *Krugovorot vremena i sudby: vospominaniya*, p. 510.

9 Leningrad oblast ispolkom order of 3 November 1941. RGASPI: Fond 17, op. 43, delo 1137, p. 8.

10 Andrei Dzeniskevich, ed., *Leningrad v osade: sbornik dokumentov*, doc. 20, pp. 188–90.

11 Ibid., pp. 111–12.

12 Pavlov, *Leningrad 1941*, p. 64.

13 Quoted in ibid., p. 66.

14 See the fascinating chapters on the Solovetsky camps in Anne Applebaum's *Gulag: A History of the Soviet Camps*, pp. 40–72.

15 Vasili Grossman, *Life and Fate*, p. 465.

16 Alexander Werth, *Russia at War, 1941–1945*, p. 188.

17 Pavlov, *Leningrad 1941*, p. 55.

18 Pär Sparén et al., 'Long Term Mortality after Severe Starvation during the Siege of Leningrad: Prospective Cohort Study', *British Medical Journal* 328 (3 January 2004), pp. 11–14.

19 Pavlov, *Leningrad 1941*, p. 120.

20 Ibid., pp. 79–80.

21 Aleksandr Boldyrev, *Osadnaya zapis: blokadniy dnevnik*, p. 78 (29 March 1942).

22 Valentina Gorokhova, in Cynthia Simmons and Nina Perlina, eds, *Writing the Siege of Leningrad: Women's Diaries, Memoirs and Documentary Prose*, p. 88.

23 Pavlov, *Leningrad 1941*, p. 123. Also see an order of 26 December 1941, signed by Andreyenko, that Academicians be given a special delivery of butter, potted meat or fish, eggs, sugar, grain, chocolate, flour and wine. Dzeniskevich, ed., *Leningrad v osade*, doc. 98, p. 209.

24 Anna Ostroumova-Lebedeva, *Avtobiograficheskiye zapiski: Leningrad v blokade* p. 274 (20 January 1942).

25 Simmons and Perlina, eds, *Writing the Siege of Leningrad*, p. 32.

26 Pavlov, *Leningrad 1941*, pp. 69, 80–81.

27 Protocol 50 of the Leningrad City Party Committee, 9 January 1942. RGASPI: Fond 17, op. 43, delo 1149, p. 9.

28 Lomagin, *Neizvestnaya blokada*, vol. 1, pp. 151–2. For more such examples see Protocol 53 of the Leningrad City Party Committee, 25 February 1942. RGASPI: Fond 17, op. 43, delo 1149, p. 121.

29 Pavlov, *Leningrad 1941*, p. 73.

30 Lidiya Ginzburg, *Blockade Diary*, pp. 81–2.

31 Ivan Zhilinsky, 'Blokadniy dnevnik', *Voprosy istorii*, 5–6, 1996, p. 24 (4 January 1942).

32 Ibid., p. 3 (30 January 1942). The same ploy was widespread at the institutional level. The Stalin Metal Works, inspectors discovered, had 729 registered workers, but of these 107 had in fact been evacuated, 70 were serving in the army, 21 had been arrested and 124 were dead.

CHAPTER 9: FALLING DOWN THE FUNNEL

1 Nikolai Gorshkov's siege diary usefully records daily temperatures. It is included in Bernev and Chemov, eds, *Arkhiv Bolshogo Doma: blokadniye dnevniki i dokumenty.*

2 Ales Adamovich and Daniil Granin, *A Book of the Blockade*, p. 326.

3 Lidiya Ginzburg, *Blockade Diary*, pp. 59–60.

4 Yelena Skrjabina, *Siege and Survival: The Odyssey of a Leningrader*, pp. 28–9, 50 (15 and 20 September 1941, 1 January 1942).

5 Ibid., pp. 31–2, 35, 37 (8 October, 6 and 7 November 1941).

6 Ibid., pp. 41, 47 (24 November and 16 December 1941).

7 Olga Grechina, 'Spasayus spasaya chast 1: pogibelnaya zima (1941–1942 gg.)', *Neva*, 1, 1994, pp. 231–9.

8 Ginzburg, *Blockade Diary*, p. 27.

9 Alexander Dymov, in Adamovich and Granin, *A Book of the Blockade*, p. 384.

10 Ivan Korotkov, in ibid., p. 45.

11 Adamovich and Granin, *A Book of the Blockade*, p. 52; Marina Tkacheva, interviewee no. 14, European University at St Petersburg Oral History Project, 'Blokada v sudbakh i pamyati leningradtsev'.

12 Quoted in an NKVD report to Zhdanov of 13 December 1941. Nikita Lomagin, *Neizvestnaya blokada*, vol. 2, doc. 56, p. 252.

13 K. V. Polzikova-Rubyets, 20 January 1942. Quoted in Andrei Dzeniskevich, 'Banditizm (osobaya kategoriya) v blokirovannom Leningrade', *Istoriya Peterburga*, 1, 2001, p. 48.

14 Sofia Pavlova, in *Trudy Gosudarstvennogo Muzeya Istorii Sankt-Peterburga*, vol. 5, p. 182.

15 Interview with Dr Lyuba Vinogradova, Moscow, July 2007.

16 Elena Kochina, *Blockade Diary*, pp. 31–55 (16 June, 27 September, 9 October, 26 November, 4 and 13 December 1941).

17 Andrei Dzeniskevich, ed., *Leningrad v osade*, doc. 174, p. 411. Dmitri Pavlov, *Leningrad 1941: The Blockade*, p. 123.

18 National Archive of the USA. Reports on the situation in the USSR by the Security Police and SD, no. 136. Microfilm T-175/233, ss. 10–20. Given in Lomagin, *Neizvestnaya blokada*, vol. 2, p. 169.

19 Ibid., p. 152 (4 December 1941).

20 Sidney Monas and Jennifer Greene Kupala, eds, *The Diaries of Nikolay Punin, 1904–53*, pp. 186, 190–91.

PART 3. MASS DEATH: WINTER 1941–2

CHAPTER 10: THE ICE ROAD

1 Hockenjos's unpublished war diary, from which all the following extracts are taken, is with Freiburg's Bundesarchiv/Militärarchiv, reference numbers MSG 2/4034, 4035, 4036, 4037, 4038.

2 David Glantz, *The Battle for Leningrad, 1941–44*, p. 100.

3 A. V. Karasev, *Leningradtsy v gody blokady*, Moscow, 1959, pp. 132–3.

4 Vasili Churkin, 8 December 1941. *Voyennaya literatura: dnevniki i pisma*, www.militera.lib.ru

5 Paul Carell, *Hitler Moves East 1941–1943*, Boston, 1963, pp. 269–70. Quoted by Glantz, *The Battle for Leningrad*, p. 106. Pavlov puts the number at 7,000.

6 For a detailed account of the Ice Road's functioning see Leon Gouré, *The Siege of Leningrad*, pp. 205–11.

7 TsAMO: Fond 96a, op. 2011, delo 5, pp. 191–4.

8 Nikita Lomagin, *Neizvestnaya blokada*, vol. 2, doc. 10, pp. 38–9.

9 Charles Burdick and Hans-Adolf Jacobsen, eds, Franz Halder, *The Halder War Diary, 1939–1942*, pp. 561, 569 (22 and 29 November 1941).

10 Ibid., p. 598.

11 As Halder's deputy Günther Blumentritt complained to the British historian Basil Liddell Hart after the war: 'Only the admirals had a happy time in this war. Hitler knew nothing about the sea, whereas he felt he knew all about land warfare.'

12 Andrew Roberts, *Masters and Commanders: How Roosevelt, Churchill, Marshall and Alanbrooke won the War in the West*, p. 64.

Chapter 11: Sleds and Cocoons

1 Vera Inber, *Leningrad Diary*, pp. 38–9 (1 January 1942).

2 Vasili Chekrizov, 'Dnevnik blokadnogo vremeni', *Trudy Gosudarstvennogo Muzeya Istorii Sankt-Peterburga*, vol. 8, p. 38 (31 December 1941).

3 Yelena Kochina, *Blockade Diary*, pp. 65–7, 69 (29 December 1941 and 6 January 1942).

4 Dmitri Pavlov, *Leningrad 1941: The Blockade*, p. 123.

5 Irina Zelenskaya, 'Dnevik', in Kovalchuk, ed, '*Ya ne sdamsya do poslednego...*', p. 10.

6 Vera Kostrovitskaya, April 1942. In Cynthia Simmons and Nina Perlina, eds, *Writing the Siege: Women's Diaries, Memoirs and Documentary Prose*, pp. 50–51.

7 William Moskoff, *The Bread of Affliction: The Food Supply in the USSR during World War II*, p. 196.

8 'Dnevnik I. M. Chaiko', *Trudy Gosudarstvennogo Muzeya Istorii Sankt-Peterburga*, vol. 5, p. 115.

9 Nikita Lomagin, *Neizvestnaya blokada*, vol. 2, p. 188.

10 NKVD report to Zhdanov, 2 June 1942. Given in Lomagin, *Neizvestnaya blokada*, vol. 2, pp. 320–23. Andrei Dzeniskevich, ed., *Leningrad v osade: sbornik dokumentov*, p. 412.

11 For examples of orphans exploited by neighbours see Dmitri Likhachev, *Reflections on the Russian Soul: A Memoir*, pp. 234, 241, and Mariya Mashkova, 'Iz blokadnykh zapisei', in *V pamyat ushedshikh i vo slavu zhivushchikh: dnevniki, vospominaniya, pisma*, p. 48 (5 March 1942).

12 Dmitri Lazarev, 'Vospominaniya o blokade', *Trudy Gosudarstvennogo Muzeya Istorii Sankt-Peterburga*, vol. 5, p. 210 (January 1942).

13 Lidiya Ginzburg, *Blockade Diary*, pp. 9–10.

14 Inber, *Leningrad Diary*, p. 40 (2 January 1942).

15 Report to Popkov from the Leningrad military prosecutor, 12 February 1942. Given in Dzeniskevich, ed., *Leningrad v osade*, doc. 136, pp. 290–92.

16 Inber, *Leningrad Diary*, pp. 37–8 (26 December 1941).

17 Lazarev, 'Vospominaniya o blokade', *Trudy Gosudarstvennogo Muzeya Istorii Sankt-Peterburga*, vol. 5, p. 207 (February 1942).

18 Nadezhda Cherepenina, 'Assessing the Scale of Famine and Death in the Besieged City', in John Barber and Andrei Dzeniskevich, eds, *Life and Death in Besieged Leningrad 1941–44*, pp. 47–8.

19 Lazarev, 'Vospominaniya o blokadye', *Trudy Gosudarstvennogo Muzeya Istorii Sankt-Peterburga*, vol. 5, p. 207 (11 February 1942).

20 Richard Bidlack, 'Survival Strategies in Leningrad during the First Year of the Soviet-German War', in Robert Thurston and Bernd Bonwetsch, eds, *The People's War: Responses to World War Two in the Soviet Union*, p. 93.

21 Chekrizov, 'Dnevnik blokadnogo vremeni', *Trudy Gosudarstvennogo Muzeya Istorii Sankt-Peterburga*, vol. 8, p. 50 (5 February 1942).

22 Report to Zhdanov and Kuznetsov by Antyufeyev, 5 February 1942. TsGAIPD SPb: Fond 24, op. 2v.

23 Vladimir Garshin, 'Tam gde smert pomogayet zhizni', *Arkhiv Patologii*, vol. 46, no. 5, 1984, p. 84.

24 Inber, *Leningrad Diary*, p. 33 (25 November 1941).

25 Ales Adamovich and Daniil Granin, *A Book of the Blockade*, pp. 424, 440.

26 Geraldine Norman, *The Hermitage: The Biography of a Great Museum*, p. 252.

27 Aleksandr Boldyrev, *Osadnaya zapis: blokadniy dnevnik*, pp. 25–8 (9 and 10 December 1941).

28 Ibid., p. 56 (12 February 1942).

29 'Dnevnik I. M. Chaiko', *Trudy Gosudarstvennogo Muzeya Istorii Sankt-Peterburga*, vol. 5, p. 117 (25 March 1943).

30 Nikolai Ribkovsky, in Nataliya Kozlova, ed., *Sovetskiye lyudi: stseny iz istorii*, pp. 263–4 (15 March 1942).

31 Vera Kostrovitskaya, April 1942. In Simmons and Perlina, eds, *Writing the Siege*, pp. 47–52.

32 Nikolai Sokolov, 'Tyoplaya vanna dlya begemota: zoosad v gody voiny', *Rodina* 1, 2003. I. M. Gergilevich, *Podvig tvoi bessmerten (1942–1945)*, unpublished paper.

33 Report by the 'Burial Affairs' section of the City Communal Enterprises Management, 5 April 1943. Dzeniskevich, ed., *Leningrad v osade*, doc. 153, pp. 319–43.

34 Sofia Buryakova, in Simmons and Perlina, eds, *Writing the Siege*, pp. 100–101.

35 Lazarev, 'Vospominaniya o blokadye', *Trudy Gosudarstvennogo Muzeya Istorii Sankt-Peterburga*, vol. 5, pp. 202–4 (24 January 1942).

36 Likhachev, *Reflections on the Russian Soul*, p. 250.

37 Barber and Dzeniskevich, eds, *Life and Death in Besieged Leningrad, 1941–44*, pp. 1, 63. The Burial Trust report of April 1943 gives what it admits is a 'far from accurate' number of 1,093,659 corpses interred in the twelve months to 1 July 1942. This is generally accepted to be a substantial overestimate, driven by the fact that cemetery and corpse collection staff were paid according to productivity.

Chapter 12: 'We Were Like Stones'

1 Mariya Mashkova, 'Iz blokadnykh zapisei', in *V pamyat ushedshikh i vo slavu zhivushchikh: dnevniki, vospominaniya, pisma*, pp. 37–9 (17 February 1942).

2 Lidiya Ginzburg, *Blockade Diary*, p. 11. Pavel Gubchevsky of the Hermitage remembered marvelling at the extravagance of energy and organisation that had gone into pre-war productions at the Philharmonia and the Mariinsky – why had he not gone to concerts and the ballet more often before?

3 Aleksandr Boldyrev, *Osadnaya zapis: blokadniy dnevnik*, pp. 41–2 (11–13 January 1942).

4 Ivan Zhilinsky, 'Blokadniy dnevnik', *Voprosy istorii*, 5–7, 1996, part 3, p. 3 (30 January 1942).

5 Lidiya Ginzburg, *Blockade Diary*, pp. 62–3.

6 Boldyrev, *Osadnaya zapis: blokadniy dnevik*, p. 83 (4 April 1942).

7 Klara Rakhman, 20 December 1941. Unpublished manuscript, in possession of the diarist's family.

8 Interview with Dr Lyuba Vinogradova, Moscow, July 2007.

9 Yelena Kochina, *Blockade Diary*, pp. 86–8 (1, 5 and 7 February 1942).

10 Dmitri Likhachev, *Reflections on the Russian Soul: A Memoir*, pp. 249–50.

11 Olga Grechina, 'Spasayus spasaya chast 1: pogibelnaya zima (1941–1942 gg.)', *Neva*, 1, 1994, pp. 242–3.

12 Solomon Volkov, *St Petersburg: A Cultural History*, p. 437; Leon Gouré, *The Siege of Leningrad*, p. 201.

13 Kochina, *Blockade Diary*, p. 86 (30 January 1942).

14 Likhachev, *Reflections on the Russian Soul*, p. 266.

15 Dmitri Lazarev, 'Vospominaniya o blokade', *Trudy Gosudarstvennogo Muzeya Istorii Sankt-Peterburga*, vol. 5, p. 238.

16 Mashkova, 'Iz blokadnykh zapisei', p. 41 (18 February 1942).

17 Ibid., p. 76 (23 April 1942).

18 Interview with Dr Lyuba Vinogradova, Moscow, July 2007.

19 Boldyrev, *Osadnaya zapis: blokadniy dnevnik*, p. 58 (13 February 1942).

20 Ginzburg, *Blockade Diary*, p. 3.

21 Georgi Knyazev, 3 February 1942, in Ales Adamovich and Daniil Granin, *A Book of the Blockade*, p. 440.

22 Vera Inber, *Leningrad Diary*, p. 50 (14 January 1942).

23 Adamovich and Granin, *A Book of the Blockade*, p. 474.

24 Mikhail Steblin-Kamensky, 'The Siege of Leningrad', *Granta* 30: *New Europe!*, April 1990, pp. 183–9. First published in *Neva*, 1, 1989.

25 Geraldine Norman, *The Hermitage: The Biography of a Great Museum*, p. 255.

26 Elliott Mossman, ed., *The Correspondence of Olga Freidenberg and Boris Pasternak, 1910–1954*, p. 225.

27 Adamovich and Granin, *A Book of the Blockade*, p. 78.

28 Klara Rakhman, unpublished manuscript in possession of the author's grandson, p. 5 (7 December 1941.)

29 Lev Uspensky, 'Gordost i lyubov moya', in G. S. Melnik and G. V. Zhirkov, eds, *Radio, blokada, Leningrad*, St Petersburg, 2002, pp. 203–4.

30 Lisa A. Kirschenbaum, *The Legacy of the Siege of Leningrad, 1941–1995: Myth, Memories, and Monuments*, pp. 54, 72.

31 Ibid., p. 66. There is confusion about when *February Diary* was first broadcast. In her autobiography of 1952, Berggolts recounts that a last-minute call from the censor prevented its broadcast on Red Army Day itself, and that it was not published in full until May. Other accounts, however, describe the broadcast going ahead as planned. Extracts were certainly published in 'wall newspapers' and widely circulated before spring.

32 Aleksandr Rubashkin, *Golos Leningrada: Leningradskoye Radio v dni blokady*, p. 136.

33 See Mikhail Shkarovsky, 'Iskrenniy privet ot Stalina: religioznaya zhizn blokadnogo Leningrada', *Rodina*, 1, 2003, pp. 146–50.

34 Report on the 'Liquidation of the Archimandrite Klavdi Group', 1 October 1942. In Andrei Dzeniskevich, ed., *Leningrad v osade: sbornik dokumentov*, doc. 192, p. 446.

35 Editor's footnote to Olga Berggolts, *Zvezda*, 4, April 1991, pp. 128–41 (8 February 1942).

36 Berggolts, *Zvezda*, 4, April 1991, pp. 128–41 (4 September 1941).

37 Adamovich and Granin, *A Book of the Blockade*, pp. 261, 442.

38 Likhachev, *Reflections on the Russian Soul*, p. 244.

39 European University of St Petersburg Oral History Project, 'Blokada v sudbakh i pamyati leningradtsev', interviewee no. 42.

40 Svetlana Magayeva and Albert Pleysier, *Surviving the Blockade of Leningrad*, p. 99.

CHAPTER 13: SVYAZI

1 Anna Ostroumova-Lebedeva, *Avtobiograficheskiye zapiski: Leningrad v blokade*, pp. 271, 275 (1 January and 13 February 1942).

2 Aelita Vostrova, interviewee no. 17, European University at St Petersburg Oral History Project, 'Blokada v sudbakh i pamyati leningradtsev'.

3 Olga Grechina, 'Spasayus spasaya chast 1: pogibelnaya zima (1941–1942 gg.)', *Neva*, 1, 1994, pp. 249–50.

4 Richard Bidlack, 'Survival Strategies in Leningrad during the First Year of the Soviet-German War', in Robert Thurston and Bernd Bonwetsch, eds, *The People's War: Responses to World War Two in the Soviet Union*, pp. 93–5.

5 Yelena Skrjabina, *Siege and Survival: The Odyssey of a Leningrader*, p. 54 (15 January 1941).

6 Georgi Makogonenko, in Ales Adamovich and Daniil Granin, *A Book of the Blockade*, p. 378.

7 Olga Berggolts, 'Blokadniy dnevnik', *Zvezda*, 3, April 1991, p. 143 (25 February 1942).

8 Berggolts, 23 and 25 March 1942, in 'Ob etikh tetradyakh', *Zvezda*, 5, 1990, pp. 190–91.

9 Mariya Mashkova, 'Iz blokadnykh zapisei', in *V pamyat ushedshikh i vo slavu zhivushchikh: dnevniki, vospominania, pisma*, p. 77 (23 April 1942).

10 Andrei Dzeniskevich, ed., *Leningrad v osade: sbornik dokumentov*, doc. 210, p. 517.

11 William Moskoff, *The Bread of Affliction: The Food Supply in the USSR during World War Two*, p. 181.

12 Vera Inber, *Leningrad Diary*, p. 72 (27 March 1942).

13 Lidiya Ginzburg, *Blockade Diary*, pp. 66–7.

14 For another example, see Dmitri Likhachev, *Reflections on the Russian Soul: A Memoir*, p. 228.

15 Valerian Bogdanov-Berezovsky, *Iz dnevnikov blokadnykh let*, typescript, RGALI: Fond 1817, op. 2, yed. khr. 185, pp. 26–7 (25 January 1942).

16 See Dzeniskevich, ed., *Leningrad v osade*, document no. 216, p. 528.

17 Likhachev, *Reflections on the Russian Soul*, pp. 235–6.

18 Ibid., pp. 238–40, 264. For more examples of corruption, see Skrjabina on senior hospital staff and their families, *Siege and Survival*, pp. 68, 71 (11 February 1942).

19 Adamovich and Granin, *A Book of the Blockade*, p. 441.

20 Skrjabina, *Siege and Survival*, p. 62 (4 February 1942).

21 See James Clapperton, *The Siege of Leningrad and the Ambivalence of the Sacred: Conversations with Survivors*, Ph.D. thesis, Edinburgh University, 2006, p. 294.

22 Skrjabina, *Siege and Survival*, p. 41 (26 November 1941).

23 Tamara Neklyudova, in Cynthia Simmons and Nina Perlina, eds, *Writing the Siege: Women's Diaries, Memoirs and Documentary Prose*, p. 62.

24 Inber, *Leningrad Diary*, p. 65; Bidlack, 'Survival Strategies', p. 91.

25 Bidlack, 'Survival Strategies', p. 94.

26 Ostroumova-Lebedeva, 22 May 1942, in Simmons and Perlina, eds, *Writing the Siege*, p. 32.

27 Skrjabina, *Siege and Survival*, pp. 38, 42–3, 60 (12 and 29 November 1941, 27 January 1942).

28 Aleksandr Boldyrev, *Osadnaya zapis: blokadniy dnevnik*, p. 82 (3 April 1942); Likhachev, *Reflections on the Russian Soul*, pp. 230–31. See also Ivan Zhilinsky, 'Blokadniy dnevnik', *Voprosy istorii*, 5, 1996, 22 December 1941, p. 9, on Leningraders trading dresses and hats with the workers at the pig farm behind the Serafimovskoye cemetery.

29 Dzeniskevich, ed., *Leningrad v osade*, doc. 187, p. 436.

30 Dmitri Lazarev, 'Vospominaniya o blokade', in *Trudy Gosudarstvennogo Muzeya Istorii Sankt-Peterburga*, vol. 5, p. 234.

31 Report to Zhdanov by the head of the 'instructors' department' of the city Party Committee, Antyufeyev, 27 January 1942. TsGAIPD SPb: Fond 24, op. 2v, delo 5760.

32 Bidlack, 'Survival Strategies', pp. 96, 106; Leon Gouré, *The Siege of Leningrad*, p. 192. See also the Harvard Project on the Soviet Social System, Schedule B, vol. 2, case 260, pp. 6, 14 (available online from the Widener Library).

33 Likhachev, *Reflections on the Russian Soul*, p. 253; Vasili Yershov, untitled typescript, Research Program on the USSR, Bakhmeteff Archive, Columbia University, p. 72.

34 Nikolai Ribkovsky, in Nataliya Kozlova, ed., *Sovyetskiye lyudi: stseni i istorii*, pp. 264, 267–9, 276.

35 Nikita Lomagin, *Neizvestnaya blokada*, vol. 1, pp. 151–2.

36 See Dzeniskevich, ed., *Leningrad v osade*, doc. 126, p. 273.

37 Likhachev, *Reflections on the Russian Soul*, p. 223.

38 Report to Kuznetsov, 28 November 1941. Dzeniskevich, ed., *Leningrad v osade*, doc. 127, pp. 274–6.

39 Report of 28–29 January 1942. Lomagin, *Neizvestnaya blokada*, vol. 2, doc. 64, pp. 281, 284.

CHAPTER 14: 'ROBINSON CRUSOE WAS A LUCKY MAN'

1 Aleksandr Boldyrev, *Osadnaya zapis: blokadniy dnevnik*, p. 63 (21 February 1942).

2 Vera Inber, *Leningrad Diary*, p. 75 (31 March 1942).

3 Georgi Knyazev, 22 February 1942, in Ales Adamovich and Daniil Granin, *A Book of the Blockade*, p. 450.

4   In the second half of March, according to a report to Beria of 4 April 1942, 7,540 houses, 1,020 cows, 134 horses and 92 other livestock were confiscated. See Nikita Lomagin, *Neizvestnaya blokada*, vol. 2, doc. 9, p. 37.

5   See a report from the Oranienbaum district soviet of 1 April 1942, in Andrei Dzeniskevich, ed., *Leningrad v osade: sbornik dokumentov*, doc. 184, pp. 430–33. Also Irina Reznikova (Flige), 'Repressii v period blokady Leningrada', *Vestnik 'Memoriala'*, no. 4/5 (10/11), p. 99.

6   NKVD report of 1 October 1942. Dzeniskevich, ed., *Leningrad v osade*, doc. 190, p. 442.

7   Report to Zhdanov and Kuznetsov from Antyufeyev, 21 March 1942. TsGAIPD SPb: Fond 24, op. 2v, delo 5760.

8   Dzeniskevich ed., *Leningrad v osade*, doc. 146, p. 308.

9   Dmitri Likhachev, *Reflections on the Russian Soul: A Memoir*, pp. 245–6.

10 Yelena Skrjabina, *Siege and Survival: The Odyssey of a Leningrader*, pp. 60–61 (29 and 30 January 1942).

11 Adamovich and Granin, *A Book of the Blockade*, p. 312.

12 Ibid., p. 344.

13 Ibid., p. 388.

14 Ibid., p. 416.

15 Ibid., pp. 483–93.

16 Dmitri Pavlov, *Leningrad 1941: The Blockade*, p. 164. The war correspondent Alexander Werth equally erroneously describes the Ice Road as working 'like clockwork' (*Russia at War, 1941–1945*, p. 332).

17 Adamovich and Granin, *A Book of the Blockade*, p. 185.

18 Ibid., pp. 435–8.

19 Vladimir Kulyabko, 'Blokadniy dnevnik', *Neva*, 3, 2004, pp. 262–7.

20 For an account of an evacuation journey at the end of March 1942, see Yelena Kochina, *Blockade Diary*, pp. 101–9.

21 Pavlov, *Leningrad 1941*, p. 164.

22 Kochina, *Blockade Diary*, p. 108 (11 and 15 April 1942).

23 Report to the Leningrad oblast Party committee, 5 March 1942. Dzeniskevich, ed., *Leningrad v osade*, doc. 137, pp. 292–4.

24 Skryabina, *Siege and Survival*, pp. 78, 101–2 (25 February and 11 April 1942).

CHAPTER 15: CORPSE-EATING AND PERSON-EATING

1   Dmitri Pavlov, *Leningrad 1941: The Blockade*, pp. 127–8.

2   Yelena Kochina, *Blockade Diary*, pp. 55–6, 59 (15 and 19 December 1941).

3 See for example Ales Adamovich and Daniil Granin, *A Book of the Blockade*, pp. 82–4.

4 Letters from Kosygin to Zhdanov, 10 and 17 February 1942. Andrei Dzeniskevich, ed., *Leningrad v osade: sbornik dokumentov*, docs 106 and 134, pp. 228, 288; Richard Bidlack, 'Survival Strategies in Leningrad during the First Year of the Soviet-German War', in Robert Thurston and Bernd Bonwetsch, eds, *The People's War: Responses to World War Two in the Soviet Union*, p. 90. See also Adamovich and Granin, *A Book of the Blockade*, p. 92.

5 Report to Zhdanov by the 'organisers' department' of the Leningrad Party Committee, 4 January 1942. Dzeniskevich, ed., *Leningrad v osade*, doc. 176, p. 414.

6 Dmitri Lazarev, 'Vospominaniya o blokade', *Trudy Gosudarstvennogo Muzeya Istorii Sankt-Peterburga*, vol. 5, p. 204.

7 Report to Popkov by the head of the city food trade organisation, 15 January 1942. Dzeniskevich, ed., *Leningrad v osade*, doc. 178, pp. 418–20. Also see an NKVD report to Beria of 23 February 1942, in Nikita Lomagin, *Neizvestnaya blokada*, vol. 2, doc. 67, p. 296.

8 Report to Zhdanov and Kuznetsov from Antyufeyev, 9 January 1942. TsGAIPD SPb: Fond 24, op. 2v, delo 5760.

9 On increased security measures, see a report by the city militia to Popkov of 30 January 1942, in Dzeniskevich, ed., *Leningrad v osade*, doc. 179, p. 420. On the results see an NKVD report to Zhdanov, March 1942, in Lomagin, *Neizvestnaya blokada*, vol. 2, doc. 68, p. 301.

10 Kochina, *Blockade Diary*, pp. 60–64 (20, 21, 22 and 26 December 1941); pp. 80–83 (17, 18 and 23 January 1942).

11 Boris Belozerov, 'Crime during the Siege', in John Barber and Andrei Dzeniskevich, eds, *Life and Death in Besieged Leningrad 1941–44*, London, 2005, p. 223.

12 NKVD reports to Zhdanov of 13 December 1941, 28–29 January, 23 February and March 1942. Lomagin, *Neizvestnaya blokada*, vol. 2, docs 56, 64 and 68, pp. 255–6, 283, 295, 300. Report to Zhdanov and Kuznetsov from Antyufeyev of 9 January 1942. TsGAIPD SPb: Fond 24, op. 2v, delo 5760.

13 Report of 10 February 1942, in Lomagin, *Neizvestnaya blokada*, vol. 2, doc. 23, p. 83.

14 See also the record of a Party meeting 'on strengthened vigilance' of 9 January 1942, in Dzeniskevich, ed., *Leningrad v osade*, doc. 177, p. 418. One of the attendees complained that 'due to poor food supply we have no guards in the city'. Touring his district at one o'clock in the morning he had seen 'absolutely nobody'.

15 Harvard Project on the Soviet Social System, Schedule B, vol. 2, case 260. (Available online from the Widener Library.)

16 Interviewed by the author, September 2008.

17 Kochina, *Blockade Diary*, p. 62 (23 December 1941).

18 Olga Berggolts, 'Iz dnevnikov', 20 May 1942. *Zvezda*, 6, 1990, p. 161.

19 See Harrison Salisbury, *The 900 Days: The Siege of Leningrad*, pp. 479–81. The novel in question, Anatoly Darov's *Blokada*, was published in Nikolayev in 1943. An English-language version was published in New York in 1964.

20 Aleksei Vinokurov, in Stanislav Bernev and Sergei Chernov, eds, *Arkhiv Bolshogo Doma: blokadniye dnevniki i dokumenty*, p. 253 (14 March 1942).

21 Dmitri Likhachev, *Reflections on the Russian Soul: A Memoir*, pp. 234–5.

22 Olga Grechina, 'Spasayus spasaya chast 1: pogibelnaya zima (1941–42 gg.)', *Neva*, 1, 1994, p. 240.

23 NKVD report to Zhdanov, 13 December 1941, in Lomagin, *Neizvestnaya blokada*, vol. 2, doc. 56, pp. 256–7.

24 Report by the Leningrad NKVD to Beria, 24 December 1941, in ibid., doc. 60, p. 264.

25 NKVD report to Zhdanov, 12 January 1942, in Lomagin, *Neizvestnaya blokada*, vol. 1, doc. 63, pp. 275–6.

26 Report to Zhdanov from Kubatkin of 2 June 1942, in ibid., doc. 75, p. 322.

27 This number is derived from Leningrad NKVD chief Kubatkin's series of reports to Zhdanov and to Beria. A report by the prosecutor's office (Dzeniskevich, ed., *Leningrad v osade*, doc. 195) gives a figure of 1,979.

28 Report to Beria from Kubatkin, 3 May 1942. Lomagin, *Neizvestnaya blokada*, vol. 2, doc. 74, p. 319. See also a report by the military prosecutor A. I. Panfilenko to Kuznetsov, 21 February 1942. Dzeniskevich, ed., *Leningrad v osade*, doc. 180, p. 421.

29 NKVD report to Zhdanov, 2 May 1942. Lomagin, *Neizvestnaya blokada*, vol. 2, doc. 73, p. 316.

30 See Andrei Dzeniskevich, 'Banditizm (osobaya kategoriya) v blokirovannom Leningrade', *Istoriya Peterburga*, 1, 2001, p. 50.

31 Report to Beria from Kubatkin, 24 December 1941, in Lomagin, *Neizvestnaya blokada*, vol. 2, doc. 60, p. 264.

32 Reports to Beria from Kubatkin, 13 March, April and 2 July 1942. Lomagin, *Neizvestnaya blokada*, vol. 2, docs 69, 70 and 76, pp. 306, 310, 325–6.

33 NKVD report to Beria and Zhdanov, 28–29 January 1942. Ibid., doc. 64, p. 282.

34 Report to Beria from Kubatkin, 23 February 1942. Ibid., doc. 67, p. 297.

35 NKVD report to Zhdanov, March 1942, ibid., doc. 68, p. 302.

36 Lazarev, 'Vospominaniya o blokade', *Trudy Gosudarstvennogo Muzeya Istorii Sankt-Peterburga*, vol. 5, pp. 205–6.

Dzeniskevich, 'Banditizm', p. 50. Report by military prosecutor A. I. Panfilenko to Kuznetsov, 21 February 1942, in Dzeniskevich, ed., *Leningrad v osade*, doc. 180, p. 422.

37 Dzeniskevich, 'Banditizm', pp. 50–51.

38 Reports from Kubatkin to Beria and Merkulov, 10 and 23 February 1942. Lomagin, *Neizvestnaya blokada*, vol. 2, docs 65 and 67, pp. 286, 292.

39 Report to Zhdanov from Kubatkin, 2 June 1942, ibid., doc. 75, p. 323. This conflicts with a prosecutor's report of 1 July 1943, according to which 1,700 people had been convicted of 'special category banditry', of whom 364 had been executed and 1,336 sentenced to imprisonment (Dzeniskevich, ed., *Leningrad v osade*, doc. 195, table on p. 461).

Chapter 16: Anton Ivanovich is Angry

1 Ales Adamovich and Daniil Granin, *A Book of the Blockade*, p. 65. See also Leon Gouré, *The Siege of Leningrad*, p. 190.

2 Reports from the 18th Army to the OKW, 7 and 19 October 1941, in Nikita Lomagin, *Neizvestnaya blokada*, vol. 2, docs 13 and 19, pp. 127, 139.

3 Air defence workers were said to have formed 'opposition groups'. SD reports, 24 October and 7 November 1941, ibid., docs 30 and 31, pp. 161, 164. On Soviet POWs, see Evan Mawdsley, *Thunder in the East: The Nazi-Soviet War 1941–1945*, pp. 103–5.

4 SD report of 18 February 1941, in Lomagin, *Neizvestnaya blokada*, vol. 2, doc. 39, pp. 196–7.

5 NKVD report to Zhdanov, 28–29 January 1942, ibid., doc. 64, p. 280.

6 See for example a table from 1939, in Lomagin, *Neizvestnaya blokada*, vol. 1, doc. 7, p. 14.

7 Georgi Knyazev, 9 November 1941, in Adamovich and Granin, *A Book of the Blockade*, pp. 323–4.

8 Irina Zelenskaya, 1 September 1941, in *'Ya nye sdamsya do poslednego . . .': zapiski iz blokadnogo Leningrada*, St Petersburg, 2010, p. 20.

9 Anna Ostroumova-Lebedeva, 6 July 1941, in Cynthia Simmons and Nina Perlina, eds, *Writing the Siege: Women's Diaries, Memoirs and Documentary Prose*, pp. 27–8.

10 Quoted in an NKVD report to Zhdanov of December 1941, in Lomagin, *Neizvestnaya blokada*, vol. 2, doc. 62, p. 271.

11 Vera Inber, *Leningrad Diary*, p. 37 (25 December 1941).

12 Ivan Zhilinsky, 'Blokadniy dnevnik', *Voprosy istorii*, 5–7, part 1, p. 21 (2 January 1942).

13 Reports to Zhdanov from the 'organisers' and 'instructors' departments of the City Party Committee, 9 and 27 January 1942. TsGAIPD SPb: Fond 24, op. 2v, delo 5760.

14 Richard Bidlack, 'The Political Mood in Leningrad during the First Year of the Soviet-German War', *The Russian Review*, 59 (January 2000), pp. 110–11.

15 NKVD report to Beria and Zhdanov, 28–29 January 1942, in Lomagin, *Neizvestnaya blokada*, vol. 2, doc. 64, p. 278.

16 Reports to Zhdanov from the 'organisers' department' of the City Party Committee, 14 and 27 January 1942. TsGAIPD SPb: Fond 24, op. 2v, delo 5760. Andrei Dzeniskevich, ed., *Leningrad v osade: sbornik dokumentov*, doc. 199, p. 472.

17 Report to Leningrad NKVD head Kubatkin, 12 February 1942, in Lomagin, *Neizvestnaya blokada*, vol. 2, doc. 66, p. 290.

18 NKVD report to Beria and Zhdanov, 28–29 January 1942, ibid., doc. 64, p. 278.

19 Report to the head of the SD from Einssatzgruppe A, stationed in Krasnogvardeisk, 10 December 1941, ibid., doc. 35, p. 179.

20 Vasili Yershov, untitled typescript, Research Program on the USSR, Bakhmeteff Archive, Columbia University, p. 77.

21 NKVD report to Zhdanov, 12 January 1942, in Lomagin, *Neizvestnaya blokada*, vol. 2, doc. 63, p. 274.

22 NKVD report to Beria and Zhdanov, 28–29 January 1942, ibid., doc. 64, p. 285.

23 Report from Leningrad NKVD head Kubatkin to Alexander Kuznetsov, 12 December 1943, ibid., doc. 15, pp. 57–60. See also Michael Jones, *Leningrad: State of Siege*, pp. 286–8. A report of November 1941 mentions that letters have been sent to the leadership threatening strikes and demonstrations unless rations are increased. See Lomagin, *Neizvestnaya blokada*, vol. 2, doc. 53, pp. 243–4.

CHAPTER 17: THE BIG HOUSE

1 In his foreword to one of the best post-war studies, Leon Gouré's *The Siege of Leningrad*. Gouré, like the BBC journalist Alexander Werth, was born Russian. His Menshevik family fled the Revolution to Berlin, and the Third Reich to Paris and later New Jersey, where Leon joined the US Army and received citizenship for the first time in his life. He fought in the Battle of the Bulge and after the war worked as an interpreter for the occupying forces in

Germany, before making a career in the Rand Corporation and academia. He died in 2007, at the age of eighty-five.

2 Rimma Neratova, quoted in Lisa Kirschenbaum, *The Legacy of the Siege of Leningrad, 1941–1995: Myth, Memories, and Monuments*, p. 34.

3 An NKVD report of 1 July 1943 states that 80 per cent of convictions to date for counter-revolutionary crimes took place in the first year of the war. Nikita Lomagin, *Neizvestnaya blokada*, vol. 2, doc. 195, p. 453.

4 See Irina Reznikova (Flige), 'Repressii v period blokady Leningrada', *Vestnik 'Memoriala'* 4/5 (10/11), 1995, pp. 95–7; NKVD reports of 6 November and mid-December 1941, in Lomagin, *Neizvestnaya blokada*, vol. 2, docs 51 and 58, pp. 232, 259.

5 NKVD report of 1 October 1942. Andrei Dzeniskevich, ed., *Leningrad v osade: sbornik dokumentov*, doc. 190, p. 441.

6 Military prosecutor's report, 1 July 1943, ibid., doc. 195, pp. 257–9.

7 Dmitri Likhachev, *Reflections on the Russian Soul: A Memoir*, pp. 235, 295.

8 Orlando Figes, *The Whisperers: Private Life in Stalin's Russia*, pp. 445–6.

9 'Blokadniy dnevnik uchitelya Vinokurova A. I.', in Stanislav Bernev and Sergei Chernov, eds, *Arkhiv Bolshogo Doma: blokadniye dnevniki i dokumenty*, pp. 236–90.

10 Aleksandr Boldyrev, *Osadnaya zapis: blokadniy dnevnik*, p. 38 (31 December 1941). Anna Akhmatova's nickname for the Big House was the 'Royal Court of Wonderland'.

11 Reznikova (Flige), 'Repressii', p. 103. There is also memoir evidence of cannibalism in the Kresty: in a commemorative brochure published to mark the 100th anniversary of the prison's foundation, a siege survivor describes seeing a group of fifteen to twenty inmates sitting in a courtyard openly eating corpse meat (Richard Bidlack, 'Survival Strategies in Leningrad', in Robert Thurston and Bernd Bonwetsch, eds, *The People's War: Responses to World War II in the Soviet Union*, p. 107).

12 Report by the Leningrad Statistical Service, 5 May 1944, in Dzeniskevich, ed., *Leningrad v osade*, doc. 156, p. 349. Deaths in prison dropped slowly through the rest of 1942, before peaking again, at 815, in January 1943.

13 Petition from the Corrective-Labour Camps and Columns Directorate of the NKVD to State Defence Committee Emissary D. V. Pavlov, 31 December 1941, in Dzeniskevich, ed., *Leningrad v osade*, doc. 175, p. 413.

14 Ivan Zhilinsky, 'Blokadniy dnevnik (osen 1941 – vesna 1942 g.)', *Voprosy istorii*, 5–6, 1996, pp. 3–7 (16 January 1942).

PART 4. WAITING FOR LIBERATION: JANUARY 1942–JANUARY 1942

CHAPTER 18: MEAT WOOD

1 Winston Churchill, *The Second World War*, pp. 465, 467.

2 Hugh Trevor-Roper, ed., *Hitler's Table Talk, 1941–44*, pp. 200, 220 (12–13 and 17–18 January 1941).

3 Fritz Hockenjos, typescript, Bundesarchiv/Militärarchiv: MSG 2/4034-4038 (5, 14, 16 January and 1 February 1942).

4 Antony Beevor and Lyuba Vinogradova, eds, *A Writer at War: Vasily Grossman with the Red Army 1941–45* (September 1941); Catherine Merridale, *Ivan's War: The Red Army 1939–45*, p. 167.

5 Dmitri Pavlov, *Leningrad 1941*, p. 88.

6 On desertion, see Nikita Lomagin, *Neizvestnaya blokada*, vol. 2, doc. 11, p. 40. On food theft and embezzlement among NKVD troops see orders of 1 February, 22 April and 16 July 1942. RGVA: Fond 32912, op. 1, delo 78, pp. 10, 39, 85. A report of 21 February complains that delivery drivers stop at villages en route, where they 'behave improperly, get drunk and supply female acquaintances with food'. (RGVA: Fond 32904, op. 1, delo 80, p. 8.)

7 'Dnevnik krasnoarmeitsa Putyakova S. F', in Stanislav Bernev and Sergei Chernov, eds, *Arkhiv Bolshogo Doma: blokadniye dnevniki i dokumenty*, p. 382 (29 December 1941).

8 NKVD report to Zhdanov, 22 December 1941, in Lomagin, *Neizvestnaya blokada*, vol. 2, doc. 59, p. 261.

9 Vasili Churkin, http://militera.lib.ru (20 November 1941).

10 See for example Yelena Skrjabina, *Siege and Survival: The Odyssey of a Leningrader*, p. 55 (18 January 1942).

11 Vasili Yershov, untitled typescript, Research Program on the USSR, Bakhmeteff Archive, Columbia University, pp. 40–41.

12 Ibid., pp. 66–7.

13 Stavka directive, 10 January 1942; David Glantz, *The Battle for Leningrad 1941–44*, pp. 149–50.

14 See Harrison Salisbury, *The 900 Days: The Siege of Leningrad*, pp. 544–5 for Mekhlis's long history of recommending colleagues' arrests. In the words of an associate he was 'a remarkably energetic and vigorous man, as decisive as he was incompetent, the master of varied but superficial knowledge and self-confident to the point of wilfulness'. Donald Rayfield calls him 'Stalin's least-known but most vicious scorpion'.

15 Charles Burdick and Hans-Adolf Jacobsen, eds, Franz Halder, *The Halder War Diary, 1939–1942*, p. 599 (5 January 1942).

16 Hockenjos, typescript, Bundesarchiv/Militärarchiv, pp. 69–70 (23 February 1942).

17 Burdick and Jacobsen, eds, Franz Halder, *The Halder War Diary*, p. 608 (2 March 1942).

18 Hockenjos, typescript, Bundesarchiv/Militärarchiv: p. 84 (13 and 16 April 1942).

19 Glantz, *The Battle for Leningrad 1941–44*, pp. 202–3.

20 I. I. Kalabin, in I. A. Ivanova, ed., *Tragediya Myasnogo Bora: sbornik vospominanii uchastnikov i ochevidtsev Lyubanskoi operatsii*, pp. 139–40. For similar accounts see Glantz, *The Battle for Leningrad 1941–44*, p. 204.

21 In a letter to Zhdanov of 3 June 1942 Khozin defended himself against accusations of drunkenness and misbehaviour with two telegraph girls. The telegraph operators, he protested, joined him only to watch films, and though he took '100g of vodka before supper, sometimes even two or three little glasses', he had never been drunk in his life. (RGASPI: Fond 77, op.3, delo 133.)

22 I. I. Kalabin, in Ivanovna, ed., *Tragediya Myasnogo Bora*, p. 142.

23 I. D. Nikonov, in ibid., p. 157.

24 For a full account of Vlasov's career see Catherine Andreyev, 'Andrei Andreyevich Vlasov', in Harold Shukman, ed., *Stalin's Generals*, pp. 301–11.

25 RGASPI: Fond 83, op. 1, yed. khr. 18, pp. 91–104.

26 Glantz, *The Battle for Leningrad 1941–44*, pp. 207–8.

27 Ilya Frenklah, www.iremember.ru

CHAPTER 19: THE GENTLE JOY OF LIVING AND BREATHING

1 Alexander Werth, *Russia at War*, p. 399

2 Andrew Roberts, *Masters and Commanders: How Roosevelt, Churchill, Marshall and Alanbrooke Won the War in the West*, pp. 271, 287.

3 Ales Adamovich and Daniil Granin, *A Book of the Blockade*, pp. 63–4; Geraldine Norman, *The Hermitage: The Biography of a Great Museum*, pp. 257–8.

4 Adamovich and Granin, *A Book of the Blockade*, p. 89; Vera Inber, *Leningrad Diary*, p. 200 (25 May 1944). Fifty-two people died from eating poisonous wild plants (Andrei Dzeniskevich, ed., *Leningrad v osade: sbornik dokumentov*, doc. 147, p. 312).

5 Dmitri Likhachev, *Reflections on the Russian Soul: A Memoir*, p. 255.

6 Vasili Chekrizov, 'Dnevnik blokadnogo vremeni', *Trudy Gosudarstvennogo Muzeya Istorii Sankt-Peterburga*, vol. 8, p. 79 (19 May 1942).

7 Lidiya Ginzburg, *Blockade Diary*, p. 75.

8 Olga Berggolts, 'Iz dnevnikov', *Zvezda*, 6, p. 154 (3 April 1942).

9 Lisa A. Kirschenbaum, *The Legacy of the Siege of Leningrad, 1941–1995: Myth, Memories, and Monuments*, p. 52. See also William Moskoff, *The Bread of Affliction: The Food Supply in the USSR during World War II*, pp. 203–4.

10 On 7 January 1942 Vera Inber attended a lecture titled 'The Illness of Starvation'.

11 Lev Markhasev, 'Dva Leningradskikh radio', in G. S. Melnik and G. V. Zhirkov, eds, *Radio, blokada, Leningrad*, St Petersburg, 2005, p. 96; Catherine Merridale, *Ivan's War: The Red Army 1939–45*, p. 165.

12 Berggolts, *Zvezda*, 6, p. 163 (31 May 1942).

13 Nikita Lomagin, *Neizvestnaya blokada*, vol. 1, pp. 227–8. Markhasev, 'Dva Leningradskikh Radio', p. 97.

14 Aileen Rambov, 'The Siege of Leningrad: Wartime Literature and Ideological Change', in Robert Thurston and Bernd Bonwetsch, eds, *The People's War: Responses to World War II in the Soviet Union*, pp. 163–4.

15 Berggolts, *Zvezda*, 6, pp. 160, 164 (13 May and 3 June 1942).

16 Elliott Mossman, ed., *The Correspondence of Boris Pasternak and Olga Freidenberg, 1910–1954*, pp. 216–21.

17 Anna Zelenova, *Stati, vospominaniya, pisma: Pavlovsky dvorets, istoriya i sudba*, p. 115.

18 Roberta Reeder, *Anna Akhmatova: Poet and Prophet*, p. 269.

19 Vera Inber, *Leningrad Diary*, pp. 60–61, 70–71 (19 and 20 February, 10 and 12 March 1942).

20 Vasili Churkin, *Voyennaya literatura: dnevniki i pisma*, http://militera.lib.ru/db/churkin part 2, pp. 9–10 (27 May and 28 June 1942).

21 Reeder, *Anna Akhmatova*, p. 277.

22 Vladimir Garshin, 'Tam gde smert pomogayet zhizni', *Arkhiv Patologii*, vol. 46, no. 5, 1984, pp. 83–8. (This short memoir was originally written in 1944.)

23 OSBP and Burial Trust reports of 14 April 1942 and 5 April 1943, in Dzeniskevich, ed., *Leningrad v osade*, docs 141 and 153, pp. 299, 337–8.

24 Reports to Zhdanov from Antyufeyev, head of the 'instructors' department of the City Party Committee, of 17 January, 28 March and 1 April 1942. TsGAIPD SPb: Fond 24, op. 2v, delo 5760.

25 Inber, *Leningrad Diary*, pp. 73–4 (28 March 1942).

26 Olga Grechina, 'Spasayus spasaya chast 1: pogibelnaya zima (1941–1942 gg.)', *Neva*, 1, 1994, p. 269.

27 Aleksandr Boldyrev, *Osadnaya zapis: blokadniy dnevnik*, pp. 76–9, 84 (26–31 March and 4 April 1942).

28 Norman, *The Hermitage*, p. 256.

29 Letter to Zhdanov from Lieut Gen. Kabanov, 11 May 1942, in Dzeniskevich, ed., *Leningrad v osade*, doc. 144, p. 307. See also the city health department's report to Kosygin and Popkov, of 31 March 1942, ibid., doc. 139, p. 296.

30 RGASPI: Fond 17, op. 43, delo 1150; protocol 57, p. 54; Dmitri Lazarev, 'Vospominaniya o blokade', *Trudy Gosudarstvennogo Muzeya Istorii Sankt-Peterburga*, vol. 5, pp. 211–12.

31 William Moskoff, *The Bread of Affliction: The Food Supply in the USSR during World War II*, p. 202; Richard Bidlack, *Workers at War: Factory Workers and Labor Policy in the Siege of Leningrad*, Carl Beck Papers, 902, p. 28.

32 RGASPI: Fond 17, op. 43, delo 1138; protocol 45, pp. 13, 44; protocol 47, p. 162. RGASPI: Fond 17, op. 43, delo 1139; protocol 48, p. 32. RGASPI: Fond 17, op. 43, delo 1140; protocol 50, pp. 1, 3, 90.

33 NKVD report to the Leningrad oblast Party Committee, Borovichi, 19 December 1942. TsGAIPD SPb: Fond 24, op. 20, delo 52.

34 NKVD reports of 5 August, 5 September and 6 October 1942, Nikita Lomagin, *Neizvestnaya blokada*, vol. 2, docs 78, 79, 80, pp. 328–39.

35 Vasili Chekrizov, 'Dnevnik blokadnogo vremeni', *Trudy Gosudarstvennogo Muzeya Istorii Sankt-Peterburga*, vol. 8, pp. 87, 97–8, 102 (29 June, 26 August and 21 September 1942).

36 Inber, *Leningrad Diary*, pp. 110–11 (16 September 1942).

37 Olga Grechina, 'Spasayus spasaya chast 2: skazka o gorokhovom dereve (1942–1944 gg.)', *Neva*, 2, 1994, p. 212. See also Lazarev, 'Vospominaniya o blokade', pp. 213–14, 216, and Adamovich and Granin, *A Book of the Blockade*, pp. 111–12.

38 Anna Ostroumova-Lebedeva, *Avtobiograficheskiye zapiski: Leningrad v blokade*, pp. 280, 295 (17 April and 24 September 1942).

39 Dmitri Likhachev, *Reflections on the Russian Soul*, pp. 256–7.

40 City statistics department, 5 October 1942, in Dzeniskevich, ed., *Leningrad v osade*, doc. 148, p. 313; Bidlack, *Workers at War*, p. 27.

41 Inber, *Leningrad Diary*, p. 101 (7 August 1942).

42 Mossman, ed., *The Correspondence of Boris Pasternak and Olga Freidenberg, 1910–1954*, pp. 222, 225.

43 Dzeniskevich, ed., *Leningrad v osade*, doc. 67, pp. 160–61.

44 Pavel Gubchevsky, in Norman, *The Hermitage*, p. 257.

45 Chekrizov, 'Dnevnik blokadnogo vremeni', pp. 94–5 (10 August 1942).

46 Lidiya Ginzburg, *Blockade Diary*, pp. 37, 105. NKVD reports to Beria and

Zhdanov, in Lomagin, *Neizvestnaya blokada*, vol. 2, docs 80 and 86, pp. 336, 353.

47 Ostroumova-Lebedeva, *Avtobiograficheskiye zapiski*, p. 286 (24 and 30 May 1942).

48 Olga Berggolts, 'Dnevnye zvezdy', *Ogonyok*, 19, 5 May 1990, p. 16.

49 See for example Aleksandr Boldyrev, *Osadnaya zapis: blokadniy dnevnik*, p. 191, 28 October 1942. See also Aleksei Vinokurov, in *Arkhiv Bolshogo Doma: blokadniye dnevniki i dokumenty*, p. 266 (17 June 1942).

50 Olga Berggolts, 'Iz dnevnikov', *Zvezda*, 6, 1990, p. 166 (2 July 1942).

51 Lazarev, 'Vospominaniya o blokade', p. 218 (December 1942); Vasilisa Malysheva, 23 July–7 August 1942; RGALI: Fond 2733, op. 1, yed. khr. 872, p. 160.

52 Dmitri Lazarev, 'Vospominaniya o blokade', pp. 215–16. Similar rhymes of the time are given in O. E. Molkina, 'Nemtsy v koltsye blokady', *Istoriya Peterburga*, 3, pp. 62–4.

53 Boldyrev, *Osadnaya zapis: blokadniy dnevnik*, pp. 148, 164–5 (28 August and 22 September 1942). The NKVD put it another way. Factory managers should stop sending their weakest, least skilled employees to cut logs, a report to Zhdanov of 9 January 1942 complained, because they failed to fulfil their norms and 'sat idly about' (TsGAIPD SPb: Fond 24, op. 2v). For another description of conscription to a peatworks see Valentina Bushueva, in Cynthia Simmons and Nina Perlina, eds, *Writing the Siege: Women's Diaries, Memoirs and Documentary Prose*, pp. 136–7.

CHAPTER 20: THE LENINGRAD SYMPHONY

1 BBC Written Archives Centre: E1/1270 Countries: Russia – Material for Use in Programmes, file 1, 1941–43.

2 Aleksandr Rubashkin, *Golos Leningrada: Leningradskoye Radio v dni blokady*, p. 173.

3 BBC Written Archives Centre: E1/1281 Countries: Russia; Russian Service (Policy) file 1, 1939–44.

4 Dmitri Shostakovich, *Story of a Friendship: The Letters of Dmitry Shostakovich to Isaak Glikman, 1941–1975*, p. xxxiv.

5 Solomon Volkov, *St Petersburg: A Cultural History*, p. 429.

6 Ibid., p. 433.

7 Olga Berggolts, 'Iz dnevnikov', *Zvezda*, 6, 1990, p. 153 (29 March 1942).

8 Alexander Werth, *Russia at War, 1941–1945*, p. 272.

9 BBC Written Archives Centre: R46/297: Leningrad Symphony 1942–44.

10 Solomon Volkov, ed., *Testimony: The Memoirs of Dmitri Shostakovich*, pp. 17, 104–6.

11 Berggolts, 'Iz dnevnikov', *Zvezda*, 4, April 1991, p. 140 (7 February 1942).

12 Kseniya Matus, in Simmons and Perlina, eds, *Writing the Siege of Leningrad: Women's Diaries, Memoirs and Documentary Prose*, p. 149. See also Rubashkin, *Golos Leningrada*, pp. 163–73.

13 Harlow Robinson, 'Composing for Victory', in Richard Stites, ed., *Culture and Entertainment in Wartime Russia*, p. 71; Volkov, *St Petersburg*, p. 442.

14 Vera Inber, *Leningrad Diary*, p. 102 (9 August 1942).

15 Volkov, ed., *Testimony*, p. 118.

16 Nadezhda Cherepenina, 'Assessing the Scale of Famine and Death in the Besieged City', in John Barber and Andrei Dzeniskevich, eds, *Life and Death in Besieged Leningrad 1941–44*, p. 36.

17 Stanislav Kotov, *Detskiye doma blokadnogo Leningrada*, p. 20.

18 Galina Vishnevskaya, *Galina: A Russian Story*, New York, 1984, pp. 30–35. Vishnevskaya went on to become one of Russia's greatest lyric sopranos. She and her husband, the cellist Mstislav Rostropovich, defected to the West in the late 1960s, having courted official disfavour by befriending Solzhenitsyn. Their collection of Russian art, purchased by a Russian steel magnate in 2007, is currently on public display in St Petersburg.

19 Kotov, *Detskiye doma blokadnogo Leningrada*, p. 86.

20 Report by the City Executive Committee to Kosygin, 28 July 1942, in Dzeniskevich, ed., *Leningrad v osade*, doc. 154, p. 344. See also Kotov, *Detskiye doma blokadnogo Leningrada*, p. 149.

21 Kotov, *Detskiye doma blokadnogo Leningrada*, pp. 78–84.

22 Interviewed by the author, Vsevolozhsk, November 2006.

23 James Clapperton, *The Siege of Leningrad and the Ambivalence of the Sacred: Conversations with Survivors*, Ph.D. thesis, University of Edinburgh, 2006, p. 393; Adamovich and Granin, *A Book of the Blockade*, pp. 179–80.

24 Clapperton, *Siege of Leningrad*, p. 120.

25 Inber, *Leningrad Diary*, pp. 148–9 (28 May 1943).

26 Moskoff, *The Bread of Affliction*, p. 201, quoting an article from *The Times*, 5 January 1944.

27 Adamovich and Granin, *A Book of the Blockade*, p. 183.

28 Olga Grechina, 'Spasayus spasaya chast 1: pogibelnaya zima (1941–1942 gg.)', *Neva*, 1, 1994, p. 281.

29 Grechina, 'Spasayus spasaya chast 2: skazka o gorokhovom dereve (1942–1944 gg.)', *Neva*, 2, 1994, p. 219 (11 May 1943).

Chapter 21: The Last Year

1 Führer Directive no. 41, 5 April 1942, Hugh Trevor-Roper, ed., *Hitler's War Directives 1939–1945*, pp. 116–17.

2 Führer Directive no. 44, 21 July 1942, ibid., p. 127. 'Heavy Gustav', which could fling a seven-tonne shell twenty-three miles, needed its own cranes and tracks and took a dedicated 1,420-strong team up to six weeks to assemble and disassemble. Though transported to within thirty kilometres of Leningrad before *Nordlicht* was called off, it was only ever used at Sevastopol, where it was fired forty-eight times in total. One of its shells is on display in London's Imperial War Museum.

3 Hugh Trevor-Roper, ed., *Hitler's Table Talk, 1941–44*, p. 617 (6 August 1942).

4 Gitta Sereny, *Albert Speer: His Battle with Truth*, p. 363.

5 Fritz Hockenjos, typescript, Bundesarchiv/Militärarchiv: MSG 2/4034–4038 (28 February 1943 and 31 March 1944). For more on women in the Red Army, see Catherine Merridale, *Ivan's War: The Red Army 1939-45*, pp.143–4.

6 Antony Beevor, *Stalingrad*, p. 392.

7 Vera Inber, *Leningrad Diary*, pp. 126–7 (16 January 1943).

8 Anna Ostroumova-Lebedeva, *Avtobiograficheskiye zapiski: Leningrad v blokade* (28 January 1943).

9 Dmitri Lazarev, 'Vospominaniya o blokade', *Trudy Gosudarstvennogo Muzeya Istorii Sankt-Peterburga*, vol. 5, p. 219 (18 January 1943).

10 G. F. Krivosheyev, ed., *Rossiya i SSSR v voinakh XX veka: poteri vooruzhyonnykh sil*, p. 283; Harrison Salisbury, *The 900 Days: The Siege of Leningrad*, p. 549.

11 Hockenjos, typescript, Bundesarchiv/Militärarchiv, p. 10 (11 August 1942).

12 Mariya Mashkova, 'Iz blokadnykh zapisei', in *V pamyat ushedshikh i vo slavu zhivushchikh: dnevniki, vospominaniye, pisma*, pp. 82–126 (February–May 1943).

13 Air-defence dept report, in Andrei Dzeniskevich, ed., *Leningrad v osade: sbornik dokumentov*, attachment to doc. 169, p. 398.

14 For more detail see David Glantz, *The Battle for Leningrad, 1941–1944*, p. 130.

15 Mashkova, 'Iz blokadnykh zapisei', p. 132 (8 August 1943).

16 Vasili Chekrizov, 'Dnevnik blokadnogo vremeni', *Trudy Gosudarstvennogo Muzeya Istorii Sankt-Peterburga*, vol. 8, p. 141 (18 April 1943). Altogether 186 factories were now working again, compared to 368 pre-war. About 80 per cent of factory workers were semi-skilled women aged under twenty-four. (Richard Bidlack, *Workers at War: Factory Workers and Labor Policy in the Siege of Leningrad*, Carl Beck Papers, 902, pp. 32–3.)

17 Chekrizov, 'Dnevnik blokadnogo vremeni', p. 145 (18 July 1943).

18 Aleksandr Rubashkin, *Golos Leningrada: Leningradskoye Radio v dni blokady*, p. 195.

19 Marina Starodubtseva (née Yerukhmanova), *Krugovorot (vremena i sudby)*, typescript held by the memoirist's family, p. 550.

20 Hockenjos, typescript, Bundesarchiv/Militärarchiv, p. 45 (16 January 1943).

21 Report by the head of the Leningrad oblast partisan organisation, M. Nikitin, to Stalin, in Nikita Lomagin, *Neizvestnaya blokada*, vol. 2, appendix 5, doc. 2, p. 430; Hockenjos, typescript, Bundesarchiv/Militärarchiv, p. 130 (25 November 1943).

22 RGASPI: Fond 269, op. 1, yed. khr. 30.

23 Walther Kulik (4 December 1943). RGASPI: Fond 269, op. 1, yed. khr. 29.

24 Gerhard Buss, taken prisoner 14 January 1944. RGASPI: Fond 269, op. 1, yed. khr. 29.

25 RGASPI: Fond 269, op. 1, yed. khr. 30.

26 Elliott Mossman, ed., *The Correspondence of Boris Pasternak and Olga Freidenberg, 1910–1954*, p. 234.

27 Inber, *Leningrad Diary*, pp. 179–82 (15, 22, 27 and 28 January 1944). See also Alexander Werth, *Leningrad*, p. 187.

PART 5. AFTERMATH

CHAPTER 22: COMING HOME

1 Vasili Churkin, *Voyennaya literatura: dnevniki i pisma*, http://militera.lib.ru/db/churkin, pp. 8–9 (4 April 1944).

2 David Glantz, *The Battle for Leningrad, 1941–1944*, p. 413.

3 Fritz Hockenjos, Bundesarchiv-Militärarchiv: MGS2/4037, pp. 1–2, 37 (16 January and 12 March 1944).

4 Ibid., p. 24 (14 February 1944).

5 Irina Ivanova, née Bogdanova, interview with the author, Vsevolozhsk, November 2006.

6 Olga Grechina, 'Spasayus spasaya chast 2: skazka o gorokhovom derive (1942–1944 gg.)', *Neva*, 2, 1994, p. 246.

7 Elliott Mossman, ed., *The Correspondence of Boris Pasternak and Olga Freidenberg, 1910–1954*, pp. 237–8.

8 Yelena Kozhina, *Through the Burning Steppe: A Wartime Memoir*, p. 145; Vera Inber, *Leningrad Diary*, p. 178 (12 January 1944).

9 Lev Kopelev, *No Jail for Thought*, pp. 6, 93, 99, 101–4, 134.

10 Vasili Churkin, letter of 2 June 1944. In *Voyennaya literatura: dnevniki i pisma*, http://militera. lib. ru/db/Churkin_part4, p. 13

11 Andrei Dzeniskevich, ed., *Leningrad v osade: sbornik dokumentov*, doc. 226, p. 562.

12 See Dmitri Likhachev, *Reflections on the Russian Soul: A Memoir*, p. 256; Ales Adamovich and Daniil Granin, *A Book of the Blockade*, p. 464; and Yelizaveta Muravyeva, interviewee no. 10, European University at St Petersburg Oral History Project, 'Blokada v sudbakh i pamyati leningradtsev'.

13 Anna Zelenova, *Stati, vospominaniya, pisma: Pavlovsky dvorets, istoriya i sudba*, p. 115.

14 See Catherine Scott-Clark and Adrian Levy, *The Amber Room: The Fate of the World's Greatest Lost Treasure*, New York, 2004.

15 Alexander Werth, *Leningrad*, pp. 188–9; Harrison Salisbury, *The 900 Days: The Siege of Leningrad*, p. 567.

16 Vera Inber, *Leningrad Diary*, p. 203 (29 May 1944).

17 A. Z. Vakser, 'Nastroyeniya leningradtsev poslevoyennogo vremeni 1945–1953 gody', *Nestor*, no. 1 (5), p. 311.

18 Werth, *Leningrad*, pp. 125, 167. He made two visits to Leningrad, in September 1943 and February 1944. For more on the rumour that Leningrad might become the capital again, see Harrison Salisbury, *Disturber of the Peace: Memoirs of a Foreign Correspondent*, p. 96.

19 NKGB report of 14 March 1945, in Nikita Lomagin, *Neizvestnaya blokada*, vol. 2, doc. 17, p. 62.

20 'They Felt the Pangs of Hunger but Survived the Cruel Siege', *St Petersburg Times*, 27 January 2004.

21 Lisa A. Kirschenbaum, *The Legacy of the Siege of Leningrad, 1941–1995: Myth, Memories, and Monuments*, p. 141.

22 Cynthia Simmons and Nina Perlina, eds, *Writing the Siege of Leningrad: Women's Diaries, Memoirs and Documentary Prose*, pp. 71–4, 76.

23 Roberta Reeder, *Anna Akhmatova: Poet and Prophet*, pp. 289–93.

24 Solomon Volkov, *St Petersburg: A Cultural History*, p. 450.

25 Reeder, *Anna Akhmatova*, p. 293.

26 Richard Bidlack, 'Ideological or Political Origins of the Leningrad Affair? A Response to David Brandenberger', *The Russian Review*, 64/1 (January 2005), p. 94.

27 Yoram Gorlizki and Oleg Khlevniuk, *Cold Peace: Stalin and the Soviet Ruling Circle, 1945–1953*, Oxford, 2004, p. 86.

28 In his memoirs Khrushchev admits that he 'may have signed the sentencing order. In those days when a case was closed – and if Stalin thought it necessary – he would sign the sentencing order at a Politburo session and then pass

it round for the rest of us to sign. We would put our signatures to it without even looking at it.'

29 Simon Sebag Montefiore, *Stalin: The Court of the Red Tsar*, p. 540.
30 For a vivid description of the Yugoslav visit and Stalin's decline, see Milovan Djilas, *Conversations with Stalin*, pp. 136–53.
31 Volkov, *St Petersburg*, p. 454.
32 B. Kostyrchenko, *Tainaya politika Stalina*, Moscow, 2001, p. 234. Quoted in Donald Rayfield, *Stalin and His Hangmen*, p. 245.
33 Reeder, *Anna Akhmatova*, p. 304; Elliott Mossman, ed., *The Correspondence of Boris Pasternak and Olga Freidenberg, 1910–1954*, pp. 303–4.
34 Sidney Monas and Jennifer Greene Krupala, eds, *The Diaries of Nikolay Punin, 1904–53*, pp. 212–13, 219.
35 Likhachev, *Reflections on the Russian Soul*, p. 255.

CHAPTER 23: THE CELLAR OF MEMORY

1 For an analysis of the cult of the Great Patriotic War in relation to Leningrad, see Chapter 6 of Lisa Kirschenbaum, *The Legacy of the Siege of Leningrad, 1941–1995: Myth, Memories, and Monuments*.
2 See for example A. J. P. Taylor in the *New York Review of Books*, 10 April 1969.
3 Solomon Volkov, *St Petersburg: A Cultural History*, p. xvi.
4 For a detailed account of the debate, see ibid., pp. 542–5.
5 Cynthia Simmons and Nina Perlina, eds, *Writing the Siege: Women's Diaries, Memoirs and Documentary Prose*, p. 109.
6 Ibid., p. 206.
7 Valentina Stolbova and Aelita Vostrova, interviewees nos 12 and 17, European University at St Petersburg Oral History Project, 'Blokada v sudbakh i pamyati leningradtsev'.
8 Simmons and Perlina, eds, *Writing the Siege*, p. 109. For more on the tensions between old residents and new, see Siobhan Peeling, 'Dirt, disease and disorder: population re-placement in postwar Leningrad and the "danger" of social contamination', in Nick Baron and Peter Gatrell, eds, *Warlands: Population Resettlement and State Reconstruction in Soviet Eastern Europe, 1945–1950*.
9 Mariya Berggolts, commentary to Olga Berggolts, 'Blokadniy dnevnik', *Zvezda*, 3, April 1991, p. 144.

Bibliography

Adamovich, Ales, and Daniil Granin, *Blokadnaya Kniga*, Leningrad, 1989. Published in English as *A Book of the Blockade*, trans. Hilda Perham, Moscow, 1983.

— 'Blokadnaya kniga: Glavy, kotorykh v knige ne bylo', *Zvezda*, 5–6, 1992, p. 8.

Akhmatova, Anna, *Selected Poems*, trans. Richard McKane, London, 1989.

— *Selected Poems*, trans. Stanley Kunitz and Max Hayward, London, 1989.

Alshits, Daniil, 'Istorizm i antiistorizm – ikh rol i znacheniye v sovremennoi nauke, politike i kulture', in *Istoriya Rossii: issledovaniya i razmyshleniya – sbornik statei k 90-letiyu so dnya rozhdeniya doktora istoricheskikh nauk Valentina Mikhailovicha Kovalchuka*, St Petersburg, 2006.

Antonov, A. N., 'Children born during the Siege of Leningrad in 1942', *Journal of Paediatrics*, 1947, pp. 250–59.

Applebaum, Anne, *Gulag: A History of the Soviet Camps*, London, 2003.

Ardov, Revd Michael, ed., *Memories of Shostakovich: Interviews with the Composer's Children*, trans. Rosanna Kelly and Michael Meylac, London, 2004.

Arutyunyan, Brezh, and Arkadi Burlakov, 'Nekotorye voprosy istoriografii boyevykh deistviy v bitve za Leningrad', in E. V. Ilyin, ed., *Bitva za Leningrad: problemy sovremennykh issledovaniy*, St Petersburg, 2007.

Bagiyan, G. A., *Gatchina: goryachaya osen sorok pervogo*, Gatchina, 2005.

Bakhareva, Yu. Yu., and T. V. Kovaleva, eds, *Arkhitektory blokadnogo Leningrada* (exhibition catalogue, Gosudarstvenniy Muzei Istorii Sankt-Peterburga), St Petersburg, 2005.

Barber, John, and Andrei Dzeniskevich, eds, *Zhizn i smert v blokirovannom Leningrade: istoriko-meditsinskiy aspekt*, St Petersburg, 2001. Published in English as *Life and Death in Besieged Leningrad, 1941–44*, New York, 2005.

Barber, John and Mark Harrison, eds, *The Soviet Home Front 1941–1945: A Social and Economic History of the USSR in World War II*, London, 1991.

Beaumont, Joan, *Comrades in Arms: British Aid to Russia 1941–1945*, London, 1980.

Beevor, Antony, *Stalingrad*, London, 1998.

— *Berlin: The Downfall 1945*, London, 2002.

Berggolts, Olga, *Govorit Leningrad*, Leningrad, 1945.

— 'Iz dnevnikov Olgi Berggolts', *Vremya i my*, 6, 57 (1980), p. 270 (covers September 1941–October 1949).

— 'Dnevnye zvezdy', *Ogonyok*, 19 (5 May 1990), p. 16.

— 'Iz dnevnikov', *Zvezda*, 6 (1990), p. 153 (covers March–August 1942).

— 'Ob etikh tetradyakh', *Zvezda*, 5 (1990), p. 180 (covers July 1939–March 1942).

— 'Blokadniy dnevnik', *Aprel*, 4 (1991), p. 128 (covers September 1941–February 1942).

— *Olga: Zapretniy dnevnik*, St Petersburg, 2010.

— *Pamyat: stikhotvoreniya, poemy, proza*, St Petersburg, 2010 (includes 'Fevralskiy dnevnik' and 'Dnevnye zvezdy').

Bernev, Stanislav, and Sergei Chernov, eds, *Arkhiv Bolshogo Doma: blokadniye dnevniki i dokumenty*, St Petersburg, 2004.

Bidlack, Richard, *Workers at War: Factory Workers and Labor Policy in the Siege of Leningrad*, The Carl Beck Papers in Russian and East European Studies, 902, Pittsburgh, 1991.

— 'The Political Mood in Leningrad during the First Year of the Soviet-German War', *The Russian Review*, 59 (January 2000), p. 96.

— 'Survival Strategies in Leningrad during the First Year of the Soviet-German War', in Robert Thurston and Bernd Bonwetsch, eds, *The People's War: Responses to World War Two in the Soviet Union*, Urbana, 2000.

Bitva za zhizn: materialy nauchno-prakticheskoi konferentsii, posvyashchennoi 65-letiyu nachala blokady Leningrada, St Petersburg, 2007.

'Blokada glazami ochevidtsev. Intervyu s zhitelyami Leningrada 1940-kh gg.', *Nestor*, 6, 2001, pp. 37–267.

Bogdanov-Berezovsky, Valerian, *V gody Velikoi Otechestvennoi Voiny*, Leningrad, 1959.

Boldyrev, Aleksandr, *Osadnaya zapis: blokadniy dnevnik*, St Petersburg, 1998.

Bonner, Elena, *Mothers and Daughters*, trans. Antonina Bonis, London, 1992.

Boterbloem, C. N., 'The Death of Andrei Zhdanov', *Slavonic and East European Review*, 80, 2 (April 2002), p. 267.

Bowlt, John, *Filonov: Khudozhnik, issledovatel, uchitel*, 2 vols, Moscow, 2006.

Braithwaite, Rodric, *Moscow 1941: A City and its People at War*, London, 2006.

Brandenberger, David, 'Stalin, the Leningrad Affair, and the Limits of Postwar Russocentrism', *The Russian Review*, 63 (April 2004), p. 241.

Brodsky, Josef, *Less Than One*, New York, 1986.

Bullard, Julian and Margaret, eds, *Inside Stalin's Russia: The Diaries of Reader Bullard 1930–1934*, Charlbury, 2000.

Bullock, Alan, *Hitler and Stalin: Parallel Lives*, London, 1991.

Burov, A. V., *Blokada den za dnem: 22 iyunya 1941–27 yanvarya 1944 goda*, Leningrad, 1979.

Chekrizov, Vasili, 'Dnevnik blokadnogo vremeni', *Trudy Gosudarstvennogo Muzeya Istorii Sankt-Peterburga*, 8 (2004).

Chernov, Sergei, Stanislav Bernev and Nikita Lomagin, eds, *Arkhiv Bolshogo Doma: Plan 'D' – plan spetsialnykh meropriyatiy, provodimykh vo vremya Otechestvennoi voiny po obshchegorodskim obyektam gor. Leningrada*, St Petersburg, 2005.

Chernov, Sergei and Stanislav Bernev, eds, *Arkhiv Bolshogo Doma: blokadnye dnevniki i dokumenty*, St Petersburg, 2007.

Chistikov, Aleksandr, ed., *Chelovek v blockade: novye svidetelstva*, St Petersburg, 2008.

Chukovskaya, Lydia, *The Akhmatova Journals*, vol. 1, *1938–41*, London, 1994.

Churchill, Winston, *The Second World War*, London, 1959.

Clapperton, James, *The Siege of Leningrad and the Ambivalence of the Sacred: Conversations with Survivors*, Ph.D. thesis, Edinburgh University, 2006.

Dale, Robert, 'Rats and Resentment: The Demobilization of the Red Army in Postwar Leningrad, 1945–50', *Journal of Contemporary History*, 45 (January 2010), p. 113.

— *Re-adjusting to Life after War: The Demobilization of Red Army Veterans in Leningrad and the Leningrad Region 1944–1950*, Ph.D. thesis, Queen Mary College, University of London, 2010.

Dallin, Alexander, *German Rule in Russia, 1941–45: A Study of Occupation Policies*, London, 1957.

Darov, Anatoly, *Blokada*, New York, 1964, originally published Nikolayev, 1943.

David, V. M., ed., *Budni podviga: blokadnaya zhizn leningradtsev v dnevnikakh, risunkakh, dokumentakh*, St Petersburg, 2007.

Dayev, Vladimir, *S distantsii poluveka: ocherki blokadnogo Leningrada*, St Petersburg, 1998.

Dickinson, Jennifer, 'Building the Blockade: New Truths in Survival Narratives from Leningrad', *Anthropology of East Europe Review*, 13, 1995, p. 21.

Djilas, Milovan, *Conversations with Stalin*, trans. Michael Petrovich, London, 1962.

Dudin, Mikhail, *Izbrannoye*, 2 vols, Moscow, 1966.

Dunham, Vera, *In Stalin's Time: Middleclass Values in Soviet Fiction*, Cambridge, 1976.

Dyson, Tim, and Corman O'Grada, *Famine Demography: Endemics from the Past and Present*, Oxford, 2002.

Dzeniskevich, Andrei, ed., *Leningrad v osade: sbornik dokumentov o geroicheskoi oborone Leningrada v gody Velikoi Otechestvennoi voiny, 1941–45*, St Petersburg, 1995.

— *Blokada i politika. Oborona Leningrada v politicheskoi konyunkture*, St Petersburg, 1998.

— *Front u zavodskikh sten: Maloizuchennye problemy oborony Leningrada (1941–1944)*, St Petersburg, 1998.

— 'Banditizm (osobaya kategoriya) v blokirovannom Leningrade', *Istoriya Peterburga*, 1, 2001.

— 'Meditsinskiy aspect blokady Leningrada', *Nestor*, 2 (8), 2005, p. 57.

— ed., *O blokade Leningrada v Rossii i za rubezhom: istochniki, issledovaniya, istoriografiya*, *Nestor*, 8, St Petersburg, 2005.

— ed., *Iz raionov oblasti soobshchayut ... Svobodnye ot okkupatsii raiony Leningradskoi oblasti v gody Velikoi Otechestvennoi voiny 1941–1945: sbornik dokumentov*, St Petersburg, 2006.

— 'The Social and Political Situation in Leningrad in the First Months of the German Invasion: The Social Psychology of the Workers', in Robert Thurston and Bernd Bonwetsch, eds, *The People's War: Responses to World War Two in the Soviet Union*, Urbana, 2000.

Ehrenburg, Ilya, *Men – Years – Life*, vol. 5, *The War Years 1941–1945*, trans. Tatiana Shebunina, London, 1964.

Erickson, John, *The Road to Stalingrad: Stalin's War with Germany*, vol. 1, London, 1975.

— *The Road to Berlin: Stalin's War with Germany*, vol. 2, London, 1983.

— *The Soviet High Command: A Military-Political History*, London, 2001.

'Ermitazh v gody Velikoi Otechestvennoi Voiny: dokumenty arkhiva Gosudarstvennogo Ermitazha', *Istoriya Peterburga*, 2, 2005, p. 71.

Fadeyev, Aleksandr, *Leningrad in the Days of the Blockade*, Westport, 1971.

— *Aleksandr Fadeyev – pisma i dokumenty: iz fondov Rossiiskogo gosudarstvennogo arkhiva literatury i iskusstva*, Moscow, 2001.

— *In the Name of Kirov*, www.sovlit.com

Feinstein, Elaine, *Anna of All the Russias: The Life of Anna Akhmatova*, London, 2005.

Figes, Orlando, *Natasha's Dance: A Cultural History of Russia*, London, 2002.

— *The Whisperers: Private Life in Stalin's Russia*, London, 2007.

Filonov, Pavel, *Dnevnik: Pavel Filonov*, St Petersburg, 2000.

Fitzpatrick, Sheila, *Everyday Stalinism: Ordinary Life in Extraordinary Times –*
Soviet Russia in the 1930s, New York, 1999.

Fridenberg, Olga, 'Osada cheloveka', *Minuvsheye,* 3, Paris, 1987, pp. 20–21.

–– *The Correspondence of Boris Pasternak and Olga Freidenberg, 1910–145,*
ed Elliott Mossman, London, 1982.

Ganzenmüller, Jörg, *Das belagerte Leningrad 1941–1944: Die Stadt in den Strategien*
von Angreifern und Verteidigern, Paderborn, 2005.

Garshin, Vladimir, 'Tam, gde smert pomogayet zhizni', in *Iz istorii meditsiny,*
Riga, 1960, and *Arkhiv Patologii,* 46, 5 (1984).

Gavrilov, V. I., *Dolina smerti: tragediya i podvig 2-y Udarnoi Armii,* Moscow, 2006.

Ginzburg, Lidiya, *Chelovek za pismennym stolom,* Leningrad, 1989.

–– *Blockade Diary,* trans. Alan Myers, London, 1995.

–– *Zapisnye knizhki, vospominaniya, esse,* St Petersburg, 2002.

Gladkikh, Pavel, *Zdravookhraneniye blokadnogo Leningrada, 1941–1944 gg.,*
Leningrad, 1985.

Gladkikh, Pavel, and A. E. Loktev, *Ocherki istorii otechestvennoi voyennoi meditsiny.*
Sluzhba zdorovya v Velikoi Otechestvennoi Voine 1941–1945 gg., St Petersburg, 2005.

Glantz, David, *Barbarossa: Hitler's Invasion of Russia 1941,* Stroud, 2001.

–– *The Battle for Leningrad, 1941–1944,* Lawrence, 2002.

–– *Colossus Reborn: The Red Army at War 1941–1943,* Lawrence, 2005.

Glinka, M. S., ed., *V. M. Glinka: vospominaniya, arkhivy, pisma,* 2 vols, St
Petersburg, 2006.

Gloster, V. I., 'Towards the History of Daniil Kharms's Last Arrest and Death',
Russkaya Literatura, 1, 1991.

Golovina, T. I., and N. N. Zozulina, eds, *Vspominaya vnov . . . sbornik,* St Petersburg,
2004 (published by the Akademiya Russkogo Baleta imeni A. Ya. Vaganovoi).

Golubeva, T. M., and N. B. Vetoshnikova, eds, *Mediki i blokada: vzglyad skvoz*
gody – vospominaniya, fragmenty dnevnikov, svidetelstva ochevidtsev, dokumental-
nye materialy, St Petersburg, 1997.

Gorlizki, Yoram, and Oleg Khlevniuk, *Cold Peace: Stalin and the Soviet Ruling*
Circle 1945–1953, Oxford, 2004.

Gorshkov, Nikolai, 'Blokadniy dnevnik', in Stanislav Bernev and Sergei Chernov,
eds, *Arkhiv Bolshogo Doma: blokadniye dnevniki i dokumenty,* St Petersburg,
2004.

Gotkhart, Sofya, 'Leningrad, blokada', in V. L. Vikhnovina, ed., *Dve sudby v*
Velikoi Otechestvennoi voine, St Petersburg, 2006.

Gouré, Leon, *The Siege of Leningrad,* Stanford, 1962.

Grechina, Olga, 'Spasayus spasaya chast 1: pogibelnaya zima (1941–1942 gg.)',
Neva, 1, 1994.

— 'Spasayus spasaya chast 2: skazka o gorokhovom dereve (1942–1944 gg.)', *Neva*, 2, 1994.

Grigoryev, V. G., *Leningrad blokada 1941–1942: vospominaniya byvshego shkolnika blokirovannogo Leningrada*, St Petersburg, 2003.

Grossman, Vasily, *Life and Fate*, trans. Robert Chandler, London 1995.

— *Everything Flows*, trans. Robert and Elizabeth Chandler, London, 2009.

— *A Writer at War: Vasily Grossman with the Red Army 1941–1945*, ed. Antony Beevor and Lyuba Vinogradova, London, 2005.

Halder, Franz, *The Halder War Diary, 1939–1942*, ed. Charles Burdick and Hans-Adolf Jacobsen, London, 1988.

Hodgson, Katharine, *Voicing the Soviet Experience: The Poetry of Olga Berggolts*, Oxford, 2003.

Ignatieff, Michael, *Isaiah Berlin: A Life*, London, 1998.

Ilyin, E. V., ed., *Bitva za Leningrad: problemy sovremennykh issledovaniy*, St Petersburg, 2007.

Inber, Vera, *Izbrannaya proza*, Moscow, 1952.

— *Leningrad Diary*, trans. Serge Wolff and Rachel Grieve, London, 1971, first published as *Pochti tri goda*, Moscow, 1946.

— *Dusha Leningrada: stikhi*, Leningrad, 1979.

Ivanov, V. A., 'Reaktsiya Leningradtsev na chrezvychainye usloviya osady . . .', *Nestor*, 2005, 2 (8), 2006, p. 102.

Ivanova, I. A., ed., *Tragediya Myasnogo Bora: sbornik vospominanii uchastnikov i ochevidtsev Lyubanskoi operatsii*, St Petersburg, 2005.

— *Za blokadnym koltsom: sbornik vospominanii zhitelei Leningradskoi oblasti vremen germanskoi okkupatsii 1941–1944 gg.*, St Petersburg, 2007.

Jahn, Peter, ed., *Blockades Leningrads: Dossiers 1941–1944* (exhibition catalogue, Museum Berlin-Karlshorst), Berlin, 2004.

Jones, Michael, *Leningrad: State of Siege*, London, 2008.

Ketlinskaya, Vera, 'Nastya', in *Den prozhitiy dvazhdy*, Moscow, 1964.

Kharms, Daniil, 'The Old Woman', in *Russian Short Stories from Pushkin to Buida*, trans. Robert Chandler, London, 2005.

— *Incidences*, trans. Neil Cornwell, London, 2006.

Khordikainen, Lyusi, *Zhizn v okkupatsii. Pushkin, Gatchina, Estoniya: dnevnik Lyusi Khordikainen*, St Petersburg, 1999.

Kirby, David, *A Concise History of Finland*, Cambridge, 2006.

Kirschenbaum, Lisa A., 'Gender, Memory and National Myths: Olga Berggolts and the Siege of Leningrad', *Nationalities Papers*, vol. 28, 3 (September 2000), p. 551.

— *The Legacy of the Siege of Leningrad, 1941–1995: Myth, Memories, and Monuments*, Cambridge, 2006.

Kleinfeld, Gerald, and Lewis Tambs, *Hitler's Spanish Legion: The Blue Division in Russia*, Carbondale, 1979.

Kochina, Yelena, *Blockade Diary*, trans. Samuel Ramer, Ann Arbor, 1990.

Kopelev, Lev, *No Jail for Thought*, trans. Anthony Austin, London, 1977.

Korkonosenko, Nataliya, 'Blokadnitsy', *Leningradskaya panorama*, 8 (1991), p. 28.

Kosogor, O. N., A. A. Melua and S. K. Yegorov, eds, *Zhenshchina i voina: o roli zhenshchin v oborone Leningrada 1941–1945 – sbornik statei*, St Petersburg, 2006.

Kotov, A. V., 'Legendarniy "Nevsky Pyatachok"', *Znaniye i obshchestvo*, 718 (2004), p. 66.

Kotov, Stanislav, *Detskiye doma blokadnogo Leningrada*, St Petersburg, 2002.

Kovalchuk, V. M., A. I. Rupasov and A. N. Chistikov, eds, *Dozhivyom li my do tishiny? zapiski iz blokadnogo Leningrada*, St Petersburg, 2009.

— '*Ya ne sdamsya do poslednego . . .' zapiski iz blokadnogo Leningrada*, St Petersburg, 2010.

Kovalenko, S. A., ed., *Anna Akhmatova: sobraniye sochineniy v shesti tomakh*, Moscow, 1998–2005.

Kozhina, Yelena, *Through the Burning Steppe: A Wartime Memoir*, trans. Vadim Mahmoudov, London, 2000.

Kozlova, Nataliya, ed., *Sovetskiye lyudi: stseny iz istorii*, Moscow, 2005.

Krammer, Arnold, 'Spanish Volunteers against Bolshevism: The Blue Division', *The Russian Review*, 32, 4 (October 1973), p. 388.

Krivosheyev, G. F., ed., *Rossiya i SSSR v voinakh XX veka: poteri vooruzhyonnykh sil – statisticheskoye issledovaniye*, Moscow, 2001.

Kryukovskikh, A. P., *Leningradskoye opolcheniye*, St Petersburg, 2006.

— 'Podvig opolcheniya', in *Istoriya Rossii: issledovaniya i razmyshleniya – sbornik statei k 90-letiyu so dnya rozhdeniya doktora istoricheskikh nauk Valentina Mikhailovicha Kovalchuka*, St Petersburg, 2006.

Kuchumov, A. M., *Pavlovsky dvorets: istoriya i sudby*, St Petersburg, 2004.

Kulyabko, Vladimir, 'Blokadniy dnevnik', *Neva*, 1, 2004, p. 210 (covers 9–20 September 1941).

— *Neva*, 2, 2004, p. 235 (covers 30 September 1941–14 January 1942).

— *Neva*, 3, 2004, p. 262 (covers 31 January–12 March 1942).

Kuznetsov, Admiral Nikolai, *Na kanune*, Moscow, 1989.

Lazarev, Dmitri, 'Vospominaniya o blokade D. N. Lazareva, N. V. Lazarevoi and E. D. Yakubovich', *Trudy Gosudarstvennogo Muzeya Istorii Sankt-Peterburga*, 5 (2000).

Liddell Hart, Basil, *The Other Side of the Hill: Germany's Generals, Their Rise and Fall*, London, 1948.

Likhachev, Dmitri, 'Kak my ostalis zhivy', *Neva*, 1, 1991, p. 15.

— *Reflections on the Russian Soul: A Memoir*, trans. Bernard Adams, Budapest, 2000.

Likhonov, M. I., L. T. Pozina and E. I. Finogenov, *Partiinoye rukovodstvo evakuatsiei v perviy period Velikoi Otechestvennoi Voiny 1941–2*, Leningrad, 1985.

Lomagin, Nikita, *Soldiers at War: German Propaganda and Soviet Army Morale during the Battle of Leningrad, 1941–44*, The Carl Beck Papers in Russian and East European Studies, 1306, Pittsburgh, 1998.

— *V tiskakh goloda: blokada Leningrada v dokumentakh germanskikh spetssluzhb, NKVD*, St Petersburg, 2000.

— *Neizvestnaya blokada*, 2 vols, St Petersburg, 2004 (document collection and commentary).

— 'Nastroyeniya leningradtsev v zerkale politicheskogo kontrolya v preddverii napadeniya Germanii na SSSR', in E.V. Ilyin, ed., *Bitva za Leningrad: problemy sovremennykh issledovaniy*, St Petersburg, 2007.

Loskutova, M. V., ed., *Pamyat o blokade: svidetelstva ochevidtsev i istoricheskoye soznaniye obshchestva – materialy i issledovaniya*, St Petersburg, 2005.

Lovyagina, V. E., ed., *Blokadniy dnevnik: zhivopis i grafika blokadnogo vremeni* (exhibition catalogue, Gosudarstvenniy Muzei Istorii Sankt-Peterburga), St Petersburg, 2005.

Lukacs, John, *June 1941: Hitler and Stalin*, New Haven, 2006.

Luukkanen, Eino, *Fighter over Finland*, trans. Mauno A. Salo, London, 1963.

Malaparte, Curzio, *The Volga Rises in Europe*, trans. David Moore, London, 1957.

Mashkova, Mariya, 'Iz blokadnykh zapisei', in *V pamyat ushedshikh i vo slavu zhivushchikh: pisma chitatelei s fronta; dnevniki i vospominaniya sotrudnikov Publichnoi Biblioteki 1941–1945*, St Petersburg, 1995.

Maslova, A. N., ed., *Publichnaya Biblioteka v gody voiny, 1941–1945*, St Petersburg, 2005.

Massie, Suzanne, *Pavlovsk: The Life of a Russian Palace*, Boston, 1990.

Mawdsley, Evan, *Thunder in the East: the Nazi-Soviet War 1941–1945*, London, 2007.

Mazower, Mark, *Hitler's Empire: Nazi Rule in Occupied Europe*, London, 2008.

Melnik, G. S., and G. V. Zhirkov, eds. *Radio, blokada, Leningrad*, St Petersburg, 2005.

Meretskov, Marshal Kirill, *Serving the People*, Moscow, 1971.

— *Nekolebimo, kak Rossiya*, Moscow, 1965.

Merridale, Catherine, *Night of Stone: Death and Memory in Russia*, London, 2000.

— *Ivan's War: The Red Army 1939–45*, London, 2005.

Molkina, O. I., 'Nemtsy v koltse blokady', *Istoriya Peterburga*, 3, 2006.

Moreno Juliá, Xavier, *La División Azul: Sangre Española en Rusia, 1941–1945*, Barcelona, 2006.

Moskoff, William, *The Bread of Affliction: The Food Supply in the USSR during World War II*, Cambridge, 1990.

Mossman, Elliott, ed., *The Correspondence of Boris Pasternak and Olga Freidenberg, 1910–1954*, trans. Elliott Mossman and Margaret Wetlin, London, 1982.

Munting, Roger, 'Soviet Food Supply and Allied Aid in the War, 1941–1945', *Soviet Studies*, 36, 4 (October 1984), p. 582.

Neratova, Rimma, 'Zhizn v leningradskoi blokade', *Zvezda* (1996).

Nicholas, Lynn, *The Rape of Europe: The Fate of Europe's Treasures in the Third Reich and the Second World War*, London, 1994.

Nikitin, Vladimir, ed., *Neizvestnaya blokada/Unknown Blockade. Leningrad 1941–1944*, St Petersburg, 2009.

Nikulin, N. N., *Vospominaniya o voine*, St Petersburg, 2008.

Nikulin, Yuri, 'Zapiski soldata', *Zvezda*, 6, 2001, p. 108.

Norman, Geraldine, *The Hermitage: The Biography of a Great Museum*, London, 1997.

Osipova, Lidiya, 'Dnevnik o zhizni v prigorodakh Leningrada', in Lomagin, *Neizvestnaya blokada*, vol. 2, St Petersburg, 2004, p. 441.

Ostroumova-Lebedeva, Anna, *Avtobiograficheskiye zapiski: Leningrad v blockade*, Moscow, 2003.

Overy, Richard, *Russia's War*, London, 1998.

Pavlov, Dmitri, *Leningrad 1941: The Blockade*, trans. John Adams, Chicago, 1965.

Peeling, Siobhan, 'Dirt, disease and disorder: population re-placement in postwar Leningrad and the "danger" of social contamination', in Nick Brown and Peter Gatrell, eds, *Warlands: Population Resettlement and State Reconstruction in Soviet Eastern Europe, 1945–1950*, London, 2009.

— *'Out of Place' in the Postwar City: Practices, Experiences and Representations of Displacement during the Resettlement of Leningrad at the end of the Blockade*, Ph.D. thesis, University of Nottingham, forthcoming.

Perlina, Nina, *Olga Freidenberg's Works and Days*, Bloomington, 2002.

Peterson, Viktor, 'Skorei by bylo teplo!', *Neva*, 1, 2001, p. 167.

— 'Iz blokady – na Bolshuyu Zemlyu', *Neva*, 9, 2002, p. 152.

Pleysier, Albert, and Svetlana Magayeva, *Surviving the Blockade of Leningrad*, Lanham, 2006.

Plotkin, Konstantin, *Kholokost u sten Leningrada*, St Petersburg, 2005.

Pohlman, Hartwig, *Wolchow: 900 Tage Kampf um Leningrad*, Bad Nauheim, 1962.

Polzikova-Rubets, K. V., *Oni uchilis v Leningrade: dnevnik uchitelnitsy*, Moscow, 1948.

— *Dnevnik uchitelya blokadnoy shkoly: 1941–1946*, St Petersburg, 2000.

Punin, Nikolai, 'Dnevnik', *Zvezda*, 1, 1994 (ed. Irina Punina).

— *The Diaries of Nikolay Punin, 1904–53*, ed. Sidney Monas and Jennifer Green Krupala, Austin, 1999.

Putyakov, Semen, 'Dnevnik krasnoarmeitsa', in Stanislav Bernev and Sergei Chernov, eds, *Arkhiv Bolshogo Doma: blokadniye dnevniki i dokumenty*, St Petersburg, 2007.

Rambow, Aileen, *Überleben mit Worten: Literatur und Ideologie während der Blockade von Leningrad, 1941–1944*, Berlin, 1994.

— 'The Siege of Leningrad: Wartime Literature and Ideological Change', in Robert Thurston and Bernd Bonwetsch, eds, *The People's War: Responses to World War Two in the Soviet Union*, Urbana, 2000.

Ratner, Lazar, 'Dva blokadnykh epizoda', *Neva*, 1, 2001, p. 151.

Rayfield, Donald, *Stalin and his Hangmen*, London, 2005.

Reeder, Roberta, ed., *The Complete Poems of Anna Akhmatova*, trans. Judith Hemschemeyer, Edinburgh, 1992.

— *Anna Akhmatova: Poet and Prophet*, London, 1995.

Reznikova, Irina, (Flige), 'Repressii v period blokady Leningrada', *Vestnik 'Memoriala'* 4/5 (10/11), 1995.

Roberts, Andrew, *Masters and Commanders: How Roosevelt, Churchill, Marshall and Alanbrooke Won the War in the West*, London, 2008.

Rubashkin, Aleksandr, *Golos Leningrada: Leningradskoye Radio v dni blokady*, St Petersburg, 2005.

Salisbury, Harrison, *The 900 Days: The Siege of Leningrad*, London, 1969.

— *Disturber of the Peace: Memoirs of a Foreign Correspondent*, London, 1989.

Sebag Montefiore, Simon, *Stalin: The Court of the Red Tsar*, London, 2003.

Selivanov, V. N., *Stoyali kak soldaty: blokada, deti, Leningrad*, St Petersburg, 2002.

Selivanova, Inessa, ed., *Ryadovoi blokadnoi epopei: khudozhnik Vasili Selivanov*, St Petersburg, 2005.

Sereny, Gitta, *Albert Speer: His Battle with Truth*, London, 1995.

Shishkin, A. A., ed., *Zabveniyu ne podlezhit: statyi, vospominaniya, dokumenty*, issues 5 and 6, St Petersburg, 2005 and 2006.

Shkarovsky, M. V., 'Iskrenniy privet ot Stalina: religioznaya zhizn blokadnogo Leningrada', *Rodina*, 1, 2003.

— 'Religioznaya zhizn blokadnogo Leningrada po novym dokumentalnym istochnikam', in E. V. Ilyin, *Bitva za Leningrad: problemy sovremennykh issledovaniy*, St Petersburg, 2007.

Shostakovich, Dmitri, *Story of a Friendship: The Letters of Dmitry Shostakovich* to Isaak Glikman, 1941–1975, with a commentary by Isaak Glikman, trans. Anthony Phillips, London, 2001.

Shukman, Harold, ed., Stalin's Generals, London, 1993.

— Stalin and the Soviet-Finnish War 1939–40, London, 2002.

Shulgina, Elena, 'V dvadtsat let oni posedeli', Smena, 7, May 1995.

Shvarts, Yevgeni, Zhivu bespokoino . . . iz dnevnikov, Leningrad, 1990.

Simmons, Cynthia, and Nina Perlina, eds, Writing the Siege of Leningrad: Women's Diaries, Memoirs and Documentary Prose, Pittsburgh, 2002.

Simonenko, V. B., S. V. Magayeva, M. G. Simonenko and Yu. V. Pakhomova, Leningradskaya blokada: meditsinskiye problemy – retrospektiva i sovremennost, Moscow, 2003.

Skrjabina, Yelena, Siege and Survival: The Odyssey of a Leningrader, trans. Norman Luxenburg, Carbondale, 1971.

Smelser, Ronald, and Edward Davies, The Myth of the Eastern Front: The Nazi-Soviet War in American Popular Culture, Cambridge, 2008.

Sokolov, Boris, B plenu i na rodine, St Petersburg, 2004.

Sokolov, Nikolai, 'Tyoplaya vanna dlya begemota: zoosad v gody voiny', Rodina, 1, 2003.

Sotnikov, Nikolai, 'V blokadniy gorod yekhal . . . tsirk!', Neva, 6, 2002, p. 222.

Sparén, Pär, et al., 'Long term mortality after severe starvation during the siege of Leningrad: prospective cohort study', British Medical Journal, 328 (January 2004), p. 11.

Speer, Albert, Inside the Third Reich: Memoirs, London, 1970.

— The Slave State: Heinrich Himmler's Masterplan for SS Supremacy, trans. Joachim Neugroschel, London, 1981.

Steblin-Kamensky, Mikhail, 'The Siege of Leningrad', in Granta, 30: New Europe! (April 1990).

Stites, Richard, ed., Culture and Entertainment in Wartime Russia, Bloomington, 1995.

Telyashkov, Rakhim, Tatary v Velikoi Otechestvennoi Voine i blokade Leningrada, St Petersburg, 2005.

Trevor-Roper, Hugh, ed., Hitler's Table Talk, 1941–1944, trans. Norman Cameron and R. H. Stevens, London, 1953.

— Hitler's War Directives, 1938–1945, London, 1964.

Trudy Gosudarstvennogo Muzeya Istorii Sankt-Peterburga, vol. 5, Materialy k istorii blokady Leningrada, St Petersburg, 2000.

— vol. 8, Vasili Chekrizov, Dnevnik blokadnogo vremeni, St Petersburg, 2004.

Tumarkin, N., The Living and the Dead: The Rise and Fall of the Cult of World War II in Russia, New York, 1994.

Tuyll, Hubert van, *Feeding the Bear: American Aid to the Soviet Union, 1941–1945*, New York, 1989.

Vakser, A. Z., 'Nastroyeniya leningradtsev poslevoyennogo vremeni 1945–1953 gody', *Nestor*, 1, 5, 2001.

— *Leningrad poslevoyenniy, 1945–1982 gody*, St Petersburg, 2005.

Varshavsky, Sergei, and Boris Rest, *Ordeal of the Hermitage*, trans. Arthur Shkarovsky, New York, 1986.

— *Podvig Ermitazha*, 4 vols, Leningrad, 1987.

Velichenko, M. N., et al., eds, *Leningradsky tramvai 1941–1945*, St Petersburg, 1995.

Verbrechen der Wehrmacht: Dimensionen des Vernichtungskrieges 1941–1944, (Austellungskatalog, Hamburger Institut für Sozialforschung), Hamburg, 2002.

Vinokurov, Aleksei, 'Blokadniy dnevnik', in Stanislav Bernev and Sergei Chernov, eds, *Arkhiv Bolshogo Doma: blokadniye dnevniki i dokumenty*, St Petersburg, 2007.

Vishnevskaya, Galina, *Galina: A Russian Story*, San Diego, 1984.

Volkogonov, Dmitri, *Stalin: Triumph and Tragedy*, trans. Harold Shukman, London, 1991.

Volkov, Solomon, *St Petersburg: A Cultural History*, New York, 1995.

— *Testimony: The Memoirs of Dmitri Shostakovich*, London, 1979.

Volkovsky, N. L., *Blokada Leningrada v dokumentakh rassekrechennykh arkhivov*, Moscow and St Petersburg, 2005.

Voronina, Tatyana, I. E. Gusintseva and V. V. Kalendarova, 'Blokada glazami ochevidtsev. Intervyu s zhitelyami Leningrada 1940-kh gg.', *Nestor*, 6, 2003, p. 37.

Voronina, Tatyana, and Ilya Utekhin, 'Rekonstruktsiya smysla v analize intervyu: tematicheskiye dominanty i skrytaya polemika', in M. V. Loskutova, ed., *Pamyat o blokade: svidetelstva ochevidtsev i istoricheskoye soznaniye obshchestva*, St Petersburg, 2005.

Voyevodskaya, A., *Chetyre goda zhizni, chetyre goda molodosti*, St Petersburg, 2005.

Werth, Alexander, *Moscow '41*, London, 1942.

— *Leningrad*, London, 1944.

— *Russia at War, 1941–1945*, London, 1964.

Wilson, Elizabeth, *Shostakovich: A Life Remembered*, London, 1994.

Yarov, Sergei, 'Rasskazy o blokade: struktura, ritorika i stil', *Nestor*, 6, 2003, p. 422.

Zelenova, Anna, *Stati, vospominaniya, pisma: Pavlovsky dvorets, istoriya i sudba*, St Petersburg, 2006.

Zhenshchiny Leningrada v gody blokady (Tezisy nauchnoi konferentsii 10–11 marta 2005 g.), St Petersburg, 2005.

Zhilinsky, Ivan, 'Blokadniy dnevnik', *Voprosy istorii*, 5, 1996, p. 5 (covers 21 December 1941–15 January 1942).

— *Voprosy istorii*, 5–6, 1996, p. 3 (covers 16–30 January 1942).

— *Voprosy istorii*, 5–7, 1996, p. 3 (covers 31 January–31 March 1942).

Zhukov, Georgi, *Marshal of the Soviet Union G. Zhukov: Reminiscences and Reflections*, 2 vols, trans. Vic Schneierson, Moscow, 1985.

Zhuravlev, D. A., 'Frontovik v tylu: kontrol za nastroyeniyami voyennosluzhash-chikh v leningradskikh gospitalyakh vo vremya sovetsko-finlyandskoi voiny 1939–1940 gg.', *Nestor*, 6, 2003, p. 402.

ARCHIVES

St Petersburg:

Oral History Center, European University at St Petersburg (Blokada v sudbakh i pamyati leningradtsev).

Tsentralniy Gosudarstvenniy Arkhiv Istoriko-Politicheskikh Dokumentov Sankt-Peterburga (TsGAIPD SPb).

Tsentralniy Gosudarstvenniy Arkhiv Kinofotofonodokumentov Sankt-Peterburga (TsGAKFFD SPb).

Moscow:

Gosudarstvenniy Arkhiv Rossiiskoi Federatsii (GARF).

Rossiisky Gosudarstvenniy Arkhiv Literatury i Isskustva (RGALI).

Rossiisky Gosudarstvenniy Arkhiv Sotsialnoi i Politicheskoi Istorii (RGASPI).

Rossiisky Gosudarstvenniy Voyenniy Arkhiv (RGVA).

Tsentralniy Arkhiv Ministerstva Oborony (TsAMO).

Elsewhere:

Bakhmeteff Archive of Russian and East European Culture, Columbia University.

BBC Written Archives Centre, Caversham.

Bundesarchiv-Militärarchiv, Freiburg.

Hoover Institution Archives, Stanford University.

Widener Library, Harvard University (Harvard Project on the Soviet Social System).

Index

A NOTE ON THE AUTHOR

Anna Reid read law at Oxford and Russian History at UCL's School of Slavonic and East European Studies. She started her career in consultancy and business journalism; from 1993 to 1995 she lived in Kiev, working as Ukraine correspondent for the *Economist* and the *Daily Telegraph*, and from 2003 to 2007 ran the foreign affairs programme at the think-tank Policy Exchange. Here previous books are *The Shaman's Coat: A Native History of Siberia* and *Borderland: A Journey Through the History of the Ukraine*. She lives in west London with her husband and sons.

A NOTE ON THE TYPE

The text of this book is set Adobe Garamond. It is one of several versions of Garamond based on the designs of Claude Garamond. It is thought that Garamond based his font on Bembo, cut in 1495 by Francesco Griffo in collaboration with the Italian printer Aldus Manutius. Garamond types were first used in books printed in Paris around 1532. Many of the present-day versions of this type are based on the *Typi Academiae* of Jean Jannon cut in Sedan in 1615.

Claude Garamond was born in Paris in 1480. He learned how to cut type from his father and by the age of fifteen he was able to fashion steel punches the size of a pica with great precision. At the age of sixty he was commissioned by King Francis I to design a Greek alphabet, for this he was given the honourable title of royal type founder. He died in 1561.